# SIR NIGEL GRESLEY

## The L.N.E.R.'s First C.M.E.

Simon A.C. Martin

Strathwood

*Fig. 1. Sir Nigel Gresley poses for a photograph next to the locomotive named for him, No.4498 Sir Nigel Gresley. Colourised Image by Ian MacCabe, The Gresley Society.*

# SIR NIGEL GRESLEY

## The L.N.E.R.'s First C.M.E.

*Celebrating the Centenary of the L.N.E.R.*
*Flying Scotsman's Centenary*
*The Diamond Jubilee of The Gresley Society*

Written by
SIMON A.C. MARTIN

Foreword written by
BEN GODFREY

Colourised images and history
of The Gresley Society by
IAN MACCABE

# SIR NIGEL GRESLEY

## The L.N.E.R.'s First C.M.E.

This edition first published in 2023
by Strathwood Publishing

Other books available in this series:
Edward Thompson: Wartime C.M.E.

ISBN 978-1-913390-88-4

# CONTENTS

# Foreword

*Gresley's Legacy*

*Fig. 2. Ben Godfrey, grandson of Sir Nigel Gresley, stands proudly next to the statue of his late grandfather at King's Cross. This was on the day it was first unveiled.*

On the 1 April 2023, I attended the Gresley Society's Spring Meeting via Zoom and I listened to a fascinating online presentation about my Grandfather, Sir Nigel Gresley, by Simon A.C. Martin.

I subsequently learned that Simon had written a book about my Grandfather, and I was able to have the chance to read the draft of this book just before it was published.

This book contains so much information that has been really well researched by Simon, and it provides a balanced view of what my Grandfather achieved during his time with the LNER.

Clearly a lot of effort has been put into writing this book by Simon and I would like to thank him for producing a fine piece of work.

**Ben Godfrey**
**C.ENG, MIMechE.**

# Preface

*The Author's Story*

*Fig. 3. The author stands next to preserved Gresley A3 No.60103 Flying Scotsman in November 2022, 28 years after first meeting the locomotive at the Llangollen Railway in Wales. Simon A.C. Martin*

The year was 1994. The sights and sounds of a steam railway at work could be heard for miles around the Welsh valleys. There were families, parents, and children, everywhere, clamouring for a sight of the famous steam locomotive, backing down onto their train. The dark green tender first loomed into view, passing underneath a bridge, and as the full locomotive came into the light, one child looked up with innocent eyes and spied the brass and black nameplate, which proclaimed *Flying Scotsman* as the massive steam locomotive, panting, slowed to a halt, gently touching the buffers of the cream and red coaches behind.

This story was true for many children that day. For myself, it was the first time I had ever seen a steam engine, and that powerful image of a dark green steam locomotive, with orange and black lining, and cream numerals reading "60103" would stay with me my entire life. There was always something about the locomotives of Sir Nigel Gresley that seemed to evoke a real sense of adventure and speed.

Even standing still, the bulk of *Flying Scotsman* always screamed out "racehorse" to me, and to this day the locomotive, regardless of whether it carries apple green or not, looks fast even when at rest. Gresley's express passenger locomotives have stood the test of time with their designs still looking modern despite nearing ninety years of operation.

On another such occasion, and whilst driving with my family through the south of England, there was smoke and steam in the distance – a flash of blue paint – and a call from myself to my father, driving, that we'd passed *Sir Nigel Gresley* on the Watercress Railway. He didn't believe me! I was five years old, after all.

How could I have known what it was from just a short glance from the back seat of a car? Ten minutes of arguing led to the car being turned around, and on arrival at Ropley, he inquired with the stationmaster there what the next locomotive arrival would be.

"It's *Sir Nigel Gresley*, Sir". My father's response – "Two platform tickets please!" To this day I cannot forget the joy on my father's face when he came face to face with the express passenger blue painted No.60007 that day. A moment with my father I will always treasure.

When all is said and done, the fact that we can still enjoy a relatively good spread of Sir Nigel Gresley's designs (both locomotive and rolling stock) in comparison to that of his successors and his predecessors likely says much about the affection and respect held for this unique and loveable railway engineer.

I certainly will always hold a candle for the Gresley locomotive that started it all for me, still running in its centenary year, and hopefully for many years to come.

**Simon A.C. Martin**
**BA, HNC (Railway Engineering Systems)**
**EngTech, TMIET**

# Introduction

*The Use of Engine Power*

*Fig. 4. Gresley A4 No.4900, Gannet, pulls into King's Cross in the late 1930s. Strathwood Library Collection.*

## The beauty of railway history

The best moments in reading are when you come across something – a thought, a feeling, a way of looking at things – which you had thought special and particular to you. And now, here it is, set down by someone else, a person you have never met, someone even who is long dead. And it is as if a hand has come out and taken yours.
*Alan Bennett, English playwright.*

There was a moment where I felt a hand had reached out and taken mine when I sat in the National Archives at Kew. It was mid-afternoon in 2018, during the midst of my research into Edward Thompson, when I found a letter signed by Sir Nigel Gresley for the first time. The letter was to the point and kindly written, asking Thompson to arrange for the fitting of the Kylchap chimney to the water tube boiler locomotive, the W1. Gresley thanked Thompson for his support in the matter of the modifications: Thompson was of course now the head of Darlington Works.

There was a warmth to Gresley's requests and in Thompson's responses that I couldn't quite shake from my mind. Was this me projecting an idea onto this evidence? Subjectivity exists in every interpretation of the primary evidence.

I felt determined after completing my tome on Thompson that I should return to Gresley and follow up with a book I had always wanted to write.

The more I delved back into the archives, looking through letters, reports, drawings, graphs, board minutes and the rest, the more convinced I was that the issues between the two men had been played up and exaggerated greatly over the years. The substance of the communications between them was always couched in professional terms.

When I discovered the Use of Engine Power document (a report which gave average annual mileages and availability statistics for every locomotive class operating on the railway) I was astonished at the amount of data that was available to analyse for the L.N.E.R. That this document survived to the modern day is remarkable. What was perhaps more remarkable is that until my book on Thompson in 2021 no one else had ever acknowledged its existence in print.

Where Edward Thompson was concerned it was easier to step back and let the figures do the bulk of the talking. The *Use of Engine Power* document was explicit in showcasing the excellence of his design work during the Second World War and nothing more was required to be said.

Where Gresley is concerned the very same document shows us a different side to his work. This is a very good thing. Far from what some would anticipate would be an undoing of Gresley's reputation, my findings are likely to further cement that well-deserved reputation. There is no doubt that he provided the G.N.R. and then L.N.E.R. ample new motive power that covered the requirements of these railways needs.

There is also little doubt that Gresley innovated beyond all other locomotive engineers at every aspect of the railway including locomotive and Carriage & Wagon design, signalling, track, electrification and many more besides.

It is not unfair to state that the modern East Coast Main Line (E.C.M.L.) owes much to Gresley's work throughout his life. Without Gresley proving the clear advantages of streamlining an entire train, the benefits of articulation, the need for a bigger picture thinking for high-speed operations, it is doubtful that the United Kingdom would have been at the forefront of many of the technical innovations that has led to the modern railway.

What we see being designed for High Speed 2 (HS2) now in terms of infrastructure, rolling stock and signalling equipment are all echoes of that Gresley was pushing for in the 1930s. Gresley gave the world its first truly high-speed railway. Nothing before and nothing since has made the same level of impact that *Silver Link* did in September 1935.

## Notes on how the data is presented and interpreted

At the end of each locomotive section within this book there will be a summarisation of the statistics taken from the London & North Eastern Railway (L.N.E.R.)'s internal *Use of Engine Power* document. These statistics are in relation to the individual classes' average annual mileages and availability.

This document, available in the National Archives at Kew, is a record of statistics on every locomotive class that was owned or operated by the L.N.E.R. during the Second World War. These statistics record the following data:

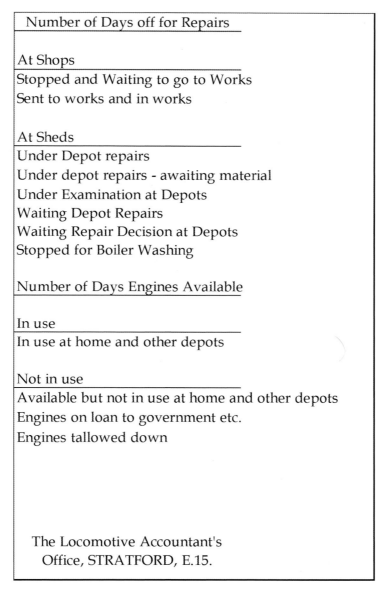

Fig.5. How data was recorded in the Use of Engine Power Document.
Simon A.C. Martin, from the Use of Engine Power Document.

These statistics were collated centrally from the Locomotive Accountant's Office in Stratford originally. The associated papers attached to this part of the L.N.E.R.'s archive suggest strongly that Sir Nigel Gresley originally initiated the production of this document to have an overview of and to investigate more fully the availability issues of the L.N.ER.'s locomotive stock in the run up to the Second World War.

On examination of the original document, I took the decision to collate the entire database into a modern format, in the form of a spreadsheet. This process took around three years with much discussion amongst peers on how to fully analyse the data. It was realised early on that the dataset the document held allowed, potentially, a closer view at the day-to-day performance of the locomotives being used. The solution was the production of a tailored Availability formula, as outlined below:

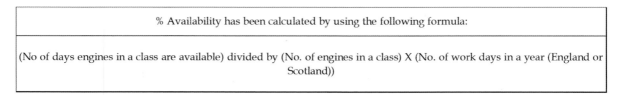

| % Availability has been calculated by using the following formula: |
| --- |
| (No of days engines in a class are available) divided by (No. of engines in a class) X (No. of work days in a year (England or Scotland)) |

*Fig. 6. How availability of a locomotive class in a year is calculated.*
*Simon A.C. Martin, from the Use of Engine Power Document.*

This formula adjusts for the different number of days available for work in England and Scotland, within the database I produced.

For the purposes of the consistency of the database the original figures are maintained with appropriate explanations in the notes. This leaves us with a modern version of the *Use of Engine Power* document.

The L.N.E.R. split these statistics into four basic areas of the railway, as outlined below (including their letter codes):

| SAW | Southern Area Western Section |
| --- | --- |
| SAE | Southern Area Eastern Section |
| NEA | North Eastern Area |
| SCO | Scottish Area |
| WHL | Whole Line |

*Fig. 7. How availability of a locomotive class in a year is calculated.*
*Simon A.C. Martin, from the Use of Engine Power Document.*

For the purposes of analysing the data that we have, the *Whole Line Averages* will be used to illustrate the relative availability and mileages of any given class across the whole of the L.N.E.R.

| 1942 | |
|---|---|
| Total number of locos: | 6237 |
| Total number of loco classes: | 164 |
| Total number of boiler types: | 193 |
| Average availability for whole fleet: | 71% |
| Total Fleet Mileage: | 151,829,377 |
| Difference in number of locos: | N/A |
| Difference in number of classes: | N/A |

| 1943 | |
|---|---|
| Total number of locos: | 6401 |
| Total number of loco classes: | 163 |
| Total number of boiler types: | 199 |
| Average availability for whole fleet: | 71% |
| Total Fleet Mileage: | 155,311,171 |
| Difference in number of locos: | 164 |
| Difference in number of classes: | -1 |

| 1944 | |
|---|---|
| Total number of locos: | 6430 |
| Total number of loco classes: | 160 |
| Total number of boiler types: | 173 |
| Average availability for whole fleet: | 73% |
| Total Fleet Mileage: | 151,782,938 |
| Difference in number of locos: | 29 |
| Difference in number of classes: | -3 |

| 1945 | |
|---|---|
| Total number of locos: | 6273 |
| Total number of loco classes: | 162 |
| Total number of boiler types: | 172 |
| Average availability for whole fleet: | 71% |
| Total Fleet Mileage: | 155,377,464 |
| Difference in number of locos: | -157 |
| Difference in number of classes: | 2 |

| 1946 | |
|---|---|
| Total number of locos: | 6451 |
| Total number of loco classes: | 162 |
| Total number of boiler types: | 172 |
| Average availability for whole fleet: | 68% |
| Total Fleet Mileage: | 156,619,241 |
| Difference in number of locos: | 178 |
| Difference in number of classes: | 0 |

*Fig. 8. An overview of some of the war years 1942–46. This high-level overview of the whole L.N.E.R. locomotive fleet gives an indication of the railway's issues and successes. Simon A.C. Martin, from the Use of Engine Power Document.*

The dataset we have is huge. It covers between 6200 to 6500 steam locomotives in any given year, sub divided into around 160 classes, covering four major areas of the L.N.E.R. with a further set of statistics covering the rest of the L.N.E.R. That gives us around 60,000 individual data entries over the five years recorded.

*The Use of Engine Power* document tells us far more about the clear day to day workings of the railway than any simplified set of works visits or withdrawal dates. For the first time, we can see the real picture of the L.N.E.R.'s locomotive stock in work.

For the purposes of this book, only the designs directly attributable to Gresley have been included. For further information on later designs from Edward Thompson please refer to Edward Thompson: Wartime C.M.E. that is also available from Strathwood Publishing.

The examination of each classes' individual performances by way of the *Use of Engine Power* document is specific to the war years and should be considered in that context. It may inform how they performed in peacetime to some degree, and for each locomotive class some supposition may be observed. Where we have more data, such as that from the Engine Record Cards held at the National Railway Museum (N.R.M.) we can use this to contrast with, or emphasise further, the *Use of Engine Power* data.

# Chapter 1
# Early Life & Influences

*Fig. 9. A young Herbert Nigel Gresley near the beginning of his railway career. The Gresley Society.*

On 19 June 1876, the future Sir Nigel Gresley was born in the house at 32 Dublin Street, Edinburgh. Strictly speaking, he was Herbert Nigel Gresley. Herbert, so named for one of his godfathers and also incorporating a family name, Nigel, that had been with the dynasty since Norman times.

Born to the Reverend Nigel Gresley and his wife (the artist and author Joanna Beatrice Wilson) in a little under three weeks the young Nigel Gresley would make his first journey by rail from Edinburgh to the sleepy village of Netherseal in Derbyshire. Though he loved Scotland and would spend time there throughout his life, Gresley was very much an Englishman. Gresley's childhood was spent at the Rectory in Neatherseal, surrounded by his large family, a cook, housemaid, parlourmaid, and a governess, together with a Swiss nursemaid in his early years who taught him French.

Gresley went to the preparatory school of Barham House in St. Leonards, before heading to Marlborough College in 1890 when he turned 14. He was clearly gifted, winning multiple awards across his years at Marlborough College in a range of activities (including but not limited to a Science Prize in 1892).

Leaving school in 1893, preferring practical experience than continuing through to Sixth Form (and leaving his future colleague Edward Thompson behind), Gresley joined the London & North Western Railway (L.N.W.R.) at Crewe Works as a premium apprentice under Francis Webb. Between 1893 and 1899 he had progressed to the job of fitter.

During his time on the L.N.W.R. Gresley would no doubt have had great experience of the experimentation of compounding, including observing a triple expansion locomotive and various types of fireboxes.

In 1898, Gresley moved across to the Lancashire & Yorkshire Railway (L.&Y.R.) as a pupil of John Aspinall, the Chief Mechanical Engineer. In this role he worked primarily in the drawing office. After his pupillage ended, he then went into the materials testing laboratory for around six months.

Gresley's next role was in the sheds, as running shed foreman at Blackpool for the summer of 1899. Around this time, he attended one of the Bolton Assembly Balls and met Ethel Frances Fullagar, an accomplished musician a few years older. They were engaged within a year.

This was not without controversy. Ethel's father disapproved the match but with the support of the Aspinalls (including Ethel lodging with them for a time, having left home) the two were wed on 17 October 1901 with the service conducted by the Reverend George Nigel Gresley (Gresley's older brother).

The first of their children, Nigel, and Violet were born on 25 June 1903 and 5 May 1904 respectively. During this period Gresley had been transferred to the Carriage and Wagon Department of the L.&Y.R., later receiving a further promotion to Assistant Manager of that department at the works at Newton Heath.

On 1 April 1902, he was promoted again, doubling his wage to £450 through becoming the Assistant Carriage & Wagon Superintendent to the Chief Mechanical Engineer.

This was followed in 1904 by moving to Beyer, Peacock & Co. Ltd as a managing director. From there, Gresley was able to gain an interview with Henry Ivatt for the position of Carriage & Wagon Superintendent at the Great Northern Railway (G.N.R.), coming into the role on 20 February 1905, with a wage of £750.

It has been reported that Aspinall may have had a hand in this by a few secondary sources, and the primary evidence including what remains of the G.N.R. Locomotive Committee notes appear to confirm this. He had a hand in this by way of persuading Ivatt to interview Gresley, perhaps recognising that Gresley wanted the top job, and was unlikely to achieve it on the L.&Y.R. in the time frames desired.

Two more children, Roger, and Marjorie, followed on 15 July 1906 and 15 September 1908.

By 1911, Ivatt was ready to retire and Gresley was in the frame for the top role. However, Gresley suffered an injury in 1910, whilst out hunting. This injury took some time to heal, and so Ivatt postponed his retirement to the end of 1911, allowing for a changeover period to facilitate Gresley to fully recuperate.

Gresley's appointment as the Mechanical Engineer (M.E.) of the G.N.R. was agreed at the board meeting on 8 August 1911 and was effective from 1 October 1911.

Nigel Gresley, Mechanical Engineer, had arrived.

*Fig. 10. Older, and now ready for the top job at the G.N.R., Nigel Gresley is seen here in this relaxed pose, impeccably dressed as always. The Gresley Society.*

# Chapter 2
# The G.N.R.

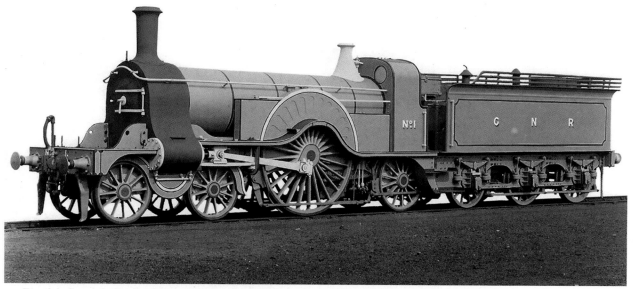

*Fig. 11. Patrick Stirling's prototype single "Eight-footer" express passenger locomotive, appropriately numbered No.1. Works photograph, Doncaster Works, 1870.*
*Tim Robbins Collection.*

## Influences of the G.N.R.

The influence on Gresley's career up unto the point that he became the M.E. of the Great Northern Railway (G.N.R.) involved a wide variety of locomotive designs and rolling stock.

Having worked for the L.N.W.R. and L.&Y.R., Gresley was well aware of locomotive development outside of the sphere of Doncaster works and there were further internal influences on his work as he developed his skills and understanding of locomotive and rolling stock design.

## The Stirling Eight Foot Single

The Patrick Stirling "Eight foot" single locomotives were at the time being taken out of service in favour of the larger Ivatt 4-4-0s and Atlantic locomotives, with the biggest influx of new locomotives happening whilst Gresley was in his early years of employment with the G.N.R. under Henry Ivatt.

When Patrick Stirling had been the Chief Mechanical Engineer of the G.N.R., he had looked to create a level of standardisation across the locomotive fleet, together with appropriate wheelbases for the work involved. A "single-wheeler" tender locomotive was borrowed from the Great Eastern Railway (G.E.R.) and from there he and his engineers produced two prototypes of the 2-2-2-wheel arrangement, both entering service in 1868.

These locomotives had 7ft 1in diameter wheels. These two prototypes led to a further prototype with 8ft 1in wheels for expresses between London and York. This locomotive featured outside cylinders and a front four-wheel bogie. This engine was Stirling's Single, No.1, and it was the first of a truly iconic class.

Between 1870 and 1895, fifty-three of these locomotives would be built at Doncaster Works, in three batches. There were a few developments within this class, the most notable of which was the later fitting of domed boilers.

*Fig. 12. Patrick Stirling's "Eight-footer" express passenger locomotive No.776. Works photograph, Doncaster Works, 1887. This was taken after rebuilding with a new domed boiler and with the cut-outs removed on the splasher. Tim Robbins Collection.*

The Singles could haul up to 280-ton trains at an average of 50 mph, but were known to have exceeded this speed in short bursts of up to 85 mph. They were no slouches, with No.775 making a time of 1 hour and 16 minutes between Grantham and York, averaging the trip at a speed of around 65 mph.

Gresley would have witnessed the final examples of the class, hard at work, still hauling passenger services until 1916. Stirling Single No.1 was preserved whilst he was C.M.E. and was brought into working order in the 1930s to provide a contrast with Gresley's newest express passenger locomotives.

*Fig. 13. Henry Ivatt's prototype Atlantic express passenger locomotive, No.990. This locomotive was the first locomotive of this wheel arrangement in Britain. It would later be named Henry Oakley. Works photograph, Doncaster Works, 1898. Tim Robbins Collection.*

## Ivatt's First Atlantic

In 1898, Henry Ivatt produced the first of his Atlantic locomotives. No.990 was also the first Atlantic locomotive to work in the United Kingdom and with its four-wheel bogie and rear trailing wheels under the cab, probably presented the first clear outline of the locomotives to follow.

Two outside cylinders of 18 ¾in diameter and four coupled 6ft 7 ½in driving wheels were married to a boiler of 4ft 8in diameter. The firebox had a grate of approximately 27 sq. ft with a total heating surface of 1442 sq. ft, and a working pressure of 175lb.

No.990 weighed 58 tons, coupled to the largest capacity tender built for the G.N.R. at that time, with space for 5 tons of coal and 3670 gallons of water.

No.990 was later rebuilt with a larger diameter boiler, and named *Henry Oakley*, after the Chief General Manager of the time. A total of 22 Class C2s were built.

## The Start of the Big Engine Policy

By December 1902, Ivatt had recognised that his Atlantic could be improved, and took the basic design and enlarged it. His prototype, No.251 made quite the stir. This, arguably, was the beginning of the "Big Engine" policy, and Gresley would join the G.N.R. just at the time that many of these locomotives were coming into service.

With train lengths and speeds increasing, the C1 Atlantics came into traffic and provided the G.N.R. with excellent service. 6ft 8in diameter driving wheels would be employed on the C1s, and all subsequent express passenger locomotives introduced thereafter on the G.N.R. and L.N.E.R.

*Fig. 14. Henry Ivatt's prototype large boilered Atlantic express passenger locomotive, No.251. This locomotive, it can be argued, started the "large engine policy" of the G.N.R. and formed a very successful class, working through to the early days of British Railways.*
*Works photograph, Doncaster Works, 1902.*
*Tim Robbins Collection.*

Ninety-four of the improved Atlantic design would be built over the years, the larger 5ft 6in diameter boiler providing a total heating surface of 2500 sq. ft. and with this heavier boiler fitted came improved adhesive weight, which in turn gave prodigious performance out on the road.

The firebox was the main point of interest: this was the first of the wide firebox, round topped boilers that Gresley would see in his career, and there is no doubt that the experiences of the G.N.R. at Doncaster in building this type of boiler would filter its way into Gresley's overall design ethos.

The Atlantics were originally fitted with slide valves. Some of the class had these replaced with piston valves later improving the performance markedly. Like the C2 Atlantics before them, the C1s were capable of higher speeds and pulling heavier trains. 90 mph running was reported with the C1 Atlantics throughout their working life, but these claims are unauthenticated.

*Fig. 15. Henry Ivatt's prototype large boilered Atlantic express passenger locomotive, No.251. Date unknown. Location is King's Cross. The description on the photograph read "Not in original condition, but with some variations around the firebox".*
*Tim Robbins Collection.*

The Atlantic boiler was fitted with four safety valves of the Ramsbottom type, enclosed in a circular casing on the firebox. These were adjusted to blow off at a pressure of 175lb. The larger boiler gave No.251 gave a total weight for the engine of 68 tons 8 cwt.

The tender was virtually identical to No.990's but had been fitted with the new water pick up apparatus, allowing for filling up with water on the move by passing over water troughs and lowering a scoop.

In 1905, Ivatt was experimenting in compounding, and the release of modified C1 Atlantic No.292 showed some interesting developments. Although the boiler and chassis arrangement were virtually identical, No.292 featured four cylinders. The outside cylinders were the high-pressure pair, 13in diameter with a stroke of 20in, with slide valves fitted and powering the rear driving wheels.

*Fig. 16. Henry Ivatt's prototype large boilered Atlantic express passenger locomotive, No.292. This locomotive was a high pressure four-cylinder compound and was one of the first British locomotives fitted with outside Walschaerts valve gear. Works photograph, Doncaster Works, 1902.*
*Tim Robbins Collection.*

The inside cylinders were 16in diameter and had a stroke of 26in, powering the front driving wheels by way of Stephenson link motion. The valves were placed back-to-back between the four cylinders. There was a valve fitted over the low-pressure steam chest that allowed the locomotive to run on the low-pressure cylinders in simple working, or in compound mode, as required.

This would not have been Gresley's first experience of compounding (having worked at the L.N.W.R. previously), but this would have been his first experience with Walschaerts valve gear.

No.292 was not considered successful and was withdrawn in 1924, after having been rebuilt as a two-cylinder locomotive in 1917.

*Fig. 17. Henry Ivatt's prototype large boilered Atlantic express passenger locomotive, No.1300. This locomotive was a "balanced" compound and may have contributed to Gresley's experiences in this area. This locomotive featured a unique boiler and firebox arrangement.*
*Works photograph, Vulcan Works, 1905.*
*Tim Robbins Collection.*

## Compounding & Four Cylinders

At the same time as No.292 was being designed and built, the Vulcan Foundry were creating their own interpretation of Ivatt's Atlantic design with their locomotive, No.1300. Ivatt had, with the consent of the G.N.R. board, put out a tender to build a further compound four-cylinder locomotive. The Vulcan Foundry had bid and won the tendering process and had based their locomotive design mostly on the De Glehn arrangement. De Glehn's compound locomotives were becoming well known internationally and it is unsurprising that a railway company would want to emulate such success.

No.1300 was set up as a four-cylinder compound, with the high-pressure cylinders on the outside, 14in diameter and 26in stroke, with Walschaerts valve gear and piston valves fitted and driving the rear driving wheels. The inside low-pressure cylinders were also actuated by Walschaerts valve gear and piston valves and were 23in diameter with a stroke of 26in.

No.1300 had a few unique features. It used a starting valve, which admitted steam at a reduced pressure to the receiver when starting. The steam supply was automatically cut off when steam reached the low-pressure cylinders. The reversing gear was also unique, allowing one reversing screw to operate both high and low-pressure valve gears at the same time. This allowed for variable cut-offs for both sets of motion, adjustable whilst the locomotive was running and without interfering with the operation of either of the two sets of valve gear.

The boiler was entirely unique to No.1300 and the design was not perpetuated by either the G.N.R. or the Vulcan Foundry thereafter. It was originally intended to be built with a square topped, Belpaire firebox but some limits at the extremes of the G.N.R. loading gauge forced a different design, with a round topped pattern that was wider than the 5ft 1 and 5/8in boiler barrel employed. It had a total heating surface of 2514 sq. ft. with a grate of 31 sq. ft. and a working pressure of 200lb.

The locomotive weighed 71 tons in service and pulled the same standard G.N.R. tender as previous Atlantics. On paper, this locomotive had great potential. It did not perform well, being involved in comparison trials with No.292 and the standard Atlantic No.294 (with boiler pressure upped from 175lb to 200lb) in the October of 1905. It was the least economical of the three locomotives, with the results given below:

| Test Conditions | No.292 | No.294 | No.1300 |
|---|---|---|---|
| Mileage in tests | 11,415 | 11,415 | 11045 |
| Average Load (tons) | 238 | 234 | 230 |
| Average Speed (mph) | 49.9 | 49.58 | 49.02 |
| Coal Consumption (lb/mile) | 43.98 | 45.31 | 45.84 |
| Lubricating Oil (pints/100 miles) | 7.18 | 6.22 | 7.34 |

Fig. 18. Test results of the Atlantic Comparative study. Simon A.C. Martin, derived from L.N.E.R. statistics.

No.1300 was also unreliable: its total recorded mileage between July 1905 and September 1921 the sum of 390,798 miles. By comparison, one of the standard Ivatt Atlantics, No.1407, had reached over 625,000 miles in a similar time frame. No.1300 was rebuilt as a two-cylinder simple in 1917, with the outside cylinders now driving the leading coupled wheels. It was withdrawn in this form in 1924.

Although not successful as a design, the importance of comparison testing between locomotives intended for similar work, and with differing methods of propulsion, was following a scientific process and no doubt the results would have influenced Gresley's thinking. No more four-cylinder compounds were built for the G.N.R., and the only compound locomotive that Gresley produced with four-cylinders would emerge in 1929 as the sole example of his high-pressure locomotive, the W1.

There was one more four-cylinder locomotive, however, with Gresley having Ivatt C1 No.279 rebuilt as a four-cylinder simple in 1913. No.279 had outside Walschaerts valve gear which operated the inside piston valves by means of rocking shafts and pendulum levers. This locomotive predated the 1915 four-cylinder Pacific outline but shared some striking similarities in the proposed setup.

# Carriage & Wagon Design

Gresley started in his role as Carriage & Wagon Superintendent in February 1905. Following after Frank Howlden who had occupied this role since 1877, producing a range of bogie coaches with clerestory roofs, very much based on American practice, using either four-wheel or six-wheel bogies. Internally, side corridors had been introduced to the coaches, together with gangway connections and toilets. There were also special types of coaches for the first time on the G.N.R., including Restaurant and Sleeping cars.

Improvements in safety had also been introduced using the Gould, then the buckeye coupler type, and continuous braking along trains with the fitting of vacuum brakes. Most of this had been introduced shortly after Ivatt had visited America and reported back to the board and engineering departments on his experiences. Despite the welcome renewal of stock that Howlden had undertaken, in 1905 a significant percentage of the G.N.R.'s rolling stock was made up of four and six-wheel short wheelbase coaches, with low seating capacity and roofs well below the railway's generous loading gauge.

Gresley adopted, in all but the most specialist of coach designs, a basic standard for his rolling stock. This standard was made up of all-steel under-frames, buckeye couplers and Pullman type vestibules, high elliptical roofs with sloping ends, maintaining the outwards finish by way of teak panelling. These coaches, instantly recognisable, remained something of a trademark for Gresley and the G.N.R., and the L.N.E.R. right up until his death in 1941.

The first Gresley coach to emerge from Doncaster was a corridor composite coach in 1905. This coach initially had two six-wheel bogies, in time being replaced with two four-wheel bogies of an improved design. Open thirds and brake thirds shortly after this coach, with some additional accoutrements such as electric lighting included.

One of Gresley's first projects was a pair of new Royal Saloons for the King and Queen, with one vehicle to be built at Doncaster and the other at York. These had the six-wheel bogies fitted and their interiors were lavish, in the style of Louis XVI; the King's saloon had a Jacobean oak fitted smoking room. Neither of the two saloons carried the insignia of the G.N.R. nor the East Coast Joint Railways (E.C.J.S.R.), but they did carry the Royal Coat of Arms on the centre panels on each side.

By the end of 1906, more new carriages in Gresley's style were coming into service, particularly for work between London King's Cross, Sheffield, and Manchester (gaining the moniker of "Sheffield stock"). These, together with new restaurant cars, first- and third-class coaches began to form complete trains of all Gresley rolling stock. As has been customary, these coaches were not known as Gresley stock when released to traffic, instead attributed to Ivatt.

By the grouping of 1923, Gresley had introduced over 400 mainline coaches of around 40 diagrams for the G.N.R., not including over 100 conversions of Howlden four and six-wheel coaches to articulated bogie coaches, and the various diagrams of articulated non-corridor suburban stock in triplet and quadruplet sets.

# Chapter 3
# G.N.R. Locomotive Designs

## G.N.R. 536 Class (L.N.E.R. Class J6) 0-6-0 1911)
Number built (G.N.R.): 110

*Fig 19. Gresley J6 No.554, works photograph. Colourised by Ian MacCabe, The Gresley Society.*

Strictly speaking, the Class J6 was the final development of the Ivatt line of G.N.R. 0-6-0 locomotives, however, by L.N.E.R. days it was recognised those changes made by Gresley with the superheated versions were significant enough to justify being classified differently to the earlier Ivatt locomotives.

A total of 95 J6s were built under Gresley's direction, all at Doncaster works in ten batches over the course of a decade with the original Ivatt-era locomotives being added to the Gresley development to create a total class of 110 locomotives.

All the J6s were initially built with standard G.N.R. Ramsbottom safety valves. As boilers came up for repair in the L.N.E.R. era, the J6s were gradually converted to being fitted with the L.N.E.R.'s chosen standard, Ross Pop safety valves.

There were various experiments with superheaters on the J6s with the first few batches being built with Schmidt superheaters with 18 elements. There were also five locomotives which were fitted with Robinson superheaters, and six fitted with a type of superheater colloquially known as the "Doncaster Straight Tube" type. This type differed from the others in that it had vertical headers which held the elements in place. In the boilers fitted with this arrangement there were separate saturated and superheated headers.

The fourth type of superheater was applied to one locomotive only in 1913 (No.563) which was a Gresley design known as a "Twin Tube" superheater. This was then replaced by a "Triple Tube" superheater two years later. Improvements included an increase in superheated surface area and had 17 elements.

The trials gave a mixture of results, and by the early 1920s the class had the choice of superheater reduced to two types; the Schmidt type (fitted to nine locomotives) and the other 101 locomotives used the Robinson design. By 1927 the L.N.E.R. had fully standardised on the Robinson design of superheater across their locomotive fleet and the remaining J6s with Schmidt type superheaters were converted accordingly.

Gresley under the G.N.R. experimented with feed water heating and several types provided by different companies between 1916 and 1918. These experiments were followed up with feed water equipment being fitted to other Gresley locomotives over the next two decades on the L.N.E.R., including classes A3, B12, O2 and P2. The feed water heaters ranged from Dabeg to Auxiliaires des Chemins de Fer (A.C.F.I.) equipment and without exception were all removed after short periods of time in service. Three members of Class J6 received such equipment in 1928, with the feed water heaters being removed by the end of 1932.

*Fig 20. Gresley's modification to one of the Ivatt built 0-6-0s with a feed water heater. 1917.*
*Tim Robbins Collection.*

The J6s were initially intended as fast mixed traffic locomotives for pulling express goods trains, but by the grouping in 1923 had been cascaded down onto coal trains and local goods trains.

Fig. 21. Gresley J6 No.3593 sits on shed awaiting its next turn of duty. Note the overall grime and condition of the locomotive. The Gresley Society.

They were mostly concentrated in the western area of the Southern section of the L.N.E.R. with a large allocation at Colwick over the years (between 35 and 40). A good number were also allocated at Doncaster and New England with the rest spread sporadically across the L.N.E.R., including a pair kept in London for some time too. There were seven members of the class which were sent to cover a group of overhauled J25s that had been loaned to the Great Western Railway (G.W.R.) in 1940 but with the return of the latter engines they were sent back to their usual haunts. The Nottinghamshire based J6s were only displaced from passenger services with the arrival of brand-new Thompson L1 tank locomotives in the early 1950s.

## Wartime Mileages & Availability

The mileages and availability of the Gresley J6s throughout the Second World War has been recorded in the *Use of Engine Power* document. They achieved respectable availability, with little change year on year and remaining in and around the 80% availability mark. Their average mileages peaked in 1942, falling in 1943, with a small improvement in 1944 but for the next two years continued to fall. This was in line with the average fleet availability and with only a few thousand miles on average a year less than those a few years earlier.

The J6s were not included in Thompson's standardisation scheme and were also absent from L.N.E.R. literature through to British Railways days. Although all the Gresley J6s survived the Second World War by British Railways days they were beginning to show their age and the first withdrawals started in 1955. By the end of 1962, the entire class had been scrapped.

| Year | Mileages | Availability |
|---|---|---|
| 1942 | 24475 | 81% |
| 1943 | 22411 | 79% |
| 1944 | 23331 | 85% |
| 1945 | 22525 | 81% |
| 1946 | 21544 | 80% |

*Fig. 22. J6 Mileages & Availability Statistics. Simon A.C. Martin, from the Use of Engine Power Document.*

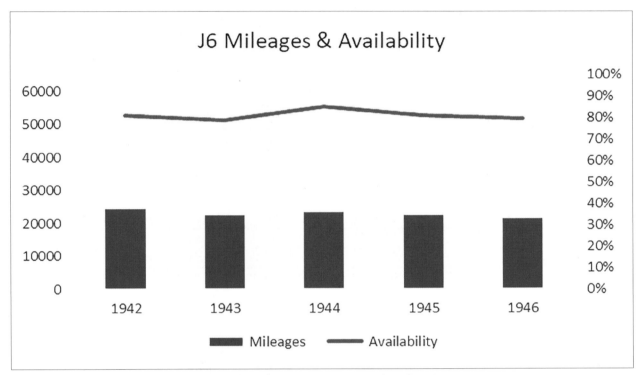

*Fig. 23. J6 Mileages & Availability Graph.*
*Simon A.C. Martin from the Use of Engine Power Document.*

The J6s were not included in Thompson's standardisation scheme and were also absent from L.N.E.R. literature through to British Railways days. Although all the Gresley J6s survived the Second World War by British Railways days they were beginning to show their age and the first withdrawals started in 1955. By the end of 1962, the entire class had been scrapped.

| Class J6 | | |
|---|---|---|
| Cylinders | (inside) x 2 | 19x26in. |
| Motion | | Stephenson |
| Valves | | 8in (Piston) |
| Boiler | Diagram: | No. 7 |
| | Max. Diameter: | 4ft 8in |
| | Pressure: | 170lb |
| Heating Surface | Total: | 1129 sq. ft. |
| | Firebox: | 118 sq. ft. |
| | Superheater: | 192 sq. ft. (18x1.25in) |
| | Tubes: | 562 sq. ft. (118x 1.75in) |
| | Flues: | 257 sq. ft. (18x 5.25in) |
| Grate Area | | 19 sq. ft. |
| Wheels | Coupled: | 5ft 2in |
| | Tender: | 4ft 2in |
| Tractive Effort | At 85% boiler pressure | 21,875lb |
| Wheelbase | Total: | 38ft 10in |
| | Engine: | 16ft 3in |
| | Tender: | 13ft 0in |
| Weight (full) | Total: | 93 tons 12 cwt |
| | Engine: | 50 tons 10 cwt |
| | Tender: | 43 tons 2 cwt |
| Max. Axle Load | | 18 tons 0 cwt |

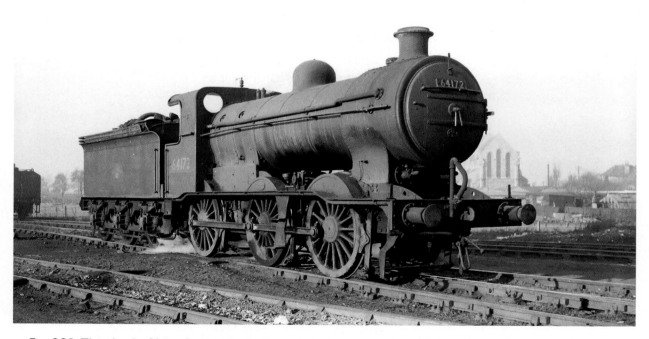

*Fig. 23B. The third of her class to be built and dating from September 1911 and numbered now as 64172, she was showing 35A New England as her allocation during the mid-1950s. By 1960 and allocated finally to 40F Boston, she would be one of twenty-three of her class withdrawn that year, leaving just seven examples to soldier on into 1961, their final year. Strathwood Library Collection.*

# G.N.R. Class H2 (L.N.E.R. Classes K1 and K2) 2-6-0 (1912)

Number built (G.N.R.): 8 (K1s), 67 (K2s)
Total built: 75

*Fig. 24. Gresley K2 No.1683, works photograph. Colourised by Ian MacCabe, The Gresley Society.*

In 1912, the G.N.R. was accelerating its freight services utilising the larger passenger locomotives available. This caused some issues in the operational departments, and availability of these locomotives started to wane. 40mph was the intended speed for goods traffic and Gresley was keen to introduce a new Mogul (2-6-0) to the G.N.R. after the railway's experience of the American designed Baldwin built moguls over the last decade.

These locomotives (given the classification "H1" by the G.N.R.) had their parts built in the United States, but most were assembled at Ardsley Shed. These locomotives employed two outside cylinders with Stephenson valve gear and a 3500-gallon capacity bogie tender with coal rails. The H1s seemed to be intended as a stop gap in the G.N.R.'s locomotive fleet and were like other Baldwins ordered by the Great Central Railway (G.C.R.) and Midland Railway (M.R.) around the same time.

Although the short lives of these early G.N.R. moguls are highlighted by other historians, their effect on the engine policy of the G.N.R. is notable. Gresley, when C.M.E., looked to introduce a similarly proportioned locomotive. The simple two-cylinder setup was translated by Gresley and his design department into a round topped 2-6-0 using a double swing-link pony truck design.

*Fig. 25. G.N.R. Baldwin Mogul No.1190, ex-works. Note the bogie tender. The Gresley Society.*

This design of swing link pony truck became the standard for all future Gresley classes built with a pony truck, and whilst suitable in the 1910s and 1920s, by the 1930s and 1940s the increase in line speeds, train weights, and the state of the permanent way made the swing link pony truck design inadequate for the largest locomotives, being replaced where required on classes like the Gresley V2s. The superheated boiler of the Ivatt Q1s and Q2s was used as a basis for the new design with a shorter barrel. An 18-element Schmidt superheater was fitted to compensate for the restrictions on the diameter of the now shorter boiler barrel. Walschaerts valve gear with a two-bar assembly was used, in conjunction with 10in diameter piston valves.

*Fig.26. Gresley K1 No.1630, works photograph. The Gresley Society.*

The prototype was completed and in service by 1913, with nine further examples following shortly after. A small difference between the prototype and those which followed was the change from 3ft 8in on the pony truck wheels of the prototype to the 3ft 2in wheels which became standard for the class thereafter. These locomotives, given the classification by the G.N.R. as H2, were allocated to Colwick, Doncaster and King's Cross and put to work on braked goods trains, and some heavy passenger services.

A larger boiler was designed for the next batch of 2-6-0s, with a firebox 6in longer and a larger diameter barrel. This was designed primarily for the fitting of a Robinson type superheater, and to accommodate these changes, the frames were lengthened, and the pony truck was fitted 4in further forward of the leading coupled driving wheels. This design was originally classified by the G.N.R. as the H3 class but would later become the L.N.E.R.'s K2. Between 1914 and 1921, sixty-five of these Mogul locomotives would be built in five batches, with Doncaster and the North British Locomotive Co. Ltd (N.B.L.) sharing two batches each, and the final batch being onstructed by Kitson & Co.

*Fig. 27. Gresley K2 No.1640, works photograph. The Gresley Society.*

The earlier K1s would later be rebuilt to K2 specification. The first rebuild was No.4635 in 1922, and the rest following suit between 1931 and 1937, rendering the original K1 class extinct. To distinguish the original locomotives and the as-built K2s, they would be split into subgroups of K2/1 (all locomotives originally built as K2s) and K2/2 (locomotives rebuilt from K1 to K2 specification). Class K1 was fitted with shorter chimneys by the L.N.E.R. in 1923 to allow them to work on lines which had restrictive loading gauges, such as the ex-Great Eastern (G.E.R.) and ex-North British (N.B.R.) lines.

This, in addition with fitting shorter dome covers, flatter cab roofs, replacement of their tall Ramsbottom safety valves with the shorter Ross Pop variety, and moving the placement of the whistles, would seem to be a pre-emptive move towards displacing older locomotives on those lines. They would only be cascaded in this way when larger numbers of Gresley's K3 class became available later.

The split of the class between East Anglia and Scotland provided a contrast by the time of British Railways: The Scottish examples had side window cabs fitted so that the crews could endure more inclement weather. Any K2s which were transferred to Scotland would have their cabs similarly rebuilt. Whereas around 20 of the K2s found in East Anglia would be fitted with Westinghouse pumps to work passenger services out of Liverpool Street, mostly on the Cambridge and Colchester lines.

## Wartime Mileages & Availability

During the Second World War, the K2 class was putting in respectable mileages and availability, however this started to tail off by the end of the war (as it was, in fairness, for all L.N.E.R. locomotive classes that had not been built new during the war) and in 1946 the classes' annual average mileages dipped below 25,000 miles, around 5000 miles a year less than it had been in 1942, with availability 12% lower overall.

| Year | Mileages | Availability |
|------|----------|--------------|
| 1942 | 30219 | 79% |
| 1943 | 27582 | 77% |
| 1944 | 25579 | 77% |
| 1945 | 25643 | 73% |
| 1946 | 24975 | 67% |

Fig. 28. K2 Mileages & Availability Statistics.
Simon A.C. Martin, from the Use of Engine Power Document.

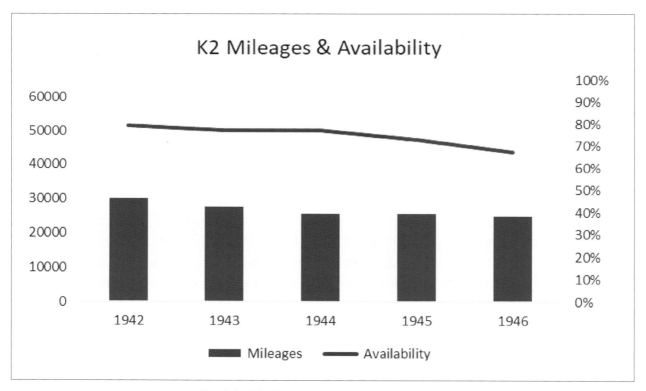

Fig. 29. K2 Mileages & Availability Graph.
Simon A.C. Martin from the Use of Engine Power Document.

The K2s survived intact until 1955, with the first being withdrawn that year and withdrawals continuing (including some used as stationary boilers) until 1962. The last of the class, No.61756, was scrapped in the summer of the following year.

| Classes K1 and K2 | | | |
|---|---|---|---|
| | | Class K1 | Class K2 |
| Cylinders: | (2x outside) | 20x26in. | 20x26in. |
| Motion: | 10in piston | Walschaerts | Walschaerts |
| Boiler: | Max. Diameter: | 4ft 8in | 5ft 6in |
| | Pressure: | 180lb | 180lb |
| | Diagram No.: | 6 | 3 |
| Heating Surface: | Total: | 1309 sq. ft. | 1934.5 sq. ft. |
| | Firebox: | 136 sq. ft. | 152 sq. ft. |
| | Superheater: | 230 sq. ft. (18x 1.25in) | 305 sq. ft. (24x 1.25in) |
| | Tubes: | 647 sq. ft. (118x 1.75in) | 1082 sq. ft. (197x 1.75in) |
| | Flues: | 296 sq. ft. (18x 5.25in) | 395.5 sq. ft. (24x 5.25in) |
| Grate Area: | | 24.5 sq. ft. | 24 sq. ft. |
| Wheels: | Leading: | 3ft 2in | 3ft 2in |
| | Coupled: | 5ft 8in | 5ft 8in |
| | Tender: | 4ft 2in | 4ft 2in |
| Tractive Effort: | At 85% boiler pressure | 23,400lb | 23,400lb |
| Wheelbase: | Total: | 46ft 10.25in | 47ft 7.5in |
| | Engine: | 24ft 10in | 25ft 2in |
| | Tender: | 13ft 0in | 13ft 0in |
| Weight (full): | Total: | 104 tons 16cwt | 107 tons 10cwt |
| | Engine: | 61 tons 14cwt | 64 tons 8cwt |
| | Tender: | 43 tons 2cwt | 43 tons 2cwt |
| Max. Axle Load: | | 18 tons | 18 tons 16cwt |

*Fig. 29B. One of the original K2/1 locomotives sent to work in Scotland for the West Highland Line and rebuilt with a side window cab in June 1951 was No.61721. Strathwood Library Collection*

# G.N.R. Class O1 (L.N.E.R. Class O3) 2-8-0 (1913)

## Number built (G.N.R.): 20

*Fig.30. Gresley O1 No.459, works photograph. Colourised by Ian MacCabe, The Gresley Society.*

In the early 1910s the G.N.R. was utilising Ivatt designed 0-8-0 tender engines, which were found wanting as traffic and train lengths increased. In particular, the required coal traffic from Peterborough to London was exceeding the capacity of the Ivatt designed freight engines with train lengths of around eighty wagons and up to 1300 tonnes of coal to be hauled. The need for a new heavy goods locomotive was clear and by 1913 Gresley's first design for the G.N.R., the 2-6-0 K1, was in service and performing adequately.

Gresley took the design of the K1 further forward by effectively developing a 2-8-0 version, albeit with a larger boiler that was based on the Ivatt C1 Atlantic but with the wide firebox substituted for a narrow type, a 24 element Robinson superheater and Ramsbottom safety valves fitted. The 10in piston valves and Walschaerts valve gear of the K1 were reused almost verbatim as was the double bolster swing link pony truck at the front end.

The order for the first batch of the Class O1 was placed in May 1913 and was for five locomotives but providing them with six boilers. This was a curious arrangement and so it proved in 1918 when the sixth boiler was finally used, but fitted to the prototype of the O2 class, the first three-cylinder 2-8-0 on the G.N.R. Further batches were quoted from Doncaster, but no more orders were placed.

Early in 1916, quotations were sought for fifteen more Gresley O1s. The First World War was in full swing and capacity for building these locomotives in the United Kingdom could not be found, so the G.N.R. looked overseas and summarily ordered boiler plates, frame plates, and axles from the United States of America (U.S.A.) during August 1917, with the locomotives put together by N.B.L. in April 1918. This order represented ten locomotives, with a further five added later in 1919 to give a final complement of 20 locomotives.

*Fig.31. Gresley O1 No.3457, pulling a goods train mostly made up of private owner wagons and one van towards the front of the train. The Gresley Society.*

The development of the three-cylinder 2-8-0 led to the curtailment of the development of the two-cylinder 2-8-0, meaning that the O1 class would be the last two-cylinder tender locomotive designed for the G.N.R. though not the last two-cylinder tender locomotive Gresley would design. That honour fell to the Class J39 of 1926.

The first batch of O1s were fitted with double admission valves of the standard Doncaster pattern, designed to open at the same time and increase the amount of steam into the cylinder, which greatly benefited the locomotives when running. On starting this caused carbon deposits within the supplementary port ways and would lead to a loss of power, with the lead steam becoming insufficient because of the build-up. These were modified between 1914 and 1915 with the ports being opened slightly.

*Fig.32. Gresley O1 No.3465, pulling a train including bogie brick wagons. Note the branding of N.E. with the space between them taken up by the word "Brick". The Gresley Society.*

The O1s and O2s had a standard boiler design (the No.2) and over the 30 years of production of the latter class no further development in the boiler design was attempted. The O1s would be withdrawn before diagram 100A boilers were fitted.

The class was subject to Gresley's experiments using feed water heaters of the Weir, Worthington and Gresham and Craven types. All of which were removed by the end of 1932. Class member No.459 was noted for the experimental fitting of a second dome hidden underneath a single long cover between the front and rear domes. Cold water would be fed into the top of the boiler and in collection trays in the second dome.

Eventually when No.459 was overhauled, the boiler was swapped for a standard diagram No.2 boiler. The experimental boiler was then fitted to No.3461 (the prototype of the O2 class) and took part in further experiments with top feed without further classmates being modified in the same way.

The piston valves on the O1s were originally a split ring design sprung inside the steam chest liner. This was to aid fitting in building the locomotives and subsequent overhauls and to provide a steam-tight fit. Unfortunately, this design was difficult to lubricate well, with the split rings exchanged for an improved design over time.

Both the O1s and O2s were to become known as "Tangos" to enthusiasts and railwaymen, the original O1s introduction to the railway coming at the time that the Tango was becoming a popular dance in the United Kingdom. Why exactly this was applied to these classes is unclear. However, it was also applied to the Gresley J50 tank locomotives which were introduced around the same time. This moniker did not stick in the same way with the tank engines as it did with the 2-8-0s.

From their inception, the twenty O1s were allocated to Peterborough's New England shed and were all employed on the heavy coal traffic, a role which they were well suited, pulling a significant amount more than their predecessors. By 1920 there were two coal trains a day from Colwick to New England and several O1s were moved there to cover this work. Between 1920 and 1926 there was a bit of shuffling of O1s around the two depots with four eventually to stay at Colwick more permanently until the mid-1930s. The O1s were to be seen taking empty trains of wagons up to Doncaster, returning with full loads, until 1925 when Robinson O4s would take over these duties permanently.

The O1s were to be moved around more in the 1930s as train speeds started to increase once again and were replaced on the old G.N.R. mainlines by Gresley's newer and faster K3 2-6-0 locomotives. Half the class were moved to Doncaster from Peterborough as a result, with the rest of the class moving to Grantham by 1942. The mid 1940s saw the O1s in the twilight of their careers. They were reclassified from O1 to O3 by 1944 as the first of Edward Thompson's own O1 design locomotives were being rebuilt from Robinson O4s and put into service.

In 1945, every member of the class not already at Doncaster was then allocated there, with the Grantham iron ore traffic being taken over by new members of Gresley's O2 class (which had continued to be built under Thompson). It would only be a short sojourn and the entire class would be passed around Frodingham, Immingham and then Retford. The class started to be withdrawn in 1947, and by 1952 had become extinct.

| Year | Mileages | Availability |
|------|----------|--------------|
| 1942 | 25382 | 75% |
| 1943 | 22372 | 71% |
| 1944 | 22545 | 73% |
| 1945 | 27379 | 80% |
| 1946 | 21869 | 71% |

*Fig. 33. O1 Mileages & Availability Statistics.*
*Simon A.C. Martin, from the Use of Engine Power Document.*

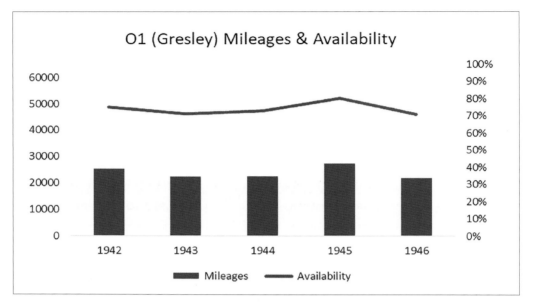

*Fig. 34. O1 Mileages & Availability Graph.*
*Simon A.C. Martin from the Use of Engine Power Document.*

The O1s in comparison to other 2-8-0s the L.N.E.R. employed during World War Two were performing well with their average mileages and availability remaining consistent throughout the war. In line with most of the railway's fleet, by 1946 the class was tired, and mileages and availability fell to their lowest levels of the war.

It must be remembered that the oldest members of the class were nearly thirty years old at this time. Their availability to do work was superior to some newer Gresley designs that were being employed on similar work such as the K3s.

| Class O1 | | |
|---|---|---|
| Cylinders | (outside) x 2 | 21x28in. |
| Motion | | Walschaerts |
| Valves | | 10in (Piston) |
| Boiler | Diagram: | No. 2 |
| | Max. Diameter: | 5ft 6in |
| | Pressure: | 180lb |
| Heating Surface | Total: | 2463 sq. ft. |
| | Firebox: | 163.5 sq. ft. |
| | Superheater: | 430.5 sq. ft. (18x1.25in) |
| | Tubes: | 1340 sq. ft. (118x 1.75in) |
| | Flues: | 528 sq. ft. (18x 5.25in) |
| Grate Area | | 27.5 sq. ft. |
| Wheels | Coupled: | 4ft 8in |
| | Tender: | 4ft 2in |
| Tractive Effort | At 85% boiler pressure | 33,736lb |
| Wheelbase | Total: | 51ft 4in |
| | Engine: | 26ft 4in |
| | Tender: | 13ft 0in |
| Weight (full) | Total: | 119 tons 6 cwt |
| | Engine: | 76 tons 4 cwt |
| | Tender: | 43 tons 2 cwt |
| Max. Axle Load | | 17 tons 12 cwt |

*Fig.34b. The elegance of these G.N.R. 2-8-0s is clear to see in this view taken at Hornsey.*
*Strathwood Library Collection*

# G.N.R. Class J23 (L.N.E.R. Class J51 and later J50) 0-6-0T (1914)

Number built (G.N.R.): 10 (J50s), 30 (J51s)
Number built (L.N.E.R.): 62 (J50s)
Total built: 92

*Fig.35. Gresley J50 No.215, works photograph. Colourised by Ian MacCabe, The Gresley Society.*

In the early 1910s the G.N.R. was using a wide range of 0-6-0 tender locomotives that were increasingly elderly and starting to struggle with train loads. The Stirling era J3s, J4s and J7s were highlighted as struggling on the heavily graded lines in the West Riding for local runs and shunting. Gresley's solution was to design a compact and powerful tank locomotive.

The biggest advantage of using a tank locomotive design was in increasing the adhesive weight over the driving wheels by use of the water tanks. Gresley however did not favour the normal saddletank design of the G.N.R.'s shunting locomotives, and this was rejected in favour of side tanks along the full length of the running plate. These had a sloping front to aid the driver's view ahead. Cut-outs in the tanks between the front and middle driving wheels would provide access to the motion.

The boilers for the first thirty locomotives came from Ivatt R1 0-8-2T tank locomotives. This class was at the time being fitted with a new larger boiler of 4ft 8in diameter compared with their original boilers that were 4ft 2in in diameter.

Twenty members of the J51 class were built with a boiler of diameter 4ft 5in and with slightly shorter fireboxes. These two later batches of tank locomotives were originally designated J23 in linem with the first batch of 30 locomotives: but at the grouping in 1923, the original thirty locomotives were designated as J51 by the L.N.E.R., and the twenty with the larger boiler were designated J50.

*Fig. 36. Gresley J50 No.589, waiting on shed. The smoke is coming from a locomotive on the opposite side of the J50. This J50 has had its bunker modified by way of platework welded in behind the coal rails. The Gresley Society.*

The J51s were rebuilt between 1929-35 with larger boilers and were reclassified as J50. Gresley was satisfied enough with the final J50 design that it became one of the group standard designs eventually numbering 102 examples.

Variations in the locomotives by way of left or right-hand drive, different bunker arrangements and similar were recognised by the L.N.E.R. which introduced sub-divisions to the class as follows:

- J51/1. 10 examples built in 1914 with the 4ft 2in boiler, vacuum brake, right-hand drive, short bunker.

- J51/2. 20 built between 1914–19. Same as the J51/1 but fitted with a longer bunker.

- J50/1. 10 examples that were rebuilt between 1929–35 from J51/1, with the new 4ft 5in diameter boiler.

- J50/2. 20 of these were built between 1922–24, from Class J51/2 but now fitted with the 4ft 5in diameter boiler. These were joined by a further 20 rebuilt between 1929–34 from J51/1 and again fitted with the 4ft 5in diameter boiler.

- J50/3. 30 built between 1926–30 with the 4ft 5in boiler, steam brake, now left-hand drive and with the longer bunker.

- J50/4. 14 examples built (the only ones not built at Doncaster works, but instead at Gorton) between 1938–39, as the final batch incorporating the 4ft 5in boiler, vacuum brake, left-hand drive and a new longer bunker with hopper.

The Gresley J50 was later included as one of the second L.N.E.R. C.M.E.'s Edward Thompson's *New Standard Classes*. However, no further examples were built and the order for more J50s was replaced by the third L.N.E.R.'s C.M.E. Arthur Peppercorn, with new examples of the N.E.R. designed J72 class instead.

*Fig. 37. An unidentified Gresley on a mixed traffic goods train at Ferme Park, these J50s were utilised as both shunters and for goods trains such as these in their working lives. Note the hopper type bunker. The Gresley Society.*

Withdrawals of the J50s began in 1958 as new diesel shunters were being delivered, and by 1963 all had been withdrawn from normal service. Seven examples were retained for departmental stock, and these worked up until 1965, when they were withdrawn and scrapped. None of the Gresley J50s survived into preservation.

| Year | Mileages | Availability |
|------|----------|--------------|
| 1942 | 21294 | 84% |
| 1943 | 22319 | 84% |
| 1944 | 22443 | 87% |
| 1945 | 21606 | 84% |
| 1946 | 20827 | 83% |

*Fig.38. J50 Mileages & Availability Statistics.*
*Simon A.C. Martin, from the Use of Engine Power Document.*

The Gresley J50s during World War Two were among the most reliable and high mileage of the L.N.E.R. tank locomotives of their size and power. They bucked the trend of the other classes by a good ten to fifteen % higher availability overall. Their mileages and availability remained high, with a slight jump in availability and mileages in 1944.

The J50 should rightly be considered as one of Gresley's most successful designs and it certainly ranks among his most distinctive and recognisable designs.

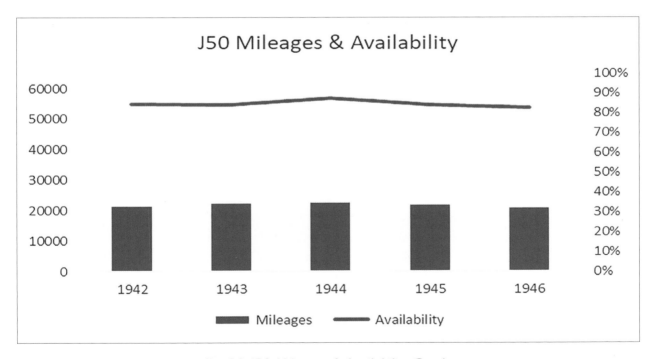

*Fig. 39. J50 Mileages & Availability Graph.*
*Simon A.C. Martin from the Use of Engine Power Document.*

| Classes J50 and J51 | | | |
|---|---|---|---|
| | | J50 | J51 |
| Cylinders (x2): | (inside) | 18.5x26in. | 18.5x26in. |
| Motion: | | Stephenson | Stephenson |
| Valves: | | Slide | Slide |
| Boiler: | Diameter (max): | 4ft 5in | 4ft 2in |
| | Length: | 10ft 1in | 10ft 6in |
| | Diagram No: | 11 | 12 |
| | Boiler Pressure: | 170lb | 175lb |
| Heating Surface: | Total: | 1119 sq. ft. | 979.85 sq. ft. |
| | Firebox: | 103 sq. ft. | 111.4 sq. ft. |
| | Tubes: | 1016 sq. ft. | 868.45 sq. ft. |
| Grate Area: | | 16.25 sq. ft. | 17.8 sq. ft. |
| Wheels: | | 4ft 8in | 4ft 8in |
| Total Wheelbase: | | 16ft 3in | 16ft 3in |
| Tractive Effort: | (at 85% boiler pressure) | 22,963 lb | 23,636 lb |
| Length: | | 32ft 2.5in to 33ft 4in | 32ft 2.5in to 33ft |
| Weight: | | 56t 6cwt to 58t 3cwt | 56t to 56t 16cwt |
| Max. Axle Load: | | 19t 5cwt to 20t | 19t 5cwt to 19t 16cwt |
| Water Capacity: | | 1500-1520 gallons | 1500-1520 gallons |
| Coal Capacity: | | 2t to 5t 5cwt | 2t to 3t 10cwt |

*Fig.39B. One of the Gorton built locomotives classified as a J50/4 with a larger hopper type bunker rests at Sheffield Darnall in 1952. Strathwood Library Collection.*

# G.N.R. Class O2 2-8-0 (1918)

Number built (G.N.R.): 11
Number built (L.N.E.R.): 56
Total built: 67

Fig. 40. Gresley O2 prototype No.461, works photograph. The Gresley Society.

Gresley's first conjugated valve gear locomotive was the prototype locomotive for Class O2, No.461. This locomotive started a significant trend in design for Sir Nigel Gresley. Though not all his future locomotives would feature conjugated valve gear and three cylinders, ultimately this locomotive would be the progenitor to all his future iconic steam locomotive designs.

## The Conjugated Valve Gear

The development of Gresley's patented conjugated valve gear warrants specific attention as for many years it has been the subject of back-and-forth discussion on whether it truly can be considered to be Gresley's own work. Appendix 5 of this book gives Gresley's full patent document of 1915 together with copies of the original drawings that were presented by Gresley's agent at the time to the Patent Office

There has been a measure of controversy regarding Gresley's conjugated valve gear, and whether it was close to the patent of Harold Holcroft, an engineer working for the South East and Chatham Railway (S.E.C.R.) at the time. The facts remain that Holcroft's patent had expired in 1913 (whether through allowing it to lapse, or fees had not been paid) and Gresley was at great pains in his patent application to note how his conjugated gear differed from the Joy's patent of 1884.

When Gresley's patent was accepted on 12th October 1916, the frames for what would become the prototype O2, No.461, had already long been laid (work had started in February of that year) and the engine order was then given in December 1916.

There are variations of the story told as to Gresley's conjugated valve gear with probably the most balanced account in Geoffrey's Hughes biography of Gresley. In this report the two engineers met in January 1919 at Gresley's suggestion. Holcroft and Gresley are presented as engineers that are discussing the pros and cons of the designs on offer by Gresley for his conjugated valve gear. Holcroft provided the benefits of his experience with some suggestions.

We know from primary evidence that both Holcroft and Gresley were proponents of three-cylinder locomotives, by way of their papers presented to the iMechE. Both believed in the advantages of removing the third set of valve gear and in some way conjugating the motion from the outside cylinders to the centre cylinder. They did so in different ways, Gresley preferring to conjugate by way of the *2 to 1 lever* described in his patent.

Gresley's patent as given in Appendix 4 shows that before the meeting in January 1919 with Holcroft to discuss his work, Gresley had already provided what would be the final version of his conjugated gear entirely separately to Holcroft within the body of his 1915 patent documents.

To continue to describe the valve gear as "Gresley-Holcroft" in terms of describing the form of G.N.R. and then L.N.E.R. conjugated valve gear as fitted post 1918 is therefore incorrect. Some reconsideration of the primary evidence is now required from an historical standpoint. If Gresley had already designed what would become the final layout of his conjugated valve gear in 1915 then Holcroft's influence on this interpretation of conjugated valve gear was minimal at best if not negligible.

Holcroft is reported in many secondary sources as providing suggestions on how to improve Gresley's own conjugated valve gear by skewing the cylinder and valve axis to retain valve events at what would now be considered the correct relationship. This had already been done by Gresley and described as such within his patent of 1915 too.

Gresley was apparently suitably impressed with Holcroft and secondary sources report that he approached Holcroft's superior on the S.E.&C.R. to enquire if Holcroft could be released to work for him. The response has been reported as a firm "no" from Holcroft's manager, one Richard Maunsell.

## The Conjugated Valve Gear Prototype: No.461

No.461 was the first conjugated valve gear locomotive built under Gresley's direction, but it differed from all later variants of the conjugated valve gear G.N.R. and L.N.E.R. fleets by way of rocking shafts to operate the middle valve gear.

Fig. 41. Gresley O2 No.477 sits simmering on shed. Strathwood Library Collection.

Fig. 42. Gresley O2 No.3500 in the 1930s. Note the somewhat bulbous feedwater heater on the running plate. Strathwood Library Collection.

The more steeply inclined outside cylinders and valve gear are a result of this unique alternate arrangement and correspond closely to the first of the two forms of conjugated valve gear as seen in Gresley's patent in Appendix 5.

No.461 has gone under the radar of G.N.R. and L.N.E.R. writers to date. From the reports given at the time the success of no.461's entry into traffic cannot be disputed. The prototype's performances directly led to Gresley making an announcement that he would concentrate on three-cylinder designs with only a few exceptions (those being classes N2, J38 and J39).

No.461 continued to work with its unique valve gear arrangement until its withdrawal in May 1948 after 30 years use. As a prototype locomotive it was subject to a few changes of boiler but was otherwise unaltered from its entry into service to its withdrawal. As such, it should be considered something of a triumph for Gresley and it is a great shame that it was scrapped before the preservation era kicked in.

*Fig. 43. Gresley O2 No.3495, works photograph. The Gresley Society.*

The production Gresley O2 locomotives came out looking quite different at the front end, with first introduction of the style of running plate that eventually became something of a Gresley trait. The reverse curves of the prototype's being ditched for the quadrant and S-curves of the final design. These locomotives benefitted from the appointing of N.B.L. to build them as they made changes to the cylinder and steam chest layout. This would become what is considered to be the standard version of the Gresley conjugated valve gear. These engines were designated as O2/1 accordingly.

At the grouping the Class O2 comprised the prototype and the first ten built at the N.B.L.'s Atlas Works. Fifteen further engines were promptly ordered with some changes made to the cab and chimney to fit the new composite loading gauge of the L.N.E.R. Their designation was accordingly, O2/2.

The prototype O2 and the G.N.R. built O2/1s were originally built with split-ring piston valves. Like the Gresley O1 class before them these suffered from lubrication and wear issues and from 1923 were all replaced with the Knorr-type piston valves when shopped for repair. Fifty more Gresley O2s were to be built and had been ordered in 1924's building programme. These were cancelled due to the proliferation of Robinson designed ex-Railway Operating Division (R.O.D.) Class O4 2-8-0s being made available for purchase. It would be 1929 before the next batch of Gresley O2/2s would be built. Eight engines were built out of an authorised batch of fifteen.

The next set of eight locomotives appeared from 1932 and were complete by March 1934. These had a further modification to their cabs and fittings to clear the more restrictive ex-G.E.R. section and were now being turned out with the new 4200 Group Standard six-wheel tenders. Further modifications included the fitting of long travel valve gear. These O2s were classified as O2/3.

Fig. 44. Gresley O2 No.3491, exists the tunnel at Ganwick on a coal train. Note the early G.N.R. cab and tender. The Gresley Society.

No further O2s were to be built until 1941 despite appearing in the 1935 programme. There was an authorisation by the Railway Executive in 1940 for 100 more of the type (as many of the Robinson O4s had been requisitioned for overseas work) but in the event only 25 more O2/3s were built. These were in service by 1943. The total class number was 67.

In 1943 one of the class, No.3479, was fitted with a diagram 100A boiler. This was the same boiler being fitted to the new Thompson standard locomotives that were being built at the time. This boiler was pressed to 180lb. No.3479 would remain unique until 1944 when four more O2s were fitted with the new standard L.N.E.R. boiler. These engines would be reclassified as O2/4. Side window cabs matching the O2/3s would later be fitted to those conversions that didn't already carry them.

These engines could be recognised quite quickly by a study of the boiler and smokebox arrangements. The diagram 100A boiler had a shorter barrel than the original design, so an extension to the smokebox together with a different placement of the snifting valve on the extension itself was necessary. This was done with a bracket to the boiler just in front of the dip in the running plate. This arrangement was later applied to all the O2/1s, O2/2s and O2/3s as their boilers came up for renewal or replacement with the diagram 100A type.

The allocation of the O2s were split by region and by batch. The first, No.461, was allocated to New England to provide comparison to the two-cylinder O1s that worked from there. Then the Class O2/1s and O2/2s followed when built but all were moved in 1942 to working from Doncaster when the first of the Class O7 War Department "Austerity" 2-8-0s were brought into service. The O2/3s were allocated to March shed and worked coal trains on the ex-G.E.R. lines between Temple Mills at Stratford in East London and Whitemoor Yard. The improvements made to the sidings of the latter in terms of refuge sidings increased the size of the coal trains up to eighty wagons at a time.

The O2/4s were kept at Doncaster between 1942 and 1944 until a move to Colwick to assist with the significant uplift in wartime traffic ahead of D-Day. Most of these engines were then moved to New England before the whole allocation of New England's O2s were split. They went to Colwick, Doncaster, Grantham, Langwith and March over the next few years.

Grantham's O2s were used primarily for iron ore workings to and from the High Dyke area. The Langwith O2s were used for coal trains over the Woodhead route to Manchester and in the Mansfield area. After nationalisation of the railways in 1948 the Gresley O2s were further moved around with a number allocated to Frodingham until 1955. These examples also were set to work heavy iron ore traffic.

The next withdrawal of a Gresley O2 would happen in 1960, twelve years after the prototype had been withdrawn. Withdrawal of the entire class took only three years with the last 40 of the class withdrawn in 1963. None survived into preservation.

*Fig.44B. Built in 1924 at Doncaster and now as Class O2/4, 63945 was captured ex-works at Doncaster in the summer of 1962, only to be withdrawn in September of the following year. During 1956 the locomotive received a Thompson 100A boiler and side window cab.*
*Ian Turnbull - Rail Photoprints*

## *Wartime Mileages & Availability*

| Year | Mileages | Availability |
|---|---|---|
| 1942 | 29130 | 77% |
| 1943 | 27947 | 81% |
| 1944 | 21509 | 70% |
| 1945 | 27702 | 82% |
| 1946 | 21825 | 69% |

*Fig. 45. O2 Mileages & Availability Statistics.*
*Simon A.C. Martin, from the Use of Engine Power Document.*

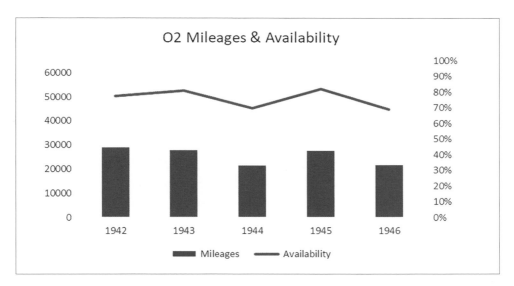

*Fig. 46. O2 Mileages & Availability Graph.*
*Simon A.C. Martin from the Use of Engine Power Document.*

The *Use of Engine* Power document shows that, with only two minor dips during, and at the end of the Second World War, the mileages and availability of the Gresley O2s was very competitive in relation to the performances of the other 2-8-0 classes in use on the L.N.E.R.

The O2 class gained some new examples during the war which helped significantly in their availability for work, but with some locomotives being withdrawn for boiler changes in 1944 and 1946, the average mileages dipped accordingly.

The excellence of the Gresley O2 design should not be underestimated by enthusiasts. The O2 prototype and its successors showed a way forward for the conjugated valve gear. The prototype, however, suffered from having a more complicated arrangement with its rocking shafts having more pins and joints than the later type, or indeed a third set of valve gear would have required.

Doncaster Works is on record as stating they were "never able to set the valve gear correctly" yet it is also factual that No.461 remained throughout its entire working life a very reliable runner.

Gresley's V2 class locomotive is often held up as one of the locomotives that "won for the war" for the L.N.E.R. and the country: perhaps the role of the Gresley O2 in the many freight trains pulled (with coal, munitions, and other mixed traffic work) should also be recognised.

| Class O2 | | | |
|---|---|---|---|
| | | O2, O2/1, 2 & 3 | O2/4 |
| Cylinders (x3): | Conjugated | 18.5x26in. | 18.5x26in. |
| Motion: | | Walschaerts | Walschaerts |
| Valves: | | 8in Piston | 8in Piston |
| Boiler: | Diameter (max): | 5ft 6in | 5ft 6in |
| | Length: | 16ft 1in | 14ft 1in |
| | Diagram No: | 2 | 100A |
| | Boiler Pressure: | 180lb | 180lb |
| Heating Surface: | Total: | 2462.5 sq. ft. | 2020 sq. ft. |
| | Firebox: | 163.5 sq. ft. | 168 sq. ft. |
| | Tubes: | 1340.5 sq. ft. | 1048 sq. ft. |
| Grate Area: | | 27.5 sq. ft. | 27.9 sq. ft. |
| Wheels: | | 4ft 8in | 4ft 8in |
| Total Wheelbase: | | 26ft 4in | 27ft 2in |
| Tractive Effort: | (at 85% boiler pressure) | 34,523 lb | 36,470 lb |
| Length: | | 53ft 3in | 53ft 3in |
| Weight: | | 75tons 16cwt | 74tons 2cwt |
| Max. Axle Load: | | 17tons 16cwt | 17tons 3cwt |
| Water Capacity: | | 3500 gallons | 4200 gallons |
| Coal Capacity: | | 6tons 10cwt | 7tons 10cwt |

# G.N.R. Class H4 (L.N.E.R. Class K3) 2-6-0 (1920)

Number built (G.N.R.): 10
Number built (L.N.E.R.): 183
Total built: 193

*Fig 47. Gresley K3 No.1003, works photograph. Colourised by Ian MacCabe, The Gresley Society.*

By 1917 train loads were increasing beyond the capabilities of Gresley's largest moguls, the
G.N.R. Class H3s (L.N.E.R. K2). Gresley and his team started looking into whether this design
could be further modified in line with the needs of the railway. There was a scheme sketched
with different diameter cylinders and the same boiler, with pressure raised to 180lb. This would
have given a higher tractive effort than the original K2. The potential two-cylinder design would
have had to increase the size of the bearing surfaces for the coupling and connecting rod crank
pins to take these greater piston loads.

Most secondary sources on Gresley's life and work give this as a reason as to why a further
two-cylinder mogul did not proceed, but the more likely reason was the success of Gresley's
first three-cylinder design, Class O2 No.461. The K3 design then morphed into a three-cylinder
mogul with 18.5in cylinder diameter, and a boiler of 6ft diameter, with pressure capped at 180lb,
which gave a net increase in tractive effort of around 40% higher than the previous K2s moguls
to 30,031lb. The middle cylinder had to be steeply inclined to clear the leading coupled axle, to
have all three cylinders drive onto the centre axle of the driving wheels. The outside cylinders
were almost horizontal by comparison.

*Fig 48. The prototype Gresley K3 No.1000, in a works photograph. Note the squared off buffer beam, tall chimney, and the additional lamp iron on the left-hand side. Rail Archive Stephenson.*

*Fig. 49. Gresley's second K3, No.1001, works photograph. The Gresley Society.*

In F.A.S. Brown's book, *Nigel Gresley: Locomotive Engineer* it is stated that Mr K.J. Cook (who later moved from his position as the G.W.R. C.M.E.E. to help with British Railways Eastern Region engineering and maintenance facilities between 1951 and 1959) confirmed that the Gresley K3 Class was originally built with 1 ½ in. steam lap and a maximum cut-off of 75%. The maximum valve travel was 6 3/8 in. If true, this would mean the Gresley K3s were fitted with long-travel valves in 1920, ahead of the G.W.R./L.N.E.R. exchange trials of 1925 and should have shown a marked superiority over the Pacifics in this regard.

The prototype K3, No.1000, showed a marked over travel of the middle valve when coasting at high speeds. This over travel was to be found in all Gresley's conjugated valve gear locomotives and in many cases led to Gresley ordering the maximum cut-off on engines so fitted to 65%. This reduced the travel of the valve but also restricted performance by way of increased fuel consumption. The K3s suffered from this and by this quirk also received their nickname, "Jazzers" due to the distinctive syncopated (or "Gresley") beat from their exhausts.

The first batch of K3s had a reasonable similarity to Gresley's first moguls by the fitting of the similarly proportioned G.N.R. Ivatt style cabs. Later batches incorporated the lessons learned by Gresley and side window cabs and padded seats would be fitted. These locomotives when introduced settled into mixed traffic work well and were often used on express passenger services when other classes were unavailable.

After the grouping of 1923, the K3 class was selected by Gresley to become one of the group's standard designs. 193 examples of Class K3 were built in seven batches up until 1937, with minor variations between the classes and each batch giving:

- K3/1 (1920)

- K3/2 (1924)

- K3/3 (1929)

- K3/4 (1930)

- K3/5 (1931)

- K3/6 (1934)

The differences between K3/2, K3/3, K3/4, K3/5 and K3/6 were minor and in 1935 all but K3/3 were reclassified as K3/2. K3/1 became extinct in 1940 when all were modified to the L.N.E.R. composite loading gauge and were also reclassified K3/2.

The Class K3 was subject to several potential rebuilds, with one scheme drawn out in 1931 featuring a smaller version of the W1's water tube boiler, and plans between 1932 and 1933 showing articulated bogies, larger driving wheels, and potentially a double chimney. Nothing came of these plans, and the Gresley V2 was instead substituted for any further K3 builds.

*Fig. 50. Gresley K3 No.227, being turned at Doncaster shed. Note the short-lived top feed running along the length of the boiler. The Gresley Society.*

*Fig. 51. Gresley K3 No.1102, sat on shed alongside one of the Raven Pacifics. The Gresley Society.*

Development by Edward Thompson of a two cylindered version of the K3, the K5, brought with it the potential for a new boiler type, and from 1945 diagram 96A boilers started to be fitted to the K3s, though downrated in boiler pressure to 180lb to match the original K3 boiler.

The K3/2 and K3/3 classifications were summarily dropped in 1947 and the entire surviving class of 192 locomotives became Class K3.

## Wartime Mileages & Availability

| Year | Mileages | Availability |
|------|----------|--------------|
| 1942 | 29165 | 71% |
| 1943 | 27432 | 70% |
| 1944 | 25054 | 67% |
| 1945 | 30684 | 71% |
| 1946 | 29773 | 69% |

*Fig. 52 K3 Mileages & Availability Statistics.*
*Simon A.C. Martin, from the Use of Engine Power Document.*

Class K3 was performing satisfactorily throughout the war years, in terms of being in and around the 70% average availability of the overall fleet.

Annual average mileages peaked in 1945. This was possibly due to the wartime traffic. Availability only dropped from the previous year by a few percent. In relation to other moguls that the L.N.E.R. owned and ran, the Class K3 was performing as well as those with two cylinders, with perhaps slightly lower availability. Average mileages dropped in 1944, but always remained between 25,000 and 30,000 miles per year. This was, if anything, still in line with the expectations of the class pre-war.

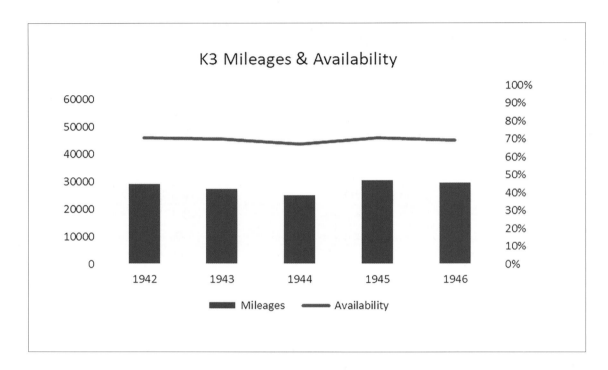

*Fig. 53. K3 Mileages & Availability Graph.*
*Simon A.C. Martin from the Use of Engine Power Document.*

*Fig.53B. From this angle the 1925 built 61853 from Ardsley shed looks a chunky and powerful locomotive indeed as seen on 3 November 1962 at Gloucester Midland shed. Peter Simmonds*

| Class K3 | | |
|---|---|---|
| Cylinders (x3): | | 18.5x26in. |
| Motion: | Outside: | Walschaerts |
| | Inside: | Gresley |
| | Valves: | 8in piston |
| Boiler: | Max. Diameter: | 6ft |
| | Pressure: | 180lb |
| | Diagram No.: | 96 and 96A (at 180lb) |
| Heating Surface: | Total: | 2308 sq. ft. |
| | Firebox: | 182 sq. ft. |
| | Superheater: | 407 sq. ft. (32x 1.25in) |
| | Tubes: | 1192 sq. ft. (217x 1.75in) |
| | Flues: | 527 sq. ft. (32x 5.25in) |
| Grate Area: | | 28 sq. ft. |
| Wheels: | Leading: | 3ft 2in |
| | Coupled: | 5ft 8in |
| | Tender: | 4ft 2in / 3ft 9in |
| Tractive Effort: | At 85% boiler pressure | 30,031lb |
| Wheelbase: | Total: | 49ft 1in |
| | Engine: | 25ft 2in |
| | Tender: | 13ft 6in |
| Weight (full): | Total: | 123 tons 14cwt |
| | Engine: | 71 tons 14cwt |
| | Tender: | 52 tons 0cwt |
| Max. Axle Load: | | 20 tons |

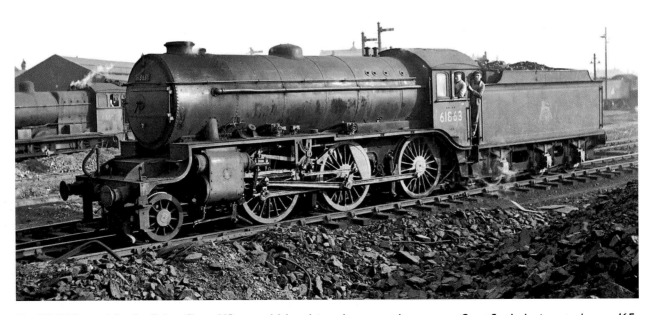

*Fig.53C. The oddball of the Class K3s would be this sole example seen at Stratford, designated as a K5. Edward Thompson converted this one into a two-cylinder locomotive. Strathwood Library Collection*

# G.N.R. Class N2 0-6-2T (1920)

Number built (G.N.R.): 60
Number built (L.N.E.R.): 47
Total built: 107

*Fig. 54. Gresley N2 No.1608 works photograph. The Gresley Society.*

Gresley's first tank locomotive design went through several different stages before Gresley settled on a reboilered version of Ivatt's useful N1 class 0-6-2T locomotive. Designs included different wheelbase arrangements of 2-6-2T and 2-6-4T. The L.N.E.R. would only get these kinds of locomotives much later in the form of the three-cylinder Gresley V1 (1930) and the two-cylinder Thompson L1 (1945).

Gresley's N2 was virtually another Ivatt N1 in certain details, with an identical wheelbase and general layout but fitted with piston valves, larger diameter cylinders, a superheated boiler and larger tanks for greater water capacity (including at the rear and under the coal space of the bunker).

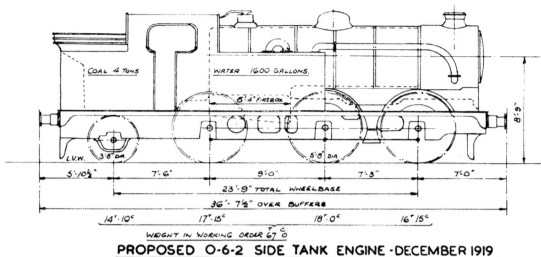

COAL 4 TONS      WATER 1600 GALLONS.

6'-4" FIREBOX

L.V.W.    3'-8" DIA      5'-8" DIA

8'-9"

5'-10½"    7'-6"    9'-0"    7'-3"    7'-0"

23'-9" TOTAL WHEELBASE

36'-7½" OVER BUFFERS

14'-10ᶜ    17'-15ᶜ    18'-0ᶜ    16'-15ᶜ

WEIGHT IN WORKING ORDER 67 ᵀ 0ᶜ

**PROPOSED 0-6-2 SIDE TANK ENGINE · DECEMBER 1919**

*Fig. 55. Gresley N2 Line Drawing, Doncaster Works. Courtesy of the R.C.T.S.*

The class was originally destined for lines running over the old Metropolitan Railway, so these were fitted with short, squat chimneys and condensing equipment for their work in the tunnels. The first batch, later classified as N2/1, was built by Doncaster Works and the N.B.L. Atlas Works. These examples went into service during 1920 and 1921 and there were some issues with the axle box journals. The issues were later resolved in part by the fitting of a Wakefield no.7 lubricator (another would be fitted for cylinder and steam chest lubrication). This type became standard across the entire class.

The original locomotives suffered from issues with the condensing equipment. With the stop-start nature of the suburban traffic they pulled caused water to surge from their tanks through the pipes and into the blastpipe area. This caused water ingress into the cylinders which would result in broken piston rings (and in more serious cases bent cotters as well). A slight change to the diameter of the condensing drain pipe was trialled but this had little effect. Baffle plates in the tanks were trialled as well with some small success but didn't fully resolve the problem.

The second batch, classified as N2/2, were built by outside contractors Beyer, Peacock & Co. These featured several significant changes to the first batch among which was the fitting of left-hand drive instead of right-hand drive. These locomotives had been built to the L.N.E.R. composite loading gauge and had a taller chimney than the N2/1s. Hulburd No.6 mechanical lubricators were fitted to feed the axle boxes and a sight feed lubricator was fitted in the cab for the cylinders and steam chest. These were intended for use in Scotland however in 1932 they were displaced south to London and were promptly fitted with condensing gear and

*Fig. 56. Gresley N2 No.2663 is seen at Broad Street in the final few months of the Second World War in 1945. Note the wartime condition of plain black livery with just N.E. on the side tanks. Rail Archive Stephenson.*

shorter chimneys to suit the ex-G.E.R. lines.

Shortly after the N2/2 batch were ordered, Doncaster Works undertook the building of a third batch of Gresley N2s in 1925. These were classified as N2/3. With lessons learned from the original batch, Doncaster Works fitted Wakefield no.7 lubricators for the axle box journals which were now a larger diameter. These were fitted together with new springing arrangements which improved the running. A sight feed lubricator in the cab was fitted for the steam chest and cylinders. This batch would not be fitted with condensing gear.

The L.N.E.R. ordered a fourth set of Gresley N2s. These were later classified as N2/4 and were built in two batches by two more outside contractors (the Yorkshire Engine Co. Ltd and Hawthorn, Leslie & Co. Ltd). These engines were built with a deeper ashpan: an improvement that allowed the fitting of a damper door at the rear end. This modification would be carried out on most of the previous batches of locomotives. Another change to this batch was the fitting of dry sanders instead of steam sanders as had been fitted to all previous batches.

*Fig. 57. Gresley N2 No.4758 pulls into King's Cross & St Pancras. Of note is the line to the left, as part of the fourth rail electrified underground system of the Metropolitan Widened Lines.*
*Strathwood Library Collection.*

The original condensing equipment on the N2/1s had given much trouble but the G.E. style gear as fitted to the N2/2s was proving more adequate. So, an arrangement based on the G.E. style gear was designed and fitted. The lack of a U-bend in the pipes like the previous gear meant that water surges were more common. Additional baffle plates were added but did little. The final solution was to create drainage holes in the vertical pipes in the tank. The water forced out of the tank by the surges would then only go out by means of the air vent mounted behind the cab. This vent was then modified to send the excess water onto the coal in the bunker.

Fig. 58. Gresley N2 No.4611 waits for its next duty at King's Cross in the rapidly darkening evening on 30 March 1936. Note a shed mate, likely No.4743, in the shadows to the left. Les Hanson-David Hanson Archive/Rail Online

This seemed to work and all N2s that had the G.E. arrangement of condensing pipes were modified as and when they were shopped from 1929 onwards. The Yorkshire Engine Co. Ltd was given another order for Gresley N2s and these locomotives when released to traffic were classified as N2/3. However, the major details of this batch more closely matched the N2/4 batches. None of the engines were fitted with condensing gear. Four of this batch would be moved to the ex-G.N.R. section and would later be modified with the shorter chimneys and condensing gear of the original N2/3s. This brought them completely into line with the specification of the N2/4s. They were not reclassified as such until 1939.

The N2s were at first concentrated at King's Cross working on the ex-Metropolitan Railway lines. By the end of 1925 there were forty N2s working out of King's Cross on a range of workings, including the suburban traffic and empty coach workings for the expresses. These engines displaced aging Ivatt C12s and N1s. Although there were still issues with water surges in the tanks the London crews were happy with their charges and some N2s were to stay in London throughout their working lives. The construction of more N7s for the ex-G.E.R. lines displaced some of these N2s to Scotland.

The Gresley N2s were less well received by Scottish crews. These locomotives were often to be found working on heavy goods trains in addition to their intended suburban passenger duties. This including transfer workings. Allocated to Dundee, Dunfermline, Eastfield, Haymarket, North Berwick and St Margaret's, the locomotives were not well liked and were reputed to spread the track in the North Berwick area. This led to a temporary speed restriction being applied of 40mph. Although the National Archives in Kew and at those at the National Railway Museum York did not yield any evidence for the claim of track spreading, there was a recorded derailment of a Gresley N2 near Gartmore on an Aberfoyle bound train in 1929.

The immediate reaction of the Scottish area to this incident was to ban the entire class from Scottish branch lines. There does not seem to have been a full investigation into the causes of the derailment. Given the somewhat more restrictive curves and sections of the ex-Metropolitan Railway lines, the idea that the N2s spread the track when there were other tank and tender locomotives with longer wheelbases (and heavier axle loading) in use seems somewhat unlikely. Nevertheless, when new Gresley V1 2-6-2Ts became available twenty-eight Gresley N2s from the Scottish group were permanently moved back to London. Those that remained were not well utilised except occasionally in use as pilots or shunters.

Some N2s were trialled in the West Riding area in the late 1920s and were liked enough to then form an allocation to Ardsley and Bradford sheds in 1931. This was relatively short lived and by 1945 all these N2s were moved back to London or were moved to the Nottingham area. The singular highlight of the West Riding N2s work was a portion of the high-speed and streamlined West Riding Limited being pulled by a double headed pair of N2s. The first withdrawal for scrapping was in 1955 but further withdrawals would not commence until 1957.

*Fig. 59. The Gresley Society's beloved N2 at work on the North Norfolk Railway during the society's Golden Jubilee year of 2013. Completing the scene is the preserved N.N.R. Gresley articulated suburban set similar to that which the engine regularly hauled from Kings Cross for over 40 years. Jason Cork, The Gresley Society.*

By then dieselisation was in full force with the entire Class N2 withdrawn from traffic by the end of 1962.

Happily, No.69523 (one of the first Gresley N2s built by the N.B.L. in 1921) was purchased by The Gresley Society and preserved in 1963. It has had a very fruitful career in preservation. It was one of the star locomotives in the famous film, The Railway Children, featuring Jenny Agutter. It ran as the locomotive in charge of "The Scotch Flyer" in its L.N.E.R. style black livery as No.4744, although the L.N.E.R. was blacked out.

It has operated on the Keighley and Worth Valley Railway (K.W.V.R), the preservation era Great Central Railway (G.C.R.), and at the time of writing is currently based on the North Norfolk Railway (N.N.R.) but is undergoing an overhaul at a contractor. Recently resplendent in G.N.R. livery as no.1744, it has been matched with a preserved "Quad-art" set of coaches that it would have pulled in its working life.

| Year | Mileages | Availability |
|------|----------|--------------|
| 1942 | 21946 | 79% |
| 1943 | 22324 | 77% |
| 1944 | 21472 | 79% |
| 1945 | 21277 | 79% |
| 1946 | 21854 | 74% |

*Fig. 60. N2 Mileages & Availability Statistics.*
*Simon A.C. Martin, from the Use of Engine Power Document.*

Gresley's oldest N2s were approaching twenty years old by the time of the Second World War. Other classes of a similar vintage did not achieve the average annual availability of the L.N.E.R. fleet, but Class N2 exceeded the 70% mark quite firmly throughout. Average annual mileages remained in line with pre-war expectations of between 20,000 and 22,000 miles a year. Overall, Gresley's Class N2 performed well in difficult conditions and where they were well liked were fully capable of prodigious performance and reliability.

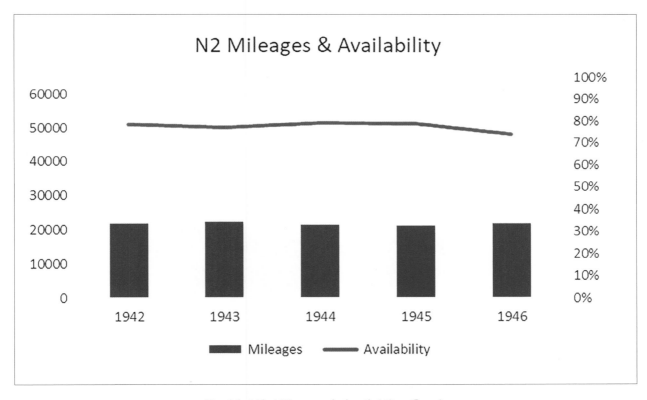

*Fig. 61. N2 Mileages & Availability Graph.*
*Simon A.C. Martin from the Use of Engine Power Document.*

# Class N2

| Cylinders (x2): | (inside) | 19x26in. |
|---|---|---|
| Motion: | Stephenson | 8in piston valves |
| Boiler: | Max. Diameter: | 4ft 8in |
| Pressure: | | 170lb |
| Diagram No.: | | 7 |
| Heating Surface: | Total: | 1205 sq. ft. |
| Firebox: | | 118 sq. ft. |
| Tubes: | | 510 sq. ft. (107x 1.75in) |
| Superheater: | | 207 sq. ft. (17x 1.25in) |
| Flues: | | 370 sq. ft. (34x 4in) |
| Grate Area: | | 19 sq. ft. |
| Wheels: | Coupled: | 5ft 8in |
| | Trailing: | 3ft 8in |
| Tractive Effort: | At 85% boiler pressure | 19,945lb |
| Total Wheelbase: | | 23ft 9in |
| Engine Weight: | (full) | 70 tons 5cwt |
| Max. Axle Load: | | 19 tons |
| Coal Capacity: | | 4 tons 0cwt |
| Water Capacity: | | 2000 gallons |

*Fig. 61B. Seen in her earlier days we find 2684 soon after being built by The Yorkshire Engine Co. in late 1928, she would become 9590 and finally 69590 before being withdrawn as a Class N2/4 in June 1957. Strathwood Library Collection.*

# G.N.R. Class A1 4-6-2 (1922)

Number built (G.N.R.): 2
Number built (L.N.E.R.): 50
Total built: 52

*Fig. 62. Gresley A1 No.4472, Flying Scotsman, as placed on display by the L.N.E.R. at the Empire Exhibition at Wembley in 1924. Colourised by Ian MacCabe, The Gresley Society.*

There are few locomotive wheel arrangements that are so intrinsically linked with a locomotive engineer more than Sir Nigel Gresley is with his Pacific locomotives designed and built for the G.N.R., and then L.N.E.R. until his final days.

The idea for a Pacific locomotive had been in Gresley's mind for a few years. In 1908 the first British Pacific locomotive had been built by the G.W.R. under George Jackson Churchward. Opinions are divided on the success or otherwise of the design. The locomotive, named *The Great Bear*, was effectively a drawn-out Star class locomotive from the front end, with the larger boiler having around 60% more heating surface area than the Star. The choice of a larger bogie fitted tender completed the overall bulk.

This locomotive had been the subject of much exposure by way of the G.W.R.'s publicity department. When built it was the largest steam locomotive on the G.W.R. and with a 23-foot-long barrel had one of the longest boilers in the country. This made for a lot of bulk but didn't necessarily translate to greater efficiency in steam raising. However, the boiler was pressed to 225lb, and the locomotive was not known as a shy steamer.

The 225lb boiler was mated to four cylinders of 15in x 26in, these being the maximum size possible for the outside cylinders to stop them from fouling the rear wheels of the front bogie. The firebox grate of the locomotive was 42 sq. ft in size, and the choice of having the wider overall size of firebox meant that trailing wheels were necessary leading to the choice of a Pacific wheelbase arrangement.

*Fig. 63. The Great Bear in 1908. G.W.R. works photograph (public domain use).*

The boiler was fitted with a Swindon No.1 superheater. The introduction of the superheater represented one of the most important improvements to locomotive design on the G.W.R. and so it proved in *The Great Bear*. The disadvantages of saturated steam were reduced as far as possible prior to *The Great Bear* by resorting to higher steam pressures to get the utmost out of boiler design within the limits of the G.W.R. loading gauge and weight restrictions.

This in turn drove up fuel consumption. Opinions on the pressing of boilers to higher and higher pressures were divided at the time. Some locomotive engineers recognised that the practice of using higher steam pressure would increase the wear and tear upon the firebox and boiler and consequently inflate the necessity for higher levels of repair and maintenance.

Churchward felt differently. He had seen on the continent how it was realised that if the water present in the steam were eliminated then the steam could be made more efficient as a superior gas possessed of greater expansion properties. Under these conditions a smaller quantity of steam would be sufficient to accomplish the desired end in a cylinder of given dimensions than if saturated steam were used. This would in theory allow the boiler pressure to be reduced and the cylinder increased in diameter to obtain the same or greater tractive effort. There could be a saving in coal and water consumption and it would reduce the maintenance costs in wastage of the firebox and boiler.

Accordingly numerous experiments with superheating were carried out on G.W.R. locomotives to devise the most efficient means for drying or "superheating" the steam. These tests were mostly carried out on earlier Saint class 4-6-0s and resulted in the superheater design that was fitted to *The Great Bear*. Further experimentation led to the fitting of a Swindon No.3 superheater in 1913 together with top-feed apparatus further improving the efficiency of the locomotive.

*The Great Bear* was used in the fastest long-distance express traffic on the G.W.R., on the through working of the summer London-Penzance trains, where high average speeds with heavy loads had to be handled over the heavy grades of South Devon and Cornwall. *The Great Bear* is normally remembered as an act of folly on the G.W.R.'s account, and it is largely regarded by railway writers and enthusiasts as a "white elephant". These points of view ignore the development work that went into *The Great Bear*.

Even as a prototype running alongside the Star class locomotives that it was derived from; it did useful work and was a good test bed for the superheating of boilers. It was also a magnificent success for the G.W.R. in terms of publicity and was the flagship locomotive for many years. It would be the largest locomotive on the G.W.R. until its withdrawal and rebuilding as a member of the Castle class under the new C.M.E. of the G.W.R., Charles Collett, in 1924.

Some writers have been unkind in their writing and have remarked that *The Great Bear* became an "embarrassment" for the G.W.R. once the more powerful Castles emerged. This overly simplistic interpretation ignores that the locomotive had run over half a million miles by the time of its withdrawal, at an average annual mileage of around 32,000 miles a year. For locomotives of its size, and as a single one-off prototype locomotive, this was still a good achievement and not too far below what was being achieved on the continent and elsewhere with similar Pacific locomotives.

The availability of *The Great Bear* was also satisfactory. It certainly had some issues, such as the rear trailing wheels of the Pacific arrangement. These were never quite sorted and probably could have done with the substitution of a cartazzi design or similar.

The oft-quoted remark by Churchward on hearing of Gresley's desire to build a Pacific for the G.N.R. is often given as "What did that young man want to build it for? We could have sold him ours!" feels apocryphal. Gresley is very likely to have seen the work and publicity surrounding *The Great Bear* and this very public development in the locomotive sphere of the United Kingdom cannot have passed him by. Tim Hillier-Graves in his book *Gresley and his Locomotives* gives a lot of background to this by way of his citations from one of Gresley's foremost assistants, Bert Spencer, and seems to indicate the importance of *The Great Bear* in the development of the A1.

The influence of *The Great Bear* on the development of Gresley's original Pacific proposal rings true when you consider the cylinder arrangements. He was also reputed to have seen the developments of the Pennsylvania Railroad K4 class and it was reported by Bert Spencer that drawings of this locomotive were kept as the development of Gresley's three-cylinder Pacific design continued apace. How much influence the K4 truly had on the final design we cannot say. The answer likely amounts to little in the way of genuine design and more by way of concept.

*Fig. 64. Pennsylvania Railroad K4, being prepared for service.*
*United States Library of Congress's Prints and Photographs Division (public domain use).*

Gresley and his design team had started the work for the Pacific design in around 1915. The earliest incarnation of Gresley's Pacific was very much a stretched-out development of his predecessor H.A. Ivatt's successful C1 Atlantic locomotives. It still featured the traditional and short G.N.R. cab. but had four cylinders. This was in line with some experiments with members of the Ivatt Atlantics (in particular No.279) and in line with contemporary The Great Bear.

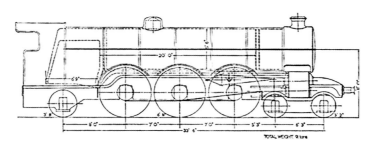

*Fig. 65. Gresley A1 Line Drawing, Doncaster Works, 1915. Simon A.C. Martin.*

This, it transpires, was to be temporary. By 1918, the first of Gresley's three-cylinder 2-8-0s was running alongside his large three-cylinder 2-6-0 and Gresley's thoughts were turning to three-cylinder propulsion together with the conjugated valve gear as the new standard. By April 1920 the design had developed much further with the 180lb round topped boiler now in its final design. The final wheelbase and cylinder sizes were now arranged as three cylinders with conjugated valve gear.

The boiler in particular represented a significant increase heating surface area and a reduction in the length of the tubes. The locomotive design still retained the G.N.R. style short cab, and the positioning of the running plate, size of the splashers over the driving wheels, and the placement of the motion bracket were more in line with Ivatt.

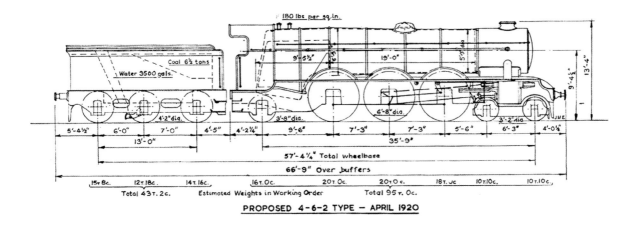

*Fig. 66. Gresley A1 Line Drawing, Doncaster Works, 1920. Courtesy of the R.C.T.S.*

By 1922, the design had been further modified into the recognisable Gresley A1 Pacific we know today. The short G.N.R. cab had been replaced by a design that was fundamentally Great Eastern Railway (G.E.R.) in layout with two side windows and deeper side sheets. It retained the G.N.R. flare with the similar cut-out under the cab roof and above the main side handrail. Other secondary sources report that Bert Spencer was responsible for the design, Gresley seeing it and approving the overall arrangement. Smaller splashers with a higher running plate allowed for a more robust outside motion bracket and Walschaerts valve gear mated with a three-slide bar arrangement.

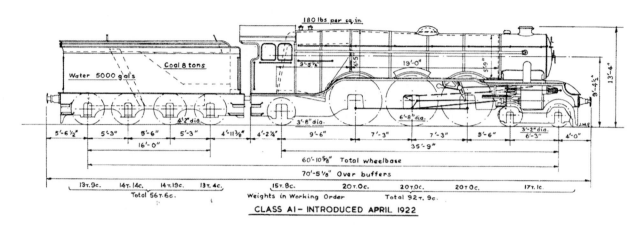

*Fig. 67. Gresley A1 Line Drawing, Doncaster Works, 1922. Courtesy of the R.C.T.S.*

The first of Gresley's Pacific locomotives had its frames laid down in the last few months of 1921, destined to become No.1470, *Great Northern*. With grouping of the railway companies only a year away, here was an opportunity to cement a firm reminder that the G.N.R. was an innovative railway with a "big engine" policy.

The new Pacific locomotive made an instant impression on Britain's railways. Gresley had claimed that it could pull trains of 600-tons: this was proven within a few months of *Great Northern's* entry into service, as a 600-ton test train taken from King's Cross to Barkston and back by sister locomotive, No.1471 (later named *Sir Frederick Banbury*).

*Fig.68. Gresley A1 No.1470, Great Northern, works photograph.*
*Colourised by Ian MacCabe, The Gresley Society.*

Fig. 69. Great Northern's frames on 10<sup>th</sup> November 1921.
The locomotive is in the E2 Shop/New Shop. Tim Robbins Collection.

Fig. 70. Great Northern's frames on 10<sup>th</sup> November 1921. The locomotive is in the E2 Shop/New Shop,
with cylinders now fitted. Tim Robbins Collection.

*Fig. 71. Great Northern's cab on 8th June 1922, with the locomotive nearing completion.*
*The locomotive is in the E2 Shop/New Shop. Tim Robbins Collection.*

*Fig. 72. The first Gresley Pacific, No.1470, Great Northern passes the Standard Telephone Company works north of New Southgate Station in 1922. Tim Robbins Collection.*

*Fig. 73. By comparison, Raven A2 Pacific No.2400 stands for its official works photograph for the N.E.R. The Gresley Society.*

The grouping in 1923 split the Class A1 between the first two examples. The next batch of ten locomotives started with No.1472 and this first emerged early in 1923. This locomotive was to begin a long and famous life as *Flying Scotsman*. Prior to its naming in 1924 it would be called on to provide an assessment that would set the tone for future development on the L.N.E.R. for years to come.

Concurrent to the development of Gresley's G.N.R. Pacific design, Sir Vincent Raven had produced for the North Eastern Railway (N.E.R.) a Pacific design of his own. This closely followed the pattern of his well-known and much liked C7 Atlantics but was drawn out over the Pacific wheelbase. The first two emerged after *Great Northern* and just before the grouping, making their test runs in December 1922 and January 1923 respectively.

Three sets of Stephenson valve gear drove onto the first axle. Some criticisms have been made of this arrangement, requiring six eccentrics and with the bearings close to each other. The design was virtually copied from the C7 Atlantic and provided no material issues in the running of the Raven Pacifics.

Far more of an issue was the valve arrangements, unchanged from the C7, as were the steam passages to the cylinders. These provided something of a throttling effect in comparison to the layout Gresley prepared for his Pacific design.

*Fig. 74. Raven A2 No.2403 presents an interesting contrast with Gresley A1 No.2571 in 1927. Note the Westinghouse pump on the running plate of the Gresley locomotive. Both locomotives have gained cut outs in each corner of their buffer beams. Rail Archive Stephenson.*

The boiler of the C7 was lengthened at the front end and the firebox widened over the trailing wheels. The grate area shortened, and was pressed to 200lb, which significantly was higher than the Gresley design. This additional boiler pressure did not translate into better tractive effort, the Raven locomotive coming in at 29,918lb compared to the Gresley A1 at 29,835lb, just below it.

The Raven Pacifics continued to be built, albeit under Gresley's directions, and the final three examples of Raven's design emerged with a cartazzi arrangement of the rear trailing wheels replacing the original trailing wheel design with inside bearings, a known issue with the first two locomotives. From the grouping, 1923 the Raven Pacifics became classified "A2", following the G.N.R.'s A1.

Over the years since the A1 and A2s emergence, a great number of writers have been critical of the efforts of Raven in relation to Gresley. Both Pacific designs employed three cylinders and drove onto one axle. Gresley preferred driving the centre axle over driving the first that Raven employed with his design.

The Raven locomotive had the higher boiler pressure, and in comparison, writings on the trials between No.2400 of the Raven A2 and No.1472 of the Gresley A1 type indicated there was at that time very little to choose between them.

*Fig. 75. Gresley A1 No.2563 William Whitelaw, in photographic grey. Note the distinct works plate on the side of the smokebox which confirms that this locomotive was built by N.B.L.*
*Strathwood Library Collection.*

Fig. 76. Gresley A1 No.2556 Ormonde takes an express through the snow at high speed in this wintry scene on 27 December 1927. Rail Archive Stephenson.

Fig. 77. Flying Scotsman, at Doncaster in 1923. The locomotive as numbered 1472 and still unnamed, as it would have been seen in the comparison trials against the Raven A2 Pacific.
Strathwood Library Collection.

Fig. 78. Seen again at Doncaster during 1923, soon No.1472 would be officially named as Flying Scotsman and renumbered as No.4472 in February 1924 to not only promote the named train service between London and Edinburgh for the L.N.E.R. but also, to make a good impression at the British Empire Exhibition taking place at Wembley from 23rd April until 1st November 1924. Most of her classmates would be named after famous racehorses whereas the Raven A2 Pacifics would take the names of cities served by the North Eastern Railway, with No. 2400 taking the name City of Newcastle.
Rail Archive Stephenson

The following graphs and tables set out the key comparisons for the trials:

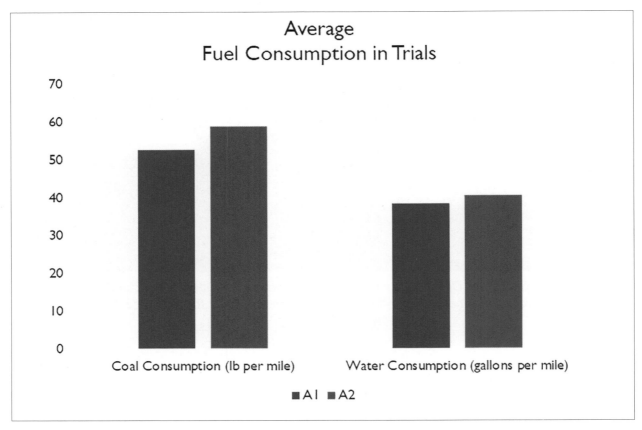

*Fig. 79. A1 Mileages & Availability Statistics.*
*Simon A.C. Martin, from the Use of Engine Power Document.*

The average coal and water consumption for the Raven A2 was 12% higher than the Gresley A1 for coal and 5% higher in terms of water consumption.

The graph shows that the coal consumption was notably higher, but the water consumption was much closer to the Gresley locomotive's performance.

| Engine Class | Coal Consumption (lb per mile) | Water Consumption (gallons per mile) |
|---|---|---|
| A1 | 52.6 | 38.3 |
| A2 | 58.7 | 40.4 |
| Difference | 12% | 5% |

*Fig. 80. Gresley A1 and Raven A2 Statistics.*
*Simon A.C. Martin, from L.N.E.R statistics.*

The additional fuel consumption didn't translate into better overall performance either.

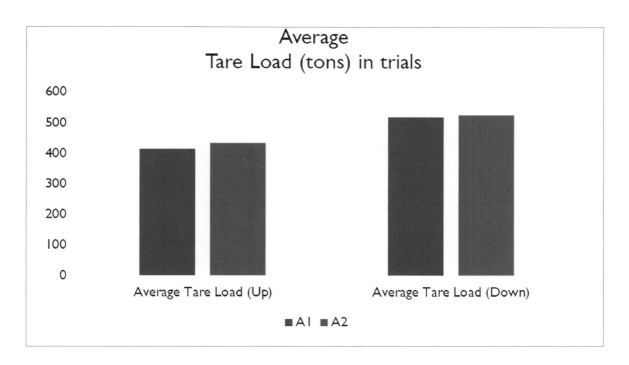

Fig. 81. Gresley A1 and Raven A2 Statistics.
Simon A.C. Martin, from L.N.E.R statistics.

The Raven A2 showed only a 2% edge in the indicated Average Drawbar Horsepower over the Gresley A1.

| Engine Class | Average Tare Load (Up) | Average Tare Load (Down) |
|---|---|---|
| A1 | 415 | 519 |
| A2 | 434 | 527 |
| Difference | 5% | 2% |

Fig. 82. Gresley A1 and Raven A2 Statistics.
Simon A.C. Martin, from L.N.E.R statistics.

The difference between the two locomotives was again, negligible, and this was being produced by one of the locomotive designs with a not insignificant difference in the boiler pressure, being 20lb lower in design. Further study of the primary data found an interesting misconception in the comparison of boiler pressures.

Cecil J. Allen criticised this aspect of the Gresley design in his book, British Pacific Locomotives, making the claim that the "North Eastern fireman kept up the better boiler pressures…whereas Flying Scotsman's [No.1472] average pressure was 164lb only".

| Engine Class | Average Drawbar H.P. |
|---|---|
| A1 | 663 |
| A2 | 673 |
| Difference | 2% |

*Fig. 83. Gresley A1 and Raven A2 Statistics.*
*Simon A.C. Martin, from L.N.E.R statistics.*

An examination of the designed boiler pressures of each locomotive against the average percentage of this pressure used produced this table:

| Engine Class | Designed Boiler Pressure | Average Boiler Pressure Pounds | % of Boiler Pressure Used |
|---|---|---|---|
| A1 | 180 | 164 | 91% |
| A2 | 200 | 197 | 99% |

*Fig. 84. Gresley A1 and Raven A2 Statistics.*
*Simon A.C. Martin, from L.N.E.R statistics.*

Although the Gresley A1 design was always producing lower boiler pressure than the Raven A2, the A1 was producing comparable performances with almost identical train loads and doing it with better overall fuel consumption. Particularly where coal was concerned. Here there was a clear advantage of the Gresley Pacific design over the Raven equivalent: efficiency. However, the mechanical criticisms aimed at the Raven design don't seem to have a basis in fact. The Raven design had an edge insomuch that although its three sets of Stephenson motion were something of a cramped front end, its overall performances from an availability and mileages point of view were good.

There was no doubt that there was little that could be done to the Raven A2 design to improve it from the valve setting and motion point of view without major reconstruction. No further development of the Raven A2s was undertaken aside from modifications made to No.2404. This was rebuilt in April 1929 using a Gresley A1 boiler when the original boiler fitted became life expired and the 180lb boiler available as a spare by the provision of newer 220lb boilers for the incoming new Gresley Pacifics.

The replacement boiler came from Gresley A1 No.2569 and was fitted with a new deeper smokebox saddle and a rearwards extension of the smokebox. A chimney very close in design (if not actually of the same design) as the Gresley A1 was also fitted. This reduced the boiler pressure from 220 to 180lb. The tractive effort was reduced accordingly to 26,926lb.

There was some consideration given in 1933 to reboilering the entire Raven A2 class with the A3 boiler instead, and although Gresley gave authority for No.2404 to be so fitted at its next overhaul, the withdrawal of the Raven class instead put paid to this, with all the class withdrawn by the end of May 1937.

So it was that the Gresley design was selected as a new standard for the fledging L.N.E.R. with No.1472 taking up her duties and a further nine Gresley A1s built and in service before the end of 1923.

In 1924, No.1472 was renumbered as No.4472 and given an "exhibition finish" to its paintwork together with nameplates which read *Flying Scotsman*. The locomotive was then put on display at the Empire Exhibition at Wembley, displayed alongside the new G.W.R. "Castle Class" No.4073 *Caerphilly Castle*. This exhibit had a sign proclaiming the G.W.R. locomotive as "The most powerful express passenger locomotive in the British Isles".

LONDON & NORTH EASTERN RAILWAY
"Pacific" Type Locomotive No. 4472.
"FLYING SCOTSMAN"
Built at Doncaster, 1923
PRINCIPAL DIMENSIONS

Cylinders (3) 20-in x 26-in    Diameter of Driving Wheels, 6-ft. 8-in
Total Heating Surface, 3,455 sq ft    Grate Area, 41¼ sq. ft.
Total weight of engine and tender, working order, 148 tons 15 cwts.
Length over buffers, engine and tender, 70-ft. 5⅜-in.

EXHIBITED AT BRITISH EMPIRE EXHIBITION, 1924.

*Fig. 85. Flying Scotsman, prepared for the Empire Exhibition at Wembley in 1924, and now No.4472. Promotional photograph, distributed at the exhibition by employees of the L.N.E.R. and costing One Shilling. Tim Robbins Collection.*

On paper, this was entirely true. The three-cylindered and 180lb boiler Gresley A1 had a tractive effort of 29,835lb. The Castle Class had four cylinders and a boiler pressed to 225lb and a tractive effort of 31,625lb.

What came next has been at best speculative by many writers in L.N.E.R. matters. In the board minutes for 1924 (as kept on record at Kew Gardens in the National Archives) we can see that the original exchange trials were proposed by Sir Felix Pole of the G.W.R., after a request was made by Gresley to the G.W.R. for the loan of a locomotive of the Castle Class. This was for comparative trials in relation to the longer valve travel the Castle class was fitted with.

Some writers of L.N.E.R. and G.W.R. matters have reported on this in mostly sporting terms, not identifying that there was serious engineering examination, debate and analysis that occurred from the trials' results. There was respectful and serious discussion between the two companies. The C.M.E.s of Gresley and Collett were less concerned about the publicity requirements of the trials and more concerned with the actual results.

| GWR Line | | LNER Line | |
|---|---|---|---|
| Engine Class | Coal Consumption Pounds Per Mile | Engine Class | Coal Consumption Pounds Per Mile |
| 4474 | 48.0 | 2545 | 57.1 |
| 4074 | 42.0 | 4079 | 53.4 |
| Difference | 12% | Difference | 6% |

*Fig. 86. Gresley A1 and G.W.R. Castle statistics.*
*Simon A.C. Martin, from L.N.E.R statistics.*

The average coal consumption of the two locomotives as given above shows an appreciable contrast in coal consumption for the G.W.R. Castle Class. Two types of coal were used in the comparison trials: Welsh coal on the G.W.R. and Yorkshire coal on the L.N.E.R., the two types differing in calorific value and overall hardness.

The different approaches of the firebox and grate design and surface area was also an appreciable factor in the coal consumption, with the larger A1 firebox requiring more coal to cover the grate space, despite the harder Yorkshire coal being better when spread thin on the wider grate.

Gresley is said to have been surprised at the difference in coal consumption between the two locomotives. The smaller boiler of the Castle Class and its smaller grate would in theory always tend towards lower coal consumption than the larger locomotive. What was the surprise was that the Great Western locomotive was doing the same work on the same lines and with a significantly lower overall coal consumption. What is also interesting is that the statistics on the G.W.R. trials indicate a broad range of coal consumption for the two classes.

| Eastbound | Run 1 | Run 2 | Run 3 | |
|---|---|---|---|---|
| Engine No. | Coal Consumption Pounds Per Mile | Coal Consumption Pounds Per Mile | Coal Consumption Pounds Per Mile | Average Consumption over Trial |
| 4474 | 50.9 | 45.2 | 40.4 | 45.5 |
| 4074 | 44.1 | 45.6 | 46.8 | 45.5 |
| Difference | 13% | 1% | 16% | 0% |

*Fig. 87. Gresley A1 and G.W.R. Castle statistics.*
*Simon A.C. Martin, from L.N.E.R statistics.*

On the eastbound runs the L.N.E.R.'s No.4474 had a first run with a significantly higher coal consumption than the latter two. The difference between the Castle's three runs was nominal. Direct comparisons of these runs shows that the lowest coal consumption for any one run was achieved by the L.N.E.R. Pacific. Average coal consumption across the three runs eastwards was identical for both locomotives at 45.5lb per mile.

| Westbound | Run 1 | Run 2 | Run 3 | |
|---|---|---|---|---|
| Engine No. | Coal Consumption Pounds Per Mile | Coal Consumption Pounds Per Mile | Coal Consumption Pounds Per Mile | Average Consumption over Trial |
| 4474 | 50 | 48.8 | 52.4 | 50.4 |
| 4074 | 40.6 | 36.8 | 37.9 | 38.4 |
| Difference | 19% | 25% | 28% | 24% |

*Fig. 88. Gresley A1 and G.W.R. Castle statistics.*
*Simon A.C. Martin, from L.N.E.R statistics.*

It was in the westbound runs that there was the biggest difference between the locomotives, with the Castle class coming out as much as 28% more efficient on coal compared to the L.N.E.R. locomotive. The average between the locomotives was a significant gulf, with the Pacific consuming over a quarter more coal per mile. The difference in grate size between the two locomotives comes out as close to a 40% larger grate size for the Pacific over the Castle. Statistically, it would have been more beneficial from the L.N.E.R.'s point of view to have been able to conduct more trials, with more crews and possibly more of each class of locomotive, to try and provide more statistical data on which to base more solid answers on the *why* questions that emerged from the testing. Gresley said as much in his own report to the L.N.E.R.'s Locomotive Committee, which was then copied to the board and discussed during the June 1925 meeting:

Fig. 89. *Flying Scotsman, prepared for the Empire Exhibition at Wembley in 1924, and now numbered 4472. Promotional photograph. Tim Robbins Collection.*

## Memorandum to the L.N.E.R. Locomotive Committee

*The trials extending over the week ending May 2$^{nd}$ between the Great Western Castle Class engine and the London and North Eastern Pacific Engine, which have caused a great amount of public interest, have shown that each engine was able to undertake the work of the other, and maintain schedules with ease.*

*On every run made by the Great Western Railway engine on the L.N.E.R. system and the L.N.E.R. engine on the Great Western system, time was made up, and in no case was time lost by the Engine.*

*The coal consumption of the engines when working over the Great Western System was as follows:*

| | |
|---|---|
| *G.W.R. Engine* | *42lbs per mile* |
| *L.N.E.R. Engine* | *48 " "* |

*When working over the L.N.E.R. system:*

| | |
|---|---|
| *G.W.R. Engine* | *53.4lbs per mile* |
| *L.N.E.R. Engine* | *57.1 " "* |

**The characteristics of the two engines are dissimilar, as the following table shows:**

|  | Great Western Engine | L.N.E.R. Engine |
|---|---|---|
| Type | 4-6-0 | 4-6-2 |
| Cylinders | 4 | 3 |
| Tractive Power | 31,625lb | 29,825lb |
| Cylinder H.P. | 2,030 | 1,946 |
| Boiler H.P. | 1,440 | 1,815 |
| Boiler Pressure | 225 | 180 |
| Weight of Engine | 79 tons 17 cwts | 92 tons 9 cwts |
| Weight of Tender | 40 tons | 56 tons 6 cwts |
| Total Weight | 119 tons 17 cwts | 148 tons 15 cwts |
| Capacity of Tender - coal | 6 tons | 8 tons |

The narrow type of the G.W. engine is more suitable for Welsh coal than the wide shallow firebox of the L.N.E. engine. When burning Yorkshire coal, a thin fire is necessary; therefore, the firebox of the L.N.E. engine should be the most suitable.

I anticipated that on Welsh coal the G.W. engine would probably be the more economical but expected that with Yorkshire coal the L.N.E. engine would give better results. Conclusive results, however, cannot be obtained from such a short trial, and so far as burning Yorkshire coal is concerned, I am confident that if the trial had been extended, the position would have been reversed.

The average coal consumption of all Pacific engines over the whole of last year running on the L.N.E. system was 54 lbs per mile, the lowest on the G.N. section being 47lbs per mile, the weight of the trains hauled up to 550 tons. The high boiler pressure of the G.W. Engine tends to economy in coal but involves higher cost in boiler maintenance. Although the tractive effort of the G.W. engine is higher than that of the L.N.E. engine, the boiler pressure is considerably less.

Fast running was therefore made by the G.W. engine on short rising grades, such as London to Finsbury Park, but on the long hill grades of the G.W. system, the Pacific engine ran faster. As to high-speed running on the flat and down grades there is nothing to choose between the two engines, which are both very free running and capable of running at high speeds.

The trials show that the road bed of the L.N.E. is superior to that of the Great Western. The Pacific engine could not be safely run at such high speeds on falling grades on the Great Western road as their own engines, probably due to the greater length, weight, and height of the Pacific engine. Strict observation had therefore to be observed on the speed limits on the curves and crossings by the Pacific engine, and consequently higher speeds were required on the up grades to maintain the schedules. The higher coal consumption is partially consequent upon this.

*It was arranged, before the trials were started, between Mr Collett, the Chief Mechanical Engineer and myself, that no results should be published without our mutual concurrence; this agreement has not been kept. The Great Western Publicity Department have obtained all the data and furnished them to the press for advertising purposes.*

*When it is remembered that the trials over the Great Western system consisted of only three trips – London to Plymouth and back – by the L.N.E. engine, it will be realised that no conclusive results could be arrived at.*
**Signed,**
**H.N. Gresley**

There are some elements of this that don't necessarily ring true, however. No comparative data was given for the claim that the G.W.R. designed boiler was more expensive by way of maintenance. It is difficult to reconcile the view, given the level of standardisation and the strict shopping regime Swindon undertook, to think that the smaller Castle boiler would be much more expensive than the Gresley A1 boiler. Obvious differences between the handling of the two locomotives has also been overlooked. The wide firebox of the Gresley locomotive required a thin spread of coal to completely cover the bars. The smaller grate of the Western locomotive required a very different firing technique which resulted in a spread of coal consumption results that ultimately don't reveal very much other than the trials required a more scientific approach in the first place.

What is perhaps missed is that the key difference between the two locomotives was the ability to run at sustained high speed for longer distances. There is no doubt given the history of the two locomotive classes that the Castle Class was superior at this specific point in time and was then entirely eclipsed by the development of the Gresley A1 arising out of these exchange trials.

In the same year as the trials, the Superheater Company of New York proposed to the L.N.E.R. a new superheater design for the Gresley A1s. The new design (Type E) was supposed to improve the steam capabilities of the Gresley A1 but was found wanting in comparison to the standard Robinson design. The key difference between the two was in the concentration of the superheater tubes in the Robinson type but could be distinguished externally by the provision of two snifter valves instead of one. This only featured on No.2562 *Isinglass*.

By 1925, the case for an increase in the steam lap setting had been made by virtue of the exchange trials. Two of the original Pacifics, No.4477 *Gay Crusader* and 2555 *Centenary*, were modified. *Centenary* was the subject of some prolonged trials which showed a dramatic decrease in coal consumption to under 40lb per mile with an absolute minimum of 39lb per mile being achieved whilst on test. This subsequently led to the rest of the class being modified when required for shopping. All of these modifications were completed by the end of 1931.

Fig. 90. No.2545 Dick Turpin and Stirling Single No.1 sit at York Station in March 1927. The contrast between the two locomotives for overall size is clear. Tim Robbins Collection.

Fig. 91. Gresley A1 No.2545 Diamond Jubilee on an express out of London King's Cross in 1924. Note the eclectic mix of carriages including a twelve wheeled clerestory G.N.R. coach. Tim Robbins Collection.

Fig. 92 No.4481 St Simon sits at Retford on an express in August 1928. Rail Archive Stephenson.

Fig. 93. Gresley A1 No.2581 Neil Gow traverses the crossover at York with an express. Note the Westinghouse pump fitted ahead of the cab and astride the rear driving wheels. Rail Archive Stephenson

*Fig. 94. Unnamed Gresley A1 No.2574 on an express at Bandon Bridge in 1925.*
*Tim Robbins Collection.*

These modifications were undertaken for Gresley under the close eye of Bert Spencer (one of his technical assistants) together with the introduction of narrow piston valve rings of the Knorr type. These piston rings were superior and led to decreased wear and damage to the valve heads. These developments overlapped with the decision to rebuild the original class members to the A3 specification. New boilers, superheater headers and other small details were fitted accordingly. The rebuilds happened between 1927 and 1947 with some of the oldest members being rebuilt after 20 years' work. Only the prototype A1, Great Northern, would not be rebuilt to Class A3.

This locomotive was rebuilt in 1945 as the prototype Thompson A1 Pacific (later reclassified as A1/1). Further information on this locomotive can be found in the previous volume in this series. The A1s prior to their rebuilding as A3s were reclassified as Class A10 by Edward Thompson, in anticipation of the new L.N.E.R. Class A1 design. The Gresley A1 Class was distinguished by a few major achievements during its lifetime. The first non-stop runs between London and Edinburgh that were undertaken by No.4472 Flying Scotsman and No.2580 Shotover respectively. The first authenticated 100 mph run in the world was achieved by No.4472 Flying Scotsman in 1934. This locomotive was also the star of Britain's first talking film, the 1929 film of the same name: The Flying Scotsman. This film was made in conjunction with the L.N.E.R. and featured several high-speed chases and many closeup shots of the titular locomotive and its star-studded cast.

Fig. 95. Gresley A1 No.4472, Flying Scotsman, just after its 100 mph run. Nigel Gresley is on the footplate. The Gresley Society.

Fig. 96. Gresley A1 No.2550, Blink Bonny waiting for the off at King's Cross in this lovely colour photograph from the 1930s. Colour Rail.

*Fig. 97. Gresley Class A1 No.1478 Hermit sits at the buffer stops at King's Cross in 1923, the original squared off buffer beam shows well in this head on view. Rail Archive Stephenson*

## Wartime Mileages & Availability

The original Gresley A1s produced good mileages and availability during the Second World War. However, their average annual mileages were lower than the higher boiler pressure locomotives of classes A3 and A4.

| Year | Mileages | Availability |
|------|----------|--------------|
| 1942 | 45308 | 70% |
| 1943 | 42628 | 75% |
| 1944 | 40637 | 73% |
| 1945 | 42028 | 73% |
| 1946 | 47188 | 76% |

*Fig. 98. A1 Mileages & Availability Statistics.*
*Simon A.C. Martin, from the Use of Engine Power Document.*

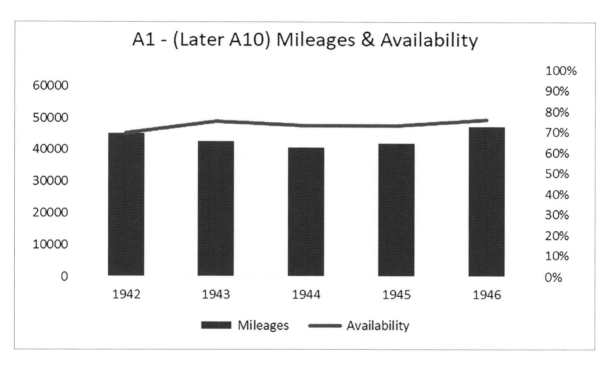

*Fig. 99. A1 Mileages & Availability Graph.*
*Simon A.C. Martin from the Use of Engine Power Document.*

Arguably, this may be down to the conversions of the class to A3. There were 36 Class A1s at the start of the Second World War and by 1946 this number was now only eight examples. The remaining locomotives produced significantly high annual mileages and availability that was over and above the average for the L.N.E.R.'s fleet during the war years.

# Class A1

| | | |
|---|---|---|
| Cylinders (x3): | | 20x26in. |
| Motion: | Outside: | Walschaerts |
| | Inside: | Gresley |
| Boiler: | Max. Diameter: | 6ft 5in |
| | Pressure: | 180lb |
| | Diagram No.: | 94 |
| Heating Surface: | Total: | 3455 sq. ft. |
| | Firebox: | 215 sq. ft. |
| | Superheater: | 525 sq. ft. |
| | Tubes: | 1880 sq. ft. |
| | Flues: | 835 sq. ft. |
| Grate Area: | | 41.25 sq. ft. |
| Wheels: | Leading: | 3ft 2in |
| | Coupled: | 6ft 8in |
| | Trailing: | 3ft 8in |
| | Tender: | 4ft 2in |
| Tractive Effort: | At 85% boiler pressure | 29,835lb |
| Wheelbase: | Total: | 60ft 10.6in |
| | Engine: | 35ft 9in |
| | Tender: | 16ft |
| Weight (full): | Total: | 150 tons 7cwt |
| | Engine: | 92 tons 9cwt |
| | Tender: | 57 tons 18cwt |
| Max. Axle Load: | | 20 tons |
| Water Capacity: | | 5000 gallons |
| Coal Capacity: | | 8 tons |

# Chapter 4
# Stepping up on the L.N.E.R.

*Fig. 100. Gresley sat at his desk in the King's Cross office. Note the photograph of an Ivatt Atlantic at speed on the back wall. The Gresley Society.*

In 1921 *The Railways Act* was passed in Parliament. This act took 120 of the country's railway companies and grouped them into four large companies: the G.W.R., L.N.E.R., L.M.S., and Southern Railway (S.R.). The intention of the act was to reduce the amount of competition between the railways and to retain some of the benefits realised during the Great War of 1914-18 when the railways had a form of government control. The provisions of this act would take effect from 1 January 1923.

Eric Geddes, minister of transport, was the act's architect. He envisaged a railway that was owned and run regionally, with workers participating in the overall running and management of the railway more heavily. He strongly felt that to fully nationalise the railways would lead to poor management, with the potential for politicisation of the railways to occur on top of this.

His cabinet paper, *Future Transport Policy*, had suggested more than just four groupings with Southern, Western, North Western, Eastern and North Eastern railway companies together with a specific transport grouping for London and separate groupings for Scotland and Ireland. Today the modern railway is closely approximating this policy from the early 1920s with Transport for London (T.F.L. or TfL) responsible for London and with many of the railway companies now coming under grouped government control by way of "operator of last resort". This is done together with the state infrastructure owner Network Rail.

Geddes' proposals became the white paper *Outline of Proposals as to the Future Organisation of Transport Undertakings in Great Britain and their relation to the state*, published in 1920. There was some disagreement within Parliament as to the splitting of Scottish interests, with the L.M.S. and L.N.E.R. groupings eventually including portions of the Scottish railways as part of their workings.

On the L.N.E.R., a level of devolution was decided, splitting the railway's three areas of Southern, North Eastern and Scottish under a Divisional General Manager for each, all reporting to the same Chief General Manager in London. There was some concern from the N.E.R. over the lack of representation for its interests in this setup, consequently Ralph Wedgwood (later Sir Ralph Wedgwood) was promoted from General Manager of the N.E.R. to Chief General Manager of the L.N.E.R.

The original plan was to separate engineering in the same way, with a different manager for each area of the company. Some internal discussion and development led to the creation of the Chief Mechanical Engineer (C.M.E.) position, to run the whole of the railway's engineering (including mechanical and electrical engineering) at a head office level.

The question now was: who should be the C.M.E.? The candidates initially looked as follows:

- Alfred Hill (G.E.R. M.E.)

- John G. Robinson (G.C.R. M.E.)

- Thomas Heywood (Great North of Scotland Railway, G.N.O.S.R. M.E.)

- Nigel Gresley (G.N.R. M.E.)

- Walter Chalmers (N.B.R. M.E.)

- Sir Vincent Raven (N.E.R. M.E.)

Of these, Hill and Chalmers looked to retire, so were out of the running. The G.N.O.S.R. was one of the smallest constituent members of the new L.N.E.R. to be formed, and so Heywood was an unlikely candidate from the outset. He had designed just one locomotive of note, what later became the L.N.E.R.'s class D40 (and even this class was based on the work of William Pickersgill). This left Gresley, Raven and Robinson in the running.

Raven took a job at Metropolitan Vickers just before the grouping, resigning as M.E. of the N.E.R. and it has been suggested that he left knowing that to hire him, as an N.E.R. man, would have been contentious and perhaps seen as a less than diplomatic move to stamp the authority of the N.E.R. onto the new company. If that was the case, it was not a viewpoint that he put forward himself.

Many secondary sources have also cited that there was a sour relationship between Gresley and Raven ahead of the grouping in any event. If this was the case, neither man commented on this directly, and Gresley ended up building or partially rebuilding and retaining several of Raven's designs (including his N.E.R. Pacifics) over the next decade.

This left Gresley and Robinson. Robinson was 66 years old compared to Gresley at 43 years old. The L.N.E.R. were to instigate a policy of staff retirement at 65 years old, which left Robinson one year adrift of this. Surprisingly, there is evidence the L.N.E.R. deputy chairman, Lord Faringdon, supported the appointment of Robinson to the top role. There may have been an element of bias to this, as Faringdon had been his former chairman on the G.C.R.

The reorganising of the major works, foundries, design houses and more required someone who had years ahead of them to fully invest into what would become a wide scale integration of the constituent companies rolling stock, workshops and more.

Several secondary sources have claimed a variety of stories in relation to how Gresley was appointed as C.M.E., including but not limited to John G. Robinson himself, writing into *The Railway Gazette* after Gresley's passing in 1941 stating that he had been offered the job, but that he had declined and instead recommended Gresley for the role.

Cecil J. Allen refuted this story, on the grounds that he believed Robinson's memory to have been "playing tricks". Geoffrey Hughes in his excellent biography of Gresley made the point that maybe there was some truth in Robinson's story, albeit perhaps that Robinson had been interviewed, and persuaded to step aside in favour of Gresley.

Eric Trask is on record as having witnessed the outcome of the meetings between Robinson and the L.N.E.R. Chief General Manager, and that of Gresley and the same. He writes that a form for the return of two N1 tank locomotives from war duty was required to be signed by the C.M.E. of the time. With no one in office, he was asked to wait outside the board room and was told by Gresley that he was waiting for the outcome of the appointment. Robinson then left the board room, Gresley entered, came out shortly after and offered to sign Trask's form, confirming his position as C.M.E.

The truth is difficult to discern, but Eric Trask's story does not contradict Robinson's, merely confirming that the former G.C.R. M.E, was present around the events of the appointment. Allen's dismissal of Robinson's claim seems unfair. Why would Robinson lie to, or mislead, *The Railway Gazette* all those years later?

It seems far more likely that Robinson was called in for his viewpoints on the appointment, and recommended Gresley in that meeting. Given the seniority of Robinson and his wide range of experience, he would have at least been a possible candidate for an interim role as C.M.E. in some form. As it stands, he was to be a consultant to the L.N.E.R. for a year after Gresley's appointment in any event, alongside Sir Vincent Raven.

There is room for Robinson's recollections being factually correct. This does not change the fact that of the two C.M.E.s, Gresley had the most years ahead of him and would have likely become C.M.E. in any event.

In the biography of his father, Anthony Bulleid reported that Gresley had in fact approached Bulleid in the October of 1922, several months before the L.N.E.R. was formed and the appointment was to be made, to encourage him to join the L.N.E.R. as his assistant. This again, does not confirm that Robinson's recollections are false, rather it confirms the suspicion that Gresley had seen in Bulleid potential on the new railway and wanted to bring him along for the new adventure.

The L.N.E.R. Board Minutes in the National Archives at Kew record that Gresley's appointment was confirmed on the 23 February 1923, with a wage of £4500.
This was recorded seven weeks from the formation of the L.N.E.R., but the decision to hire Gresley is likely to have been made much earlier, as was standard with the L.N.E.R. board in years to come.

Gresley was now latterly responsible for the following assets of the L.N.E.R:

- Over 7400 steam locomotives

- Over 21,000 coaches

- Over 300,000 wagons

- Utilities including water and electricity

- Road vehicles

- Fixed plant and machinery

- Locomotive and Carriage & Wagon Works, including Doncaster, Darlington, Gorton,

Inverurie, Stratford and several more.

- 6590 miles (10,610 kilometres) of railway lines

There was also the organisation and development of his individual departments, reorganisation of the drawing office and much more besides. Crucially, on taking over as C.M.E., Gresley made several appointments of technical assistants including Bert Spencer and Frank Day.

The latter would support Gresley in the development of carriages and wagons, the former would be highly influential in the development of his locomotive designs and in particular the use of conjugated valve gear.

*Fig.100b. In recognition of the impending grouping and some forward thinking that perhaps served to place his position and the management team of the former Great Northern Railway, first and foremost in the eyes some, Gresley's first Pacific numbered as No.1470 bore the name Great Northern. Colourised by Ian MacCabe, The Gresley Society.*

# Chapter 5
# L.N.E.R.
# Locomotive Designs
## L.N.E.R. Class P1 2-8-2 (1925)
## Number built (L.N.E.R.): 2

*Fig. 101. The first Gresley P1, No.2393, ex-works at Doncaster. Note that the locomotive is fully lined out on its running plate, boiler, tender and, at a first glance, the front pony truck wheels. Colourised by Ian MacCabe. The Gresley Society.*

By 1925, Gresley had been considering the provision of locomotives which could haul longer, and heavier freight trains on the east coast main line. In August 1923, a design for a 2-8-2 tender locomotive was submitted for consideration to the L.N.E.R. Locomotive Committee, with its intended use being between London and Peterborough in the south of England, and between Immingham and Wath Yard in the north.

The original wheelbase of the proposed locomotive had been 2-10-2, with 4ft 8in driving wheels, as opposed to the final designs' 5ft 2in diameter driving wheels. R.C.T.S. L.N.E.R. 6B states that there "must have been some doubts about the wisdom of introducing a ten-coupled design". The 2-10-2 would have been the same length as one of the Gresley A1 Pacifics, but with much greater adhesion. The issue would have been the ten coupled wheelbase being used on sharply curved track layouts.

The 2-8-2 was in effect a compromise and allowed the driving wheels to be increased in size and spaced apart more effectively. The result was a locomotive that Gresley's then assistant, Oliver Bulleid would later describe as the "most handsome" of Gresley's designs.

Fig. 102. Gresley P1 No.2393, as early on in her career. Note the distinctive large diameter piping under the cab and running plate, signifying that the locomotive is booster fitted at this time. The number and company lettering are all on the tender, as was the case with the early L.N.E.R. liveries for a few years. Strathwood Library Collection.

Fig. 103. Gresley P1 No.2393, at Potters Bar on 13 May 1939. By this time the booster equipment has been removed, as has the Westinghouse pump on the running plate. The locomotive still has its original 180lb boiler fitted at this time. The locomotive's number is now on the cab sides. George C. Lander/Rail Photoprints

The front end of the 2-8-2 design below the running plate should be recognisable, as it was based on the production Gresley O2, and certain details of the conjugated valve gear layout together with the outside Walschaerts valve gear were standard with the latter class. However, the P1s were fitted with steam reversing gear, which was useful when starting a heavily loaded train (this would allow the driver to ease the couplings throughout the train).

The 2-8-2 design and its associated documentation gave certain specific details: these locomotives would cost no more than £8000 (they ended up costing, as a pair, £20,986, or £4986 more than anticipated) and would be able to haul up to 25% more wagons in a single train than the existing classes of 2-8-0. It was a bold proposal: perhaps bolder was the omission of the words from the original proposal which stated, "sufficient loads can be found for these locomotives".

There should be little doubt that the locomotives went over their original allocated budget due in no small part to the complication of the booster engine fitted under the cabs of these engines. Additional design time and work was allocated to the Superheater Co. Ltd of New York towards this equipment and some of this was delayed whilst the company tried to design in a radial truck under the cab with the booster equipment, later admitting that Gresley's cartazzi design, which had been in use with the Pacifics for a few years, was "undoubtedly about the lightest form of suspension that could be worked out for booster application to these Mikado engines".

The boosters to be fitted to No.2393 and No.2394 were similar in layout and design to the type C-1 booster which had been previously fitted to Ivatt Atlantic C1 No.4419. The equipment was designed to increase tractive effort when starting trains (both for heavy or unusual loads and when starting on a gradient). This equipment was effectively a two-cylinder steam engine incorporated into the trailing wheels of the given locomotive, which by a gearing system would be engaged when required. No.4419's was quoted as producing 8500lb additional tractive effort when applied at 75% cut off, and there is no reason to assume the Gresley P1s' equipment did anything less. The boosters were designed to only work at full cut off and to automatically cut out when the reversing gear was notched up. When running, by means of the Westinghouse air compressor located on the running plate, the booster would be engaged before 10mph was reached and disengaged after 21mph was achieved.

In September 1925 the prototype P1, No.2393, worked a train with the dynamometer car, 101 mineral wagons and a 20-ton brakevan. This was one of the longest trains assembled, and the booster was employed in varying degrees whilst a drawbar horsepower figure of 1210h.p. was recorded. The test was satisfactory in all but one regard: the locomotive had burned coal at a rate of 150lb per mile. In operating service, the boosters were never quite reliable enough and by May 1938 both locomotives had the boosters removed (No.2394 had hers removed a year earlier in April 1937).

One downside of removing the booster equipment is that the factor of adhesion of the two locomotives was reduced from 4.16 to 3.89, by way of the redistribution of weight across the coupled driving wheels from 71 tons 10cwt to 66 tons 18cwt. When A3 boilers were fitted in 1942, and the cylinders lined up from 20in to 19in, the tractive effort went up from 38,500lb to 42,466lb but their factor of adhesion went down further to 3.65. In practice this lowering of adhesion did not seem to make much of a difference to the two locomotives performances and they were taking far lighter loads than they were intended to pull or were capable of.

*Fig. 104. The second Gresley P1, No.2394, rounding the curve at Ganwick and making light work.*
*The Gresley Society.*

There is little doubt that the two locomotives were fully capable of taking on whatever work was thrown at them. They worked mostly between New England and Ferme Park, which allowed them the ability to make up long trains and take advantage of the two locomotives' capabilities. The issue on the east coast main line at this time was that quadrupling of the major parts of the line had not happened at the time the Gresley P1s were introduced. The longer formations of trains they were able to pull ultimately had to be timetabled carefully to prevent knock on delays to other mixed traffic and express passenger services. Ultimately, the removal of these two track bottlenecks came too late in the day for the Gresley P1s. Their timetabled 100 wagon trains had fallen to one a day in 1932. The two P1s had an unusual record in that they kept their original 180lb boilers longer than any of the Gresley classes so fitted. When shopped for overhaul in 1934, both locomotives received new boilers: No.2393's boiler was in "the worst condition of any Pacific boiler [I] have ever seen" by the works manager of the time, F.H. Eggleshaw.

Incredibly, this boiler was repaired and put into use on Gresley A1 No.4481 St. Simon. No. 2394's boiler, on the other hand, was summarily scrapped.

No.2393 was notable as having taken part in the 1925 Stockton & Darlington Centenary Celebrations. Otherwise, the two locomotives were run without fuss for twenty years, before they were withdrawn, the first casualties of Edward Thompson's standardisation scheme. Their boilers went into the Gresley A3 pool of boilers and the tenders were then used for two of the rebuilds of Gresley's B17s into Thompson B2s.

## Wartime Mileages & Availability

| Year | Mileages | Availability |
|------|----------|--------------|
| 1942 | 22849 | 69% |
| 1943 | 24781 | 74% |
| 1944 | 20920 | 72% |
| 1945 | 0 | 0% |
| 1946 | 0 | 0% |

Fig. 105. P1 Mileages & Availability Statistics.
Simon A.C. Martin, from the Use of Engine Power Document.

Before withdrawal in 1945, the two Gresley P1s were performing in line with the performance seen across the L.N.E.R. fleet. They were pressed heavily in 1943 and were doing a few thousand more miles between them in that year than they were expected to. Availability remained in and around 70%, a respectable figure and in keeping with the overall expectations of that time.

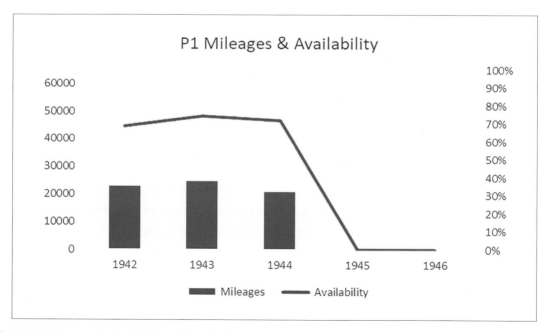

Fig. 106. P1 Mileages & Availability Graph. Simon A.C. Martin from the Use of Engine Power Document.

Their withdrawal was covered by the introduction of brand new Gresley O2/4s and other 2-8-0s that the L.N.E.R. was producing or using around the same time (including, but not limited to, Stanier Class O6/8F and Austerity Class O7).

| Class P1 | | | | |
|---|---|---|---|---|
| | | A1 boiler (1925-43) | A3 boiler (1942-45) |
| Cylinders (x3): | | 20x26in. | 19x26in. |
| Motion: | Outside: | Walschaerts | Walschaerts |
| | Inside: | Gresley | Walschaerts |
| | Valves: | 8in piston | 8in piston |
| Boiler: | Max. Diameter: | 6ft | 6ft |
| | Pressure: | 180lb | 225lb |
| | Diagram No.: | 94 | 94HP & 94A |
| Heating Surface: | Total: | 2308 sq. ft. | 2308 sq. ft. |
| | Firebox: | 182 sq. ft. | 182 sq. ft. |
| | Superheater: | 407 sq. ft. (32x 1.25in) | 407 sq. ft. (32x 1.244in) |
| | Tubes: | 1192 sq. ft. (217x 1.75in) | 1192 sq. ft. (217x 1.75in) |
| | Flues: | 527 sq. ft. (32x 5.25in) | 527 sq. ft. (32x 5.25in) |
| Grate Area: | | 28 sq. ft. | 28 sq. ft. |
| Wheels: | Leading: | 3ft 2in | 3ft 2in |
| | Coupled: | 5ft 2in | 5ft 2in |
| | Tender: | 3ft 8in | 3ft 8in |
| Tractive Effort: | At 85% boiler pressure | 38,500lb | 42,466lb |
| Wheelbase: | Total: | 59ft 8in | 59ft 8in |
| | Engine: | 36ft 2in | 36ft 2in |
| | Tender: | 13ft 0in | 13ft 0in |
| Weight (full): | Total: | 151 tons 8cwt | 151 tons 8cwt |
| | Engine: | 100 tons 0cwt | 100 tons 0cwt |
| | Tender: | 51 tons 8cwt | 51 tons 8cwt |
| Max. Axle Load: | | 18 tons 13cwt | 18 tons 13cwt |

# L.N.E.R. Class U1 Garratt 2-8-0+0-8-2 (1925)
## Number built (L.N.E.R.): 1

*Fig. 107. Gresley U1 No.2395 works photograph. The Gresley Society.*

The genesis of one of the most powerful locomotives in the British Isles is a complicated one. The Great Central Railway (G.C.R.) under its C.M.E., John G. Robinson, had been investigating the potential for a four-cylindered Garratt. This was due to a desire to reduce the number of banking locomotives required for the Worsborough Bank route, where the length and severity of the gradient (1 in 40 for three miles at its worst) made it difficult to restart trains on the ascent. As train lengths became longer up to three banking locomotives might be used to assist trains going up the incline.

The G.C.R. design called for the use of two Robinson 2-8-0 chassis with a Garratt designed boiler slung between the two units. By the time of nationalisation in 1923, Robinson had relinquished his role as C.M.E. and Gresley was now in charge of the L.N.E.R.'s inherited locomotive development plans. He switched the two-cylindered Robinson 2-8-0 units for a pair of his three-cylindered O2 design, and the tender was increased to two locomotives of such a type from Beyer, Peacock & Co. Ltd. This order was subsequently reduced to one after the initial price of £21,000 for two units was discarded in favour of £14,895 for one.

The sole U1 was reputedly built in a three-week period, the frames and boiler coming together in a hurried fashion. It was still sporting works grey when first steamed and prepared for its debut at the Stockton & Darlington Centenary Celebrations alongside the new Gresley P1 2-8-2 Mikado. The locomotive was both the first mainline Garratt in the United Kingdom and would remain the most powerful locomotive built to run in Britain.

When pressed into duty, No.2395 (following the numbering of the Gresley P1 Mikados) would make up to 18 return trips in a day up Worsborough Bank between Wentworth Junction and Silkstone Junction, pushing loaded coal trains of over sixty wagons in addition to the leading locomotive and the assisting engine at the rear as well.

The Silkstone Tunnels had always had a poor reputation for air quality, and with up to two steam locomotives ahead of any one working of the Gresley Garratt, the atmosphere was so bad for the crews that steps were taken, by means of equipment to provide the driver and fireman with fresh air. This came in the form of respirators which took in air from vents at the railhead level. The crews objected to sharing the equipment on hygiene grounds and returned to using the standard wet handkerchief wrapped around the nose and mouth.

The U1 suffered from corrosion in its tubes and firebox in the early years of its life. The suspicion is a combination of a lack of water treatment, poor coal quality and some unfamiliarity with the locomotive's design led to these issues. In any event, the Garratt's boiler, new in 1925, was completely retubed in 1926, followed by cracks in the firebox requiring repair in 1927, and in 1928 further corrosion issues led to a complete renewal of the firebox the same year, putting the locomotive out of service for nine months whilst rebuilt. The locomotive would continue to work in this role and was renumbered under the Thompson renumbering scheme as 9999.

By 1948, the locomotive had settled down to its role on the Worsborough Incline, but with the electrification of the Manchester, Sheffield and Wath lines incoming the necessity for the locomotive was in doubt. Initially stored, it was then trialled at the Licky Incline alongside the famous Midland Railway Lickey Banker, "Big Bertha" (also known variously as "Big Emma" and other names), with one significant modification being the addition of an electric headlight for visibility during darkness. Renumbered as 69999 by British Railways, the Garratt ran for just under a year at Bromsgrove before patience ran out with the local operating department, and it was returned to Mexborough and placed back into storage.

A reprieve came in 1951 when the locomotive was returned to the Worsborough Bank route and resumed its original duties for a year before going back into store, and then sent to Gorton Works for overhaul. The locomotive was to be converted to oil firing and was at Gorton Works for three years whilst this was carried out, together with a new electric headlight. It resumed work at Bromsgrove in June 1955, but this was to be short lived and the operating department there pulled the plug, the locomotive going back into store for the final time at Gorton in October 1955. There would be no reprieve and the locomotive was then hauled to Doncaster Works where it was withdrawn officially in December 1955 and then cut up in the first few months of 1956.

| Year | Mileages | Availability |
|------|----------|--------------|
| 1942 | 22117 | 75% |
| 1943 | 16215 | 62% |
| 1944 | 18474 | 74% |
| 1945 | 13438 | 64% |
| 1946 | 5170 | 28% |

*Fig. 108. U1 Mileages & Availability Statistics.*
*Simon A.C. Martin, from the Use of Engine Power Document.*

It is difficult to assess the relative value of the Gresley U1. It is one of the few classes which was not covered in documents such as the *Mileages of Locomotives Between General Repairs* published internally by the L.N.E.R. and as such, even looking at the data we have available in the *Use of Engine Power* document, has limitations without full context.

The U1 seemed to be available for somewhere between 62 and 75% of the time in any year, and her mileages went from a high 22,117 miles to as low as 5,170 miles. One suspects that this reflects the locomotive being taken out of service for repairs, since we know that she was back in work by the end of 1947. If we discount 1946, and concentrate on the statistics from the war years, the locomotive's mileages varied substantially as did its availability. 1942 however was a good year, bucking the trend of the L.N.E.R. by having better availability than the fleet average of around 70%.

*Fig. 109. Gresley U1 No.2395 works photograph. The Gresley Society.*

The relative value of this unique locomotive is very specialised to one job: banking locomotives. There is nothing similar with which to compare on the L.N.E.R., and to criticise the locomotive's design would be unfair. There certainly was a need for such a locomotive: it does not appear to have suffered too poorly from the lack of wartime maintenance, and the reduced mileages by the end of the war could be a downturn in overall wartime traffic and not necessarily the locomotive being unreliable in any form.

The criticisms of its use of conjugated valve gear don't ring true, either: on the contrary, the two O2 style units appear to have been the most reliable parts of the locomotive, the issue being by far more about the lack of a decent water treatment regime in its early years, and in later years the issues with oil firing, and the efforts to keep its large grate covered (56 square foot, bigger even any of than the L.N.E.R. Pacifics) may have contributed to its poor reputation on the Midland Region, though we cannot discount prejudice against it nor genuine operational difficulties (it has been reported anecdotally that the locomotive caused platform damage on the Midland Region. There does not appear to be any official record of such issues and as such may be considered speculative at best).

Some writers have unkindly presented the Gresley Garratt as folly on Gresley's part, and the use of two of his O2 units as a measure of arrogance. This cannot be so: a locomotive was required for a specific task, and Gresley provided it. The conjugated gear on the Garratt was no more onerous, pre-Second World War years than four sets of independent valve gears, as would have been the case on the proposed Robinson Garratt: in any event, its overall availability and mileages during the war were in line with the fleet's average.

Nothing exists on record criticising the conjugated valve gear in this application, in any event. If anything, the use of the valve gear allowed a more powerful locomotive to be built, and the gear only became worn and unreliable when over travel of the middle valve was experienced (something never encountered, of course, on the slow-moving banking work of the Gresley U1). Some views on record from those who fired it recall it was a good running, and a better riding locomotive than most. It would be trite to call Gresley's Garratt an unmitigated success, given the issues of the boiler and its potted final career at Bromsgrove, but it would also be unfair to call it a failure. There is no doubt that the U1 was built to do a job and it did that one job well for a good twenty years. To the L.N.E.R.'s board and to Gresley, that was enough.

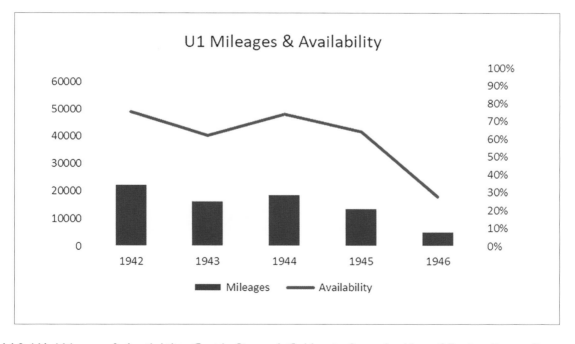

*Fig. 110. U1 Mileages & Availability Graph. Simon A.C. Martin from the Use of Engine Power Document.*

| Class U1 | | |
|---|---|---|
| Cylinders (x6): | | 18.5x26in. |
| Boiler: | Diameter: | 7ft |
| | Length: | 13ft 6 7/8in |
| | Pressure: | 180lb |
| Heating Surface: | Total: | 3581 sq. ft. |
| | Firebox: | 223.5 sq. ft. |
| | Tubes: | 1819.5 sq. ft. |
| | Superheater: | 650.0 sq. ft. |
| Grate Area: | | 56.5 sq. ft. |
| Wheels: | Coupled: | 4ft 8in |
| | Leading: | 2ft 8in |
| | Trailing: | 2ft 8in |
| Total Wheelbase: | | 79ft 1in |
| Tractive Effort: | At 85% boiler pressure | 72,940lb |
| Length: | | 87ft 3in |
| Weight: | (full) | 178t 1cwt |
| Max. Axle Load: | | 18t 6cwt |
| Water Capacity: | | 5000 gallons |
| Coal Capacity: | | 7tons |

*Fig. 110B. She was certainly an impressive exhibit when presented to the public and guests from around the world at the Stockton & Darlington Centenary Celebrations in 1925. Rail Photoprints*

# L.N.E.R. Class J38 0-6-0 (1926)
Number built (L.N.E.R.): 35

*Fig. 111. Gresley J38 No.1417, at St. Margaret's Shed in Scotland. The Gresley Society.*

In 1924 the L.N.E.R. was focused on planning for the future, and the first true group standard locomotive to be built under theirs and Gresley's auspices was to be an 0-6-0 tender engine, intended for work across the majority of the L.N.E.R. (Southern, North Eastern and Scottish areas) with an intended 103 locomotives to be built.

However, in early 1925 a large quantity of ex-R.O.D. Robinson 2-8-0s came up for sale; the Southern area of the L.N.E.R. purchased in bulk, and as a result the order for the new 0-6-0 locomotive was reduced by half, dividing the intended fleet between the North Eastern and Scottish areas of the L.N.E.R. accordingly. This would have been 55 locomotives; the final order deleted the North Eastern allocation and thus just 35 locomotives were to be built at Darlington works.

The general construction order described the new 0-6-0 as the "J27 Modified", which amongst writers on the L.N.E.R. has caused some confusion. The resulting 0-6-0 tender engine was J27 in wheel arrangement only and all other details were significantly different. If anything, the Gresley J38 had far more in common with Doncaster designed 0-6-0s including, but not limited to, the final Gresley incarnation of the Ivatt J6. This was despite the smaller driving wheels at 4ft 8in diameter. (The later Gresley J39 then used the same driving wheel diameter as the J6s, at 5ft 2in, and were discernible from the J38s by the small splashers on top of the running plate).

The cylinder size was 20in by 26in, similar in size to the J6s 19in by 26in, however the Stephenson valve gear arrangement was based on the Class A5 Pacific tank's arrangement, with minor changes to the eccentrics and rocking arms to suit. This valve gear design was later to be used, it is reported, almost unchanged on locomotives rebuilt under Gresley's direction (the next 0-6-0, Class J39 and then classes D11 and D16/3) and later Thompson's. (It was used on the lone D49/4 Class The Morpeth 4-4-0 and the Robinson 0-6-0, the J11/3). This design of valve gear was also fitted to members of Class A5 as they came up for overhaul.

The class were built with the original group standard tender, with flared sides, of 4200-gallon tanks and water pickup apparatus. This addition was curious as there were no troughs for water pickup in the areas of Scotland they operated in.

Between 1931 and 1933 some members of Class J38 had their tenders swapped out for 3500-gallon tenders, with no water pickup apparatus, and their original tenders were sent to be paired with new Gresley O2s that were being built. The engines with the 3500-gallon tenders were reclassified as J38/1 and all others were reclassified as J38/2, but this was short lived. In the 1950s, some of the class swapped tenders again, with a range of tenders coming from classes Raven A2, J39, K3 and K3.

The J38's diagram 96 boiler had the same diameter as the J27's, but with a larger firebox and grate (9ft and 26sq.ft respectively). The boiler was pitched higher than other 0-6-0 tender classes to clear the piston valves. The boiler was pressed to 180lb, in line with most of Gresley's classes to date (only Class J6 was the odd one out, having a boiler pressed to 170lb).

This boiler had a Darlington style round firehole, with a square N.E.R. style Firehole door covering it, unlike the later Class J39 which had the oval style of firehole. From 1932, J38s were fitted with diagram 97 boilers as per Class J39 as and when their original boilers were condemned. This accelerated from 1940 and in 1941 class J38 was reclassified for the second time into two parts: those with the original boiler type as J38/1 and those with the later boiler type as J38/2, now ignoring the tender types altogether.

This boiler had a Darlington style round firehole, with a square N.E.R. style Firehole door covering it, unlike the later class J39 which had the oval style of firehole. From 1932, J38s were fitted with diagram 97 boilers as per class J39 as and when their original boilers were condemned. This accelerated from 1940 and in 1941 class J38 was reclassified for the second time into two parts: those with the original boiler type as J38/1 and those with the later boiler type as J38/2, now ignoring the tender types altogether.

The J38s were specifically goods engines, and their work in Scotland reflected that. They were utilised on mineral and coal trains between Fife and Lothian to Glasgow, Edinburgh, and the ports of Scotland. Allocations of the first 30 were small and evenly split across three different sheds initially, Dunfermline, St. Margaret's, and Thornton, with five going to Dundee, and two each to Eastfield and Stirling. Stirling's allocation lasted a year, with the pair split and sent to Dunfermline and Dundee.

These allocations lasted until 1930, with the St. Margaret's engines cascaded elsewhere with the arrival of some K2 2-6-0s and the newer Gresley J39s into service.

*Fig. 112. Gresley J38 No.65900, at St. Margaret's Shed in Scotland. The Gresley Society.*

The J38s were to be maintained at Cowlairs Works, after having been built at Darlington, though some were sent to Darlington as and when space at Cowlairs was unavailable for them. From 1955, Inverurie Works also undertook limited repairs on the J38 class when Cowlairs did not have capacity.

The J38 was the first of Gresley's Group Standard designs for the L.N.E.R., and as a class it had the distinction of being the Gresley last class to remain intact when dieselisation took hold and the last Gresley designed class working for British Railways. The entire class worked into 1962 and from there withdrawals continued over the next five years until the scrapping of No.65929 rendered the class extinct.

| Year | Mileages | Availability |
|------|----------|--------------|
| 1942 | 25894 | 69% |
| 1943 | 22785 | 68% |
| 1944 | 22375 | 76% |
| 1945 | 24351 | 70% |
| 1946 | 21451 | 65% |

*Fig. 113. J38 Mileages & Availability Statistics.*
*Simon A.C. Martin, from the Use of Engine Power Document.*

Class J38 performed in line with the overall average availability of the L.N.E.R. during the Second World War, with availability in and around 70% with a high of approximately 76% in 1944. Annual mileages varied by a few thousand in a year, with the lowest coming immediately post war in 1946 with a class average of 21,451 miles achieved.

This was still within expected parameters of the class, pre-war, and although other 0-6-0 tender classes (including Gresley's earlier Class J6) performed better in terms of availability, the average mileages of the Gresley J38 were still above average and consistent throughout.

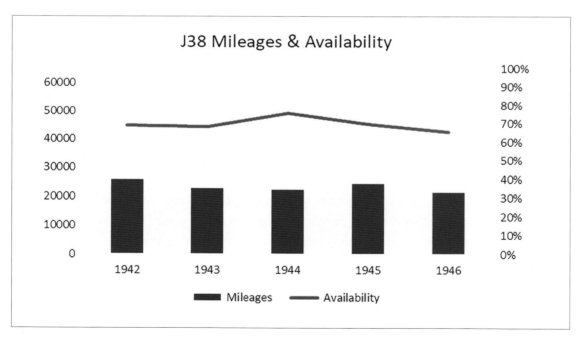

*Fig. 114. J38 Mileages & Availability Graph.*
*Simon A.C. Martin from the Use of Engine Power Document.*

# Class J38

| | | |
|---|---|---|
| Cylinders (x2): | (inside) | 20x26in. |
| Motion: | | Stephenson |
| Piston Valves: | | 8in. diameter |
| Boiler: | Max. Diameter: | 5ft 6in |
| | Pressure: | 180lb |
| | Diagram No.: | 97A |
| Heating Surface: | Total: | 1744.35 sq. ft. |
| | Firebox: | 171.5 sq. ft. |
| | Superheater: | 289.6 sq. ft. (24x 1.2") |
| | Tubes: | 912.25 sq. ft. (177x 1.75in) |
| | Flues: | 371 sq. ft. (24x 5.25in) |
| Grate Area: | | 26 sq. ft. |
| Wheels: | Coupled: | 4ft 8in |
| | Tender: | 3ft 9in |
| Tractive Effort: | At 85% boiler pressure | 28,414lb |
| Wheelbase: | Total: | 41ft 3in |
| | Engine: | 17ft 0in |
| | Tender: | 13ft 6in |
| Weight (full): | Total: | 110 tons 9cwt |
| | Engine: | 58 tons 19cwt |
| | Tender: | 51 tons 10cwt |
| Max. Axle Load: | | 20 tons 6cwt |

*Fig. 114B. Gresley J38 No.65908, as running in the 1950s as running out of 62A Thornton Junction shed. Strathwood Library Collection*

# L.N.E.R. Class J39 0-6-0 (1926)
## Number built (L.N.E.R.): 289

*Fig. 115. Gresley J39 No.1448 works photograph. The Gresley Society.*

Gresley's J39 0-6-0 goods locomotives was the most numerous of the classes designed under him, with 289 locomotives built over a 15-year period between 1926 and 1941. The locomotives were built, in the main, by Darlington Works but many of the boilers were manufactured for the L.N.E.R. by Armstrong, Whitworth & Co. Ltd, with R. Stephenson & Co also manufacturing boilers towards the class. One batch of 28 locomotives was built from 1926 by Beyer, Peacock & Co in addition to the above.

The J38 had been intended to become the group's standard 0-6-0 locomotive, however some design changes were made and the J39 class emerged with larger driving wheels (6in larger, matching the Gresley J6 at 5ft 2in in diameter) and was marginally shorter in length in the frames by 6in. Close inspection of photographs will show that the splasher arrangement of the J38 and J39 were different, the latter protruding above the running plate whereas the J38's was flush. Sub divisions in the class were made in 1930 on the L.N.E.R. and these related to tender type: those with the original 3500-gallon group standard tender became J39/1, those with the 4200 alternatives became J39/2 and any fitted with G.C.R. or N.E.R. tenders were classified as J39/3. These sub divisions were dropped in 1952.

There was a variety of braking arrangements within the 289 Class J39s, largely down to the area they operated in. The first batch of twelve locomotives had Westinghouse brakes and a vacuum brake to cover all types of train braking.

The twenty J39s that followed in East Anglia would always have Westinghouse brakes fitted, whereas the North Eastern J39s were similarly fitted from new, but in the 1930s were onverted to steam braking. The J39s built up to 1934 outside of these batches were given steam brakes for the locomotive and tender, and vacuum for the train, but from 1935 all those built were vacuum braked only. One J39, No.1270 would be fitted with a unique superheater: the Cruse-Gray superheater, which was supplied by Bolton's Superheater & Pipe Works Company. This was a one-off fitting and was replaced by the standard Robinson type of superheater in 1931, bringing it into line with the other J39s.

The J39s suffered from severe twisting forces on their axle boxes, thought to be due in part by the coupling rods being 180 degrees from their adjacent connecting rods, together with being separated by 90 degrees from each other. Edward Thompson, as the head of Darlington Works in 1938, reported to Gresley that the axle boxes were experiencing significant heavy wear, with overheating of the right-hand side occurring more often than on the left side. This was also observable in several other 0-6-0 tender locomotive designs the L.N.E.R. had inherited.

*Fig. 116. Gresley J39 No.2712, showing the use of the class on passenger trains. The Gresley Society.*

Some modifications were trialled by way of fitting divided axle box types, with six locomotives modified at Gorton Works under Arthur Peppercorn's regime. No more were converted, with the six affected then returned to the standard setup in the early 1950s as and when they were to be shopped for overhaul. In 1946 there was a proposal to fit the J39s with the Thompson L1 type boiler.

This would have reduced the weight of the class and increased the route availability. The proposal does not seem to have got much past outline drawings, and with nationalisation on the horizon was quietly dropped by 1949.

Although the class has received criticism for its axle box issues, there is no doubt of the overall excellence of the class, though conceived primarily as a goods locomotive, the use of the 5ft 2in diameter wheels made the J39s quite versatile, pulling everything from coal, oil, mixed traffic, and passenger trains throughout their working lives. The J39s were only displaced, in the main, by the newer Thompson B1s coming into traffic, but all 289 of the type survived through to 1959, with all withdrawn by the end of 1962. No.64747 is notable for having become the sole surviving class member by way of becoming a stationary boiler at Woodford Shed until late 1964.

## Wartime Mileages & Availability

| Year | Mileages | Availability |
|------|----------|--------------|
| 1942 | 24221 | 70% |
| 1943 | 22152 | 66% |
| 1944 | 22625 | 71% |
| 1945 | 23305 | 68% |
| 1946 | 20615 | 61% |

*Fig. 117. J39 Mileages & Availability Statistics.*
*Simon A.C. Martin, from the Use of Engine Power Document.*

The J39's performances during the Second World War placed it firmly below the older Gresley J6s and J38s in terms of availability, only just achieving 70% availability in 1944 and at all other times below it. This was until 1946 when a combination of factors (including a number out for repair) led to 60% availability and an average annual mileage of 20,615. In fairness the class as a whole had performed in line with the L.N.E.R.'s fleet averages for the wartime period, and annual average mileages were always above 20,000 miles.

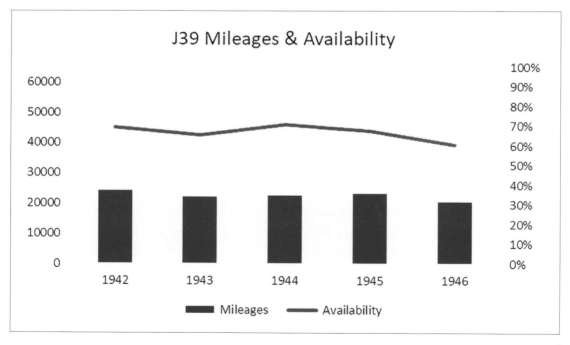

*Fig. 118. J39 Mileages & Availability Graph. Simon A.C. Martin from the Use of Engine Power Document.*

*Fig. 119. J39 No.1509 at Newport Motive Power Depot in 1940. Strathwood Library Collection.*

| Class J39 | | |
|---|---|---|
| Cylinders (x2): | (inside) | 20x26in. |
| Motion: | | Stephenson |
| Piston Valves: | | 8in. diameter |
| Boiler: | Max. Diameter: | 5ft 6in |
| | Pressure: | 180lb |
| | Diagram No.: | 97 |
| Heating Surface: | Total: | 1669.58 sq. ft. |
| | Firebox: | 171.5 sq. ft. |
| | Superheater: | 271.8 sq. ft. (24x 1.2") |
| | Tubes: | 871.75 sq. ft. (177x 1.75in) |
| | Flues: | 354.53 sq. ft. (24x 5.25in) |
| Grate Area: | | 26 sq. ft. |
| Wheels: | Coupled: | 5ft 2in |
| | Tender: | 3ft 9in |
| Tractive Effort: | At 85% boiler pressure | 25,664lb |
| Wheelbase: | Total: | 40ft 5.25in |
| | Engine: | 17ft 0in |
| | Tender: | 13ft 0in |
| Weight (full): | Total: | 102 tons 1cwt |
| | Engine: | 57 tons 17cwt |
| | Tender: | 44 tons 4cwt |
| Max. Axle Load: | | 19 tons 13cwt |

# L.N.E.R. Class A3 4-6-2 (1927)
## Number built (L.N.E.R.): 78 (52 rebuilt from Class A1)

*Fig. 120. Gresley A3 No.2750, Papyrus, on the turntable at King's Cross, being turned for its next stint hauling the Flying Scotsman service. This locomotive went on to be a record breaker with a top speed of 108 mph. Colourised by Ian MacCabe, The Gresley Society.*

The A3 development for the L.N.E.R. was born out of the sustained trials with the A1 class surrounding several key elements of the design: the superheater type, the boiler pressure, and the long lap travel valves. The revised design had its boiler pressed to 220lb rather than the 180lb. The use of a wider superheater header led to the distinctive cover plates on either side of the smokebox, behind the chimney, which allowed onlookers to distinguish the original Pacifics with the new design quite easily.

In 1927, the first two A3s were introduced by rebuilding Gresley A1s No.2544 *Lemberg* and No.4480 *Enterprise*. No.2544 would have its cylinders lined to 18.25in to compare with No.4480's original setup of 20in cylinders. Three more rebuilds were authorised, and carried out, but retained their 20in cylinders.

When new A3s started to be built in 1928, the cylinders were bored to 19in instead. This combination seemed to be optimal and no new A1s were built past 1928, with existing members of Class A1 to be rebuilt as A3s when possible, over the next 20 years.

Fig. 121. Gresley A3 No.2501 Colombo appears to be deputising for an A4 pacific as it comes through Peterborough North hauling the Silver Jubilee on 27 September 1937. Rail Archive Stephenson.

All the original A1s had been built with right-hand drive, and those rebuilt to the A3 specification retained this. All new A3 builds were left-hand drive. This meant that by the late 1930s the class would be roughly half left-hand drive and half right-hand drive. The right-drive examples of the A3s together with the remaining members of Class A1, would not be converted to left-hand drive until the end of 1954.

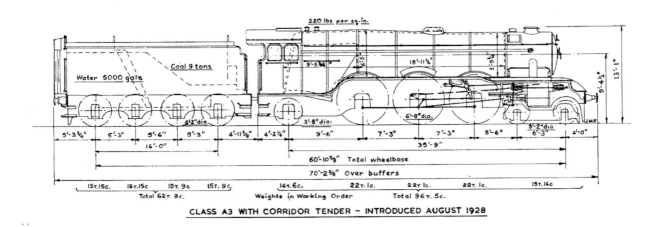

*Fig. 122. Gresley A3 Line Drawing, Doncaster Works. Courtesy of the R.C.T.S.*

Like Class A1 from which they were derived, Class A3 would pull a variety of eight-wheel tender types throughout its career, the most famous of which were the original 1928 built corridor tenders.

*Fig. 123. Gresley A3 No.2580, Shotover, fitted with an ACFI feed water header.*
*The Gresley Society.*

Fig. 124. Gresley A3 No.2751 Humorist at Doncaster Works, fitted with a partial smokebox front, including sloped internal smoke lifting air channels. 5 July 1932. Doncaster Works.
Rail Archive Stephenson.

Fig. 125. Gresley A3 No.2751 Humorist at Grantham in 1932, with a sloped smokebox and wing deflector plates and a stovepipe chimney. Note the similarities to the W1 setup and the A4 Pacifics to come in terms of format. Rail Archive Stephenson.

*Fig. 126. Gresley A3 No.2751 Humorist, as modified for smoke deflection trials. Note the slope to the smokebox together with the stovepipe shape of the chimney, echoing the streamlining work done on Gresley's W1. Strathwood Library Collection*

The original G.N.R. style tenders with coal rails lasted until the end of steam, supplemented by the corridor tenders, and two versions of the non-corridor eight-wheel tender: one "beaded" and non-streamlined, and the final type matching the non-corridor A4 type of tender. Tenders were swapped around as and when required for the non-stop services.

The class was subject to a series of trials in chimney and smoke lifting experiments, with the most famous of those modified locomotives being No.2751 *Humorist*. This locomotive became the first of the class to be fitted with a Kylchap double chimney, which eventually became a standard fitting for Thompson's Pacifics and Peppercorn's A1 design, post-war.

*Humorist* gained a reputation for being the classes' best example, but the issue of drifting smoke because of the softer exhaust of the Kylchap fitting led to a series of trials with smoke deflectors. Wing deflectors were fitted, and then replaced by a Peppercorn-like variant in 1947, which it retained until withdrawal. The other seventy-eight A3s would only start receiving double Kylchaps from 1958. Initially wing type deflectors like *Humorist*'s original pair were fitted, but further development by those at King's Cross (including Peter Townend) led to the Witte style wing deflectors being trialled instead. They were found to be a complete success and fitted to most of the A3s accordingly.

*Fig. 127. Gresley A3 No.2751 Humorist at Doncaster Works, shortly after the full-size smokebox was restored and a rimmed double chimney was fitted. Re-draughting experiments were also conducted on the W1 10000 and to A4 4468 Mallard. This photograph portrays Humorist in her most elegant form as many consider the various experiments she was subjected to, did nothing towards improving her appearance. Although she gained the name Humorist when built, she was originally allocated to be Spion Kop instead, both were racehorse names and winners of the Derby in 1921 and 1920 respectively. Tim Robbins Collection*

*Fig. 128. Gresley A3 No.60066 Merry Hampton (the second!) in B.R.'s express passenger blue livery, at Doncaster shed in April 1952. The blue liveries of B.R. days were short lived due in part to quick discoloration. Note that Merry Hampton is still right-hand drive at this time. Original G.N.R. tender. Colour Rail.*

From 1954, A4 type boilers were fitted to Gresley A3s, due to a shortage of spare A3 type boilers. These were built to work at 250lb but when fitted to the A3s were set to the A3's pressure of 220lb. This meant that some members of Class A3 would have had four types of Gresley designed L.N.E.R. boiler fitted during their lifetimes, with diagram 94 (original Class A1 boiler), 94HP (original Class A3 boiler with round dome), 94A (as before, but with the banjo dome, and then later streamlined dome) and class 107 (Class A4 boiler).

The A4 boilers were modified slightly prior to fitting on an A3 Pacific, as the running plate of the latter would obscure some mudhole doors on the lower front edge of the firebox sides. Instead of modifying the running plate, the mudhole doors were moved.

Gresley's A3 Pacifics performed well until the end of steam, with the first example withdrawn in 1959. They were displaced from the East Coast Main Line's premier services from late 1961 with the introduction of the Deltic diesel locomotives, and most were moved onto expresses into Scotland by way of the Midland route, out of Leeds. The last survivor, No.60052 *Prince Palatine*, would be withdrawn in January 1966. Class A3 was distinguished with the speed record achieved by No.2750 *Papyrus* of 108 mph in 1935. This was notable for maintaining a speed above 100mph for over 12 miles, a record at the time. This successful test in high-speed running would point the way towards the development of Gresley's Class A4 Pacific.

Fig. 129. Gresley A3 No.60067 Ladas looks in fine fettle as it flies by a group of schoolboys in the early 1960s. The train behind is made up of B.R. MkI coaches in various liveries. Colour Rail.

*Fig. 130. Gresley A3 No.60080 Dick Turpin, in its final livery. Note the single chimney fitting at this time, combined with the later B.R. crest on the tender. Colour Rail.*

*Fig. 131. Gresley A3 No.60067 Ladas, now fitted with a double chimney and presenting a very much more purposeful front end. Colour Rail.*

Fig. 132. Gresley A3 No.60045 Galtee Moore showing the final form of the Gresley A3, with the Peter Townend modifications of the double chimney and Witte style deflectors fitted at the front end, giving a very purposeful look to the aging locomotives. These fittings enabled something of an Indian Summer for the Gresley Pacifics on the E.C.M.L. Original from Peter Townend's collection. Colourised by Ian MacCabe, The Gresley Society.

The Class A3's performances during the Second World War were remarkably consistent, benefiting from each new addition to the class by way of rebuilt Gresley A1s throughout the war. Average annual mileages dipped in 1943, rising with each year into 1946. Availability was always in and around the 70% mark, in line with the rest of the L.N.E.R. fleet. The A3 Class was not singled out for criticism in E.S. Cox's report on the conjugated valve gear, his criticism was reserved for the high speed 4-6-2s (A4s), then the 2-8-2s (P2s) and 2-6-2s (V2s).

## Wartime Mileages & Availability

| Year | Mileages | Availability |
|------|----------|-------------|
| 1942 | 44875 | 66% |
| 1943 | 42578 | 66% |
| 1944 | 43102 | 71% |
| 1945 | 45895 | 67% |
| 1946 | 51606 | 71% |

Fig. 133. A3 Mileages & Availability Statistics.
Simon A.C. Martin, from the Use of Engine Power Document.

There is no doubt that issues with the conjugated valve gear during wartime, during a period of low maintenance and high intensity of traffic, influenced the overall availability of the fleet.

Although availability remained at the fleet average of 70% in 1946, the average annual mileage peaked at 51,606 miles. An impressive achievement for the class in the first year immediately following the Second World War. It should be noted that the classes' improvements came as older A1s were being converted to A3 specification.

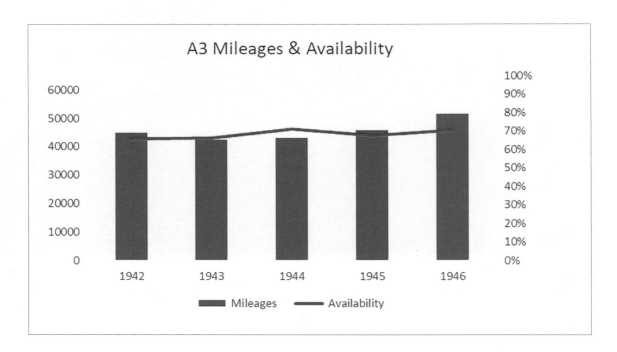

*Fig. 134. A3 Mileages & Availability Graph.*
*Simon A.C. Martin from the Use of Engine Power Document.*

*Fig. 134B. While many consider that the Witte or German style deflectors improved the appearance of the A3s and perhaps shaved years off the design's appearance, most would agree that the final appearance of 60097 Humorist with the deflectors seen in the view of the locomotive at Doncaster in 1962 as a detraction. Colour Rail.*

# Class A3

| | | |
|---|---|---|
| Cylinders (x3): | | 20x26in./18.25x26in./19x26in. |
| Motion: | Outside: | Walschaerts |
| | Inside: | Gresley |
| Boiler: | Max. Diameter: | 6ft 5in |
| | Pressure: | 220lb |
| | Diagram No.: | 94A, 94HP, 107 |
| Heating Surface: | Total: | 3981 sq. ft. |
| | Firebox: | 215 sq. ft. |
| | Superheater: | 1104 sq. ft. |
| | Tubes: | 1880 sq. ft. |
| | Flues: | 2158.8 sq. ft. |
| Grate Area: | | 41.25 sq. ft. |
| Wheels: | Leading: | 3ft 2in |
| | Coupled: | 6ft 8in |
| | Trailing: | 3ft 8in |
| | Tender: | 4ft 2in |
| Tractive Effort: (for each cylinder size) | At 85% boiler pressure | 36,465lb (20in), 30,362lb (18.25in), 32,909lb (19in) |
| Wheelbase: | Total: | 60ft 10.6in |
| | Engine: | 35ft 9in |
| | Tender: | 16ft |
| Weight (full): | Total: | 154 tons 3cwt |
| | Engine: | 96 tons 5cwt |
| | Tender: | 57 tons 18cwt |
| Max. Axle Load: | | 20 tons |
| Water Capacity: | | 5000 gallons |
| Coal Capacity: | | 8 tons |

# Flying Scotsman:
# The Centenarian's Adventures

*Fig. 135. 4472 blasts round the corner at Sharnbrook in the cold spring air on 29 March 1969. Note the holes in the buffer beam, required for the fitting of the cowcatcher on the tour of the United States. George Woods.*

The A3 class would survive by way of the preservation in 1963 of No.60103, *Flying Scotsman*, which was purchased by Alan Pegler and restored into a pseudo-L.N.E.R. form as No.4472. A single chimney and blastpipe was sourced and then fitted, and Pegler purchased a corridor tender for use with the locomotive, replacing its Class A4 non-corridor streamlined tender.

British Railways had declared its intention to be steam free on 11 August 1968. However, before this policy was established, Alan Pegler had negotiated an agreement to be able to run on the British mainline until 1971. Its success in running the first of these steam hauled mainline rail tours throughout the country no doubt influenced a change in mentality at British Railways and directly led to the creation of the charter market that we enjoy today.

Fig. 136. The final day with British Railways. Alan Pegler is seen touching the nameplate of his locomotive, newly purchased. Note the Ffestiniog Railway emblem on his cap. *Colour Rail.*

Fig. 137. Flying Scotsman on the day of its final non-stop run to Edinburgh in May 1968. This was the last occasion that an L.N.E.R. Pacific would travel non-stop between the capital cities (Scotsman repeated this feat the following day, returning non-stop to London). Colour Rail.

*Fig. 138. Fully dressed and prepared for her starring role ahead for her planned extensive publicity tour across the United States of America and into Canada, the preserved No.4472 Flying Scotsman, with L.N.E.R. crest on the cab sides and a second tender fitted certainly makes an impressive sight in this official Doncaster Works photograph, in 1968. Tim Robbins Collection.*

*Fig. 139. Preserved No.4472 Flying Scotsman, opposite angle at Doncaster Works. Doncaster Works Photograph, 1968. Tim Robbins Collection.*

Fig. 140. Preserved No.4472 Flying Scotsman, closeup of the chime whistle and bell fitted for its tour of the United States. Doncaster Works Photograph, 1968. Tim Robbins Collection.

In May 1968, No.4472 *Flying Scotsman* repeated its non-stop feats from London to Edinburgh for the first time since the 1930s. This trip, dubbed the "40th Anniversary Non-Stop" run was only made possible by the provision of the second tender, a converted corridor tender, and the retention in some places of the water troughs on route, prior to their removal due to dieselisation of the railways. *Flying Scotsman* then repeated the run, albeit down to London, three days later.

In 1969 *Flying Scotsman,* together with a full train of Pullman coaches and an observation car, was taken to the United States for a tour that was supported by Harold Wilson's government. The locomotive's tour started on 8 October 1969 in Boston, Massachusetts, running to Atlanta, Georgia via New York City and Washington, D.C., and continued to Slaton, Texas before finishing its first tour in Montreal, Canada. In 1971, the second tour left Montreal and continued through to San Francisco, the final stop. The locomotive had run 15,400 miles total during its tour, with reliability key to its success. *Flying Scotsman* remains the only L.N.E.R. locomotive and preserved steam locomotive to have run in the United States on its mainlines.

Fig. 141. A closeup of Flying Scotsman's driving wheels, whilst the locomotive waits at King's Cross to pull a rail tour northwards on 1 May 1966. George Woods.

Fig. 142. Flying Scotsman departs King's Cross with that same White Rose May Day special out and back to York on 1 May 1966. George Woods.

*Fig. 143. Flying Scotsman passes through Kibsworth on a rail tour on 22 February 1969. Note the semaphore signals and the location cases to their right. Five men are discernible standing alongside the line adjacent waiting for the famous locomotive to pass through. George Woods.*

*Fig. 144. Out of use and covered in snow, the hulk of No.4472 Flying Scotsman is pulled by a diesel shunter after returning abroad from the United States. The sea air has caused some light surface rust across many of the locomotive's surfaces. Robert Gadsdon. Originally taken by C.M. Whitehouse.*

Fig. 145. Flying Scotsman presents a forlorn sight outside the British Rail Engineering Limited (B.R.E.L.) works at Derby. Thankfully, the story did not end here, and she would soon be restored to working order once more. Ultimately becoming the national treasure, she is today, although her security in reservation would still make hearts flutter yet. Robert Gadsdon. Originally taken by C.M. Whitehouse.

Fig. 146. Flying Scotsman thunders round the curve at St. Devereux on a sunny 6 April 1974. Note that the locomotive now wears "4472" on the cab sides once more, and the second tender has now been painted to match the corporate blue of the carriages behind. George Woods.

Although a modest commercial success in its first year, by the end of 1970 Alan Pegler was bankrupt, and the locomotive holed up on a United States military base in Lathrop, California, to prevent it being taken by creditors. None of the trips on the tours carried paying passengers (Federal law rendered this illegal), and this may have contributed to the failure of the second tour.

Alan Bloom and George Hinchcliffe were instrumental in rescuing the locomotive, with businessman Sir William McAlpine purchasing the locomotive and bringing it home by ship through the Panama Canal. The locomotive was returned to service and ran more rail tours under the auspices of *Flying Scotsman Enterprises*.

*Fig. 147. Preserved No.4472 Flying Scotsman, on display with two of Victorian Railway's R Class 4-6-4s on its tour for the Bicentennial Celebrations in Australia. Not obvious straight away is the difference in track gauge between the 5ft 3in of Nos.761 and 707 and 4472's 4ft 8in. The Gresley Society.*

*Flying Scotsman* was exported to Australia in 1988 after a request by the government of Australia for it to take part in its Bi-Centennial celebrations. During this trip, it was reunited with an old British friend and friendly rival - No.4079 *Pendennis Castle*, which had been sold and sent abroad some years earlier. It was also paired with the famous New South Wales steam locomotive, No.3801, for which it double headed several steam tours.

*Fig. 148. Down under! Flying Scotsman's support crew pose for a photograph during the tour. Left to right: Pete Nutt, Sue Nutt, Roland Kennington, Pat Crisp, Colin Crisp, Steinle Jr, Dave Steinle, Tony Gooding, Dave Burgess, Fred Steinle, Dave Rollins and Edward Gardner. Ian MacCabe.*

During its tour of the continent of Australia achieved a world record for non-stop running by steam on 8 August 1989 by running 442 miles between Parkes and Broken Hill. This record still stands today.

After returning to the United Kingdom, *Flying Scotsman* was overhauled once more, but returned to British Railways form as No.60103, complete with a Kylchap double chimney and the Witte style smoke deflectors. For a time, Pete Waterman (record producer and railway enthusiast) part owned the locomotive alongside Sir William McAlpine, but the pair sold the locomotive to pay off debts accrued in 1996.

The new owner was Tony Marchington, an ambitious businessman whose plans for the locomotive included a business village in Edinburgh. *Flying Scotsman's* overhaul under Marchington was the most expensive to date, at £1 million, having been purchased together with spares and the support coach for £1.5 million.

The second tender was at this point sold to the A1 Steam Locomotive Trust, in an aborted effort to create an authentic tender for their locomotive, *Tornado*. The trust then ended up building a new eight-wheel tender to the Darlington pattern, selling the water carrier to Jeremy Hosking for use with his A4 Pacific, *Bittern*. *Flying Scotsman's* overhaul involved boring out the cylinders, and the use of a spare A4 boiler. This boiler had been purchased by Pegler in the 1960s and when overhauled was set to 250lb. This was a decision that was not taken in British Railways days on the A3 Pacifics that had been fitted with the diagram 107 boilers.

This decision increased the locomotive's tractive effort beyond that which the original locomotives had been designed for. The locomotive ran under Marchington on the mainline for just four years, Marchington and his company, Flying Scotsman Plc, being declared bankrupt in 2003. To raise funds to pay down this debt, the agency acting on their behalf put *Flying Scotsman* into a sealed bid auction.

Fearing the sale of the locomotive abroad, the National Railway Museum declared their intention to bid. Supported by the National Heritage Memorial Fund, Richard Branson and the donations of the general public, the Museum raised and bid £2.3 million for the locomotive, with which it won the auction and the locomotive together with its associated spares and the support coach. The locomotive then ran on a series of Scarborough Flyer rail tours, after which it was withdrawn for the most protracted overhaul of its preservation life. It emerged in 2016 painted in British Railways dark green, as No.60103 once more, its current form at time of writing in its centenary year. Throughout its life, *Flying Scotsman* has been loved and admired by those within railways and those outside of railways. It has won acclaim and is recognised worldwide.

The highlight of *Flying Scotsman's* recent career on the main line came on 12 June 2023 when the locomotive pulled the Royal Train, with his majesty King Charles III on board. The locomotive was resplendent with a full complement of lamps across the buffer beam and smokebox and painted with a traditional Stratford Works white roof for royal workings.

It remains the only steam locomotive to have run under its own steam on three continents, and to have circumnavigated the world. It retains the non-stop record for a steam locomotive still, and its achievements during its L.N.E.R. years as a flagship locomotive, achieving the world's first authenticated 100 mph run and in the non-stop runs London-Edinburgh leave us in no doubt of its importance to railway history. The locomotive proved beyond reasonable doubt that there was a market for leisure travel behind steam locomotives, despite British Railways' best efforts to wipe out steam, and were it not for the foresight and modest genius of Alan Pegler, the current rail tour scene might look very different today.

Flying Scotsman's small number of vocal detractors often complain of the locomotive being overhyped and of little importance in the relative scheme of things. Even a cursory glance at its history shows this to not be the case. They also overlook its influence at a cultural level in bringing new volunteers and supporters from outside the sphere of railways, together with its very real role as an ambassador for the L.N.E.R. throughout its working life. Very few other steam locomotives have captured the general public's imagination in the way that Flying Scotsman has, and its importance and mystique are very real.

One thing that is often misunderstood about the locomotive is that it is a collection of components of metal arranged in such a way as to make a working steam locomotive. It had no choice in the decisions made for it. These decisions were of the people who built, ran, managed, fixed, and saved it over the course of its 100 years of life.

It is a representation of all those peoples' hopes, dreams and achievements and as such should be seen in that very light. Hopefully, it will continue to inspire younger generations to love steam traction as it did this author in 1994.

*Fig. 149. Flying Scotsman, hauling the Royal Train, on the North Yorkshire Moors Railway on 12 June 2023. For this event, the locomotive wore the full complement of headlamps on the front and was adorned with a white cab roof, as per Stratford's tradition for Royal Train locomotives.*
*Alamy, under license.*

*Fig. 150. His Majesty King Charles III stands next to No.60103 Flying Scotsman on 12 June 2023, thereby joining the many thousands of people, of all ages across three continents who have likewise posed for their photograph to be taken alongside the World's most famous steam locomotive. Alamy, under license.*

# L.N.E.R. Class D49 4-4-0 (1927)

Number built (L.N.E.R.): 76

*Fig. 151. Gresley D49/2 No.336, Buckinghamshire, works photograph.*
*The Gresley Society.*

There was a demand for locomotives of a mixed traffic type in the North Eastern and Scottish areas of the L.N.E.R. by the mid-1920s. The older pre-grouping locomotives of mainly N.E.R. and N.B.R. locomotives with Atlantic wheelbases were to be retained and used on the main expresses, with any new design supplementing them (at least, until the routes in question were able to take the higher axle loads of the Pacific classes).

Gresley ordered Darlington to produce a new 4-4-0 design, using three cylinders and conjugated valve gear. At the same time, a six-cylinder version of a new 4-4-0 was being developed, but by 1931 was no more than a detailed arrangement drawing. The design shared the wheel arrangement and 6ft 8in driving wheels of the D49 and was effectively set up as a six cylinder uniflow engine driving twin shafts with cranks set at 120 degrees. This proposal was quietly dropped by the end of 1931.

By the end of 1926, the first engine diagrams for the conventional three-cylinder locomotive had been issued and by October 1927, the first of the class, No.234 and named *Yorkshire*, emerged. It had the distinction of being the first passenger locomotive designed for the L.N.E.R., all other designs to that date had been either freight, or pre-grouping designs.

151

The design utilised the same design of boiler as Class J39, though boiler swaps with this class were rare, and only recorded in the final years of steam. The boilers for all class members were identical, but built by Darlington Works, Cowlairs and outside contractor Robert Stephenson & Co. All boilers were fitted with Ross Pop safety valves. These boilers were long lived, some lasting upwards of twenty years in service.

*Fig. 152. Gresley D49/2 No.336, Buckinghamshire, closeup of the Lentz gear, works photograph. The Gresley Society.*

There were three sub-groups in class D49 between 1927 and 1935, with the following details (given chronologically):

- D49/1 – built in three batches between 1927 and 1929. These locomotives had conventional Walschaerts valve gear for the outside cylinders and a form of Gresley's conjugated valve gear for the inside cylinder. These locomotives were in the main designed by the Chief Locomotive Draughtsman at Darlington Works, one R.J. Robson, under Gresley's direction. It was interesting that a reversion to some of Vincent Raven's N.E.R. practice was to be observed on the D49/1s, with monobloc cast cylinders and steam chest in one casting, inside steam pipes and 12-spoke bogie wheels following Darlington's pattern of 3ft 1 1/4in diameter. Twenty-eight locomotives were built.

The D49/1s had a further unique feature. There was a large rectangular box just ahead of the first splasher on each side of the running plate. These covered the top of the expansion link in the outside valve motion: owing to space constraints these extended above the footplate on both sides.

All the D49/1s that had been originally built as D49/1s were named after Shire Counties.

- D49/3 – six locomotives in one batch built by the end of 1928. Although sub classified as Part 3, these locomotives entered service before the D49/2 batches. These locomotives represented the most experimental of the Class D49, featuring oscillating-cam operated Lentz poppet valves combined with Walschaerts valve gear on the outside cylinders and valve spindle ends replaced by hanging arms and extension rods. The Lentz poppet valves were each in individual valve boxes on top of each cylinder, with four valves each with an admission and exhaust valve. The Gresley conjugated gear was used for the centre cylinder, but arranged to work in a vertical plane, again due to space constraints.

All the engines in this sub class suffered from issues with the oscillating camshaft associated with the middle cylinder, where the valve gear would physically bend under heavy stresses, normally in full forward gear. The riding of these locomotives was particularly poor and was felt on the footplate quite markedly. Things became so serious that No.329 was fitted with a horizontally arranged 2 to 1 lever in 1929, to try to alleviate the issues. This seemed to give some improvement, and the other D49/3s were also converted. This was short lived, and No.329 failed with a damaged middle gear again, the rocking lever and valve rod locked due to excess backward travel, bending the camshaft in the process.

The issue was circumvented by way of reducing the available cut-off to 62% and restricting the locomotives' loadings on trains. By 1938, when all the sub class required new cylinders, the decision was taken to rebuild them, and they were converted to conventional outline as D49/1s with piston valves. This included removal of the outside steam pipes.

- D49/2 – built in one batch between 1929 and 1935 with rotary cam operated Lentz gear. These were largely the same in detail outside of the valve gear arrangements however, they had outside steam pipes of the Doncaster style fitted. This was the most visible difference between the D49/1s and the D49/2s.

Gresley's first P2 Class Mikado locomotive, No.2001 Cock O' The North (covered elsewhere within this volume) was fitted with a similar version of the D49/2 gear, as were the two N.E.R. Atlantics Gresley converted to Class C7. The latter retained their valve gear to withdrawal whereas No.2001 would be converted to piston valve when withdrawn for overhaul.

This may have been in part due to a series of trials that Darlington Works undertook to determine the relative advantages of the Lentz gear in comparison to the piston valve fitted D49s. The latter showed significant advantages across the board, not least in maintenance costs and overall fuel economy. Two members of the D49/2 Class were fitted at different times with the Reidinger infinitely variable rotary cam poppet valve gear. This had the valves controlled by steam pressure instead of springs.

The first, No.365 *The Morpeth*, had this fitted between January 1940 and February 1941.

*Fig. 153. Gresley D49/2 No.365, The Morpeth, showing its unusual Reidinger gear, works photograph. The Gresley Society.*

The gear gave some trouble, to the extent that when damage to the camshaft was sustained, a decision was taken under Edward Thompson's auspices to rebuild the locomotive as a two-cylinder locomotive, with inside Stephenson's valve gear. The availability of locomotives was at dire levels and anything that was capable of being run, by way of the condition of the boiler, was preferable to standing idle. More details on this locomotive can be found in the previous work in this series.

The Reidinger gear was laid aside for some years, until British Railways ordered an investigation into the type of poppet valve gear. The gear was then fitted to No.361, emerging as British Railways No.62764 *The Garth*, with the major alteration to the fitting being a reversion to spring-controlled valves (identical in setup to the existing D49/2 locomotives). After 5000 miles of running, the locomotive was tested on the Rugby Testing Station, and the valve gear stayed with the locomotive until it was withdrawn.

The class were subject to several changes of lubricators throughout its life, with the first sub class, D49/1, initially fitted with Wakefield six-feed lubricators for the piston valves, and oil boxes in the cab for the axle boxes. Additional feeds from the mechanical lubricators were fed to the outside cylinders to improve the overall condition of the lubrication system, but it was difficult to fit a similar feed to the middle cylinder.

The D49/3s retained the six-feed mechanical lubricators but the D49/2s were fitted with two eight feed lubricators instead.

The conversion of the D49/3s to piston valve locomotives would indicate a desire for some standardisation, but by the advent of the Second World War, the D49/2s were performing reasonably and any expenditure for a wholescale rebuilding of the class was unlikely to have been authorised. Class D49 was included within Thompson's standardisation programme, as one of the "non-standard, to be maintained" classes.

In the late 1920s, allocations of the locomotives were concentrated on the North Eastern and Scottish areas of the L.N.E.R., the D49s running alongside the much-loved N.B.R. C11 Atlantics and the Scottish "Director" D11 4-4-0s.

In the case of the Atlantics, there was some controversy and in October 1930, whilst giving a lecture on the 3-cylinder conjugated valve gear to members of the Royal Technical College in Glasgow, Gresley was questioned by some railwaymen on whether the intention was for the D49s to replace the Atlantics.

Gresley is described in R.C.T.S. Part 4 as "vehemently denying" this, and in respect to Gresley this seems to be entirely true, particularly at the level of primary evidence for which there are no records alluding, intimating, or outright stating that the D49s were intended to replace or displace the Reid Atlantics.

Gresley would have been justified, however, in responding differently: built between 1905 and 1910, many of the Atlantics were coming up for thirty-years old and the condition of their boilers was coming into question. The C11s would be withdrawn between 1933 and 1937 as the numbers of the D49s increased to their full complement by 1935.

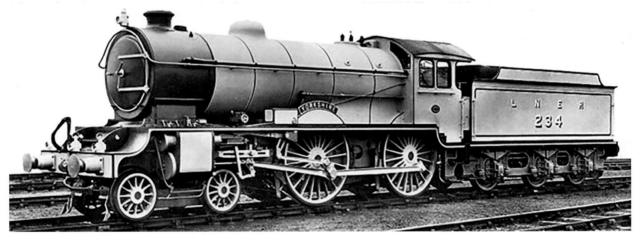

*Fig. 154. Gresley D49/1 No.234, Yorkshire, outside Walschaerts and conjugated fitted example, works photograph. The Gresley Society.*

During the late 1930s, improvements in the condition and axle loading of many routes led to classes A3 and V2 displacing the D49s from their main express passenger services. The advent of the Thompson B1 Class coming into service from 1942 onwards led to the D49s to be further cascaded away from their usual duties.

Coupled with a high axle loading of their own, D49s were not displaced to branch lines but in terms of the duties they hauled, now including much freight including coal trains, for which with their 6ft 8in driving wheels and four coupled wheelbase they were not ideal for.

The overall condition of the D49s going into the Second World War led them to also being fitted with the "stink bomb" for the middle big end, to detect overheating and prevent failure and damage. Although not singled out for criticism by E.S. Cox within his report on the conjugated valve gear, the D49s seemed to suffer a higher proportion of failures throughout the Second World War.

This, in combination with the advent of diesel locomotives, and diesel multiple units within their areas of operation, led to further reduced work for the Gresley D49s, with withdrawals starting in earnest in September 1957, and complete by July 1961. Happily, one of the D49/1s has been preserved, No.62712 *Morayshire*, which at time of writing is undergoing a restoration to working order.

## Wartime Mileages & Availability

| Year | Mileages | Availability |
|------|----------|--------------|
| 1942 | 32835 | 64% |
| 1943 | 30881 | 62% |
| 1944 | 29055 | 63% |
| 1945 | 32730 | 65% |
| 1946 | 27911 | 58% |

*Fig. 155. D49 Mileages & Availability Statistics.*
*Simon A.C. Martin, from the Use of Engine Power Document.*

The war years were not kind to the Gresley D49s, and their overall availability was always below the average for the entire fleet of 70%. Things came to a head by 1946, however, with the condition of the class leading to availability and mileages falling well below that expected for the class, and similarly sized locomotives on the same principal duties.

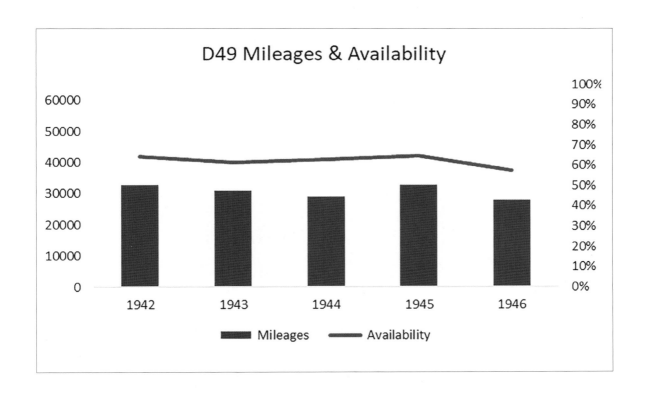

Fig. 156. D49 Mileages & Availability Graph.
Simon A.C. Martin from the Use of Engine Power Document.

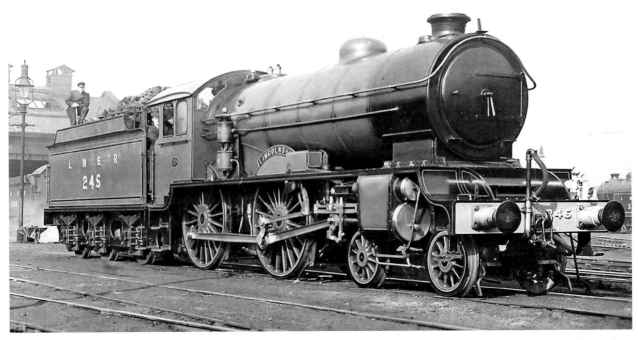

Fig. 156b. In this view Class D49/1 No.245 Lincolnshire looks resplendent in her apple green livery, by
the autumn of 1960 as No.62710 in a scruffy lined British Railways black livery she would join the last
of her class in the scrap lines at Darlington Works. Strathwood Library Collection

# Class D49

| Sub Class | | D49/1 | D49/2 | D49/3 |
|---|---|---|---|---|
| Cylinders (x3): | | 3x 17x26in. | | |
| Motion: | | Walschaerts, Conjugated | Lentz, Rotary | Walschaerts, Lentz cam |
| Boiler: | Max. Diameter: | 5ft 6in | | |
| | Pressure: | 180lb | | |
| | Diagram No.: | 97 | | |
| Heating Surface: | Total: | 1669.58 sq. ft. | | |
| | Firebox: | 171.5 sq. ft. | | |
| | Superheater: | 271.8 sq. ft. (14x1.1in) | | |
| | Tubes: | 871.75 sq. ft. (177x 1.75in) | | |
| | Flues: | 354.53 sq. ft. (24x 5.25in) | | |
| Grate Area: | | 26 sq. ft. | | |
| Wheels: | Leading: | 3ft 1.25in | | |
| | Coupled: | 6ft 8in | | |
| | Tender: | 3ft 9in | | |
| Tractive Effort: | At 85% boiler pressure | 21,556lb | | |
| Wheelbase: | Total: | 48ft 5.25in | 48ft 5.25in | 48ft 5.25in |
| | Engine: | 24ft 11in | 24ft 11in | 24ft 11in |
| | Tender: | 13ft 6in | 13ft 6in | 13ft 6in |
| Weight (full): | Total: | 118 tons 4cwt | 117 tons 3cwt | 118 tons 7cwt |
| | Engine: | 65 tons 11cwt | 64 tons 10cwt | 65 tons 14cwt |
| | Tender: | 52 tons 13cwt | 52 tons 13cwt | 52 tons 13cwt |
| Max. Axle Load: | | 21 tons 5cwt | 21 tons | 21 tons 2cwt |
| Water Capacity: | | 4200 gallons* | | |
| Coal Capacity: | | 7tons 10cwt* | | |

# L.N.E.R. Class B17 4-6-0
## (1928) Number built (L.N.E.R.): 73

*Fig. 157. Gresley B17 No.2870, Tottenham Hotspur, on display.*
*Colourised by Ian MacCabe, The Gresley Society.*

Strictly speaking, the B17 class has no place in a volume on Gresley. His involvement with the development of the classes' final design and building was minimal, with the L.N.E.R. eventually farming out the work to N.B.L. instead, after several years of requests for a workable 4-6-0 for the ex-G.E.R, region had met with little response from Doncaster.

It is arguable that those in charge of the G.E. section under the L.N.E.R.'s auspices were being particularly unreasonable with their demands. Upgrades to the axle loading of the main lines and branch lines and changes to the length of the turntables would have allowed for a wider variety of locomotives, including Gresley's Pacifics, to venture further into Anglia. This would have allowed for an acceleration of the services and, principally, the increase in the number of vehicles in trains. (This is perhaps exemplified by the fact that over 20 years later, 94-ton Pacifics would be allowed on the ex-G.E.R. mainlines and would be allowed to run at more than 90 mph.)

The loading gauge for the G.E. section was more constrained than the G.N. mainline too, and the main demand from the G.E. section for the heavy Southend services was for a 2-6-4T tank locomotive, with the Cambridge services ably handled by the existing B12s. With the acceleration of the services and the increasing lengths and weights of the trains, a more potent locomotive was required, 4-6-0 or otherwise. Gresley had built additional B12s, which allowed the tank locomotive proposal to be quietly dropped, but the G.E. section persisted with the desire for a new 4-6-0.

The Doncaster design was reportedly a rearrangement of D49 components, with three cylinders and conjugated valve gear with outside Walschaerts fitted. The design reputedly would have had a tractive effort of about 25,000lb and an axle loading of 17 tons. However, this still required the bogie to carry 20 tons and the overall weight of the locomotive was significantly higher than the B12s, at 71 tons total. The boiler was to be tapered, and fluted brake hangers were proposed for the overall reduction of weight.

The Locomotive Running Department did not approve the design, and Gresley together with the design office did no further work on the proposal. Things became altogether strained, to the extent that the Chief General Manager was called in, together with the principal officers and Gresley himself. The outcome was clear; Doncaster would do no further work on a 4-6-0 and the L.N.E.R. went to N.B.L. thereafter, with the acceptance of the contract undertaken on the 1 December 1927.

The N.B.L. Co already had some experience with Gresley's overall design ethos, having built for the G.N.R. a batch of his O2 locomotives. From this project, and work relating to the Gresley Pacifics, they had a considerable quantity of drawings from which to produce a new design, with A1, K3, O2 drawings from Doncaster, bogie arrangements from Darlington Works and the G.E.R. pattern tender from Stratford Works, that would be employed for this design due to the length of the turntables on the route.

*Fig. 158. Gresley B17 No.2813 Woodbastwick Hall. Note the shorter G.E.R. tender and the fitting of a Westinghouse Pump in comparison to the previous shot of No.2870 Tottenham Hotspur. Colourised by Ian MacCabe, The Gresley Society.*

*Fig. 159. In her final rebuilt guise as a Class B17/6 No.61659 East Anglian shuffles back and forth towards the turntable at Liverpool Street station whilst Britannia No.70041 Sir John Moore waits to get into its platform on 11 July 1958. Two of the B17s were chosen in 1937 to be rebuilt with streamlining in a style similar to the Class A4 Pacifics, to work the East Anglian named service from Liverpool Street to Norwich Thorpe as part of the publicity departments activities for the L.N.E.R.. These two streamlined locomotives were given straight nameplates as East Anglian and City of London. Both locomotives were stripped of their streamlining during 1951. Once they were both fitted with Type 100A boilers of the type fitted to Thompson's Class B1, both locomotives were classified as Class B17/6 as were ultimately fifty-five members of the class by the end of 1957. Strathwood Library Collection.*

Fig. 160. Streamlined B17 No.61670 City of London races towards Haughley Junction in this post war scene. The locomotive is in plain black but with British Railways numbering and branding. Note the short-formed train of just four Gresley designed teak carriages. Dr. Ian C. Allen/The Transport Treasury

*Fig. 161. Whilst still classified as a B17/5 No.61659 East Anglian sits awaits her next duty at Liverpool Street with Thompson B1 No.1047. As we have already seen East Anglian was later rebuilt back to conventional outline from the streamlined form presented here in this rare colour photograph. Strathwood Library Collection.*

There was some discussion regarding the quantity of locomotives to be built by N.B.L., with just ten locomotives and their tenders eventually agreed. Even then, the original axle loading of 17 tons could not be met, and the lighter of N.B.L.'s designs (with an 18-ton axle loading) was chosen and approved for construction. The requirement was quietly changed from a design "for all G.E. lines" to "certain G.E. main lines". It should be noted, that had the G.E. section accepted this compromise in the first place, there is every likelihood that the original Doncaster proposal might have seen the light of day.

The B17 design that eventually emerged was recognisably Gresley in outline without having his direct influence or being produced by his drawing office. The A1 Pacifics' cylinder and valve gear arrangements were copied very closely. Unlike the Pacifics, and with a nod to the Royal Scot class that the N.B.L. Co had produced for the L.M.S., the centre cylinder was pushed forward and higher above the front bogie, driving onto the front axle while the outside cylinders, with their Walschaerts valve gear, drove the centre driving wheels. Like the Class D49, the conjugated gear was behind the cylinders on the B17 class. The boiler and cab were minor alterations of the O2 and K3 designs.

The first batch emerged in 1928 and the L.N.E.R. promptly put in an order with Darlington Works to produce another twelve locomotives of the type. It is reported that the N.B.L. Co wrote in 1929 asking for an additional order, but this was turned down and forty more locomotives were constructed at Darlington instead, with the final eleven built by Robert Stephenson & Co.

All seventy-three locomotives were constructed between 1928 and 1937, forming four parts as B17/1, B17/2, B17/3, and B17/4, with the distinctions between them being the springing arrangements. The earlier locomotives were eventually brought into line with the same springing arrangements as B17/4, and were amalgamated into B17/1 from 1937, their major distinction from Class B17/4 now being the G.E.R. pattern tenders they pulled rather than the larger group standard 4200 gallons the latter had.

The B17 class received a further two sub divisions. The first came when two members were streamlined (as per the A4 Pacifics) for the pulling of the East Anglian in 1937, becoming B17/5. Their streamlining was extended to their tenders too, and chime whistles were also fitted. When their streamlining was removed in 1951, they had by then been fitted with the diagram 100A boiler and were made B17/6 in line with all other B17s that were being fitted with the higher-pressure Thompson standard boiler.

The prototype was No.2800 and named Sandringham, and the rest of the B17s fitted with the G.E.R. type tenders were also named after English country houses within the L.N.E. R.'s territory. The B17/4s were known as the "Footballers" owing to being named after Football Association teams. All seventy-three locomotives would be named, with a few changes made (such as the streamlined pair which became City of London and East Anglian) within the company's boundaries.

*Fig. 162. Gresley B17 No.2800 Sandringham, the prototype, preparing to take a passenger train out of Liverpool Street in the late 1920s. Colourised by Ian MacCabe, The Gresley Society.*

The B17s were split between Cambridge workings and Colchester workings, with the class popular with Cambridge crews, but less so with Ipswich crews. This seems to have been down to the gradients on the London-Ipswich line, which with heavier services required harder running. Further B17s would be moved onto Great Central services to displace older Atlantic locomotives, with allocations at Gorton, Leicester, Neasden, and Sheffield. All of these would be moved to East Anglia at the outbreak of the Second World War.

By 1939 it was recognised that new boilers with thicker plating was desirable, and Gresley did have drawings prepared for a higher-pressure version of the B17 boiler. It was not until Edward Thompson took over in 1941 that there was a suitable boiler to fit: as previously mentioned, the diagram 100A boiler (which was designed for his two-cylinder 4-6-0, the B1). Fifty-five of the seventy-one locomotives would be fitted with the diagram 100A boiler and would be reclassified as B17/6. In the meantime, those fitted with the original boilers had the pressure reduced to 180lb from August 1943 in an attempt to reduce overall maintenance and overhaul demands.

Between 1945 and 1947 ten of the B17 class would be rebuilt with two cylinders and the diagram 100A boiler, becoming Thompson's Class B2. The prototype, No.2871 Manchester City, was compared to B17/1 No.2827 Aske Hall in a series of comparison runs on the same workings between Cambridge and Liverpool Street.

The trains were loaded to around 400 tons for both locomotives. In this first set of trials the lower pressure 180lb boiler of the B17 was noted as a major difference between the two, besides the conjugated gear and three cylinders compared to two-cylinder setups. The B2 was reported as having 10% better overall fuel economy, but the separate figures for coal and water do not appear to have survived.

Further trials were requested under Arthur Peppercorn's auspices and were carried out, this time with the N.E.R. dynamometer car in attendance, with B17/7 No.1622 Alnwick Castle and B2 No.1607 Blickling. This time, both locomotives had the 225lb diagram 100A boiler fitted, and the B17 now had the advantage of a higher tractive effort. The results were conclusive; the B17/6 now had the edge on the two-cylinder B2 with a 10% improvement in power and around 6% better fuel economy (although again, it must be noted that individual statistics for the coal and water do not appear to have survived).

No more B2s were built but most of the B17s would be converted to the B17/6 configuration over the years as their original lower pressure boilers came up for replacement. Class B17 had some of the earliest withdrawals of Gresley's classes, with the first withdrawn in 1952, and two more before the end of 1953. The remaining 57 locomotives were withdrawn between 1958 and 1960 rendering the class extinct.

Two groups were formed to build a new B17, though at time of writing one group had disbanded, donating their major components (an unrestored group standard tender, buffers, and other components) to the B17 Steam Locomotive Trust. The building of their locomotive, No.61673 *Spirit of Sandringham*, is well underway with frames cut and assembled and all major wheelsets cast at time of writing.

## Wartime Mileages & Availability

| Year | Mileages | Availability |
|------|----------|--------------|
| 1942 | 35072 | 68% |
| 1943 | 35061 | 64% |
| 1944 | 33353 | 67% |
| 1945 | 34205 | 64% |
| 1946 | 34617 | 61% |

*Fig. 163. B17 Mileages & Availability Statistics.*
*Simon A.C. Martin, from the Use of Engine Power Document.*

With boiler pressure reductions and overall availability significantly poorer than other similar classes (such as Class B12) it is clear the B17s struggled during the Second World War, however the average annual mileages as a class remained high and competitive with other similarly sized locomotives utilised on similar traffic of a similar age.

By the end of 1946 Thompson's B1 class, a locomotive of similar size but with smaller diameter driving wheels, was doing similar work, and achieving significantly better overall mileages and availability. This comparison however must be tempered with the caveat that Thompson's B1s were brand new and simpler machines.

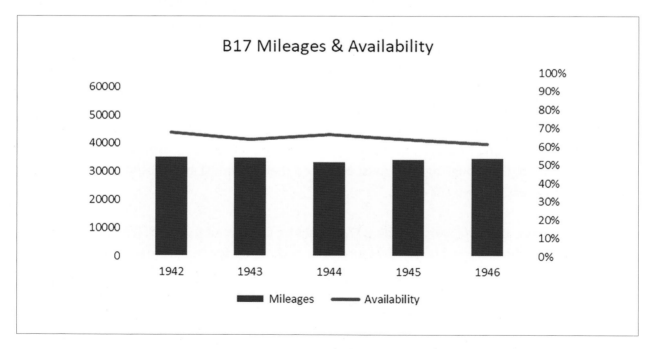

*Fig. 164. B17 Mileages & Availability Graph.*
*Simon A.C. Martin from the Use of Engine Power Document.*

The issue of mileages for the B17s was affecting their overall shopping into works too, to the extent that serious conversations between Thompson and the mechanical engineers were had on the mileages achieved between shopping. In the National Archives, file Rail 394/225 gives a report into these mileages dated 1st May 1946.

The report gives the shopping mileages for the B17s that had not achieved 70,000 miles before shopping (Appendix 3: Mileages of Locomotives between General Repairs (1937) of this book shows that the intended mileage between shopping for the B17s was targeted to be 75,000 miles). The report identified that 48 locomotives out of the 73 extant had not achieved the desired mileages, giving the results shown on the next page.

Overall, the B17 class could not be considered one of the L.N.E.R.'s better designs. Despite being derived from some of Gresley's most successful locomotive classes, the overall mileages between overhauls and mileages annually, together with quantifiably lower overall availability for work indicate a locomotive class that required more attention than others working alongside it.

It could be argued quite cogently that in attributing the class to Gresley, we do him a disservice by way of association. Criticising Gresley for the classes' pitfalls when he was not entirely involved seems unfair too. This was the locomotive design he had the least oversight on throughout the design and building process.

The Class D49 which Gresley did have a hand in and had a similar setup by way of divided drive, and conjugated valve gear driven behind the cylinders rather than in front, suggest that dividing the drive for conjugated gear locomotives may have been a factor in their performance issues. This however, is speculative at best.

There was never any doubt of the classes' ability once the diagram 100A boiler was fitted, however, and the 220lb boiler together with three cylinders and conjugated valve gear produced a very potent locomotive design, capable of excellent timekeeping and performances on all the services the class undertook.

*Fig.164b. Another short-lived variation of livery for 61659 East Anglian at Colchester on 13th August 1949. Strathwood Library Collection*

| No. | Date of Shopping | Mileage at Shopping |
|-----|------------------|---------------------|
| 2823 | Jan-37 | 56000 |
| 2844 | Jan-37 | 68000 |
| 2808 | Jan-37 | 60540 |
| 2821 | Feb-37 | 50700 |
| 2846 | Feb-37 | 57500 |
| 2830 | Feb-37 | 61900 |
| 2851 | Feb-37 | 61231 |
| 2834 | Mar-37 | 47900 |
| 2829 | Mar-37 | 36700 |
| 2804 | Mar-37 | 58310 |
| 2853 | Mar-37 | 60820 |
| 2809 | Apr-37 | 44600 |
| 2841 | Apr-37 | 57800 |
| 2834 | Apr-37 | 58081 |
| 2846 | Apr-37 | 53229 |
| 2847 | Apr-37 | 53282 |
| 2855 | Apr-37 | 60305 |
| 2838 | Jun-37 | 29000 |
| 2839 | Jun-37 | 58927 |
| 2859 | Jul-37 | 64627 |
| 2806 | Sep-37 | 42800 |
| 2817 | Oct-37 | 56056 |
| 2861 | Oct-37 | 60021 |
| 2858 | Oct-37 | 65546 |

| No. | Date of Shopping | Mileage at Shopping |
|-----|------------------|---------------------|
| 2807 | Dec-37 | 69602 |
| 2818* | Jan-38 | 40350 |
| 2818* | Jan-38 | 55398 |
| 2820 | Jan-38 | 67383 |
| 2840 | Jan-38 | 55924 |
| 2862 | Jan-38 | 66483 |
| 2867 | Jan-38 | 62163 |
| 2833 | Feb-38 | 58000 |
| 2866 | Feb-38 | 50013 |
| 2828 | Mar-38 | 40400 |
| 2840 | Mar-38 | 61000 |
| 2805 | Mar-38 | 48736 |
| 2864 | Mar-38 | 60431 |
| 2810 | Apr-38 | 65000 |
| 2836 | Apr-38 | 48900 |
| 2826 | Apr-38 | 52000 |
| 2825 | Apr-38 | 67170 |
| 2814 | Apr-38 | 62669 |
| 2803 | May-38 | 65784 |
| 2837 | Jun-38 | 65700 |
| 2860 | Jun-38 | 33751 |
| 2842 | Jul-38 | 61800 |
| 2818* | Sep-38 | 31000 |
| 2821 | Nov-38 | 50442 |

*2818 is listed in the report three times, but twice in January 1938. It is logical that one of these is a misreporting of recorded data and may be reflective of another member of Class B17.

# Class B17

| Sub Class | | B17/1, /2, /3, /4, /5 | B17/6 |
|---|---|---|---|
| Cylinders (x3): | | 17.5x26in. | 17.5x26in. |
| Motion: | Outside: | Walschaerts | Walschaerts |
| | Inside: | Gresley | Gresley |
| Motion: | Piston valves: | 8in diameter | 8in diameter |
| Boiler: | Max. Diameter: | 5ft 6in | 5ft 6in |
| | Pressure: | 220psi | 225psi |
| | Diagram No.: | 100 | 100A |
| Heating Surface: | Total: | 2020 sq. ft. | 2005 sq. ft. |
| | Firebox: | 168 sq. ft. | 168 sq. ft. |
| | Superheater: | 344 sq. ft. (24x 1.2in) | 344 sq. ft. (24x 1.2in) |
| | Tubes: | 1048 sq. ft. (191x 1.75in) | 1048 sq. ft. (191x 1.75in) |
| | Flues: | 460 sq. ft. (24x 5.25in) | 460 sq. ft. (24x 5.25in) |
| Grate Area: | | 27.5 sq. ft. | 27.9 sq. ft. |
| Wheels: | Leading: | 3ft 2in | 3ft 2in |
| | Coupled: | 6ft 8in | 6ft 8in |
| | Tender: | 4ft 1in / 3ft 9in | 4ft 1in / 3ft 9in |
| Tractive Effort: | At 85% boiler pressure | 25,380lb (22,842lb at 180lb pressure) | 28,553lb |
| Total Wheelbase: | | 27ft 9in | 27ft 9in |
| Max. Axle Load: | | 18 tons | 18 tons 3cwt |

*Fig.164c. An early British Railways' apple green livery interpretation for 61661 Sheffield Wednesday seen in 1948. Strathwood Library Collection*

# L.N.E.R.

## Class W1 4-6-2 -2(1929)

Number built(L.N.E.R.): 1

*Fig. 165. Gresley W1 No.10000 At Doncaster in 1929. The locomotive's unusual boiler casing is shown to good effect here. Strathwood Library Collection.*

Gresley's prototype high-pressure experimental locomotive, known as the W1, has been the subject of several articles, papers, books and even films on the pros and cons of what was, at a first glance, a not particularly successful entry into compounding and high-pressure experimentation for Gresley. In its original form it achieved a lifetime mileage of around 90,000 miles.

The best source for information on this intriguing locomotive (outside of the extensive file kept in Search Engine at the National Railway Museum) is, in this author's view, found in the book *Hush-Hush: The Story of LNER 10000* by William Brown, due to the significant amount of primary material that is provided for the reader to study and analyse, including a well detailed bibliography, timeline of events and photographic evidence. Some secondary sources that have been written prior to his tome have significant factual inaccuracies, and it is best to treat these with caution, particularly in the record of some of its early trips and issues.

For the purposes of this book, it would be helpful to recount the locomotive's development history, which began in 1924. In the September of that year Gresley had held a meeting with the eminent marine-boiler engineer Harold Yarrow. They discussed, amongst other details, impressive reliability and efficiency measurements recorded for water tube boilers on locomotives Yarrow had been involved with. Yarrow and his company were fundamentally involved from the beginning of the project. It was Gresley's intention to build a steam locomotive of comparable power output to his existing 1922 designed A1 Pacific, but with far greater efficiency in the use of steam.

This would lead to improved fuel economy overall, the original A1 Pacifics having proved somewhat heavier on coal than originally anticipated. In the event, with long lap travel valves, improved drafting, and driver/fireman familiarisation would produce a considerable improvement in the A1's efficiency.

To maximise the anticipated benefits of high-pressure steam, it would be necessary to produce a new locomotive as a *compound*. In a simple-expansion locomotive, steam is sent to the cylinders effectively in a parallel circuit. In a compound, the high pressure and low-pressure cylinders are arranged in series: the steam is expanded into one or two high-pressure cylinders first and then, after heat and pressure drops, is exhausted into the receiver, which then feeds the low-pressure cylinders.

This extends the thermodynamic cycle of the steam. The volume ratio of the high and low-pressure cylinders must be balanced to counter balance the piston thrusts between them, and this is done usually either by increasing the diameter of the low-pressure cylinders or by lengthening the stroke of the piston.

Gresley had been aware of compounding for some time, having been at Crewe Works, L.N.W.R., during the Francis Webb era of locomotive design. Webb's compounds were a mixed bag, generally down to the wheelbase arrangements, with divided drives between the high and low-pressure cylinders. These were all three-cylinder compounds, however, and these together with the drawings provided by the L.M.S. of its contemporary three-cylinder Midland Compounds likely focused Gresley's thoughts towards a compound three-cylinder design of his own.

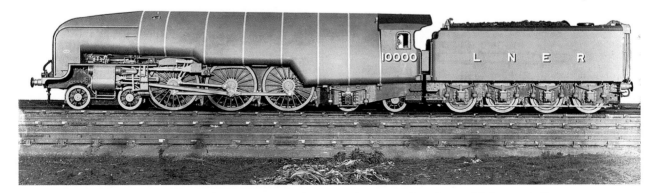

*Fig.165b. An early works portrait in photographic grey. Strathwood Library Collection*

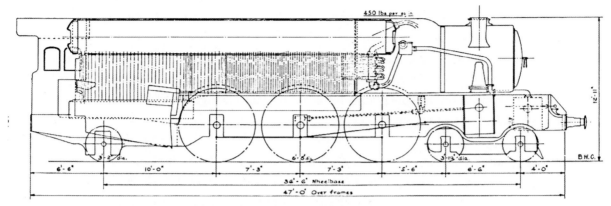

450 lbs per sq in

3'-2" dia.    6'-8½"    3'-1½" dia.    B.W.C.

6'-6"    10'-0"    7'-3"    7'-3"    5'-6"    6'-6"    4'-0"

36'-6" Wheelbase
47'-0" Over frames

PROPOSED 4-6-2 TYPE – JUNE 1927

*Fig. 166. Gresley W1 Line Drawing, Doncaster Works, 1927. Note that at this late stage of development, the locomotive retains a Pacific wheelbase arrangement. Courtesy of the R.C.T.S.*

The initial proposals for the project envisaged a three-cylinder Pacific locomotive with an inside high-pressure cylinder driving the second coupled axle. It was envisaged that two D49 locomotives would also be designed and built as three-cylinder compounds in order to gain some operating experience of the compound type.

In 1926, after reviewing the schematics for the Midland Compounds, and with reference to the work on several proposed compound options by Professor W.E. Dalby at the City & Guilds Engineering College, both the D49 locomotives and the three-cylinder version of the W1 compound were quietly dropped. The latter in favour of a four-cylinder compound locomotive, which would prove to be Gresley's first and last four-cylinder locomotive.

The final configuration of the valve gear, with four cylinders and two sets of Walschaerts valve gear was worked out in November 1926. The inside valves were driven off the outside radius rod with a half expansion link. This arrangement of the valve gear was unique to this locomotive and never repeated.

To reverse the locomotive, the outside expansion link was utilised. The inside half link enabled the inside cut off to vary to be longer or shorter than that applied on the outside cylinders, allowing for maximum cut off to be 90% in the high-pressure cylinders and 75% in the lower cylinders. In 1927 an alternate configuration with Lenz poppet valve gear was considered but rejected.

The boiler's design was largely dictated by the dimensions of the high and low-pressure cylinders. The original pressure was 350lb. This was eventually finalised to operate at 450lb.

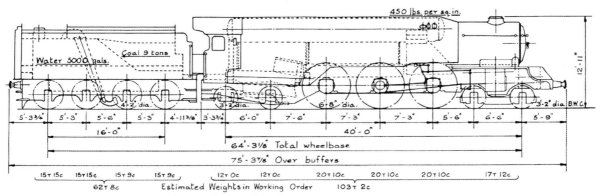

450 lbs. per sq. in.

Water 5000 gals.    Coal 9 tons

12'-11"

4'-2" dia.    3'-2" dia.    6'-8" dia.    3'-2" dia. B.W.Ct

5'-3¾"   5'-3"   5'-6"   5'-3"   4'-11¾" 3'-3¾"   6'-0"   7'-6"   7'-3"   7'-3"   5'-6"   6'-6"   5'-9"

16'-0"             40'-0"

64'-3⅛" Total wheelbase

75'-3⅞" Over buffers

15т15c   15т15c   15т9c   15т9c    12т0c   12т0c   20т10c   20т10c   20т10c   17т12c

62т8c       Estimated Weights in Working Order     103т2c

## PROPOSED 4-6-4 HIGH PRESSURE ENGINE – OCTOBER 1928

*Fig. 167. Gresley W1 Line Drawing, Doncaster Works, 1928. The W1 is now a 4-6-4. Debates have been waged on whether this was a 4-6-4 or 4-6-2-2 ever since its debut, but the L.N.E.R. considered it a 4-6-4 and labelled it as such. Courtesy of the R.C.T.S.*

The boiler consisted of a central steam drum, with two further smaller drums fitted either side of the fire grate, and two others fitted further forward between the frames. The water drums were connected to the steam drum by tubes through which the water was circulated. The central steam drum was exactly 30ft long when built and took up much of the locomotive's length.

The grate area was a bone of contention for some time, with the draughtsmen proposing 41 sq. ft and Gresley repeatedly wishing it reduced. Drawing office and C.M.E. were at cross purposes; Gresley was adamant that he wanted to produce a more efficient locomotive than the A1 class with comparable power whereas the design team wanted to produce a more powerful locomotive. Later in the locomotive's life, this grate area was reduced even further to 33.5 sq. ft., and this did not seem to affect the boiler's ability to produce steam.

The boiler was constructed by Yarrow & Co Ltd in Glasgow, and its size and bulk dictated that the locomotive be stretched from the Pacific format into what the L.N.E.R. officially recorded as a 4-6-4HP tender locomotive. With the separation of a rear carrying Bissel truck, and a cartazzi ahead of it, it was in fact a 4-6-2-2 by the Whyte notation standard.

By February 1929, the boiler had been built and tested at Yarrow's. Meanwhile, Darlington Works had been building the chassis of the locomotive, with a hydraulic test of the high-pressure cylinders made, up to 750lb (300lb higher than the intended boiler pressure). The chassis was to be transferred to Yarrow's in Glasgow for the fitting of the boiler.

Gresley and his team working on the locomotive worked on the project in great secrecy, aware that the L.M.S. were also working on their own high-pressure locomotive (the erstwhile Fury, whose own design foreshadowed that of the nuclear industry in its boiler design). Yarrows could only be reached on LMS metals, so the locomotive was sheeted both there and back. This may have been where the name Hush-Hush was originally coined. Some men of Darlington Works reputedly referred to the chassis, boiler-less, as a "hush-hush job".

Whatever the truth, the name was to stick with the locomotive throughout its life.

*Fig. 168. The W1's prototype boiler, at Yarrow's where it was built. This unusual view of the boiler shows well, the peculiar shape that the cladding would need to take to provide a more aerodynamic shape for the locomotive. The Gresley Society.*

Various secondary sources have speculated on the locomotive's form, some disputing the claim that here was Britain's first truly streamlined steam locomotive. It is clear from the file on the W1 kept at the National Railway Museum, that the remit for the National Physics Laboratory (N.P.L.) was to primarily design the front end to deflect smoke from the chimney (a single blastpipe at this point), together with a drafting arrangement by way of the three front ducts (incorporated into the deflectors and casing ahead of the smokebox) to improve the draw of primary air around the fire grate, under Gresley's explicit instruction.

In October 1928, Darlington Works provided what would be almost the final outline drawing of the locomotive, with everything bar the smokebox and deflector arrangement in situ: the wind tunnel tests had not yet been carried out. The standard A1 smoke box was drawn, and indeed when the locomotive was being put together with its boiler at Yarrow, an A1 type of smokebox was used.

By April 1929 Professor W.E. Dalby was in the L.N.E.R.'s employ on this project and had been conducting wind tunnel tests on wooden models of the W1, helping to perfect the shape of the locomotive's front end and overall casing and in discussion with Gresley. The added benefit of Professor Dalby's work was to make the locomotive more streamlined, anticipating high-speed running in future and predating the work done on the Gresley A4 by six years. This reduced the locomotive's drag across the casing but maximised the air flow into the air ducts and over the centre line of the smokebox, deflecting the smoke higher into the air.

The W1 can be considered Britain's first scientifically designed streamlined steam locomotive, and certainly the first whose outer casing was dictated by the results of wind tunnel experimentation. The later Gresley A4 and L.M.S.' Coronations classes probably had lower drag, but this was not the primary aim of the design, which in the W1 required preheating the air for the draughting of the unique boiler and grate design.

This pre-heating was achieved by way of three air intakes. There were two obvious small openings under the deflectors and the third, less obvious, but larger open inlet was in the centre of the locomotive's front, also forming access to the smokebox door (the flap above the inlet was hinged. Either by coincidence or by design, this top hinged part of the smokebox is very close to the design fitted to the A4 Pacifics later).

Cold air would go into these intakes, passing under the casing of the boiler and by the time it reached the fire, had been significantly preheated by the water-tubes, thereby eliminating issues by way of cold air circulating around hot air in the firebox and out of a secondary need to deflect smoke away from the driver's vision.

Fig. 169. Gresley W1 No. 10000 portrait, just after completion at Doncaster Works. The shape of the streamlined casing and the curvature across the front end is more apparent from this angle.
Strathwood Library Collection.

(On a side note, looking at the Gresley P2 which Bulleid also worked on, shows a similar deflector setup. When overlaying the W1's shape onto the A4's, however, one can see that the profile of the hinged front of the W1's smokebox casing, together with the single chimney casting, is not a million miles away from the final shape of the A4 Pacifics. An unintentional foreshadowing of the more aerodynamic design to come).

Templates were used to modify the smokebox in accordance with the outcomes of the wind tunnel testing, and the familiar sloping front was in place by the September of 1929 together with all the cladding, the deflectors, the front hinged plate, ducting and the cab.

The cab itself was flat fronted, but with the bare minimum of surface area (in fact occupying a much smaller overall profile than other cabs to date). Its cab roof and its sloping slides added to the overall streamlined shape and completing the overall profile. However, the use of the standard eight-wheel corridor broke the effect with its vertical sides. As would be discovered with the A4 Pacific later, maintaining the overall profile of an entire train's streamlining was of the greatest importance to reducing drag.

By December 1929, the locomotive had been returned to Darlington, with final fit out completed, and had been paired with its corridor tender, which had been slightly modified to suit the locomotive's cab. (This tender still exists, together with its unique features, and is to be preserved at the museum of John Cameron, owner of Gresley A4 *Union of South Africa*, which was paired with it in preservation and has towed it for many miles of mainline running throughout the United Kingdom, until its retirement in 2022).

On 15 December 1929, the locomotive, finished in battleship grey with stainless steel boiler bands, and numbered 10000, went out on its first trial run to Croft Junction, towing only the N.E.R. dynamometer car. Gresley was in attendance and was photographed inspecting the locomotive closely.

Between this first run, in steam, and its first official public outing, was just 28 days: around one month's worth of checks, tests, and very close monitoring by its designer. Gresley was again in attendance for many of these tests, with some of his family including his daughters supporting him throughout. It would not be an understatement to say that he was putting his all into the W1, its design representing at the time the ultimate development of much of his work to date. There were concerns with the injectors, and larger cones were ordered (the existing Davies & Metcalfe type were considered inadequate) but there were also issues with the Gresham & Craven high-pressure injector (with the company offering as a courtesy replacements, despite not being responsible for the damage found on the existing one).

*Fig. 170. This unusual shot of the W1 shows well the complex curvature of the smoke deflectors and the main casing around the smokebox. The shape of the upper part of the locomotive, together with its teardrop profile single chimney in particular stand out. Note also that the locomotive cab does not fully protect the tender in terms of streamlining and is exposed at the outer edges.*
*The Gresley Society.*

The locomotive was then taken to King's Cross on the 8 January 1930. It was a high-profile affair, with the press in attendance (including British Pathé News, whose film of the W1's arrival and turning on the King's Cross turntable can still be seen on their website), and many photographs were taken. Gresley was in attendance with his family: one sad absence was that of his wife, who had passed away the previous year.

There is much photographic evidence of this event and there is clear pride in the machine from all present, despite the internal knowledge that it was not performing as intended. It was a prototype and the first of its kind: although not the first water tube boiler locomotive in the United Kingdom, it was undoubtedly the largest and most ambitious.

*Fig. 171. Gresley W1 No.10000, with Gresley and his daughters on hand as part of the locomotive's public entry into traffic. Note that the electric lighting system has yet to be fitted.*
*The Gresley Society.*

It was apparent by this time that the locomotive's boiler had significant advantages over traditional types of boiler. Removing the cladding showed that the air spacing between the water tubes and the outer cladding was beneficial in preventing the build-up of ash, making the job of clearing out the ash deposits much easier.

Fig. 172. Gresley W1 No.10000 portrait, just after completion at Doncaster Works. The shortness of the cab footplate can be seen clearly here, together with the unusual shape of the roof, dictated by the height of the boiler and casing. Strathwood Library Collection.

Further, the boiler gained a reputation for never leaking, and certainly this was something Gresley was very proud of and wrote of in one of his papers on the locomotive's design. What was less satisfactory was the boiler's behaviour when underway with trains: the locomotive would gain a reputation for poor steaming. There were repeated issues with the auxiliary equipment, almost always the injectors and over the course of 1930 numerous changes were made with little success. The manufacturers, the designer, the engineering team, and the operating department were unsure of the reasons why.

Fundamentally there were no issues with the boiler's design. What was not understood was that a combination of factors was working against it. The auxiliaries were not producing the required levels of water; this effectively choking the locomotive. It would be two years before changes were made that allowed the locomotive to be fit for purpose.

Trips with the dynamometer car and various test loads were undertaken, with the locomotive registering some interesting statistics in relation to its coal consumption and indicated brake horse power, both poorer than anticipated (the latter around 1300 HP and the average coal consumption on its Scottish outing over the Forth Bridge on 23 February 1930 at 64.2lb per mile).

Over 1930 and 1931 the locomotive was in and out of the works and by September 1932 a permanent solution had been found for the injectors' issues. By feeding 450psi directly from the boiler rather than the manifold, the boiler was producing steam at the rate required: at last, the W1 was showing what was possible with its unique setup, but it still wasn't enough. Tests continued, alongside genuine work (such as repeated use on the *Flying Scotsman* service) and exhibitions at which it was always a star attraction.

The locomotive was still not quite showing what it was capable of, with modifications made to the cylinders and compound settings that were never quite optimal. By 1934 the Gresley P2s were in service and the double Kylchap chimney was proving itself. Oliver Bulleid had been very involved with the W1 design up to this point, and now was the turn of mechanical engineer Edward Thompson, whose team at Darlington undertook the design, and then fitting out, of the W1's double chimney to fit the bought in Kylchap equipment. (In 1937, Gresley A3 No.2751 Humorist was fitted with a double Kylchap arrangement based on the W1's).

With this improvement, the locomotive was proving far more potent, and in 1935 there was an additional change: the boiler was now regularly operating at 475lb instead of the 450lb as originally designed. The compound settings were being investigated with steps in the cut offs of 25%, 35%, 45% and 55% for the low-pressure cylinders and 30%, 40% and 50% for the high-pressure cylinders. William Brown states in his book that if the cut off in the high-pressure cylinders had been 90%, the potential horsepower would have been "just short of 4000HP".

Fig. 173. Gresley W1 No.10000 on the Forth Bridge under test. Rail Archive Stephenson.

*Fig. 174. Gresley W1 No.10000 on an express passenger service, pulling into King's Cross.
The Gresley Society.*

Reliable and effective fuel economy was still tantalisingly out of reach. Chapelon later produced No.242A1, a 4-8-4 steam locomotive which was set up very similarly to one of the W1's trialled formats, effectively as a three-cylinder compound. William Brown asserts in his book that Gresley came close to achieving that Chapelon did: but ten years earlier. This is speculative of course, but one cannot help but wonder.

By August 1935 the W1 had been fitted with a smoke cowl between the deflectors and had been running well. However, it was now out of service pending a decision on its future. The success of the Gresley A4s coming into service put paid to the future development of the water tube boiler. No.10000 was retrieved from the Darlington Works paint shop and taken to Doncaster works for rebuilding. The bold experiment was finally over, but the vision had been correct and the results so close to achieving excellence.

When withdrawn, the W1 had achieved Gresley's aim of a locomotive with comparable performance achieving superior fuel economy to his original Pacifics. This aim and achievement have been repeatedly overlooked by secondary sources for decades, reducing the W1 from what it was: a bold and well-developed locomotive design to a "grey galloping sausage".

## The Hush-Hush - the underrated machine

In the interests of balance, however, it would be remiss not to try and dispel a few of the more widely held myths. The first among them being that No. 10000 was a failure: there is no doubt that the water tube boiler was an excellent piece of design and the fact that it ran continuously with little modification for over a thirty-year period, outliving the rebuilt locomotive by way as a static boiler for Darlington Works, is probably indicative of the robustness of the original design.

*Fig. 175. Gresley W1 No. 10000 on an express passenger service. This shot shows two specific aspects of the W1 design: the ability to lift the smoke clear of the boiler casing at the front end, and the width of the water tube boiler at the rear of the locomotive. The Gresley Society.*

In service, the valve gear arrangement gave virtually no problems whatsoever and hot big ends or overheating of any kind, were not experienced in any meaningful way. There is also no doubt that when fitted with the Kylchap double chimney, and with the auxiliaries set up closer to that originally intended, that the W1 was capable of being more efficient on fuel.

Even prior to the 1935 and 1934 modifications, the W1 with its smaller grate was recording coal consumptions as follows:

| W1 Locomotive Coal Consumption 1932 | | | |
|---|---|---|---|
| Date of Run | Load (tons) Out Run | Load (tons) Return | Coal Consumed (lb per mile) |
| 17-Oct | 331 | 393 | 44.1 |
| 31-Oct | 336 | 378 | 44.3 |
| 01-Nov | 329 | 355 | 42.4 |
| 02-Nov | 368 | 360 | 44.2 |
| 03-Nov | 273 | 358 | 46 |

*Fig. 176. The W1's coal consumption figures. Despite being set up in a way that was not optimal, the locomotive was already recording impressive fuel economy with a grate no larger than 35 sq. ft. Simon A.C. Martin, from the W1 File at the N.R.M, Search Engine.*

This with similar tractive effort and performance, made it better than most of Gresley's A1s and arguably the locomotive in its final form prior to complete rebuilding was more than the equal of a Gresley A3, but without the complications of the issues of conventional boilers or the issues of the conjugated valve gear when run down. The drawbacks in the use of compounding and the familiarisations of its crews with firing and driving it notwithstanding, of course.

Throughout its lifetime as a water tube boiler locomotive, the W1 never failed with a hot axle box or valve gear, which, as observed by William Brown in his book, made it unique amongst Gresley's express passenger locomotive designs. No.10000 is also criticised repeatedly for its days spent out of work, compared to days recorded in works. The issue with these statistics is that an assumption was made that every time the locomotive was out of service, it was at Darlington Works.

In its role as a prototype, it was constantly being checked, worked on, parts adjusted, tested, and maintained. It was also rolled out on display, photographed continuously, filmed, and was almost the new Flying Scotsman insomuch that the L.N.E.R. press team had a field day with the locomotive. It was on posters, pamphlets, in newspapers, in cinema and whether by design or by luck, "Hush-Hush" was anything but: as everyone, including the public, was aware of this extraordinary locomotive.

That it was not doing the same work as the conventional steam locomotives is a red herring: it wasn't meant to be, this was a prototype locomotive with serious scientific development and testing behind it. A good comparison would be the role of the prototype Concorde aircrafts, 001 and 002, which were to undertake many flights, less than a third of which were supersonic, and spent much time on the ground not doing work because their various systems and components were being checked, tested, and calibrated towards data accumulation. This is exactly what the W1 was doing, and for this it has been called a failure.

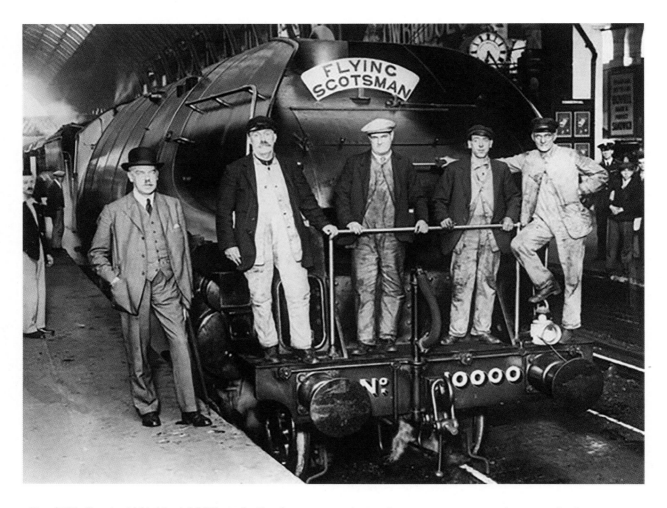

*Fig. 177. Gresley W1 No. 10000, with Gresley posing alongside its crew, prepared to run the locomotive non-stop to Scotland whilst pulling the Flying Scotsman. The locomotive ran to time and without mechanical issues, which was no mean feat. Note that the electric lighting system is now fitted, with a conduit running at the top of the buffer beam. The Gresley Society.*

On that note, what has been most perplexing is the number of secondary sources calling the locomotive an outright *failure*. In looking at the primary evidence (of which we have an *abundance* of material at the National Railway Museum at York, including carefully labelled photographic evidence which directly contradicts, and there calls into question many of the accepted secondary sources that have written on this locomotive) there are many records of the locomotive struggling on trains for sustained high pressure steam, but no actual records of *failing* to run trains.

There's repeated mention of having to work the boiler hard, particularly in the early years, to maintain required pressures, but once the cut offs to the cylinders had been adjusted and the double chimney fitted, the locomotive was performing work to a very high standard and with excellent fuel economy. We now know that in its original form, and perhaps retaining the single chimney, with a larger receiver and with better cut offs for low and high-pressure cylinders, that it would have been fully capable of anything thrown at it, and moreover, would have been the most powerful express passenger locomotive in the British Isles without needing to be rebuilt.

On the water tube boiler itself, actual issues with the design and its major components number zero. There are no records of water leaks or issues with the boiler, and almost every issue on the W1 that was encountered lay in the auxiliary equipment fitted, and the cladding causing air leaks, not issues with the water boiler itself. Gresley's water tube boiler design was an astonishing leap forward compared to other contemporary designs and the lack of praise for his considered, thoughtful development of the water tube boiler for railway use is unfair.

There is an argument that many writers have failed to notice the almost obvious advantages of the water tube boiler, one which was highlighted almost immediately after the locomotive started running: it did not accumulate as much ash and detritus as a standard boiler and was far easier to dispose of after running. A clear maintenance advantage, particularly when one considers the damage that such detritus can cause a boiler.

Perhaps the most astonishing fact was that many years after the water tube variant of the W1 design had been shelved, Andre Chapelon produced his locomotive, No.242A1 which was set up virtually as Gresley intended for the W1 originally. This locomotive achieved some incredible horsepower figures in its short life.

Gresley's erstwhile failure with the W1 as a four-cylinder compound had been taken further by a close friend and ally and then proved beyond all reasonable doubt that Gresley's ideas were ultimately correct, albeit achieved with a compound locomotive running at 300lb.

Unfortunately, Gresley's perceived failure is lent credence whereas Chapelon's success somehow has little to do with Gresley's own developments a decade before. There is no doubt in my mind that the original W1 helped cement Chapelon's own ideas and, with the advantages of the test facilities at his disposal, was able to achieve that Gresley had sought after.

There is also the question of streamlining. The W1 was the first of Gresley's steam locomotives to showcase any form of streamlining. The P2 design and A4 designs to come would showcase several aspects of the W1's development. In the case of the former, the smoke deflectors of the W1 were copied almost verbatim onto the P2 design, with the inclusion of the double blast pipe of the P2 and more conventional smoke box arrangement making for a less streamlined front end.

On the A4, the nods to the W1's design were more subtle. The outer casing of the smoke box with the curved hinged casing covering the conventional smoke box followed very similarly the W1's shape. This had been developed because of the wind tunnel testing, with further designs that were produced by Frederick Johansen inspired in part by the previous work.
The W1 pointed the way for Gresley for scientific development and for the streamlining of locomotives and rolling stock toward high-speed running.

*Fig. 178. The W1, now rebuilt with the streamlined casing of the A4 Pacifics adapted for use and covering a conventional boiler type. Four cylinders and valve gear have given way to three cylinders and conjugated valve gear. Note the bulge over the lower portion of the front valances for the larger cylinders. The Gresley Society.*

## The Rebuilt W1

In October 1936, the W1 was transferred from Darlington Works to Doncaster for rebuilding. By November 1936 the first outline drawing of the rebuilt W1 had been produced, the drawing office closely following the pattern of the Gresley A4 Pacific in its design.

The water tube boiler gave way to a boiler of diagram 111, similar in proportion to the diagram 108 boiler on the P2 *Wolf of Badenoch*. This boiler was pressed to 250lb, as per the A4 Pacifics. Married to three cylinders of 20in by 26in diameter, activated by 8in piston valves and with conjugated valve gear applied, this increased the tractive effort of the locomotive to 41,437lb, making the W1 on paper the express passenger locomotive with the highest tractive effort in the United Kingdom.

A4 streamlining was provided, together with a new lengthy cab, based on the A4 type, that stretched to the end of the rear frames. The Bissel truck and Cartazzi arrangement was retained. It took one year of work at Doncaster Works to make the outline drawing come to life, with No. 10000 emerging in November 1937, the only member of the streamlined fleet to be unnamed across classes A4, B17, P2 and W1.

Fig. 179. The rebuilt W1 emerges from the tunnel at Ganwick in the late 1930s. Aside from the lack of a nameplate, and a careful look to the cabside area, the slight bulge to the bottom of the cylinder casing and you'd be forgiven for thinking this a member of the A4 class. Rail Archive Stephenson.

The locomotive worked up until 1939 on a variety of express passenger services, and during the war worked closely alongside the Pacifics on all kinds of work including, but not limited to, heavy troop train traffic and freight.

In 1942, and as recorded in the L.N.E.R. Emergency Board minutes, new C.M.E. Edward Thompson ordered a set of comparison trials between the W1 and the Gresley P2s. The W1, so far as we can ascertain from the board minutes of the time, did good work and its availability for this year remained superior to the P2s (69% availability compared to 57%).

The exact nature of the trials is not explicitly recorded. The comparisons were those of fuel consumption and overall availability. The W1 performed well from the information we have available. The railway press of the time was receiving much correspondence on the excellence of the rebuilt W1's performances, which is in stark contrast to the accepted views of previous L.N.E.R. writers.

The use of a six-coupled express passenger locomotive being sent for trials on the routes the P2s worked strongly suggested that Thompson was looking ahead to a time when the Mikados would be replaced with other six-coupled locomotives. If a six-coupled express passenger locomotive could do the same work as the P2s and be more reliable, then the business case for keeping the six Mikados starts to fall away.

## Wartime Mileages & Availability

| Year | Mileages | Availability |
|------|----------|--------------|
| 1942 | 48799 | 69% |
| 1943 | 52580 | 76% |
| 1944 | 36840 | 60% |
| 1945 | 42073 | 57% |
| 1946 | 36833 | 50% |

Fig. 180. W1 Mileages & Availability Statistics.
Simon A.C. Martin, from the Use of Engine Power Document.

The W1's overall availability, as recorded in the Use of Engine Power statistics gave a peak of 76% reliability and 52,580 miles achieved in 1943, which then led to a decline towards the end of the war, with only 50% availability and 36,833 miles achieved in 1946, and it is interesting that the locomotive had some of its best availability in Scotland.

This may have been down to the use of specific crews allocated to specific locomotives, which was different to other parts of the country where there was a strict common user policy. There was no doubt that the boiler was the most significant factor. Having no spare boiler for the locomotive increased the amount of time spent in works significantly.

The decision to have no spare boiler, or to fit a standard boiler with the Pacifics has always puzzled, as classes A2/2, A2/3, Peppercorn A1 and A2 all ended up sharing the similarly proportioned diagram 118 boiler.

The W1 would have benefitted enormously from joining the same pool of boilers as any delay in returning to service swiftly almost always centred on overhauling its unique nonstandard boiler.

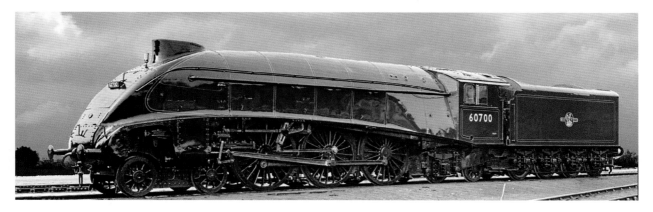

Fig. 181. The lone W1, as rebuilt but in its final form and livery as British Railway's No.60700. This may be a shot of the locomotive at Doncaster Works shortly after its final overhaul prior to withdrawal at the end of the 1950s. Colourised by Ian MacCabe, The Gresley Society.

The W1 eventually settled down to working Kings Cross to Doncaster and Kings Cross to Leeds expresses. In 1955 the W1 was involved in a derailment at Westwood Junction, Peterborough, overturning onto its side. This was put down to weld defects from a rushed repair in the bogie frames, which was the same type as that applied to the B17 class. The locomotive was able to soldier on until 1959, with its major issue being its nonstandard boiler.

By June 1959, No.60700 (as it had become under British Railways, retaining its original number 10000 right through the Thompson re numbering scheme) had been withdrawn. Even in its rebuilt state, it had a mixed reputation.

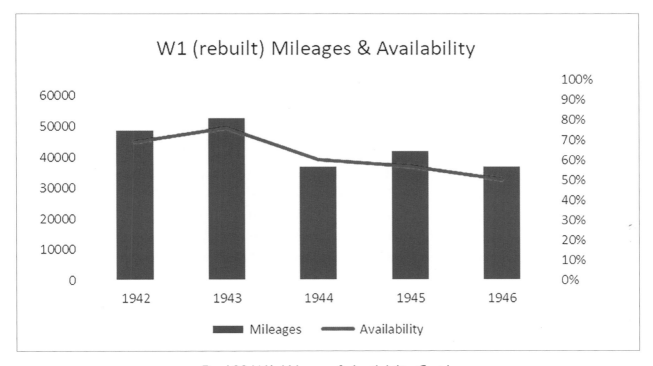

Fig. 182. W1 Mileages & Availability Graph.
Simon A.C. Martin from the Use of Engine Power Document.

## The Forgotten Influence

Gresley's W1 has at times suffered from certain prejudices and misconceptions: about what it had been designed to achieve, what it actually achieved, and whether in its water tube boiler form it was of any benefit to the L.N.E.R. It is my contention that Gresley would not have been able to produce the A4 Pacific without going through the W1's development. This is based on simple factual analysis of the primary evidence that we have available, which shows a clear change in Gresley's approach to locomotive design and scientific experimentation over nearly a decade of work for the L.N.E.R.

Nobody should be claiming that the W1 was a perfectly streamlined locomotive. It wasn't. It had several areas across its design that were not optimised for reduction of drag and high-speed running. However, in its original water tube boiler form, the front end was specifically designed to channel air in such ways that its front-end casing was superior to other conventional outline locomotives, including contemporary designs and some which came after, such as Gresley's P2 locomotives, which also benefitted from the wind tunnel testing and experimentation that had been undertaken (and produced the original distinctive smoke deflectors on the former and the latter locomotives).

In the W1's distinctive casing, there are parallels with the setup of Gresley's A4 Pacific, including the hinged panel access creating a more streamlined smoke box casing, and a teardrop shaped chimney profile for single and double chimney formats. What is perhaps most intriguing is how the W1 sits between the two design formats, with the distinctive, recognisable shapes and dimensions of its front end closely matching two of Gresley's most famous steam locomotive classes to come. It was the first of Gresley's locomotives to have been designed in such a way that would produce such aerodynamic results, and it seems, probably the first steam locomotive in the United Kingdom to benefit directly from a more scientific approach to design, testing using models, and adjust as necessary with retesting. The P2 design's smoke deflectors speak for themselves, the influence is obvious.

That this was all a by-product of the work done to improve the draughting for the fire grate by way of the air ducting at the front end, and the channelling of air up and over the boiler casing and the cab for smoke deflection purposes is somewhat irrelevant. Just because the intention to create a streamlined design wasn't there originally does not mean Gresley and the L.N.E.R didn't take advantage of this when the further significance of this was fully understood. On the contrary, the L.N.E.R. wasted no time in adjusting the promotional material on the W1 locomotive, describing it as streamlined until it was withdrawn for rebuilding.

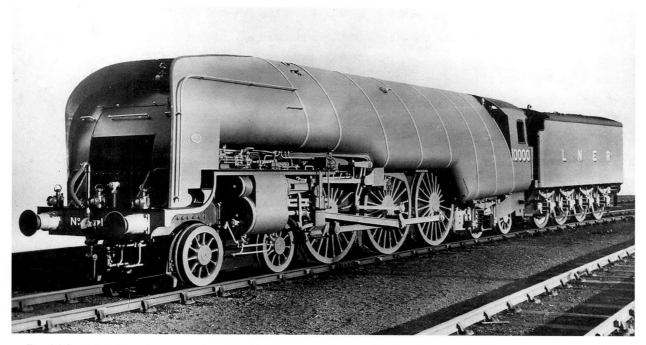

Fig. 183. Official works portrait of the W1 as complete at Darlington works. The shape of the casing and the boiler underneath necessitated partially covering the middle and rear driving wheels, requiring splashers inset to those parts of the casing. Strathwood Library Collection.

For many years the locomotive has been branded a failure and misunderstood. Perhaps in hindsight writers and historians dismissing it out of hand could consider the following influences that it had on Gresley's designs:

- Designed by work in a wind tunnel producing streamlined results

- Chimney shape's design optimised for the P2 and A4 classes

- Deflector design influenced the P2's

- Smoke box casing and components at the front end influenced the A4 shape to come

- Overall experimental development taken forward by way of incorporating scientific techniques

Out of this, the very clear success that the W1 provided was the impetus to continue the development of a streamlined locomotive and then a fully streamlined train thereafter. Had it not proved successful in this area, it may have taken longer for Gresley to achieve the desired shape from a design point of view for the A4 Pacific. Certainly, its influence on later locomotive designs, arguably the A4 benefitting the most, has been underplayed to the extent that its link to this class has been all but rendered extinct in secondary evidence and literature. Equally, without the W1's notable success in achieving great publicity as a prototype locomotive, Gresley may not have been able to later persuade the L.N.E.R. board of the advantages a fully streamlined train may bring. The latter is speculative, the former is evidential.

Perhaps more surprising is that the claim for the first streamlined steam locomotives in the world lies with two American steam locomotives that came out five years after the W1's entry into service. The first of these locomotives, the Commodore Vanderbilt, was outshopped as a streamlined locomotive in December 1934, from a conversion of a conventionally built Class J3 "Hudson" 4-6-4 locomotive for the New York Central Railroad. The second design, the Milwaukee Road Class A Atlantic locomotives, have laid claim as the first steam locomotive class in the world to be designed fully streamlined and these first engines emerged in May 1935.

Given that these locomotives have appeared five and six years after the Gresley W1 entered traffic, and with the knowledge that the W1 *was* intended to be, and *was* streamlined, both through scientific design development and in practical application of its building, the historical record now needs to be updated. To the list of Sir Nigel Gresley's achievements we can perhaps now also claim the first *truly* streamlined steam locomotive produced for a major railway company, worldwide.

Was the W1 a failure? On the contrary, the W1 was a brave experiment that led the way for Gresley's greatest achievements in so many ways. Without the work done on this unique and inspiring locomotive, it is doubtful that Gresley's later successes would have happened.

*Fig. 183b. Proudly displayed at the Liverpool & Manchester Railway centenary exhibition at Wavertree in 1930, it is easy to see how futuristic 10000 would have appeared to the visiting public and in all of the L.N.E.R.'s publicity. Rail Archive Stephenson/Rail Online*

| Class W1 | | | |
|---|---|---|---|
| Sub Class | | Water Tube Boiler | Conventional |
| Expansion: | | Compound | Simple |
| Cylinders: | | Inside HP: 12"x26"<br>Outside LP: 20"x26" (4) | 20"x26"<br>(3) |
| Motion: | | Walschaerts/Rockers to Inside Cylinders | Walschaerts/Conjugated Valve Gear |
| Boiler: | Max. Diameter: | 3ft drum | 6ft 5in |
| | Pressure: | 450lb | 250lb |
| | Diagram No.: | 103 | 111 |
| Heating Surface: | Total: | 1986.5 sq. ft. | 3346.5 sq. ft. |
| | Firebox: | 919 sq. ft. | 252.5 sq. ft. |
| | Superheater: | | 748.9 sq. ft. |
| | Tubes: | 872 sq. ft. | 1281.4 sq. ft. |
| | Flues: | N/A | 1063.7 sq. ft. |
| | Combustion chamber: | 195 sq. ft. | N/A |
| Grate Area: | | 34.95 sq. ft. | 50 sq. ft. |
| Wheels: | Leading: | 3ft 2in | 3ft 2in |
| | Coupled: | 6ft 8in | 6ft 8in |
| | Trailing: | 3ft 2in | 3ft 2in |
| | Tender: | 4ft 2in | 4ft 2in |
| Tractive Effort: | At 85% boiler pressure | 32,000lb | 41,437lb |
| Total Wheelbase: | Engine: | 40ft | 40ft |
| | Tender: | 16ft | 16ft |
| Weight (full): | Engine: | 103 tons 12cwt | 107 tons 17cwt |
| | Tender: | 62 tons 8cwt | 64 tons 19cwt |
| | Total: | 166 tons 0cwt | 172 tons 16cwt |
| Max. Axle Load: | | 21 tons | 22 tons |
| Water Capacity: | | 5000 gallons | 5000 gallons |
| Coal Capacity: | | 9 tons | 9 tons |

# L.N.E.R
## Class V1 2-6-2T (1930)
### Number built (L.N.E.R.): 82

*Fig. 184. Gresley V1 No. 2900, works photograph. The Gresley Society.*

The development of Gresley's first three-cylinder passenger tank locomotive took two years and went through numerous changes, most in relation to the boiler, the cylinders, smokebox saddle and the cab design. Intended for working on the Metropolitan City Widened Lines initially, the first draft of this locomotive design in 1928 included condensing equipment and shortened fittings including the chimney. By the end of 1928, the route availability intended for these locomotives had changed, and these fittings had been discarded: the locomotives were now to be sent for work in Scotland and the condensing equipment was entirely dispensed with.

The opening design had been based on the original Gresley K1 Mogul design, incorporating the boiler and coupled wheelbase of this class, but with three cylinders of 16in by 26in, Gresley conjugated valve gear and a tractive effort of 22,464lb.

An intermediate to the design included the use of the D34 (Glen) type boiler. This was almost entirely discarded, with the new boiler design taking cues from the Gresley K3 class boiler.

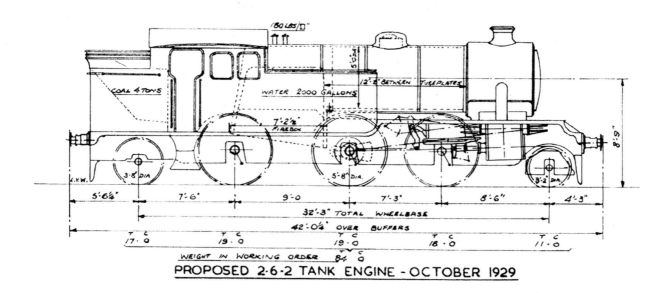

Fig. 185. Gresley V1 Line Drawing, Doncaster Works, 1929. Courtesy of the R.C.T.S.

A monobloc casting incorporating the cylinders, but not the smokebox saddle, was to be fitted, together with a larger side window cab, also based on the Gresley K3. The front pony truck was the same as that fitted to the K3s, but the rear was a radial truck that had been copied from the Gresley N2 tank locomotive.

The first batch of twenty-eight locomotives was built between September 1930 and December 1931, as part of the 1929 building programme. There were to have been twenty-six in the 1930 programme, but this was reduced substantially to thirteen locomotives, delayed until the 1931 programme. This was due in no small part to the depression being felt at the time in the railway industry and Class V1 was not the only casualty of this tightening of financial belts across the L.N.E.R. The running department put in a request for more V1s in September 1930, but this was rejected. The programme of works was further altered, reduced to six locomotives, for 1932, with the remaining twenty on order eventually cancelled.

The 1930 programme was for twenty-six, but thirteen were cancelled completely, and the other thirteen delayed until the 1932 programme. These were completed between 1933 and 1934. This would be the end of the V1's building programme, as will be explained in later in the chapter on the Gresley V3s. The first batch, comprising twenty-eight locomotives, had some difficulty with coaling at various sheds on the Scottish region, so different types of bunkers were fitted to replace the original coal rails. Later built V1s would have coal hoppers instead. Both the Scottish and North Eastern areas would have ample allocations for many years, with one notable change of allocation coming during the Second World War when a few of the Tyneside based examples were moved to Leeds to support the R.O.D. at Thorpe Arch.

*Fig. 186. Gresley V1 No.2908, waiting to be coupled to a train bound for Edinburgh. Note the brackets on the top of the smokebox for the fitting of the unusually curved destination board.*
*The Gresley Society.*

The Great Eastern section had allocations at Stratford, Norwich, and King's Lynn, with the most held at Stratford and for working suburban traffic. By 1948, allocations of Thompson L1 locomotives were coming, and these locomotives were sent to the North East and Scotland to add to the existing allocations. The numbers of Class V1 would decrease steadily as boiler replacement dictated whether they would be converted into Class V3 (covered later in this book) and eventually the numbers reversed with Class V1 becoming the minor class and V3 with the higher-pressure boiler forming the majority.

The last examples of Class V1 survived until 1960, with withdrawals starting as the bulk of their suburban passenger work was taken over by diesels and diesel rail cars. By the end of 1962, the remaining members of Class V1 had been withdrawn and scrapped.

## Wartime Mileages & Availability

Gresley's Class V1 was by far one of the stand-out locomotive classes of the L.N.E.R. during World War Two. Mileages were always consistently above 30,000 miles in every year of the conflict, married to astonishing availability, completely bucking the trend of the rest of the Gresley conjugated valve gear fleet and significantly above the L.N.E.R.'s own fleet average in every year.

| Year | Mileages | Availability |
|------|----------|--------------|
| 1942 | 30822 | 75% |
| 1943 | 30787 | 76% |
| 1944 | 32082 | 78% |
| 1945 | 30352 | 78% |
| 1946 | 31091 | 79% |

*Fig. 187. V1 Mileages & Availability Statistics.*
*Simon A.C. Martin, from the Use of Engine Power Document.*

With availability peaking at almost 80% in 1946, matched to an impressive average of 31,091 miles that year, the Gresley V1s, even with some examples as much as fifteen years old, were one of Gresley's most exemplary classes.

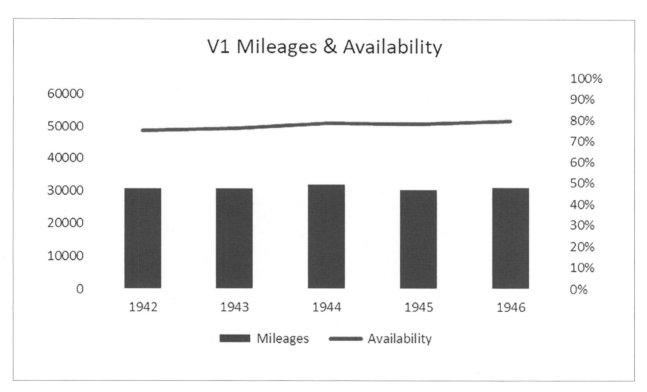

*Fig. 188. V1 Mileages & Availability Graph.*
*Simon A.C. Martin from the Use of Engine Power Document.*

| Class V1 | | |
|---|---|---|
| Cylinders (x3): | | 16x26in. |
| Motion: | Outside: | Walschaerts |
| | Inside: | Gresley |
| | Valves: | 8in piston |
| Boiler: | Max. Diameter: | 5ft |
| | Pressure: | 180psi |
| | Diagram No.: | 102 |
| Heating Surface: | Total: | 1609 sq. ft. |
| | Firebox: | 127 sq. ft. |
| | Superheater: | 284 sq. ft. |
| | Tubes: | 830 sq. ft. (149x 1.75in) |
| | Flues: | 368 sq. ft. (22x 5.25in) |
| Grate Area: | | 22.08 sq. ft. |
| Wheels: | Leading: | 3ft 2in |
| | Coupled: | 5ft 8in |
| | Trailing: | 3ft 8in |
| Tractive Effort: | 22,464lb | At 85% boiler pressure |
| Total Wheelbase: | | 32ft 3in |
| Engine Weight: | (full) | 57 tons 1cwt |
| Coal Capacity: | | 4 tons |
| Water Capacity: | | 2000 gallons |
| Max. Axle Load: | | 19 tons 5cwt |

*Fig.188b. An official posed image of the first built new Class V1 in photographic grey in 1930.*
*Strathwood Library Collection*

# L.N.E.R
## Class P2 2-8-2 (1934)
Number built (L.N.E.R.): 6

*Fig. 189. Gresley P2 No.2001 Cock O'The North, waiting for the "right away" to take the Aberdonian on. Colourised by Ian MacCabe, The Gresley Society.*

Gresley's Class P2 locomotives remain one of his most iconic designs. Indeed, class prototype No.2001 Cock O' The North is rightly known as one of the most distinctive, and handsome steam locomotives ever built. In the modern day, its legend is being carried forward by the P2 Locomotive Trust, building the "next in class" P2 locomotive, (but retaining the handsome lines of the prototype together with a more robust version of the Lentz valve gear fitted). Andrew Hardy's book, Gresley's Class P2 Locomotives, written to support the P2 Trust's efforts, remains the definitive book on this class of locomotives and is highly recommended as the starting point for further reading on the class. For the purposes of this book, a summary of the classes' development is included below together with commentary on the performance during the war years.

One thing is very clear about the development of the P2. Gresley signed off on the design, and was involved from the outset, but the main instigators of the locomotive design were the operating department, requesting for suitable motive power on the Edinburgh to Aberdeen, also from O.V.S. Bulleid, one of Gresley's assistants. This line has steep gradients and tight curves throughout and had for many years resorted to double heading on the heaviest trains.

The N.B.R.'s esteemed Atlantics were still the mainstay of services by the 1930s and normally acted as either the train engine or the pilot when operating services double-headed. Double heading the existing Pacifics was not allowed due axle loading requirements.

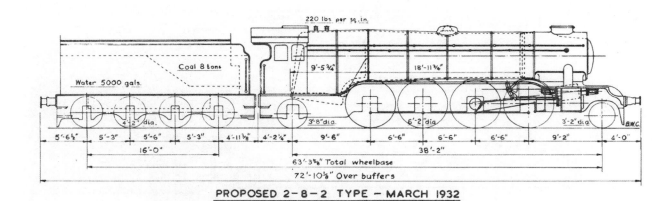

Fig. 190. Gresley P2 Line Drawing, Doncaster Works, 1932. Note the similarity to the Gresley P1 in outline, and the use of outside Walschaerts valve gear. One surprise is the inclusion of the cutaway below the chimney and above the smokebox door, like the experimental arrangement Humorist was fitted with in 1932. Courtesy of the R.C.T.S.

Initial plans for an A3 styled Mikado 2-8-2 locomotive were put together during 1932. There was an element of Deja-vu about these designs, as the first few outlines bore a great similarity to the existing P1 Mikados, albeit with 6ft 2in driving wheels.

This design began to evolve and, on reviewing the material built up from the W1 project, certain aspects of the latter were integrated into the design, which was also tested in a wind tunnel for the express purpose of optimising its smoke deflection, the double Kylchap chimney being added to the design early on.

The issues of smoke deflection were well known with the W1's experimental deflectors and streamlined shape, and the other tests that were being conducted on the A3 Pacifics around the time providing valuable data for analysis which would then influence the P2's project.

The final design was strikingly similar in concept to the W1's, but with the more conventional smokebox and large double chimney with Kylchap applied, subtle changes to improve the deflective propensity of the plates was taken, including making the sides vertical from the bottom, and curving in more sharply towards the top end and the top of the boiler casing.

This, like the W1 before it, was produced by experimentation in a wind tunnel by way of Professor W.E. Dalby with chalk dust introduced to show air flow over a wooden model of the locomotive.

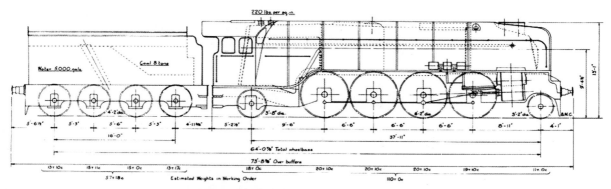

PROPOSED CLASS P2 – MARCH 1934

*Fig. 191. Gresley P2 Line Drawing, Doncaster Works, 1934. The smoke deflectors and Lentz gear are now present, together with a higher running plate and a vee-shaped cab. Courtesy of the R.C.T.S.*

This experimentation also influenced the design of the cab, with the first use of the vee-shaped cab front married to cab sides that more closely followed the format of his A3 Pacifics. This both improved the smoke deflecting ability of the locomotive's overall shape and provided an unexpected advantage by reducing glare to the driver's vision, by way of the angled glass in the cab spectacles.

The first two P2 locomotives were originally to have been more similar than they turned out. For the first, No.2001, Lentz valve gear and an ACFI water heater were to be fitted, giving the No.2001 a distinctly continental look. The use of Lentz gear harked back to the trials on L.N.E.R. classes J20, B12, C7 and D49. These trials spanned almost a decade, starting with J20 No.8280 in 1925 and culminated with the prototype P2 in 1934, becoming the largest steam locomotive to have been fitted with the valve gear in the United Kingdom.

No.8280 was later rebuilt in 1937 with standard piston valves, bringing it back into line with the other twenty-four locomotives in the class. That the locomotive lasted over a decade in this form is probably indicative of the general robustness of this version of the Lentz gear.
In the case of the Holden B12s built in the 1920s with Lentz gear, they were to be rebuilt to B12/3 specification complete with piston valves from 1931. These locomotives were fitted with monobloc cylinders and these cracked, leading to expensive replacement. Andrew Hardy in his book on the P2s exercises caution, pointing to the position of the inlet and exhaust ports likely leading to excessive stressing in the casting.

In any event, the rebuilding of these Lentz gear fitted locomotives to long travel piston valve fitted locomotives under the direction of Edward Thompson at Stratford Works should not be taken as a criticism of the Lentz valve gear directly. Thompson was tying into the overall push by Gresley for some standardisation of L.N.E.R. boilers, with the Belpaire type of the B12/2s and B12/1s being replaced by a round topped boiler based on the B17s type.

*Fig. 192. Gresley P2 No.2001 Cock O'The North, on its first visit to King's Cross. To the right of the picture is Sir Nigel Gresley. Colourised by Ian MacCabe, The Gresley Society.*

Round topped boilers would remain the L.N.E.R.'s preference, in defiance to the other members of the Big Four who embraced the square cornered Belpaire with gusto. The change to piston valves did also bring them into line with most other locomotives running on the Great Eastern section, including the similarly transformed D16/3s.

In late 1933, the first of two C7 Atlantics, No.732, was rebuilt with Lentz gear, and the second, No.2212. was fitted similarly, work starting in 1934 by removing its Uniflow cylinder arrangement and not finishing the conversion until January 1936.

With the D49s, comparisons by way of close testing between the three sets of valve gear fitted showed no discernible advantage for the Lentz gear over the Walschaerts/Conjugated valve gear locomotives (see the D49 section in this book). These locomotives however were never rebuilt and the D49/2s continued in service with their Lentz gear until the end of steam.

The P2 version of the Lentz gear was not quite like the D49's and operated by way of two camshafts set above the outside cylinders and set at right angles. These camshafts were synchronised to work with the rotation of the driving wheel axles. Mounted onto these two camshafts were six scroll cams that controlled the admission and exhaust valves.

These allowed for an infinitely variable cut-off setting. In forward gear this was between 10% and 70%, and between 31% and 70% in reverse gear.

The clear advantage of this design was the potential for providing perfect valve events across the range of cut off positions, but in both forward and reverse, something not attainable on more traditional valve gears such as Walschaerts, with a bias for events in forward running noted.

The steam circuit was optimised to reduce overall thermal losses and to produce more efficient use of steam. This echoed much of the work done with the W1 from its early development through the early 1930s when modifications were still being undertaken on the water tube boiler locomotive.

No.2001 was to receive the first all welded tender, one of the new non-corridor eight-wheel tenders. This tender remained with No.2001 for all its life and was unique amongst the P2 classes' tenders in being fitted with spoked wheels (of which the new build P2's tender, No.2007, will also feature).

With sweeping deflectors and eight large driving wheels married with the iconic apple green livery of the L.N.E.R., No.2001 swept onto the scene in May 1934 and captured the minds of the public straight away, appearing at open days, in the news (British Pathé News again covered the first runs). The locomotive followed in the footsteps of Gresley's other iconic express passenger locomotives, some more closely than others, being the subject of a feature film titled *Cock O' The North*, much like *Flying Scotsman* had been in 1929.

*Fig. 193. Gresley P2 No.2001 Cock O' The North on the rollers at the Vitry Testing Station in France. The Gresley Society.*

*Fig. 194. Gresley P2 No.2001 Cock O'The North emerging from Gasworks Tunnel, undergoing indicating tests with a wooden shelter mounted on the front buffer beam and around the smoke deflectors. The Gresley Society.*

Cock O' The North underwent a series of indicator tests and high-speed runs on L.N.E.R. metals prior to a sojourn abroad in France for intense observation at the Vitry Testing Station in France, starting in December 1934. The locomotive ran under its own steam whilst in France, equipped with large French pattern headlights and accompanied by a French engineer and inspector whilst being ably driven by its assigned Doncaster crew.

The best summary of the testing in France can be found in Andrew Hardy's tome, but a general summary would conclude that sufficient data was not able to be recorded on the locomotive's performance due to consistent issues with the axle boxes in the first three weeks of testing.

The second period, with modifications made to the nature of the tests, and with great care and attention resulted in a maximum power output record of 2250 horsepower being made on the Vitry rollers. On the road in France, one test run for the locomotive resulted in a maximum power output recorded as 1910 horsepower, running at an average of 80.7 kph.

Whilst No.2001 was undergoing its testing and modifications, a second P2 had been started and would be completed to enter service in October 1934. No.2002, named *Earl Marischal*, was effectively the prototype's conventional sister and was fitted with the familiar Walschaerts and conjugated valve gear set up of the Gresley Pacifics. It did not feature an ACFI water heater, this equipment proving troublesome on No.2001 throughout its use on the locomotive.

No.2002's early days of testing revealed a propensity for drifting smoke obscuring the driver's vision, something not experienced on No.2001 to the same degree. The overall conclusion was that the softer exhaust and draughting characteristics of No.2002 were different because of the use of the piston valves in comparison to the Lentz gear on No.2001. Additional smoke deflectors were then fitted, giving the locomotive a unique appearance.

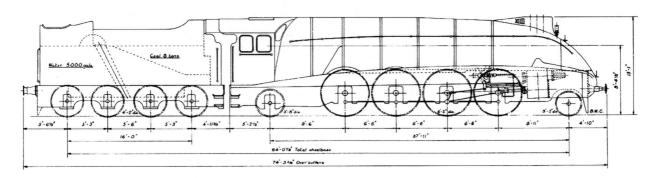

PROPOSED CLASS P2—MARCH 1936

*Fig. 195. Gresley P2 Line Drawing, Doncaster Works, 1936. The influence of the A4 Pacific is now obvious with a complete change at the front end to the streamlined casing. To fit the cylinder block as designed, some modification was made to the casing to incorporate the steam pipes. Note that the drawing shows a cab, running plate and valances like the A4 Pacifics, which was not fitted to the production locomotives. Courtesy of the R.C.T.S.*

The reasonably successful introduction of Nos.2001 and 2002 to work in Scotland led to an order for four further locomotives, and these were completed during 1936. The introduction of the A4 Pacifics in 1935 had highlighted the excellence of the streamlined front end for smoke deflection, and with the issues of No.2002, and to a lesser extent, No.2001 well known, the remaining P2s were to emerge with a variation of the A4 streamlined casing, with steam pipes more prominent and with a slight bulge over the cylinder covers.

*Fig. 196. An unidentified member of the Gresley P2 under construction, showing the complex shape of both the front of the valances and the teardrop shape of the casing over the smokebox. Note the running plate at the cab end follows the design of that fitted to the Gresley A3s, not the A4 Pacifics. The Gresley Society.*

At its general overhaul in 1936, *Earl Marischal* was rebuilt to conform with the other four locomotives. *Cock O'The North* followed suit in 1937, with a more in-depth conversion during the overhaul by way of replacing its Lentz gear with the now standard conjugated valve gear and outside Walschaerts fitted. The six P2 locomotives by 1938 were all in service but represented some variations on the same theme. This is best summarised, as seen below:

- No.2001 *Cock O The North* had been built as the sole Lentz gear fitted locomotive, rebuilt to streamlined form in 1937 and had a non-corridor eight-wheel tender with spoked wheels. This was classified as P2/1 when built and became P2/2 when rebuilt. Tablet catcher apparatus was only fitted to the locomotive just prior to entering regular service in Scotland.

- No.2002 *Earl Marischal* had been built as the sole semi-streamlined piston valve fitted locomotive, rebuilt to streamlined form in 1936. It was always classified as P2/2, the significant difference between P2/1 and P2/2 being the piston valves fitted to the latter. Tablet catcher apparatus was only fitted to the locomotive just prior to entering regular service in Scotland.

- No.2003 *Lord President* was the first of the streamlined P2/2s and featured a change to the tender type with an A4 style streamlined non-corridor tender fitted, and tablet catcher apparatus fitted from new.

- No.2004 *Mons Meg* was largely identical to *Lord President* but was unique amongst the P2s in being fitted with a bypass valve to divert a portion of its exhaust from the blastpipe.

- No.2005 *Thane of Fife* was again largely identical to *Lord President*, except for being fitted with a single blastpipe and chimney instead of the double Kylchap arrangement on all the other P2s. This reversion to the single chimney undoubtedly contributed to this locomotive's reputation being poorer in relation to the rest of the class.

- No.2006 *Wolf of Badenoch* was also almost identical to *Lord President*, however featured additional roof vents (like that seen on the A4 Pacifics), together with a larger combustion chamber in its boiler. This difference in boiler diagram led to the locomotive being sub classified as P2/3. The boiler, diagram 108, would be unique and was largely based on the diagram 107 boiler of the A4 Pacifics. It would later form the template for the standard Thompson/Peppercorn diagram 118 boiler.

The P2s were diagrammed to run Edinburgh-Dundee and Dundee-Aberdeen, with an engine change made at Dundee in both directions. This was a change of policy from the original intention of the P2s running Edinburgh-Aberdeen without changing locomotive. Some secondary sources have suggested that the locomotives presented issues for single crew working, with the coal consumption high and the effort required by the fireman significant. In the short time between coming into service as a class, and the start of the Second World War, the locomotives suffered from some mechanical issues, which increased in regularity and seriousness as the war intensified. This issues were in part due to the design of the locomotives and the significant reduction in manpower for maintenance tasks across the railway. The main issues of failure concerned the pony truck, axle boxes and the crank axles.

In the case of the pony truck, the design as used on the P2 was an almost verbatim copy of that fitted to Gresley's K3 2-6-0 locomotive. The running characteristics of this pony truck were well known, and though suitable for the smaller and less powerful mogul type, the heavier and more powerful P2 type seemed to make this pony truck become run down more quickly. This, in combination with the tight curvature of the Edinburgh-Aberdeen line, led to a constant myriad of overheating and wear issues.

*Fig. 197. Gresley P2 No.2001 Cock O'The North sits on shed. This atmospheric photograph shows well the curvature of the smoke deflectors and the casing at the rear of the chimney. This was designed, like the W1, to channel air up and away from the Driver's vision. Strathwood Library Collection.*

It has been reported by several secondary sources that the main issue was the swing links. The swing link holes would wear down more quickly, resulting in the pony truck to not guide the locomotive into corners as designed, the main stresses in fact being placed on the front set of driving wheels. This resulted in significant wear on the coupling rods and outside crankpins, with the latter replaced more often than was usual for L.N.E.R. locomotives.

*Fig. 198. Gresley P2 No.2001 Cock O' The North, on its first visit to King's Cross. To the right of the photograph is the preserved Gresley N2 No.4744. Colourised by Ian MacCabe, The Gresley Society.*

This pony truck issue also led to overheating the driving wheel axle boxes, with locomotives being stopped for re-metalling of the axle boxes more often than the Pacific classes.

The piston loads of the P2s was 34 tons, one of the highest figures recorded for L.N.E.R. locomotives fitted with the conjugated valve gear and outside Walschaerts. The middle end bearings suffered the most, these being a slightly enlarged version of the A3 classes' type (and these locomotives had a max piston force of 30 tons by comparison). Overheating of the middle big end was a perennial problem for the P2s, and unlike the A1s, A3s and A4s, in the most extreme cases the stresses on the crank axles would cause structural failure.

There are three officially recorded crank axle failures on the Gresley P2s, as outlined below:

- 18 July 1939. *Thane of Fife* fractures its crank axle leaving Stonehaven with an Aberdeen – King's Cross train.

- 27 May 1942. *Mons Meg* fractures its crank axle leaving Kirkcaldy with an Edinburgh – Aberdeen Express.

- 29 July 1944. *Lord President* fractures its crank axle two miles out of Aberdeen whilst hauling an Aberdeen – Edinburgh Express.

One notable trend between the first two officially recorded instances of crank axle failure is that the locomotives had been in service for some time and were starting trains of over 500 tons tare in weight. In the third instance the failure happened some time into the trip.

There are two further records of crank axle failures on No.2002 *Earl Marischal* and No.2006 *Wolf of Badenoch,* however these are in relation to their maintenance records and further details are not available at present for public viewing. Only the prototype P2 No.2001 *Cock O' The North* was not recorded with such a failure of its crank axle. Speculatively speaking, this could be down to the locomotive's conversion from Lentz valve gear to piston valve gear, a new crank axle perhaps fitted during the locomotive's heavy overhaul.

With five out of the six locomotives suffering from crank axle failure, that represented a very high failure rate amongst the class. There was also a question of safety, and a mark would have been recorded against any chief mechanical engineer who failed to act on something so significant as a crank axle failure on a passenger train, never mind multiple over a period of ten years.

Post-war, the Merchant Navy class Bulleid Pacific *Bibby Line* fractured its crank axle at Crewkerne station at high speed (between 70 and 80 mph). It is more by luck than by design that the train did not derail and cause both death and damage. The entire class of locomotives was withdrawn from service for close examination, and it was discovered that the fractures, caused by metal fatigue, was a common fault amongst the class. A redesigned crank axle was provided for the class. Gresley V2s and Thompson B1s from the Eastern Region were drafted in to cover the absent Merchant Navy locomotives.

In *Locomotives of the L.N.E.R. Part 6B*, it is stated that the "annual mileage figures, and mileages between shopping to works of the P2s were on a par with those of the Scottish Pacifics". This statement has been used by other secondary sources as evidence that the reliability and availability issues of the P2s were not significant.

However, during the research for writing my previous work *Edward Thompson: Wartime C.M.E.*, primary evidence from the L.N.E.R. was found at the National Archives at Kew known as the *Use of Engine Power* document, together with full copies of the six locomotives' engine record cards.

These primary sources show that the P2s mileages were significantly less than the Scottish Pacifics working alongside them. At their best they achieved 12,000 miles per year less than other locomotive classes that were employed on either the same or similar work on the same route.

Fig. 199. Gresley P2 No.2002 Earl Marischal as built, waiting on shed. With outside Walschaerts valve gear but fitted with the same deflectors as No.2001, No.2002 represented a midway point between the final streamlined Mikados and the Lentz gear fitted Cock O'The North.
Colourised by Ian MacCabe, The Gresley Society.

Fig. 199b. Seen from a slightly wider angle here at Dundee in 1935, we can see the curvature of the smoke deflectors to better advantage. William Clark/Rail Archive Stephenson

This difference in annual average mileage isn't easily explained away. The statistics below give the lifetime and average annual mileages for the six P2s and in their A2/2 format:

| Loco No. | Date Built | Date Rebuilt | Date Withdrawn | No. years as P2 | Total Mileage as P2 | Average Annual Mileage | No. years as A2/2 | Total Mileage as A2/2 | Average Annual Mileage |
|---|---|---|---|---|---|---|---|---|---|
| 2001 | May-34 | Sep-44 | Feb-60 | 10 | 362,136 | 36,214 | 15 | 616,461 | 41,097 |
| 2002 | Oct-34 | Jun-44 | Jul-61 | 9 | 360,907 | 40,101 | 17 | 673,947 | 39,644 |
| 2003 | Jun-36 | Dec-44 | Nov-59 | 8 | 246,283 | 30,785 | 14 | 508,498 | 36,321 |
| 2004 | Jul-36 | Nov-44 | Jan-61 | 8 | 294,243 | 36,780 | 16 | 694,797 | 43,425 |
| 2005 | Aug-36 | Jan-43 | Nov-59 | 6 | 225,739 | 37,623 | 16 | 673,464 | 42,092 |
| 2006 | Sep-36 | May-44 | Apr-61 | 7 | 287,187 | 41,027 | 16 | 629,013 | 39,313 |
| Class Average | N/A | N/A | N/A | 8 | 296,083 | 37,088 | 16 | 632,697 | 40,315 |

*Fig. 200. P2 and A2/2 Mileages Statistics. Simon A.C. Martin, from the Use of Engine Power Document & Engine Record Cards.*

## Wartime Mileages & Availability

The locomotives performed poorly during the early years of the Second World War. Although noted on troop trains between Perth and Newcastle, there were periods where the number of P2s available to run services was minimal, with Gresley's Pacifics stepping in and doing their work on several occasions.

| Year | Mileages | Availability |
|---|---|---|
| 1942 | 34784 | 57% |
| 1943 | 25357 | 46% |
| 1944 | 0 | 0% |
| 1945 | 0 | 0% |
| 1946 | 0 | 0% |

*Fig. 201. P2 Mileages & Availability Statistics. Simon A.C. Martin, from the Use of Engine Power Document.*

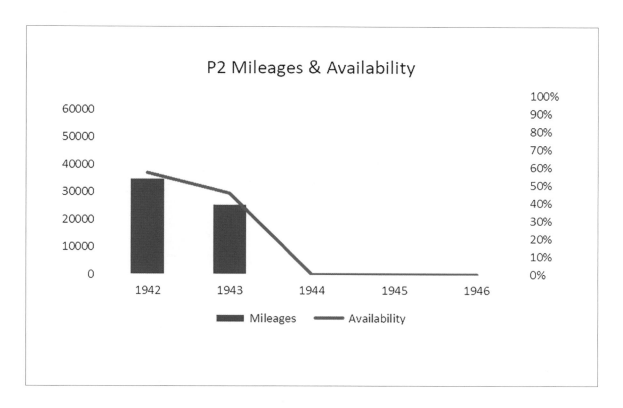

*Fig. 202. P2 Mileages & Availability Graph.*
*Simon A.C. Martin from the Use of Engine Power Document.*

## Overall Conclusions

Where the Gresley P2s are concerned, there are clear facts that need to be understood when writing on them. Those facts are as follows:

•       The front pony truck was not robust enough for the P2 design.

•       The pony truck caused further wear and uneven tear on other parts of the locomotive, including driving wheel flanges, coupling rods, axle boxes and more.

•       The crank axle was not robust enough for the P2 design.

•       The adhesive weight of the eight coupled driving wheels will have also contributed to the crank axle failure, by way of preventing slipping in high torque conditions. Slipping driving wheels alleviates stresses on the various crank pins and axles in a manner like the Gresley Pacifics.

•       The curvature of the Scottish mainline was also a significant factor in the continued degradation of the locomotive's running and valve gear components, because of the issues with the core features of the locomotive's design.

*Fig. 203. Gresley P2/2 No.2002, Earl Marischal, on a fast fitted fish train soon after rebuilding. Note the water tanker in the train a couple of vans behind the tender. The Gresley Society.*

Some secondary sources have claimed that if the P2s were not in use on certain trains that double heading of locomotives on those trains was the result. However photographic evidence and contemporary reporting shows that the Pacific locomotives, the V2s and the lone W1 were more than capable of handling the P2s stipulated maximum loads. That being the case, and with the six locomotives proving to be mechanically unreliable for most of their working lives, the argument for retaining the P2s altogether must be questioned.

In relation to the maximum loading of the P2s, one of Gresley's earliest tests of his original Pacific locomotives was a test train loaded to 600 tons tare weight. This had occurred in 1922. If the low pressure A1 Pacifics could pull such train weights and keep to time, there is little doubt of the ability of any other Pacific locomotive built after then achieving the loads of the P2s. Much is made of the P2's adhesive strength, but this was coming at great mechanical cost to the railway company. *Thane of Fife* as a Pacific worked identical trains to the remaining P2s for over a year and did over double the mileage in the same year. There can be no arguments about which class was providing a better service for the railway company at that time.

*Fig. 204. The first of the streamlined Mikados, No.2003 Lord President, on display in front of recently built prototype V2, No.4771 Green Arrow. Colourised by Ian MacCabe, The Gresley Society.*

There is also the question of safety. Whoever oversaw the railway as Chief Mechanical Engineer would have had to answer for the decision making in relation to the known issues and potential dangers of locomotives that were breaking their crank axles on passenger trains and proving unreliable in service. Much has been made of the P2s breaking their crank axles at low speed, but that the failures did not happen at speed is more by luck than entirely by design.

In acknowledging the issues of the original P2s what else is there to say? There is no doubt, given the efforts of the P2 Trust in identifying and rectifying the design issues of the Gresley P2s in their new build No.2007, that the issues of the Gresley P2s could have been sorted without rebuilding as Pacifics. However, this could only happen if those present at the time could have demonstrated that further crank axle failures would not happen again in future.

There are no easy decisions to be made in peacetime at the top, let alone in the middle of a war which saw the L.N.E.R. lose thousands of maintenance staff and nearly 90% of their workshop and foundry capacity to designing and manufacturing equipment, gun boats, aircraft, and munitions towards the war effort. Rebuilding or scrapping were the obvious answers to the poor performances of the P2 locomotives in 1942, at the time of the second much publicised failure of a crank axle.

Had the Second World War not happened, and if further development work had been undertaken, the P2s may well have improved to the required levels mechanically to ensure their legend. Arguably the controversy of their rebuilding has led to their legend being cemented regardless, albeit with many secondary sources giving an inaccurate picture of events with some unfair criticism aimed at the C.M.E. of the time.

As a founder member of the P2 Trust I believe that No.2007 *Prince of Wales* will finally prove that the original intentions of the Gresley P2 can be realised. Seeing the recreation of Lentz gear fitted P2 will also be a sight to behold. It is highly likely that the modern day P2 will prove most reliable and powerful because of the technical expertise and engineering excellence that has been applied to the redesign of the troublesome parts of the original locomotives.

*Fig 205. The bulge in the casing over the cylinders on Gresley P2 No.2004 Mons Meg is shown to good effect on the Grantham turntable. F.H. Gilford/Rail Archive Stephenson.*

*Fig 205b.Posing for her official portrait at Doncaster in 1936 No.2006 Wolf of Badenoch certainly looks modern and impressive just the image the L.N.E.R. wished to portray.*
*Strathwood Library Collection*

| Class P2 | | | | |
|---|---|---|---|---|
| Sub Class | | P2/1 | P2/2 | P2/3 |
| Cylinders (x3): | | 21x26in. | 21x26in. | 21x26in. |
| Motion: | Inside: | Lentz R.C. | Gresley conjugated | Gresley conjugated |
| | Outside: | | Walschaerts | Walschaerts |
| | Valves: | 8in & 9in Poppet | 9in Piston | 9in Piston |
| Boiler: | Max. Diameter: | 6ft 5in | 6ft 5in | 6ft 5in |
| | Pressure: | 220lb | 220lb | 220lb |
| | Diagram No.: | 106 | 106 | 108 |
| Heating Surface: | Total: | 3490.5 sq. ft | 3490.5 sq. ft | 3346.5 sq. ft. |
| | Firebox: | 237 sq. ft | 237 sq. ft | 252.5 sq. ft. |
| | Tubes: | 1354.2 sq. ft (121x 2.25in) | 1354.2 sq. ft (121x 2.25in) | 1281.4 sq. ft. (121x 2.25in) |
| | Flues: | 1122.8 sq. ft (43x 5.25in) | 1122.8 sq. ft (43x 5.25in) | 1063.7 sq. ft. (43x 5.25in) |
| | Superheater: | 776.5 sq. ft (43x 1.244in) | 776.5 sq. ft (43x 1.244in) | 748.9 sq. ft. (43x 1.244in) |
| Grate Area: | | 50 sq. ft. | 50 sq. ft. | 50 sq. ft. |
| Wheels: | Leading: | 3ft 2in | 3ft 2in | 3ft 2in |
| | Coupled: | 6ft 2in | 6ft 2in | 6ft 2in |
| | Trailing: | 3ft 8in | 3ft 8in | 3ft 8in |
| Tractive Effort: | | 43,462lb at 85% boiler pressure | | |
| Wheelbase: | Total: | 64ft 0.9in | 64ft 0.9in | 64ft 0.9in |
| | Engine: | 37ft 11in | 37ft 11in | 37ft 11in |
| | Tender: | 16ft 0in | 16ft 0in | 16ft 0in |
| Weight (full): | Total: | 165 tons 11cwt | 167 tons 6cwt | 167 tons 10 cwt |
| | Engine: | 110 tons 5 cwt | 109 tons 8 cwt | 107 tons 3 cwt |
| | Tender: | 55 tons 6 cwt | 57 tons 18 cwt | 60 tons 7 cwt |
| Max. Axle Load: | | 20 tons 10 cwt | 20 tons 14 cwt | 20 tons |

# L.N.E.R

## Class A4 4-6-2 (1935)
### Number built (L.N.E.R.): 35

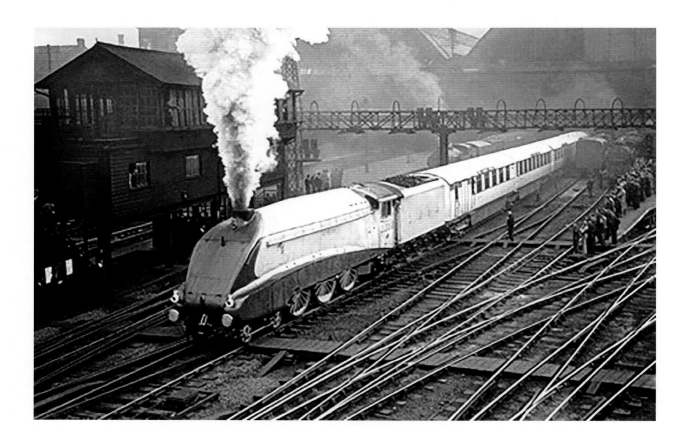

*Fig. 206. Gresley A4 No.2509 Silver Link on its inaugural press run pulling the Silver Jubilee from King's cross to Newcastle in 1935. Colourised by Ian MacCabe/The Gresley Society.*

Gresley's most iconic design was undoubtedly the A4 Pacific, with the blue streak's influence still seen today in the lining out of the front end of the modern day L.N.E.R.'s Azuma high-speed trains. The development of the A4 Pacific really started in 1915 with Gresley's original Pacific outline. There was a continual demand for longer trains and higher average speeds between capital cities and other destinations.

With the emergence of *Great Northern* by 1922, Gresley had produced the basic mechanical layout subsequently used for all future Pacific locomotives. This layout was developed into the A3 Pacific with a boiler pressure of 220lb, long lap travel valves and, in the case of No.2751 *Humorist*, the inclusion of a double chimney and blastpipe. Other influences are also evidence, not least the aerodynamic work that was carried on the W1.

A.J. Mullay in his book *Streamlined Steam* states that there was some issue of knowing where the experimentation for the A4 started, citing that Gresley's comments regarding "previous test results using one-twelfth scale models" was "downright puzzling". He also questioned over where the nature of the "wedge shaped front end" came from. The truth of the matter is quite simple: the curvature and symmetry of the A4 shape was not, in fact, wedge shaped at all. It was far more complex and more carefully thought out than that.

The original tests in question were those of the Gresley W1, done in the late 1920s to determine the best shape for smoke deflection, the pre heating intakes and the streamlining of the casing. This resulted in the first streamlined casing present on a Gresley locomotive. The W1 work influenced both the shape and design of the chimney and the overall profile of the A4's front casing, as experimentation with the W1 models in the 1920s had produced a locomotive with certain starting points for further aerodynamic development work. (As an aside, the W1's 1/12th scale model owned by the L.N.E.R was later used for streamlined testing in Frederick Johansen's experiments for the L.N.E.R.'s and L.M.S.' streamlined developments).

Tim Hillier-Graves in his books *Gresley and his Locomotives* and *Gresley's Silver Link* shows that there was significant design and development overlap in the 1930s with the L.M.S. *Coronation Scot*, where the same technical staff (including Frederick Johansen, the wind tunnel specialist) in attendance to develop the designs. The L.M.S. used their wind tunnel experiences to create the Coronation class, the L.N.E.R. used theirs to create the A4 Pacific.

The design evolved through several stages in the drawing office, informed by the wind tunnel work.

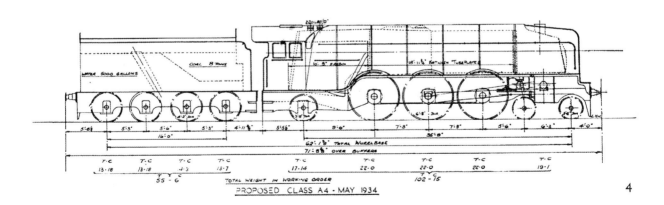

Fig. 207. Gresley A4 Line Drawing, Doncaster Works, 1934. The family resemblance to the Gresley P2 is very clear here, albeit with splashers as per the A3 Pacifics on the running plate. Note the single chimney fitted. Courtesy of the R.C.T.S.

In May 1934, the first outline drawing for the A4 Pacific had been produced and it was in effect the P2 Mikado arrangement, compete with Lentz gear, rearranged to a Pacific format. This proposal included the V-shaped front cab and splashers with a conventional boiler arrangement (pressed to 220lb, as per the A3 Pacifics) albeit identical in setup with regards the smoke deflectors at the front end to the prototype P2, No.2001. This design included a stovepipe single chimney, different from the P2s and was not to be repeated after this drawing. The trials of P2 No.2001 in its original form put paid to this early version of the A4 Pacific and it was dropped.

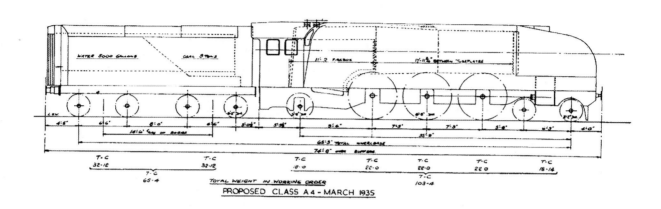

*Fig. 208. Gresley A4 Line Drawing, Doncaster Works, 1935. This time the similarities are with the Gresley W1, with the outside leading edge of the deflectors and the single chimney arrangement the biggest nods to the water tube boiler locomotive. For the first time, the driving wheels are covered with the casing a straight line from the bottom edge of the cab to the front of the locomotive. Note the streamlined bogie tender, not to be seen again after this. Courtesy of the R.C.T.S.*

The next proposal for the A4 Pacific appeared in March 1935. The starting point above the frames was the basic arrangement of the W1's front casing and chimney, together with the tapered in sides of the W1's front smoke box casing. Gresley had the V-fronted cab of the P2 incorporated again, but now with no cab cut out at the rear. The front end of the locomotive reverted mechanically to the conventional design of his Pacifics, complete with Walschaerts valve gear and conjugated gear. The smoke deflectors and the teardrop shaped single chimney of this design was almost pure W1 in approach.

However, below the smoke deflectors a casing over the driving wheels was proposed. This was the first time in the development of the A4 that it was recognised that reducing the drag as much as possible around the driving wheels was also required to produce a more optimal aerodynamic shape. This drawing was likely turned into a wooden model *or* was based on the relevant wooden model that was the first tested in the wind tunnel by Frederick Johansen and his team (of these, it seems most likely that this is related to model no.6207/2).

A further unique aspect of this design was the bogie tender, which for the first time in the classes' development featured curved ends either side of the corridor at the rear. This aspect was retained going forward, but the flat front to the tender sides were not. Some experimentation occurred physically with the modification of an A3 cab and associated tender but in the event this part of the design was discarded in the next iteration.

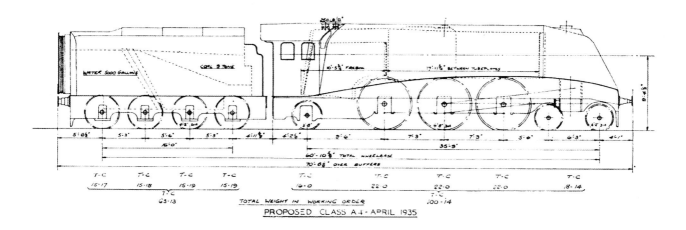

*Fig. 209. Gresley A4 Line Drawing, Doncaster Works, 1935. The wheels are covered again but this time the aerofoil shape has made its first appearance. The front of the locomotive is distinctly angled in relation to the chimney. There is no corresponding wooden model for this locomotive drawing. The tender's front edges have reverted to something closer to the original eight-wheel tenders of the L.N.E.R. Pacifics. Courtesy of the R.C.T.S.*

The wind tunnel testing appeared to produce some new results, with a further drawing being issued of a new profile with a separate casing over the driving wheels and the replacement of the bogie tender with a streamlined version of the normal eight-wheel L.N.E.R. corridor tender. The covering over the driving wheels was now separate from the boiler casing and formed a more aerofoil shape than the previous version, but not as high in profile, nor as long, ending at the front of the cab rather than towards the rear on the final design.

The front end of the locomotive was now heavily slanted with an unusual arrangement of the single chimney. The profile was split into two flat lines of differing angles, with a curve between them. Like the previous drawing, the cab cut outs were omitted at this time, and presented something of a foreshadowing of the Peppercorn A1 and A2 designs which would later have these straight cab side sheets and semi-V shaped front ends. The buffers at the front seem to have been intended to be the standard type as fitted to classes A1, A3 and P2 at this point. The tender, by comparison, was much closer to the final design, with the eight-wheel fixed wheelbase restored, as were the distinctive cut outs at the front end in the side sheets, but the top of the tender included several layers of streamlined covering, each level slightly lower towards to the rear third of the tender.

By September 1935, further wind tunnel testing and design work had produced the final version of the A4 Pacific. Whereas the L.M.S. had chosen a shape developed by Frederick Johansen that was more in line with that of the developments in Germany, Gresley and the L.N.E.R. eventually went for the front-end drawing 6207/5, with a teardrop shaped front end arrangement and chimney shape.

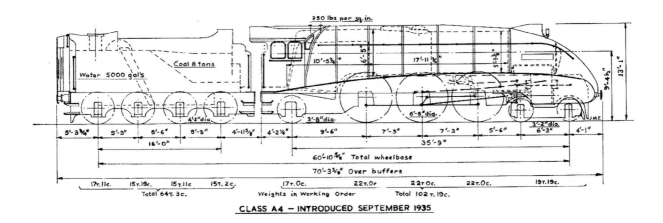

CLASS A4 — INTRODUCED SEPTEMBER 1935

*Fig. 210. Gresley A4 Line Drawing, Doncaster Works, 1935. The final form, as introduced in September 1935. The wind tunnel testing and influences from the P2, W1 and elsewhere have come together to produce an aerodynamically superior, and striking, locomotive shape. The tender is also now close to its final form, featuring the streamlined rear around the corridor connection that would be a feature of the early A4 Pacifics. Courtesy of the R.C.T.S.*

The valances over the wheels were also now more teardrop in profile, echoing the overall shape of the casing at the front end. There was a cut out just behind the cylinders, running along the bottom line of the locomotive and in line with the bottom edge of the tender tank, with cut outs in the valances provided for maintenance access for the outside valve gear, but otherwise the geometry and curvature followed the teardrop shape providing a theoretically low drag coefficient over the valances.

The tender design of the A4 was a further development in streamlining. Great care had been taken for the new design of corridor tender to match the profile of the train behind it, retaining the curved rear section either side of the corridor connection as in previous versions. There was now no beading, as with earlier types, and the tender sides were entirely smooth.

The rear of the tender, where the water filler cap was located, now had a new streamlined fairing to help with the full streamlining of the locomotive and train behind. (During the course of the testing of the W1 and 4472 1/12th scale models, a significant discovery was that a locomotive of poorer aerodynamic shape would in fact help to "shield" the train behind it, where a locomotive of superior aerodynamic shape, if this was not continued onto the tender and train behind, would create more drag on the tender and train behind).

*Fig. 211. An unidentified A4 Pacific being built in April 1938. This is likely to have been one of the last A4s to be built, with only Nos. 4900, 4901, 4902 or 4903 not in service by that time. The arrangement behind the fitter is likely a double chimney setup, given the size of the cut-out, which reduces the potential candidate to just 4902 Seagull or 4903 Peregrine. Note also, the shape of the casing and the front frames, confirming the teardrop outline of the design in a vertical plane. The similarity of the frame design and the placement of the chimney is strikingly like the original W1's. The Gresley Society.*

*Fig. 212. No.2509 Silver Link on one of its first runs in September 1935 passes New Southgate at speed. Rail Archive Stephenson.*

The fairing on the tender, though aerodynamically useful, would ultimately be removed in service as it presented issues when filling the tender with water, and restricted the amount of coal that could be piled up on the tender. The A4 Pacific became a workable compromise between useability and streamlining.

The smokebox's complex curvature from the narrow section between the buffers to the curvature at the top was the most challenging. In contrast to smooth flow over the casing on the rest of the locomotive it was necessary to channel air upwards from the chimney to clear the driver's vision.

The chimney design was developed from the W1's and was also teardrop in profile, albeit in its horizontal cross section, with the main difference between the two designs being the curves around the base of the A4's chimney, in comparison to the vertical, almost stovepipe profile of the W1 chimney design.

The W1 and P2 chimneys had been set at the same height as their smoke deflectors, which due to the loading gauge profile meant the chimney was below the maximum height at the centre of the gauge. Gresley and his team decided this had been an error, and the A4 chimney was increased to the maximum permitted in the LNER composite gauge.

There was one more innovation to come on the chimney side, for which Eric Bannister, one of Gresley's technical assistants, has recorded in full the unintentional moment of genius:

> There was much visiting between the King's Cross and Doncaster offices in connection with the design of the A4. I met Mr Bert Spencer and got to know him. One day he told me to go at once to the Physical Laboratory at Teddington and take with me a wooden model of the A4 to test in the wind tunnel. I was to observe the action of the smoke. I met Professor Dalby whom I had seen before when the streamlining tests had been carried out.
>
> The smoke was simulated by French chalk and took the expected way along the higher part of the boiler and to the cab windows. The fairing at the back of the chimney was shaped level with the top of the boiler and we could think of no way of deflecting chalk other than by providing some [smoke] deflectors at the side of the smokebox. Professor Dalby had some stiff card available for trials, so at first, we tried the model just as it had been supplied from Doncaster and then lifted it out.
>
> When it [the model] was on the table, we noticed a depression in the plasticine fairing behind the chimney, apparently made by one of us when we had lifted out the model from the wind-tunnel. It looked like the mark made by the pressure of a thumb. Professor Dalby said, 'Let's put the wind on and see what happens'. To our surprise, the chalk 'smoke' passed along the boiler but lifted well above the cab windows. We tried it a second time, with the same result.
>
> So Professor Dalby commented, 'it looks as though our accident has found the answer'. We tried again measuring carefully with an instrument now known as a mimic. Our conclusion was that the slight depression seemingly caused a vortex which caused the French chalk to be

## Gresley and Stanier's Pacifics: wind tunnel testing

Some railway writers, including O.S. Nock, have put forward the point of view that the L.M.S.'
Coronation locomotives had superior streamlining to the A4 Pacifics.

There are two main issues to consider here. That of surface area and of shape, both incredibly
important for the flow of fluids and cases around objects. The Stanier design does not conform
to the required shapes for reducing drag: in actuality, the flat vertical front of the Coronation
locomotive creates greater drag. This combined with the circular profile of the casing, meant
that the overall profile of the locomotive from railhead to the top of the chimney was much
wider and less aerodynamic overall.

Not so on the Gresley A4 design, which came in three parts: the valances over the driving
wheels on each side, and the central section covering the smoke box. The three elements came
together with tapers down to the buffers, reducing the overall surface area of the locomotive
further. Gresley's choices here would go on to be echoed in the present day by virtually all high-
speed trains, including the modern day L.N.E.R.'s Hitachi built Azumas.

The L.M.S and L.N.E.R. railway companies would pick the basis of their front-end designs on the
wind tunnel experiments conducted under Frederick Johansen for Professor Dalby. Recently in
Tim Hillier-Graves tomes on Gresley, and his A4 Pacifics, there have been for the first-time
published photographs of many of the front-end models used, which we can then cross
reference with the known line drawings that exist for the A4 Pacific development.

Some secondary sources have pointed to other influences as well. Certainly, a commonly held
belief is that Ettore Bugatti's petrol rail car had an influence on the shape of the Gresley Pacific.

*The shape of the streamlined front end was modelled on the French Petrol Railcar
designed by Bugatti. The final arrangement was obtained by Doncaster from the results
of wind tunnel experiments.*

*Locomotives of the L.N.E.R. Part 2A, page 92 (1973 Edition)*

It is difficult to ascertain how true this was. There are however echoes of similar shapes
between the Ettore Bugatti designed rail cars and the Gresley designed steam locomotive.
Viewed head on, the narrow central section under the buffers rising out to a wider form whilst
retaining the overall teardrop shape in profile is unmistakable on both, but by no means
identical.

It seems more likely that Bugatti and Gresley came to similar conclusions on the overall shape of their front ends entirely independently. There is certainly no internal reference to Bugatti's designs within the L.N.E.R. archives at Kew or the N.R.M. in relation to the rail cars. There was another assertion made by a secondary source in relation to the shape of the A4 Pacific's aerofoil shape over the wheels:

> ...Even whilst No.2509 was under construction, changes were being made to the streamlined casing. When Gresley saw that the shape of the casing over the wheels was not following his ideas (though it did in fact literally follow his rough pencil sketches), the chief draughtsman was told to put the matter right. Gresley said that what he wanted was a true aerofoil shape. Technical journals were hastily searched, and a drawing was found of the R-101 airship, which had the desired shape.

*Locomotives of the L.N.E.R. Part 2A, page 93 (1973 Edition)*

This appears to be backed up by the archives of Frederick Johansen, who worked for the L.M.S. and L.N.E.R. at the N.P.L. in the early thirties. Amongst his archives was found technical drawings and references to the R101 test model, which was put into a wind tunnel for experiments as early as 1926. The use of the R101 shape as inspiration for the aerofoil shape has legitimacy in terms of the scientific development of aerodynamics. It conforms to the known parameters in shape that are known to improve air flow around objects.

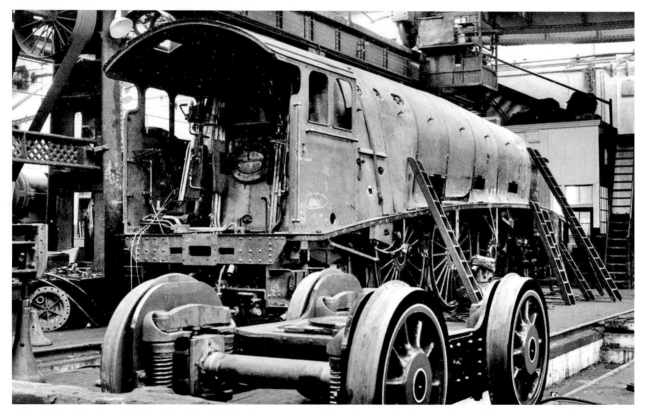

*Fig. 213. Gresley A4 Pacific, No.4491 Commonwealth of Australia being built. Of note is the four-wheel bogie in the foreground, of the Pacific type and likely intended for a Gresley A3 or A1.*
*The Gresley Society.*

Based on the primary evidence that has been presented, together with the known dimensions and shapes inherent in the Gresley A4, it would be more accurate to describe the overall shapes present on the A4 Pacific as *teardrop* in outline and thereby conforming more closely to the best principles of streamlining in aerodynamics and fluid mechanics, rather than "wedge shaped", which at one stage of the drawing development it *was* (see the April 1935 drawing) but was *definitely not* after great refinement to the final shape by way of the wind tunnel experiments and even when physically working on the prototype, No.2509 *Silver Link*.

*Fig. 214. The prototype Gresley A4 No.2509 Silver Link, at King's Cross in its first few weeks of service in September 1935. Note the short buffer shanks, and the recessed coupling at the front of the casing. This would be modified to long buffer shanks and the coupling further forward after an accident during shunting when a worker was crushed and died. The reason for recessing the coupling and shortening the buffers was for streamlining the locomotive. R.C.T.S. Collection.*

## Silver Link and The Silver Jubilee

By March 1935, the order had been increased to four locomotives for the specific purpose of hauling the planned *Silver Jubilee* train. This too was undergoing great development and the carriages were also streamlined. This was achieved by placing curved valances between the bogies of each coach body down to 10in above rail head and by utilising curved steel sheets across the coach sides.

Crucially the locomotive and train were designed hand in hand, with the gaps between the coaches being covered with an aluminium-coloured rubber sheeting, further streamlining the vehicles. The roofs of the coaches were smooth, the only components breaking the air flow being those of the ventilation system.

The train itself originally consisted of seven coaches, arranged in two articulated pairs and one triple (with the centre coach, the restaurant coach body, riding on two bogies and forming an articulated triplet). Later this would be extended to eight coaches with the rear twin converted into a triplet with the addition of another vehicle.

The seating arrangements were originally comprised of 28 seats in the first-class restaurant car, 48 seats in the third class and brake set, with 72 further passengers in the third-class cars, 32 in the twin first class and brake coaches and the open section seating 18 passengers.

This gave an original total seating of 198 passengers for 220 tons tare weight. The chief architects in the design of the train were Robert Thom, (Mechanical Engineer at Doncaster Works), Alfred Willetts (Chief Carriage & Wagon Draughtsman), Frank Day (Technical Assistant at King's Cross) and Norman Newsome (Doncaster Apprentice and Draughtsman, later promoted into Alfred Willetts' role).

These four men together with Bert Spencer supported Gresley in realising his vision, with much of the design work and construction of the *Silver Jubilee* train set carried out at Doncaster Works.

The L.N.E.R produced a pamphlet to advertise the train, for which the following showcases the train, its accommodation, and its point-to-point timings. This can be found in Appendix 8 at the back of this book. On the rear of the pamphlet was this quotation, picked out in silver lettering:

> *True love's the gift which God has given*
>
> *To man alone beneath the heaven...*
>
> *...It is the secret sympathy,*
>
> *The silver link, the silken tie,*
>
> *Which heart to heart, and mind to mind*
>
> *In body and in soul can bind.*
>
> *Lay of the Last Minstrel, Canto V, Stanza XIII, Sir Walter Scott*

There seems no doubt that the name for the prototype A4 Pacific, *Silver Link*, was derived from the line of this verse in Sir Walter Scott's *Lay of the Last Minstrel*.

From the order in March 1935 for the first four A4 Pacifics, to the unveiling of the class

*Fig. 215. Gresley A4 Pacific, No.2509 Silver Link as outshopped from Doncaster Works. Note that the black parabolic curve has yet to be painted on the side of the smokebox casing, and that she carries nameplates, instead of having the name painted on the casing as when finally in service.*
*The Gresley Society.*

Fig. 216. The L.N.E.R. did not hesitate in making the most of its promotional material for Britain's "First streamlined train" as this poster from 1935 demonstrates ably. The Gresley Society.

prototype *Silver Link* in September 1935, the bulk of the design and manufacturing of the *Silver Jubilee* train had taken just over a six-month period. It was an extraordinary turn around, even by the high standards of Gresley and the L.N.E.R.

*Silver Link* undertook the trial publicity run for the new service on 27 September 1935, a few days before the train would enter full service. It is not an understatement to say that nothing quite like this had been achieved before, and certainly nothing the like since. It was reported extensively throughout the world's press, with the following from *Railway Wonders of the World*:

> *The ability of "Silver Link" - the first engine of the new class - to travel at the requisite speed was demonstrated in an astonishing fashion at the trial trip which was made on September 27, 1935, three days before the introduction of the new service. Several world's railway records were broken once the train had got into speed. After mounting the initial incline to Holloway, the engine reached 70 miles an hour on the short level stretch to Wood Green, and slowly but steadily accelerated up the long 1 in 200 to Potter's Bar until the summit was breasted at 75 miles an hour. Then the "Silver Jubilee" fairly flew. A speed of 98 miles an hour was attained as the Lea was crossed beyond Hatfield, followed by 88 miles over the summit level near Knebworth, and 95 miles at Langley Troughs. Then the long descent to Huntingdon began. At mile post 30 the magic "hundred" line was crossed.*

> *For the next twenty-five miles the speed never once fell below one hundred miles an hour, and twice rose to 112 - near Arlesey and between Biggleswade and Sandy. This stretch of twenty-five miles was covered at an average rate of 107.5 miles an hour and formed part of a total distance of forty-three miles covered at the one hundred average.*

> *No such figures have been previously known on rails, whether with steam, diesel, or electric propulsion. It is only in the single particular of the maximum speed attained that the "Silver Jubilee" has to acknowledge a superior, for the new German streamlined 4-6-4 express engine touched, on trial with a train of only 196 tons, a momentary maximum of 119½ miles an hour.*

> *The detailed times and speeds on this wonderful journey, in which the writer was privileged to participate, are fully set out in the table. Over no fewer than seventy miles continuously up hill and down dale, from Wood Green until the brakes were applied at Fletton Junction for the slowing through Peterborough, the speed averaged 91.8 miles an hour - yet another clear record for steam. Peterborough was passed in 55 minutes 2 seconds from King's Cross, or ten minutes less than the schedule of the "Silver Jubilee" service, and after but little more than a quarter of the journey had been accomplished. It was small wonder that signal checks soon followed, for "Silver Link" had caught up the regular express which had left London forty-five minutes previously. The trial trip was from London to Grantham and back, and as a performance of a locomotive barely a month old was in every way an amazing demonstration of ability.*

*It is in view of the exceptional speed and comfort provided by the "Silver Jubilee" that a supplementary fare over and above the ordinary ticket is made for its use. The charge is five shillings to first-class and three shillings to third-class passengers. For many years past the only "extra fare" trains in Great Britain have been those composed exclusively of Pullman cars; but the "Silver Jubilee" represents a definite inquiry by the LNER as to whether the British public really does desire facilities of this description.*

*The gain in time over the best ordinary all-the-year-round service between London and Newcastle is no less than sixty-seven minutes, so that the benefit conferred is considerable. Further justification for the additional charge is found in the new rolling stock which has been built specially for the service, and for the disturbance of other and slower-moving traffic which cannot be avoided when a time-table path has to be found for an ultra-speedy express such as this. The aim of the LNER operating authorities is to keep the train to that path with strict punctuality. The "Silver Jubilee" was put into regular daily service on September 30, 1935, and the "Pacific" locomotive No. 2509 "Silver Link", although scarcely a month old, and therefore not fully run in, showed itself capable of continuous running involving journeys of over 536 miles a day at average speeds considerably in excess of 70 miles an hour, for the first fortnight continuously, until the second engine "Quicksilver" was ready to share the work, without any trace of mechanical defect. This is in itself a fine testimony to the excellence of both the workmanship and the design.*

*Since its record-breaking run the locomotive, the first of its class, has shown itself capable of handling the express in accordance with the schedule without recourse to excessive speeds on favourable stretches of line. The general public, as soon as this new service became available to them, were quick to convey their appreciation of the smooth running and comfortable appointments of the train.*

*Railway Wonders of the World, Volume 15, Famous Trains*

The first run by No.2509 included an absolute maximum top speed of 112 mph, but more impressive was the sustained running of over 100 mph for 25 miles between Arlesey and Sandy. No other steam locomotive to that date had achieved sustained high-speed running of this kind, and it was also well above the average figures for diesel and electric trains to that date. There can be no doubt that the streamlining of the locomotive and train was a significant factor in the successful running.

That *Silver Link* then went on to be the sole locomotive running the *Silver Jubilee* train for the next two weeks, whilst its sister locomotives were completed at Doncaster, with no train failures or late running recorded at all. No.2509 completed 536 miles continuous running every single day, with over 8000 miles run total over that period with no train failures. This was an extraordinary achievement without equal in Britain's railway history. That *Silver Link* never seems to be mentioned for this achievement outside of L.N.E.R. circles, is something of an oversight on the part of many railway commentators.

*Fig. 217. Gresley A4 Pacific, No.2509 Silver Link as prepared for the new Silver Jubilee service.*
*The Gresley Society.*

This locomotive and its rolling stock worked "straight out of the box" and is a testament to the scientific principles, engineering know-how, hard work and support that Gresley, his design team, hired in contractors (e.g., Frederick Johansen and Professor W.E. Dalby), the staff at Doncaster works, the crews on the train and those maintaining the signalling equipment and permanent way showed in the development of the *Silver Jubilee* train. It remains one of Sir Nigel Gresley's greatest achievements as a railway engineer and this train pointed the way forward for all high-speed trains to come.

There was one disappointment with the train, which happened eleven months after the first scheduled services. On a run into King's Cross *Silver Fox* achieved a top speed of 113 mph, a new speed record. However, the middle big end overheated, but the train did arrive at King's Cross, albeit seven minutes late with *Silver Fox* then removed for repair. This record would later be taken by the L.M.S.' Coronation Scot, achieving 114 mph.

*Fig. 218. The interior of the beavertail observation car on The Coronation. Note the arm chairs and the shape of the window at the rear. Happily, both of the observation cars have survived to the present day and No.1729 has been restored to its original form. Strathwood Library Collection.*

## The Coronation

The second streamlined train developed for the L.N.E.R. came into service on 3 July 1937. The development of this streamlined train directly followed that of the Silver Jubilee, incorporating articulated twin coach sets, streamlined sides and valances and, with the summer timetable, the introduction of a streamlined observation coach.

*The Coronation* was timed to cover the 188 miles between King's Cross and York in just 157 minutes, at an average speed of just under 72 mph. The train would then run non-stop to Edinburgh in 200 minutes for 205 miles at an average speed of just over 61 mph. The tare load was 312-ton gross. In the opposite direction, *The Coronation* ran Edinburgh to Newcastle, 124 miles done in 120 minutes at an average speed of 62 mph. It then ran from Newcastle to King's Cross (268 miles) at an average speed of 68 mph in 237 minutes.

The L.N.E.R produced a pamphlet to advertise the train, for which the following showcases the train, its accommodation, and its point-to-point timings. This can be found in Appendix 8 at the back of this book.

Fig. 219. Gresley A4 No. 4492 *Dominion of New Zealand thunders through Peterborough North with the Coronation on 27 September 1937. Rail Archive Stephenson.*

*Fig. 220. Gresley A4 No.4484 Falcon is examined by a member of its crew in this rare colour photograph of the A4s in the late 1930s. Note the black top to the tender above the beading and the colour of the wheels throughout, painted red to the edges of the tyres. Colour Rail.*

The locomotives for this train were painted in a blue livery, with red wheelsets and with the black smokebox and parabolic curve to be lined out in white and red. In a similar fashion to the secondary sources pointing towards Bugatti for the shape of the locomotive, much has been made of the French blue racing colours used on his race cars and the new blue livery of the A4 Pacifics that were prepared for pulling *The Coronation* train, and the slight variation (without stainless steel numerals and lettering) which became the standard for the entire A4 fleet. There seems to be no official instruction or mention of the Bugatti livery anywhere in archive L.N.E.R internal documents and literature.

There is therefore nothing in the way of primary evidence to link Bugatti and Gresley's work, yet even in the 21st Century, the myth pervades with such things as a poster in 2011 that was prepared for the Retromobile classic car show in Paris showed one of Bugatti's race cars being passed by a Gresley A4 in garter blue and pulling *The Coronation* train. *The Coronation* train was painted in specific colours alluding to the 1937 Coronation of King George VI. The Railway Magazine reported the following at the time of entry into service:

> *The engines are painted garter blue, with dark red wheels, and stainless-steel letters, numbers, and mouldings. The train, too, is garter blue below the waistline but Marlborough blue above; stainless steel is also used for lettering, each coach carrying the name "Coronation" in the centre of the body and again across the full width of the rear end of the tail car, below the windows.*

*The Railway Magazine, Page 81, August Edition, 1937*

So, the Bugatti link to the A4's most iconic livery may yet be a myth. It cannot be denied, however, that the blue of the racing cars to this day bears a distinctly striking resemblance to that applied to the A4 Pacifics.

*Fig. 221. Gresley A4 No.4487 Sea Eagle in its short-lived version of the L.N.E.R. apple green livery as applied to some of the A4s. Note the straight black rear edge to the smokebox casing, which on other locomotives was painted as a parabolic curve. Strathwood Library Collection.*

## The Flying Scotsman

During the same year as the introduction of *The Coronation*, A4 Pacifics began working the *Flying Scotsman* train in the summer of 1937. This train had been the preserve of the Gresley A1s and A3s for an uninterrupted nine years, with only the prototype W1 high pressure steam locomotive also working the train in the 1930s. The A4s ran the non-stop service highly successfully, and their appearance at the front of the train led to further improvement on the timings and workings of this prestigious train.

## The West Riding Limited

The *West Riding Limited* was introduced in 1937 as the final streamlined train, operating between London King's Cross and Leeds and Bradford. The train was timed to run at an average speed of 64 mph across the route. The coaches used for the *West Riding* were identical to *The Coronation* sets of 1935 and comprised four twin articulated coaches with two kitchen cars in each train set. There were seats for 48 first class and 168 third-class passengers. The service started on 27 September 1937 when the first train was hauled by No.4492 *Dominion of New Zealand*.

The L.N.E.R produced a pamphlet to advertise the train, for which the following showcases the train, its accommodation, and its point-to-point timings. This can be found in Appendix 8 at the back of this book.

*Fig. 222. Gresley A4 No.4467 Wild Swan has lamps fitted for the express passenger code, in preparation for pulling the Aberdonian. Normally the preserve of the Gresley P2s up to this point, the A4s proved masters of their work and were fully capable of taking the heavy train and maintaining the required timings. Strathwood Library Collection.*

Fig. 223. No 4487 Sea Eagle is waiting in the paint shop to be released to traffic. This version of the L.N.E.R.'s apple green livery was short lived, giving way to garter blue by the Second World War for all that were outshopped in green. Rail Archive Stephenson.

Fig. 224. No 4482 Golden Eagle passes Sandy with an express. Note that unlike Sea Eagle, the black smokebox has a full parabolic curve painted, instead of being painted straight back to the first boiler band. Les Hanson/David Hanson Archive/Rail Photoprints.

Fig. 225. Gresley A4 No.4496, still unnamed as yet at Doncaster Works in 1937, but she will take up the name Golden Shuttle. Postwar she would become Dwight D. Eisenhower in recognition of his service as Supreme Commander of the Allied Expeditionary Force in Europe. In addition, the locomotive would become the first of the class to be restored to her pre-war blue livery when named at Marylebone on 27 September 1945. Note the curve of the rear tender tank and the matching curve to the stainless-steel strip at the rear of its base. Strathwood Library collection.

Fig. 226. Gresley A4 No.4900 Gannet passes Potters Bar with the up Yorkshire Pullman. Note the position of the headboard, between the lamps. George C. Lander, Rail Photoprints.

Fig. 227. Gresley A4. No.4468 Mallard flies past onlookers at Ganwick in 1938. In due course, this locomotive would become world famous. Rail Archive Stephenson.

*Fig. 228. Mallard pauses ahead of its fast run during the braking tests on 3 July 1938, the Dynamometer car will do little for the train's streamlining.*
*Strathwood Library Collection.*

## Mallard

By the end of 1937, Gresley and his team were working on an upgrade for the A4 Pacific. The Gresley P2s and the W1 had been fitted with the Kylchap double chimney and this fitting was compared with the single chimney P2, *Thane of Fife*, and the single chimney A4s already in service. The double Kylchap had created a marked improvement in the performance of the water tube W1 locomotive in particular, whereas *Thane of Fife* as a single chimney P2 was proving shyer of steam compared to the rest of its class so fitted.

The order was made for locomotives No.4468, 4901, 4902 and 4903 to be fitted with the new blast pipe arrangement when built. The revised drawings were submitted in January 1938. In March 1938 No.4468, *Mallard* was the first A4 to be outshopped with the Kylchap double chimney. Entering service alongside the single chimney A4s, this locomotive was to be run in for the next three months with a close eye on its work.

The loss of the world speed record from *Silver Link* to the L.M.S., and then this record to the Nazis, was met with frustration from the L.N.E.R. side. In the case of the former, two days after the L.M.S.' *Coronation Scot* had achieved 114 mph, No.4489 *Dominion of Canada*, with *The Coronation* set, was sent out to try and retake the record on the press trip. 109 ½ mph was the top recorded speed, and the disappointment was palpable. Gresley was known to be unhappy at the failure to retake the record.

There was no doubting the superiority of the streamlined A4 for sustained high-speed running, particularly above 100 mph. In the years to come, the A4s would continue to work the top end expresses with such speeds: the issue now was proving that the speed record should rightly belong to the L.N.E.R. and to Gresley.

*Fig. 229. Workers pose alongside DRG No.05 001 as it steams for the first time in March 1935. The class was the fastest steam locomotive to run in continental Europe and held the world speed record for steam traction for two years. This locomotive, number 05 001, is the only member of the class to be preserved. German Federal Archive.*

By June 1938, the world speed record for steam hauled traction was held by Nazi Germany with the DRG Class 05 No. 05 002 achieving a top speed of 124.5 mph on 11 May 1936. This run was exceptional and though the class of three locomotives (two streamlined, and one cab forward streamlined, No.05 003) was used for experimental high-speed running, the speed record was the only real output of the class, with their post war work limited to average speeds significantly lower than that of the Gresley A4 Pacifics (around 87 mph). Still, they were no slouches, and it was with great pride for Nazi Germany that No.05 002 held the record, being recorded in their contemporary press with great aplomb.

The German record had been recorded by way of dynamometer car; the same way that *Papyrus* and *Flying Scotsman* had been recorded for their specific speed runs before. The dynamometer car worked by marking one second time intervals across one foot of paper. The paper was propelled by the turning of the 12ft circumference measuring wheel outside of the coach, applied to the running rail. This gave an accuracy to within a ¼ mph of the speed.

*Fig. 230. Mallard is examined ahead of starting the run. It is likely that one of the men on the right is Eric Bannister or Norman Newsome, who were on the train. Strathwood Library Collection.*

The time was recorded by an electromagnetic pen that was controlled by chronometer, speed being calculated by way of a graduated scale at 5 second intervals.

The choice of 3 July 1938 for the record attempt was obvious: it would be one year to the day of the introduction of *The Coronation* service. This service had become the fastest train schedule to appear in Britain's railway timetables. There was some trepidation approaching the day of the record attempt within the L.N.E.R, and it was suggested to Gresley that their dynamometer car should be modified to make the readings more accurate. This was done by changing the measuring apparatus to record the distance/speed readouts across two feet of paper, instead of the usual one-foot width. This meant that the recording effectively doubled the sensitivity of the data recorded across the paper roll. The dynamometer car recorded one second intervals and each quarter mile travelled.

The train was carefully selected too, with three twin sets from *The Coronation* (photographs show the coaches unbranded, which suggests they formed part of the spare set). The load was 240 tons gross, together with the dynamometer car. Each coach had been fitted with Westinghouse Quick Service Application valves to the vacuum brake cylinders. These allowed air to be admitted directly to each cylinder. This new braking system required testing, and it was proposed that some high-speed test runs including braking applications should be made. This formed a good enough ruse for the day of the test run, which was to make brake applications on the outward journey at Welwyn Garden City, Stevenage, Langford Bridge and Holme, before further tests were made on the rearward journey at Connington, Tempsford, Wymondley and Digswell.

Those within L.N.E.R. circles might have sensed something was up when the crew of driver, Joe Duddington (with a reputation for hard and fast running of steam locomotives) and fireman Thomas Bray were booked specially for the 3 July 1938 run.

The attempt may have been made more obvious, when Gresley sent a letter outlining the following on 28 June 1938:

> …Whilst the brake trials will be made south of Peterborough, it is proposed to run the train to Barkston and back in order that a fast run down the bank from Stoke Tunnel to Peterborough may be recorded.

Eric Bannister, one of Gresley's assistants at the time, was present on the tests and provided this account of the day's events in his book:

> By this time, the test runs for the quick acting brake valves were almost finished and HNG [Gresley] told Norman Newsome, the Senior Carriage Assistant, that he could 'have a go'. In great secrecy, a speed run was arranged in conjunction with one of the Sunday brake tests. As I had assisted at some of the tests at Norman's request, on July 3rd 1938, I was present on the train when the Doncaster A4 No.4468 Mallard headed out of King's Cross with the 'Coronation' set of coaches and the L.N.E.R. Dynamometer car. For the benefit of the layman, the latter was fitted with instruments to record by stylo on paper rolls: speed, distance, power at the drawbar, etc, of the locomotive.

> The Westinghouse people were surprised to see the Dynamometer car added to the set of articulated 'Coronation' set of coaches as this would mean the day's run would not be comparable with previous tests. However, we proceeded to Barkston, where we turned on the triangle. D.R. Edge, the senior L.N.E.R. representative, told the Westinghouse team what was proposed and offered them a Taxi if they did not wish to return with us. They declined!

> At Barkston, Inspector Sam Jenkins asked me to help him go underneath the engine and douse the middle big end with superheater oil as precaution against possible overheating. Mr Robson, who was in charge of the dynamometer car at Darlington, told the Westinghouse team the details of our proposed speed attempt. Then we got the signal to get away and Driver Duddington turned his hat back to front – he was that sort – and off we went!

> I sat with Norman Newsome at a table in one of the first-class vehicles. HNG had loaned Newsome a large stopwatch which he used to time the distance from milepost to milepost and so estimate the speed. Approaching Grantham we slowed down as there was a permanent way check at 24 mph. Naturally we were disappointed as we wanted a good run up to the top of Stoke bank. Even so, we passed the summit at 74 ½ mph and our speed gradually increased down the bank…

> …I returned to the centre of the train where I asked Norman Newsome what speed we were doing and he said: 'Over 120'. Then Bernard Atkinson said: 'I think we'd better go up nearer the front, Eric'…

*We leaned out to see if we could smell the stink bomb which was inserted in the hollow crankpin of the middle big end and would be set off if overheating occurred.*

*We kept calling across to each other when suddenly Bernard called out 'Can't you smell anything Eric? Your nose is better than mine'. So I said 'I haven't smelt anything yet'. Then, 'It's gone. I can smell it!'.*

*So Bernard immediately signalled to Inspector Jenkins to steady up. Back at our table, Norman, who had felt the slight touch on the brake, said that the speed then had seemed to be 125 mph.*

*…When tracing the charts, I found they showed a peak of 126 mph, but the Chief declined to mention this as the duration was less than a mile.*

'Trained by Sir Nigel Gresley', pages 31 & 32 Eric Bannister, (1984).

*Mallard* was accelerated hard by Duddington on the speed record attempt. Starting from Barkston, Grantham was passed at 24 mph and then on passing Stoke signal box, the speed was 74 ½ mph, regulator wide open with 40 % cut off. The dynamometer car recorded a maximum drawbar horsepower of 1800 at 116 mph at milepost 94, with the cut off having been increased by Duddington to 45% cut off shortly beforehand. At milepost 91 the speed had risen to 125 mph, and by milepost 92 ¾, the speed record had been taken with an absolute maximum of 126 mph, reported as being attained for a short time.

On inspecting the dynamometer roll, I found evidence that suggests strongly that *Mallard* is likely to have attained a speed in excess of 126 mph in order to have recorded a speed of 126 mph by milepost 92 ¾. The dynamometer roll, when its quarter mile measurements are then put against the one second intervals recorded, show that *Mallard* was still accelerating prior to steam being shut off and records higher top speeds than the five second intervals taken on the roll. In my opinion, the 126 mph record undoubtedly stands. Other views are available.

*Mallard* herself suffered some overheating of the middle big end during the end of the high-speed run. Happily, for the locomotive, only some of the white metal had run out of the big end brasses, and she was re-metalled at New England shed shortly after the record run. Further examination at Doncaster Works and some minor attention led to No.4468 being back in traffic nine days later.

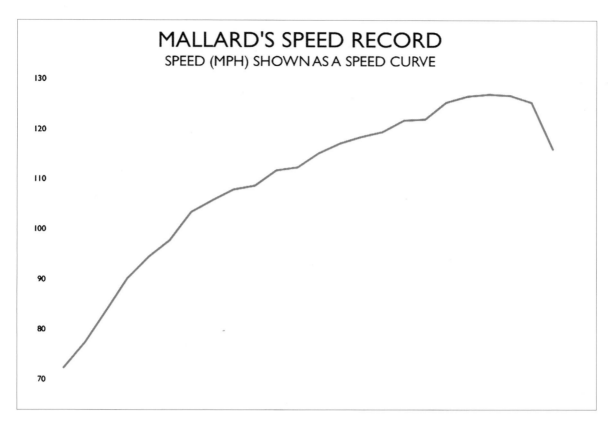

# MALLARD'S SPEED RECORD
## SPEED (MPH) SHOWN AS A SPEED CURVE

*Fig. 231. Speed curve, based on the data from the original Dynamometer roll, kindly provided for examination by the National Railway Museum's Copy Service staff. Simon A.C. Martin.*

*Fig. 232. Mallard at Peterborough shortly after the record was taken, with drive Joe Duddington and fireman Tommy Bray standing to the left and middle of the photograph. The Gresley Society.*

*Fig. 233. Mallard's Speed Record plaques, as applied in the late 1940s by British Railways Eastern Region. Strathwood Library Collection.*

## Post Speed Record

On 31 August 1939, the last streamlined services ran on the L.N.E.R. and the short period of the Gresley A4's dominance in publicity and performance was over. This was due to the enactment of the Emergency Powers (Defence) Act. The King's Cross A4 Pacifics and the streamlined trains went into store for a short time, but with availability of locomotive stock taking a nose dive throughout 1939 and 1940, they were brought back into service on main trains. The chime whistles were removed and replaced by the group standard whistles until after the war, due to fears they could be mistaken for air raid sirens. Wartime black paint with shortened branding became the norm, as per the rest of the L.N.E.R. fleet.

*Fig. 234. Gresley A4 No.4494 Andrew K. McCosh, shortly after overhaul. Of note is the wartime application: the careful removal of the valances over the driving wheels, the N.E. on the tender and the use of yellow shaded red numerals and letters. Colourised by Ian MacCabe, The Gresley Society.*

The A4s became (except in Scotland) part of the common user group of steam locomotives, and pulled everything from evacuation trains, to mixed traffic, coal, and War Department trains for the railway. When the locomotives had been built, it had been envisaged they would be pulling trains of no more than 15 coaches. This was not the case and there are records of some remarkable length trains pulled by the A4 Pacifics.

The A4s began to suffer some maintenance issues as the war went on, with the conjugated valve gear specifically criticised in the report by E.S. Cox to the L.N.E.R.'s wartime Emergency Board. These can be read in Appendix 5 of this book. There were no plans by Thompson or his team to significantly modify them, other than the removal of the valances ahead of and behind the cylinders for easing maintenance issues in wartime. Six of the A4s (including class prototype *Silver Link*) had trial modifications made with the centre cylinder lined to 17in and the cut offs modified to 75% to reduce issues on the middle cylinder, but this was short lived and not extended to the rest of the class.

No.4469 *Sir Ralph Wedgwood* became the first of the class to be withdrawn after it was severely damaged from a bomb going off during an air raid in York's shed on 29 April 1942. Whilst the locomotive was scrapped, the tender was repaired and put into service behind a new Thompson Pacific, A2/1 No.3696.

With the end of hostilities in 1945, the A4s were gradually repainted into their garter blue livery, with stainless steel numbers and letters applied to the whole of the class. Three of the A4 Pacifics were to be used in the 1948 Exchange Trials, including the by then numbered E22, *Mallard*.

Figs. 235 & 235b. Gresley A4 No.4496 Dwight D. Eisenhower, post war. The stainless-steel letters and numerals of the Coronation engines and Sir Nigel Gresley became standard for the A4s, with the eye-catching garter blue livery punctuated by the more visible red wheelsets. Renumbered as 60010 Dominion of Canada displays her bell which had been awarded by the Canadian Pacific Railway in 1938. Both: Strathwood Library Collection.

Fig. 236. Gresley A4 No.60022 Mallard, in its final livery and form under the auspices of British Railways. Note the curly numeral 6 on the smokebox numberplate, a hangover from the early days of nationalisation, and the plaque fitted to the centre of its boiler casing. Strathwood Library Collection.

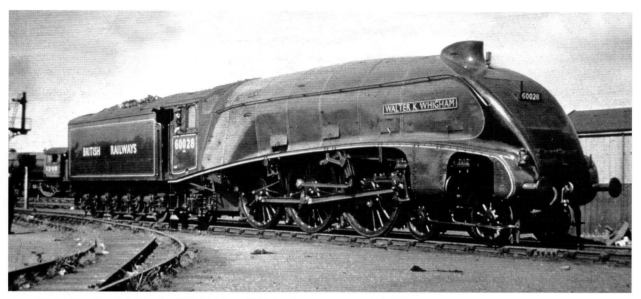

*Fig. 237. Gresley A4 No.60028 Walter K. Whigham sits on shed. This rare photograph shows the depth of colour of the experimental "purple" (or dark blue), together with the L.N.W.R. style lining out on the valances, and red/black/red boiler bands. The parabolic curve is a single red line between the black of the smokebox and the blue of the casing. Colour Rail.*

Though recording excellent coal and water consumption figures, the failure of the conjugated valve gear by way of the middle big end on several occasions throughout the trials was a mark against them. It has been suggested this was down to poor wartime maintenance, but the reality was that the war had been over for three years and all the A4s used in the trials had been recently in works to prepare for the trials. Unfamiliarity to the classes' design on the part of the regions hosting the locomotives may have been a factor.

The class returned to front line service and their work on the premier East Coast mainline expresses resumed from 1946. From the late 1940s into the 1950s, they were joined by Peppercorn A1 Pacifics on work between London King's Cross and the West Riding, and northwards up towards York and beyond. Thompson Pacifics and Peppercorn's A2 class largely supported them in their work in Scotland on their usual routes. The A4s went through several livery changes before the British Railways Dark Green was applied, with orange and black lining out, from 1952. An experimental "purple" livery was applied from 1949 to some members of the class, this was short-lived. Express Passenger blue was also applied, and short lived, between 1950 and 1953.

An important thing to note with regards all of the Gresley Pacifics working out of King's Cross and their cleanliness in the late 1950s and early 1960s was the influence of the depot's last shedmaster: Peter Townend.

*Fig. 238. Peter Townend (right) discusses matters with one of Top Shed's footplatemen in the late 1960s. Stood behind with the "cod's mouth" open is No.60006 Sir Ralph Wedgwood. The Gresley Society.*

He saw to it that the A3s and A4s running were to be looked after to a significantly improved maintenance regime, recording changes to the lubrication of the middle big ends, changes to the felt pads. The one alteration to the Gresley Pacifics which made the most remarkable improvement was the fitting of the Kylchap double chimney arrangement which Peter eventually instigated after getting management agreement on the basis of economy. The oldest engines of the Class A3 in particular were given a new lease of life and worked turn and turnabout with the much newer 8P locomotives. The old problem of smoke deflection on the A3's with double chimneys was overcome by designing a version of the German Witte type of smoke deflectors first trialled on A3 No. 60049 *Galtee More* which proved to be very satisfactory and allowed far better forward vision for the footplate crew.

These improvement during Peter's tenure at Top Shed helped to ease the introduction of diesels to the East Coast mainline. The Pacifics were able to cover for the many failures of the early express diesels when introduced to work the new intensive cyclic timetable diagram when London to Newcastle and return in 12 hours became the norm and if necessary, back to Newcastle again within a few hours. The Eastern Region management, general public and enthusiasts alike who travelled on Gresley Pacifics from London during the twilight of steam owe him their thanks for his efforts. Without Peter, the Gresley Pacifics might have gone quietly into the night, rather than enjoyed a new lease of life and performances that put newer traction to shame. By 1960, the onset of dieselisation was in full swing, with locomotives such as the Class 40s and the Class 55 "Deltics" taking over much of the A4's work. In 1962 the first A4s (other than No. 4469) were scrapped while others were placed in store or relocated to Scotland for something of an Indian summer.

The last run of an A4 Pacific in service with British Railways was on 3 September 1966, by No.60019 *Bittern*. Six of the class were preserved. No.4468 *Mallard* was retained for the fledging National Railway Museum, initially at Clapham and now latterly at York. It was restored to its speed record form, albeit with the cast plates on its casing that had been fitted post war recording its speed record run. Aside from a special return to service in the 1980s to celebrate the speed record, it has not run again in preservation. No.60007 *Sir Nigel Gresley* has been repeatedly restored to working order and run on the mainline almost continuously to the present day by the *Sir Nigel Gresley Locomotive Trust*. At the time of writing, she is now back on main line in Express Passenger Blue again after a year of trials in the fetching wartime black livery. This locomotive set a post-war speed record on 23 May 1959 whilst hauling a special for the Stephenson Locomotive Society. The speed recorded was 112 mph and is likely to remain the post war record for steam for all time.

No.60008 *Dwight D. Eisenhower* was originally named *Golden Shuttle* and was renamed post-war for the American general, in honour of his work with the allies. The locomotive was donated to the National Railroad Museum in Green Bay, Wisconsin. In 2012 it returned to the United Kingdom for The Great Gathering, where all the six surviving A4 Pacifics were put on display. It returned to the United States in 2013, after cosmetic restoration.

No.60009 *Union of South Africa* was purchased by John Cameron and has, as of 2021, retired to be an exhibit at his new museum in Scotland. We owe a debt of thanks to John Cameron for keeping the locomotive running since preservation in the 1960s. At the time of writing the locomotive had just been transferred to the new museum after being repainted at the East Lancashire Railway.

No.4489 *Dominion of Canada* was donated to the Canadian Railway Museum at Quebec. In 2012 she crossed the Atlantic to re-join her classmates for *The Great Gathering*. Originally preserved as No.60010 in British Railways Dark Green livery, the National Railway Museum as part of the agreement with her owners restored to her original form, complete with valances, single chimney, and stainless-steel trim as L.N.E.R. No.4489. The bell, donated to the L.N.E.R. by the Canadian Pacific Railroad in the 1930s, was refitted and is operational once more. In 2013 she was dispatched back across the Atlantic and put on display.

No.60019, *Bittern*, was originally bought by the Drury family and served on the mainline for many years. She has appeared as No.2509 *Silver Link* whilst waiting for overhaul in the 1980s, and *Dominion of New Zealand* in the 2010s, and has carried a plethora of the classes' liveries and forms throughout her preservation career. Her most famous moment in preservation, however, came when running as herself 2013. To celebrate the 75th anniversary of *Mallard's* record run, the locomotive was authorised to run on the mainline at 90 mph, which it achieved on three separate occasions. It now carries plaques in the same style as No.4468 and No.60007 commemorating these runs. At the time of writing, she is on display at the One:One collection in Hornby's premises at Margate, awaiting her turn for overhaul to mainline operation under her current owner.

Fig. 239. Sir Nigel Gresley is being prepared at Nine Elms on the Southern region of British Railways in this shot from February 1967. Mike Morant Collection.

Fig. 240. The first four names chosen for the A4s featured the word silver. Twenty-three were allocated names of British birds although some of these were later given names of senior L.N.E.R. office bearers and of course Dwight D. Eisenhower. However, five were to be awarded names from the Commonwealth, among these was No.4489 Dominion of Canada. Seen here as one of the stars of a show at Cambridge on 7 May 1938 having been previously named officially by their High Commissioner, the Hon.Vincent Massey at Kings Cross on 15 June 1937. When the bell was fitted the original brass nameplates were exchanged for stainless steel versions with screw affixed lettering and beading. Clearly the bell does little for the efficiency of the streamlining. In addition, all five of the Commonwealth names locomotives had painted coats of arms affixed to to their cabsides at various points during their working lives. The locomotive was restored to this form in 2012 as part of the "Great Gathering" of the class at the N.R.M., and later returned to Canada.
Strathwood Library Collection.

Fig. 241. The world record holder, No.60022 Mallard in the twilight of her career with British Railways in 1962. The diesel to the right, one of the first English Electric built Deltics (D9016 Gordon Highlander) points to the future of the east coast main line. Colour Rail.

*Wartime Mileages & Availability*

| Year | Mileages | Availability |
|------|----------|--------------|
| 1942 | 52882 | 67% |
| 1943 | 46868 | 63% |
| 1944 | 51582 | 71% |
| 1945 | 51065 | 67% |
| 1946 | 51237 | 65% |

*Fig. 242. A4 Mileages & Availability Statistics.*
*Simon A.C. Martin, from the Use of Engine Power Document.*

During the Second World War, the A4 Pacifics suffered in availability. This is only part of the overall story, however. The mileages achieved by the class per year, despite the availability issue, were significant. Even the lowest year for annual average mileages, 1943, with an availability at its lowest of 62%, the locomotives were achieving nearly 47,000 miles per year.

This remains a high figure and is testament to the excellence of the A4 Pacific's design, despite the conjugated valve gear issues. In comparison to the other large locomotives including the A1s, A3s, P2s and the Thompson Pacifics to come, the A4s were the standard to achieve in terms of mileages, culminating in three years of achieving over 50,000 miles per annum, a record that would not be beaten until Peppercorn's A1s were brought into service.

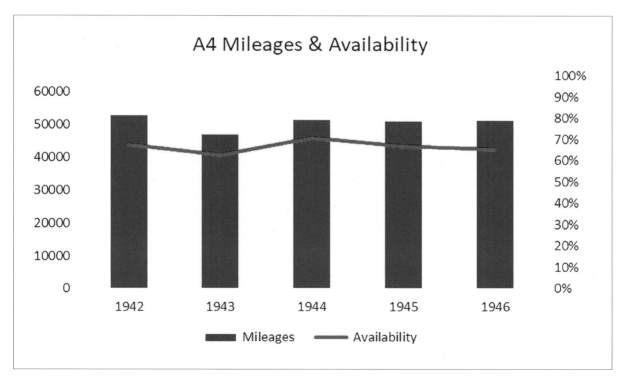

*Fig.243. A4 Mileages & Availability Graph.*
*Simon A.C. Martin from the Use of Engine Power Document.*

# Class A4

| | | |
|---|---|---|
| Cylinders (x3): | | 18.5x26in. |
| Motion: | Outside: | Walschaerts |
| | Inside: | Gresley |
| Piston Valves: | | 9in. diameter |
| Boiler: | Max. Diameter: | 6ft 5in |
| | Pressure: | 250lb |
| | Diagram No.: | 107 |
| Heating Surface: | Total: | 3325.2 sq. ft. |
| | Firebox: | 231.2 sq. ft. |
| | Superheater: | 748.9 sq. ft. |
| | Tubes: | 1281.4 sq. ft. (121x 2.25in) |
| | Flues: | 1063.7 sq. ft. (43x 5.25in) |
| Grate Area: | | 41.25 sq. ft. |
| Wheels: | Leading: | 3ft 2in |
| | Coupled: | 6ft 8in |
| | Trailing: | 3ft 8in |
| | Tender: | 4ft 2in |
| Tractive Effort: | 35,455lb | At 85% boiler pressure |
| Wheelbase: | Total: | 60ft 10.6in |
| | Engine: | 35ft 9in |
| | Tender: | 16ft |
| Weight (full): | Total: | 167 tons 2cwt |
| | Engine: | 102 tons 19cwt |
| | Tender: | 64 tons 3cwt |
| Max. Axle Load: | | 22 tons |
| Water Capacity: | | 5000 gallons |
| Coal Capacity: | | 8 tons |

# L.N.E.R

## Class V2 2-6-2 (1936)
### Number built (L.N.E.R.): 184

*Fig. 244. Gresley V2 No.4785 is seen running at speed with a mixed traffic train.*
*Colourised by Ian MacCabe, The Gresley Society.*

The V2 came out of the desire for a more powerful version of Gresley's K3 2-6-0 locomotive in 1932. Early studies included a version with a bogie between the locomotive and tender, thus articulating the two together. This was somewhat reminiscent of work already done by Gresley on one of Vincent Raven's Atlantic locomotives and would have been a 2-6-4-4 arrangement.

No further development was undertaken on the articulated version, instead the design team opted for a 2-6-2-wheel arrangement and conventional tender. With the added advantages of being able to fit a wide firebox arrangement above a cartazzi, as with the existing Pacifics and Mikados. By 1934, this had morphed into a 2-6-2 version of the P2 arrangement, complete with sloping smokebox, smoke deflectors, Lentz valve gear and an ACFI feed water heater.

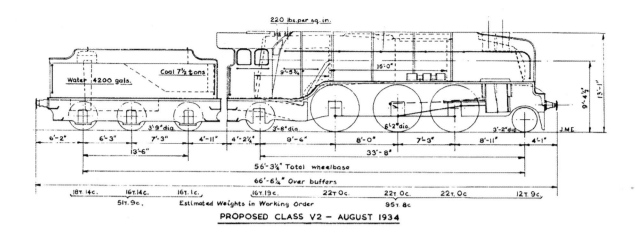

Fig. 245. The original concept for the V2 locomotive, like the A4 Pacific before it, was to draw on the family resemblance intended based on the Gresley P2. Note the double chimney that matches the P2s closely. Courtesy of the R.C.T.S.

By 1935, there was an order on the books for fourteen V2s and the design had changed again to resembling the new A4 Pacifics externally, also fitted with Walschaerts valve gear and the conjugated 2:1 motion. Surprisingly, unlike the Gresley B17s that had been streamlined to work the *East Anglian*, the tender would not be streamlined.

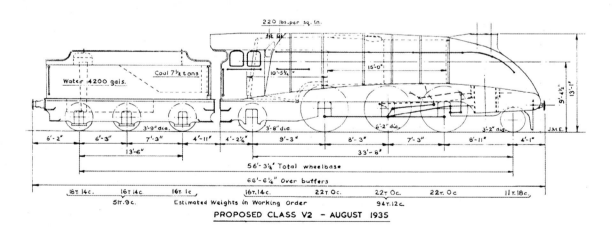

Fig. 246. The V2 design enters its streamlined phase. Interestingly the double chimney of the P2s has been retained, its setup closely aligned to the double chimney fitted P2/2s and P2/3 *Wolf of Badenoch*. Courtesy of the R.C.T.S.

Roll forward to the October of 1935, and the streamlined casing had been discarded in favour of a more conventional layout.

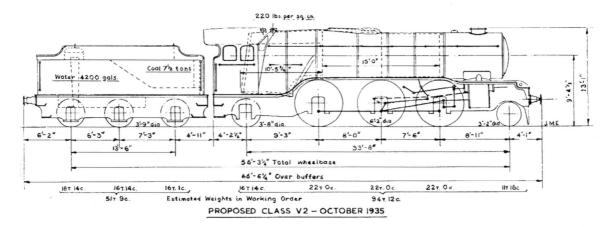

*Fig. 247. The V2 design is almost complete. The only major change would be to the tender, with a higher coping fitted on the final design. The locomotive has now been given a single chimney, as per the A4 Pacifics. Courtesy of the R.C.T.S.*

The 2-6-2, or "Prairie" arrangement for tender locomotives was well known and familiar on the continent and further abroad, but in the United Kingdom was virtually non-existent. Save for Paget's sole sleeve valve fitted 2-6-2 of 1908, the Gresley V2s were the first built for standard gauge in the country.

The design incorporated a monobloc, in the Darlington style and similar in setup to that used on the Gresley P2s with the cylinders, steam chest and passages all incorporated into the one component. This allowed for greater streamlining of the internal steam passages, however the monobloc if damaged through cracking was difficult and expensive to repair, with a crack in any of the cylinders rendering the block unfit for use.

These issues would put members of the class out of service for lengthy periods. By the mid-1950s, the decision was made to replace cracked monoblocs with separately fitted cylinders. Locomotives with this change were identifiable by outside steam pipes fitted, indicating the fitting of the separate cylinders. This change made the V2s look much closer to the Gresley A1s and A3s in appearance. Only 71 members of the class ended up being fitted with the separately fitted cylinders.

Fig. 248. Green Arrow as originally outshopped. Note the curved nameplate over the centre splasher, harking back to the original Gresley A1s and the prototype's original number of 637 on the cab sides. Shortly after, straight edged nameplates were applied to the smokebox, with the builder's plaque repositioned to the cab sides, and No.4771 replaced the original number.
The Gresley Society.

The prototype, *Green Arrow*, was named for the L.N.E.R.'s express freight service, reputedly by R.A. Thom, one of the mechanical engineers working under Gresley. No.4771 impressed from the outset and the general reputation of the class was of excellence: equally at home on fast fitted freight or deputising for the Pacifics on expresses.

The V2 quickly became the L.N.E.R.'s go-to mixed traffic locomotive. Engine crews loved them, and by 1944 over one-hundred-and-eighty-four V2s had been built in eleven batches between Doncaster and Darlington, the latter V2s when outshopped sporting green cylinder covers.

One issue of the class was its high axle loading of 22 tons, which restricted them to around 40% of the L.N.E.R.'s lines. They were allocated across the Scottish, Eastern and North Eastern regions but were barred from working in the Great Eastern area for this reason.

During the Second World War the V2s were sometimes given loads well in excess of the official maximum, particularly on evacuation and troop trains at the start of the war. This when combined with the poor maintenance standards of the locomotives and the permanent way, and the double swing link pony truck fitted, led to some incidents including derailments throughout the war, culminating into several serious accidents in 1946.

The original design was replaced with the type used on Thompson's L1s and K1/1 designs, itself based on that used on Stanier's 8F 2-8-0 (L.N.E.R. Class O6). By 1947, all the V2s had their pony trucks replaced.

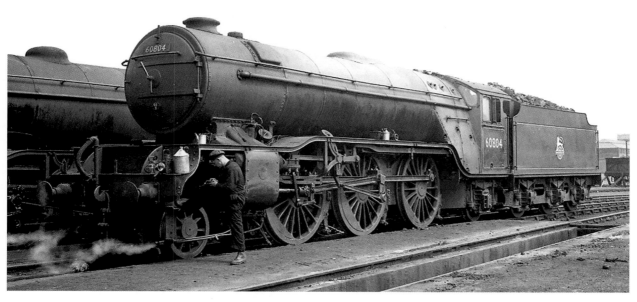

*Fig. 249. Gresley V2 No.60894 at St Margaret's shed in largely original condition, including the monobloc casting of the cylinders and inside steam pipes. Strathwood Library Collection.*

*Fig. 250. Gresley V2 No.60827 getting into its stride at Lenzie on 1 February 1962. Colour Rail.*

Fig. 251. The naming ceremony for V2 No.4844 Coldstreamer, with members of the regiment present at King's Cross Station. Steve Armitage Archive/Rail Online

Concurrently with the changes being made to the Gresley A3 class in terms of the double Kylchap chimney, some V2s underwent testing with a range of blast pipe arrangements, some based on that used in the L.M.S.' Royal Scot class. The V2s used, No.60817 and No.60963 did not produce the results expected and by January 1961 No.60817 had been converted to the Kylchap cowls together with No.60881. The improvements were impressive and a further six V2s were converted.

*Fig. 252. Gresley V2 No.60881 at the New England coal stage circa 1959. Note the double Kylchap chimney and the outside steam pipes fitted. Strathwood Library Collection.*

This improvement came quite late in the day and no more conversions happened before the first withdrawal in February 1962. Withdrawal of the entire class happened in the next four years, with No.60831 being the last in service with British Railways, dropping its fire and being withdrawn on 6 December 1966.

Class pioneer No.4771 *Green Arrow* joined *Mallard* in preservation and was a regular mainline performer for the National Railway Museum until its withdrawal, for the last time, 2008. At the time of writing *Green Arrow* is on loan to the Doncaster Museum and Art Gallery, on display alongside a fellow Doncaster built steam locomotive, Ivatt's prototype C1 Atlantic, No.251.

| Year | Mileages | Availability |
|------|----------|--------------|
| 1942 | 40248 | 71% |
| 1943 | 41276 | 75% |
| 1944 | 38560 | 76% |
| 1945 | 39497 | 71% |
| 1946 | 42226 | 70% |

*Fig. 253. V2 Mileages & Availability Statistics.*
*Simon A.C. Martin, from the Use of Engine Power Document.*

The V2 class in some L.N.E.R. secondary sources are described as one of the engine classes which "won the war", and its annual average mileages and availability suggest that it was indeed one of the L.N.E.R.'s best performing classes. A further sixty-six V2s were manufactured under Edward Thompson's auspices, the dip in overall average mileages in 1944 due in part to these examples being released to traffic during the year and therefore having less time in which to run.

Although one of the classes criticised in E.S. Cox's report, the availability of the V2 class to do work during the war was always in line with, or above, the 70% average for the entire L.N.E.R. fleet. Bearing in mind its mixed traffic role, and its versatility throughout the war, the criticism in the Cox report in relation to the V2 class should be understood in the strict context of the causes of failure within the class and not necessarily a criticism of its performances out on the road.

The excellence of the V2s during the war can perhaps be summed up with the singular exploit of No.4800 of New England Shed on 31 March 1940. With a train of twenty-six vehicles, picking up the train from Peterborough to head into London, No.4800 under the hand of its driver Mr Hensy, took the heavy train into London and lost only nine minutes on the total schedule allotted. The gross load of the train was somewhere in the region of 850 tons, very much more than the normal stipulated maximums of the class.

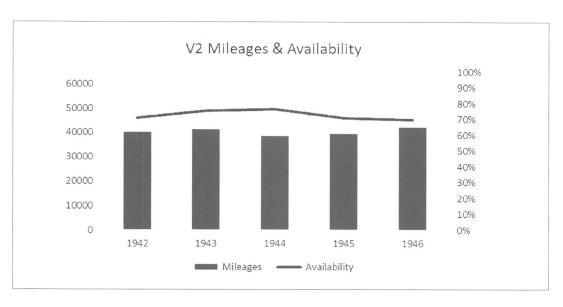

*Fig. 254. V2 Mileages & Availability Graph.*
*Simon A.C. Martin from the Use of Engine Power Document.*

| Gresley V2 | | |
|---|---|---|
| Cylinders (x3): | | 18.5x26in. |
| Motion: | Outside: | Walschaerts |
| | Inside: | Gresley |
| | Valves: | 9in dia. piston |
| Boiler: | Max. Diameter: | 6ft 5in |
| | Pressure: | 220lb |
| | Diagram No.: | 109 |
| Heating Surface: | Total: | 3110.74 sq. ft. |
| | Firebox: | 215 sq. ft. |
| | Superheater: | 679.67 sq. ft. |
| | Tubes: | 1211.57 sq. ft. (121x 2.25in) |
| | Flues: | 1004.5 sq. ft. (43x 5.25in) |
| Grate Area: | | 41.25 sq. ft. |
| Wheels: | Leading: | 3ft 2in |
| | Coupled: | 6ft 2in |
| | Trailing: | 3ft 8in |
| | Tender: | 3ft 9in |
| Tractive Effort: | At 85% boiler pressure | 33,730lb |
| Wheelbase: | Engine: | 33ft 8in |
| | Tender: | 13ft 6in |
| Weight (full): | Total: | 144 tons 2cwt |
| | Engine: | 93 tons 2cwt |
| | Tender: | 51 tons 0cwt |
| Max. Axle Load: | | 22 tons |

# L.N.E.R

## Class K4 2-6-0 (1937)
Number built (L.N.E.R.): 6

*Fig. 255. Gresley K4 No.3441 Loch Long, seen in a later works photograph. Note the cylinder covers, painted green as was the custom at Darlington Works. When new on 17 February 1938, the locomotive was reported as being in a black livery lined out in red to mingle in with the Class K locomotives on the West Highland line. After twelve months experience with this new locomotive working the heavily graded route between Glasgow and Fort William, it was decided to place an order with Darlington Works for five more on 17 February 1938. The first of these No.3442 was named as MacCAILEIN MOR very briefly on 12 July 1938. However, the spelling was deemed to be incorrect so thirteen days later No.3442 was named as THE GREAT MARQUESS after the head of the Graham family, being one of the largest landowners around Loch Lomond. The Gresley Society.*

In 1934 the existing Gresley K2s were struggling on the challenging Fort William to Mallaig line. Gresley and his team started work on different options of a new design based on the K2s. There was one set of calculations carried out which showed by way of an increase in boiler pressure, married to 21-inch diameter cylinders, a tractive effort of 31,351lb would be achieved. This came with a reduction in adhesion to a factor of around 3.7, which given the requirements for the line, was not recommended. There was provision made for one prototype 2-6-0 locomotive by the Joint Traffic & Locomotive Committee in 1935, but design work did not develop in earnest until May 1936. By July 1936, a revised outline drawing was available, and this new proposal was a development of a much earlier outline from the Doncaster drawing office (dated 1924). In the new version, a boiler based on a combination of the K2 barrel and B17's firebox was in situ, with K3 cylinders and 5ft 2in driving wheels. The boiler was now reduced in pressure to 180lb, giving a tractive effort of 32,939lb.

On 28 January 1937, the prototype K4, No.3441 *Loch Long* entered service on the Fort William line. 300-ton trains were taken without any assistance, but by June 1937, feedback from the operating department led to the boiler pressure being increased to 200lb with a corresponding increase in traction effort to 36,599lb. This improved the acceleration of the locomotive but reduced the factor of adhesion slightly. A further batch of five K4s was ordered in February 1938, with all five delivered and in service between July 1938 and January 1939.

No further K4s were built. All the K4s had modifications to their front buffer beams to take small snowploughs in the winter months. A further modification was the addition of spark arrestors from 1947. One of the K4s, No.3445, was rebuilt as a two cylinder 2-6-0 and formed the prototype for Thompson and Peppercorn's K1 classes in 1945. The K4s were much liked, but the introduction of the two Gresley V4s and Thompson B1s displaced them from the Glasgow to Fort William trains onto just the Mallaig stretch of the line. After nationalisation of the railways in 1948 the K4s were transferred over to Eastfield and were used mostly on West Highland goods trains. By 1959 the K4s were at Thornton and were used strictly on goods

Fig. 256. Gresley K4 No.61995 *Cameron of Lochiel* waiting patiently for the off, in the early 1960s.
The Gresley Society.

trains. Four of the five remaining K4s were withdrawn in October 1961, leaving just No.3442, *The Great Marquess* running. This too was withdrawn but sold into preservation. Viscount Garnock and the Garnock family owned the locomotive, running it on the mainline until sold in in the mid-2000s to John Cameron, owner of *Union of South Africa*. Restored into British Railways livery, No.61994 retired from service in 2016 and has been transferred to John Cameron's new museum in Scotland. It is now displayed alongside No.60009.

# Wartime Mileages & Availability

The war years were not kind to the K4s, whose mileages and availability suffered in the first few years of the war. With the rebuilding of No.3445, annual average mileages improved for the remaining five K4s, but availability remained always below the 70% average of the L.N.E.R. fleet.

| Year | Mileages | Availability |
|------|----------|--------------|
| 1942 | 29957 | 60% |
| 1943 | 26417 | 59% |
| 1944 | 22869 | 60% |
| 1945 | 29403 | 68% |
| 1946 | 29589 | 63% |

*Fig. 257. K4 Mileages & Availability Statistics. Simon A.C. Martin, from the Use of Engine Power Document.*

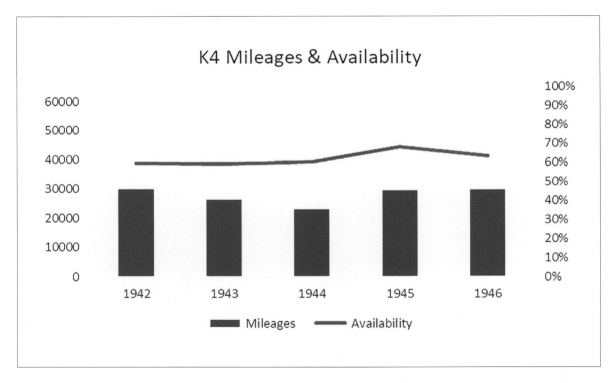

*Fig. 258. K4 Mileages & Availability Graph.*
*Simon A.C. Martin from the Use of Engine Power Document.*

| Gresley K4 | | |
|---|---|---|
| Cylinders (x3): | | 18.5x26in. |
| Motion: | Outside: | Walschaerts |
| | Inside: | Gresley |
| | Valves: | 8in piston |
| Boiler: | Max. Diameter: | 5ft 6in |
| | Pressure: | 200lb |
| | Diagram No.: | 110 |
| Heating Surface: | Total: | 1731.6 sq. ft. |
| | Firebox: | 168 sq. ft. |
| | Superheater: | 310 sq. ft. (24x 1.244in) |
| | Tubes: | 871.1 sq. ft. (164x 1.75in) |
| | Flues: | 382.5 sq. ft. (24x 5.25in) |
| Grate Area: | | 27.5 sq. ft. |
| Wheels: | Leading: | 3ft 2in |
| | Coupled: | 5ft 2in |
| | Tender: | 3ft 9in |
| Tractive Effort: | At 85% boiler pressure | 36,599lb |
| Wheelbase: | Total: | 48ft 7in |
| | Engine: | 25ft 2in |
| | Tender: | 13ft 0in |
| Weight (full): | Total: | 112 tons 12cwt |
| | Engine: | 68 tons 8cwt |
| | Tender: | 44 tons 4cwt |
| Max. Axle Load: | | 19 tons 17cwt |

*Fig.258b. In her final condition No.61993 Loch Long takes a breather from regular goods duties at Thornton Junction on 20 April 1957. Strathwood Library Collection*

# L.N.E.R
## Class V3 2-6-2T (1939)
### Number built (L.N.E.R.): 73(63 rebuilt from Class V1)

*Fig. 259. Gresley V3 No.416, works photograph. Note the wartime black livery and the hopper coal bunker at the rear. The Gresley Society.*

By 1939, the Class V1 had been in service for nearly ten years. The North Eastern region of the L.N.E.R. had considered raising the boiler pressure to at least 200lb to improve the performance of the tank locomotives. A new batch of the 2-6-2Ts was ordered with the 200lb boilers and classified as V3. Other than boiler pressures, the differences between the V1s and V3s were minimal, but the L.N.E.R. classified them as separate classes and recorded their mileages and availability entirely separately. By 1948, four of the original V1s had been upgraded with higher boiler pressure, and, and within the next ten years a further sixty-seven of the V1s would beconverted to V3s.

By 1960, withdrawal of both classes had started, with the low pressure V1s becoming extinct in 1962. The V3s held on a little longer, with the last withdrawn in 1964. Diesel railcars and the smaller types of Diesel-Electric locomotives (usually Type 2s) took over their duties as they were withdrawn.

Fig. 260. Gresley V3 No.67660, works photograph. Outshopped with a small "Cycling Lion" and in mixed traffic livery, lined out as per the old L.N.W.R. locomotives of the pre-grouping years.
The Gresley Society.

## Wartime Mileages & Availability

| Year | Mileages | Availability |
|------|----------|--------------|
| 1942 | 41537 | 74% |
| 1943 | 36984 | 73% |
| 1944 | 30962 | 72% |
| 1945 | 32858 | 72% |
| 1946 | 32732 | 68% |

Fig. 261. V3 Mileages & Availability Statistics.
Simon A.C. Martin, from the Use of Engine Power Document.

It was surprising to note, when reviewing the statistics for the two classes in this book, that the V1s had better mileages and availability. The major difference between the two classes was the 20lb higher boiler pressure of the V3s. This may have resulted in somewhat greater, or *quicker* wear and tear on these locomotives than the low-pressure engines.

A similar trend can be observed between the A1 and A3 classes. Nevertheless, the V3s still performed well at the outset of the war, with the wartime maintenance levels gradually reducing their overall availability throughout the war. It must be remembered that there were only ten examples of Class V3 by 1946, so they represented a fraction of the overall L.N.E.R. fleet.

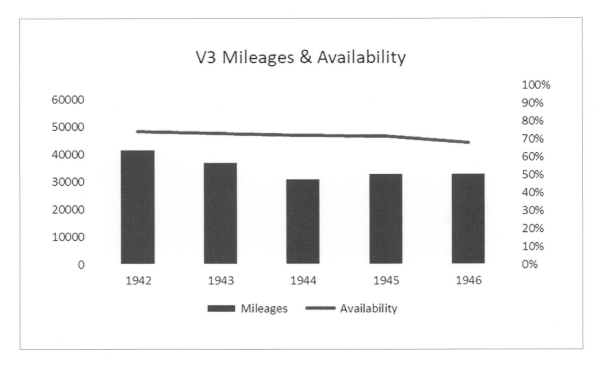

*Fig. 262. V3 Mileages & Availability Graph.*
*Simon A.C. Martin from the Use of Engine Power Document.*

*Fig.262b. Built originally as a Class V3 No.67684 stands ex-works at Darlington during the 1950's.*
*Strathwood Library Collection*

| Class V3 | | |
|---|---|---|
| Cylinders (x3): | | 16x26in. |
| Motion: | Outside: | Walschaerts |
| | Inside: | Gresley |
| | Valves: | 8in piston |
| Boiler: | Max. Diameter: | 5ft |
| | Pressure: | 200lb |
| | Diagram No.: | 102HP |
| Heating Surface: | Total: | 1609 sq. ft. |
| | Firebox: | 127 sq. ft. |
| | Superheater: | 284 sq. ft. |
| | Tubes: | 830 sq. ft. (149x 1.75in) |
| | Flues: | 368 sq. ft. (22x 5.25in) |
| Grate Area: | | 22.08 sq. ft. |
| Wheels: | Leading: | 3ft 2in |
| | Coupled: | 5ft 8in |
| | Trailing: | 3ft 8in |
| Tractive Effort: | At 85% boiler pressure | 24,960lb |
| Total Wheelbase: | | 32ft 3in |
| Engine Weight: | (full) | 59 tons 2cwt |
| Coal Capacity: | | 4 tons |
| Water Capacity: | | 2000 gallons |
| Max. Axle Load: | | 20 tons |

*Fig.262c. Originally built as Class V1 No.67662 seen at Buchannan Street on 26 May 1962 had been converted to a V3 during February 1955. Winston Cole.*

# L.N.E.R

## Class V4 2-6-2 (1941)
Number built (L.N.E.R.): 2

*Fig. 263. Gresley V4 No.3401, works photograph. The Gresley Society.*

Gresley's final steam locomotive design was also arguably one of his best. With modern construction methods, light alloys employed, and careful design, the total weight of the locomotive was brought down to around 70 tons. This gave the V4 significant route availability: out of a possible 6414 miles of L.N.E.R. lines, it could run over 5000 miles of it. By comparison, locomotives such as the larger Gresley V2 had just 2700 miles available to run on, restricted by its axle loading and overall weight.

L.N.E.R. board minutes from 1939 show that it was specifically designed to be a "go anywhere" machine: Gresley making it clear that it would initially be trialled in the Eastern sections of the L.N.E.R., where historically it had been difficult to build locomotives that could pull the heaviest services and meet fast point to point timings due to the more lightly laid lines of the region.

This was a continuing problem in Anglia. Although the N.B.L. designed B17 was reasonably successful at running most services, the boilers gave trouble, and they were somewhat underpowered for the heaviest work. Further batches of the G.E.R. B12 design had also been built to supplement the aging locomotive stock in that region. The comparisons with the K4 that been given by L.N.E.R. authors historically are interesting and may stem from the eventual move to Scotland long term that allowed the two Gresley classes a direct comparison.

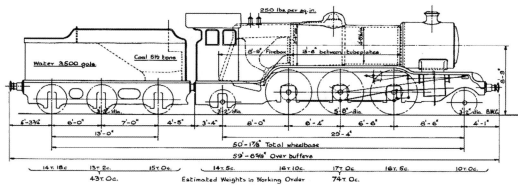

PROPOSED CLASS V4—NOVEMBER 1939

*Fig. 264. The V4 takes shape in the late 1930s. Even in this early stage, the original 300lb pressure for the boiler had been dropped to 250lb in the new design. Courtesy of the R.C.T.S.*

The design was a mix of standard components and new designs. A new boiler, originally specified at 300lb with a set of thermic siphons but when the first was built this was set to 250lb and was the smallest of the conventional wide firebox boilers designed under Gresley with the highest pressure (if the W1's original marine tube boiler is discounted).

Originally the design had thermic syphons to improve water flow, but this was changed to a 250lb boiler and only the second Gresley V4, No.3402 had the thermic syphons fitted at construction. After multiple issues with broken stays, this experiment was abandoned and a boiler standard with No.3401 was fitted to No.3402 in 1945. This may explain the class's low availability and mileages between 1945 and 1946: statistics reflect an average for one working locomotive and one engine out of service awaiting a revised boiler.

The tractive effort of the design was 27,000lb. The Gresley V2 and V3 classes provided much inspiration towards the new locomotive, with the mono-bloc casting for the cylinders derived largely from that produced for the V2, together with the same swing link pony truck design. No.3401 when outshopped was given the name *Bantam Cock*, deliberately highlighting the lightweight nature of the design. No.3402 was never given an official name but was nicknamed *Bantam Hen*. Gresley lived long enough to see both locomotives in steam before passing away. After some time working around the country, both as intended in East Anglia (but also in the north, on trains between Leeds and York), the V4s were moved to Scotland. Initially put to work on passenger services around Edinburgh, they were transferred out to the Glasgow-Fort William line. The comparisons with the K4s were instant and the general view of the crews and timekeepers were that the V4s were highly capable machines, proving faster on the stretches of line where speed was possible, but the K4s proved surer footed on the gradients of the line.

Fig. 265. Gresley V4 under construction at Doncaster Works. The driving wheels have been painted and lined. The lack of mounting points on the smokebox for nameplates strongly suggest that this is V4 No.3402. The Gresley Society.

Fig 266. Gresley V4 No.3401, running in East Anglia at speed on a long passenger service. Note the six-wheel ex-G.E.R. brake coach positioned at the front of the train immediately behind the locomotive's tender. The Gresley Society.

By 1949, enough of the Thompson B1s were coming into service that the V4s were moved to Eastfield to work on fast goods services through to Scottish towns and cities. The two engines were split up for a short time, with No.3401 (by then numbered 61700) heading to Stirling shed to work passenger trains. The V4s' final home was Aberdeen in 1954, from which the two locomotives were withdrawn in 1957.

## Wartime Mileages & Availability

| Year | Mileages | Availability |
|------|----------|--------------|
| 1942 | 40724 | 71% |
| 1943 | 38529 | 72% |
| 1944 | 33093 | 65% |
| 1945 | 32587 | 60% |
| 1946 | 22903 | 53% |

*Fig. 267. V4 Mileages & Availability Statistics.*
*Simon A.C. Martin, from the Use of Engine Power Document.*

As locomotives there was absolutely no doubt of the quality of the V4 design. High tractive effort and low axle loading, with generally well-regarded adhesive weight, made for a very potent machine. The problem with the V4 was not the design, or even the conjugated valve gear particularly: it was in the use of lighter alloys throughout the locomotive some of which were not available for locomotive building or would not be authorised for locomotive building during the Second World War. Some L.N.E.R. historians have argued that Gresley "built a Rolls Royce when a Ford was needed" and perhaps there is some truth to that. Equally, the V4 remains a "what could have been" had things been different.

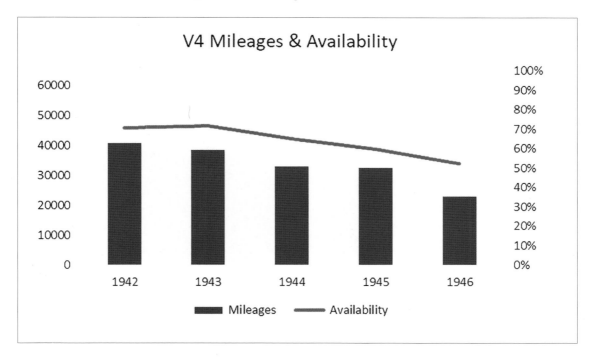

*Fig. 268. V4 Mileages & Availability Graph.*
*Simon A.C. Martin from the Use of Engine Power Document.*

Fig. 269. Gresley V4 No.61701 sits waiting for its next turn of duty. Note the combination of L.N.E.R. apple green with British Railways numbering and branding.
The Transport Treasury

# Class V4

| | | |
|---|---|---|
| Cylinders (x3): | | 15x26in. |
| Motion: | Outside: | Walschaerts |
| | Inside: | Gresley |
| | Valves: | 7in piston |
| Boiler: | Max. Diameter: | 5ft 4in |
| | Pressure: | 250lb |
| | Diagram No.: | 112 |
| Heating Surface: | Total: | 1799.9 sq. ft. |
| | Firebox: | 151.6 sq. ft. |
| | Superheater: | 355.8 sq. ft. |
| | Tubes: | 884.3 sq. ft. (143x 1.75in) |
| | Flues: | 408.2 sq. ft. (22x 5.25in) |
| Grate Area: | | 28.5 sq. ft. |
| Wheels: | Leading: | 3ft 2in |
| | Coupled: | 5ft 8in |
| | Trailing: | 3ft 2in |
| Tractive Effort: | At 85% boiler pressure | 27,420lb |
| Wheelbase: | Total: | 50ft 2.25in |
| | Engine: | 29ft 4in |
| | Tender: | 13ft |
| Weight: (full) | Total: | 113 tons 3cwt |
| | Engine: | 70 tons 8cwt |
| | Tender: | 42 tons 15cwt |
| Max. Axle Load: | | 17 tons |

# L.N.E.R.

## No.6701 Bo-Bo Electric Locomotive (1941)

Number built (L.N.E.R.): 1
Number built (B.R.): 57
Total built: 58

*Fig. 270. Gresley EM1 No.6701, works photograph. The Gresley Society.*

The difficult cross Pennine line through the Woodhead tunnel had long been considered for electrification, and in the 1930s the government made "Loan Act" finance available for railway infrastructure improvements. The L.N.E.R. decided to use this finance to electrify the Manchester, Sheffield and Wath line, including the Woodhead tunnel, and in 1935 serious planning started. In 1937 Gresley hired an Electrical Engineer, Edgar Claxton, to act as his technical assistant in these matters.

The Ministry of Transport had recommended the use of 1500V DC overhead electric lines for the project, largely down to experience gained with the Manchester, South Junction and Altrincham Line electrification, and this was chosen for the Woodhead line. Gresley as C.M.E. had worked alongside an electrical engineer, Edgar Claxton, for some years, having hired him previously as one of his team. The proposal for rolling stock included ten banking electric locomotives, nine express passenger electric locomotives and sixty-nine mixed traffic electric locomotives. The mixed traffic design was selected for development first, with the tendering process starting at the end of 1937.

By January 1939, the electrical equipment for seventy locomotives had been ordered from Metropolitan Vickers Electrical Co. Final assembly would be at Doncaster Works. However, the Second World War intervened, and the electrification of the line was halted, together with the production of all but one prototype mixed traffic locomotive.

The prototype exhibited some unusual design features for the time. Gresley had visited the South African Railways and observed their locomotives, which had also been supplied by Metropolitan Vickers. On these locomotives, no transmission of traction or braking forces came through the locomotive body. The draw gear and buffers were mounted on the bogies. The ride quality was praised, and Gresley was impressed, instructing this be adopted for the new locomotives.

*Fig. 271. "Tommy" became the first electric (rental) locomotive in the Netherlands. No.6000 is seen here in the service of the N.S. in Utrecht. City of Utrecht, Creative Commons License.*

The L.N.E.R. board had outlined concerns regarding the overall capital cost of the project and the mixed traffic locomotives were consequently designed with a Bo-Bo arrangement (two bogies with two axles on each, or four-wheel drive). Each axle was powered by a 467HP motor, married to a reduction gear with a ratio of 17:70. The two motors on each bogie was connected in series.

The locomotive was designed with 19 "notch" settings (the first fifteen were technically resistances, switched out for acceleration), and two "gears" (done by selecting series or parallel with both bogies). When accelerating from rest, the locomotive would have the bogies set up in series, and each successive resistance switched out.

Additional speed was achieved by switching from series to parallel and then switching the resistances back in. The prototype EM1 originally numbered as No.6701 was complete by August 1940, and initial trials involved no electricity whatsoever. The prototype was hauled along stretches of the East Coast main line between Doncaster and Retford to examine the riding characteristics.

*Fig. 272. No.6000 in the service of the N.S. with carriages along the platform of the N.S. station Utrecht C.S. in Utrecht. City of Utrecht, Creative Commons License.*

There seemed to be an unusual oscillation when running around 20 mph, so the prototype was modified with several different spring arrangements until the riding was considered adequate. It took until after Gresley's death in 1941 for No.6701 to be added officially to stock, and from September 1941 it carried out trials on the Manchester, South Junction and Altrincham Line. The trials consisted of a range of train weights and included empty coaching stock or wagons, loaded, or unloaded. Regenerative braking tests were undertaken by simulating a gradient by way of two J39 0-6-0 locomotives providing resistance by way of running in reverse to No.6701.

The trials showed that when hauling trains there was still some degree of oscillation between 20 and 25 mph. No.6701 was returned to Doncaster in mid-October and then stored for the rest of the war. In 1947, the electrification project was resumed, and No.6701 was brought out of storage. It was renumbered as No.6000, and more running trials were undertaken after servicing of the bogies. It was sent on loan to the Netherlands State Railway in September 1947, where intense testing over 10,000 miles revealed further issues with the ride quality of the locomotive.

*Fig. 273. No.6000 in the service of the N.S. with a freight train. City of Utrecht, Creative Commons License.*

More drastic measures were required, and modifications including upper-structure springing were fitted. This seemed to work, and the modifications remained in place when No.6000 returned to Britain five years later in February 1952. It was then officially named *Tommy*, a name used by the Dutch working on the locomotive. This was a reference to the nickname given to the British liberation forces in Holland.

Orders for further examples of the type (now known as EM1) were made from July 1946, with firm production to start in earnest from after nationalisation of the railways in 1948. Darlington had an order of twenty-four examples: this was cancelled. Gorton Works had an order for fifty-seven examples, and this went ahead with all of them being delivered between October 1950 and August 1953. The electrical equipment was prepared at Dukinfield, together with the traction motors. Externally, the placement of the cab doors and side windows were changed compared to the prototype No.6000.

All of the production locomotives were fitted from new with the modified bogie and springing arrangements that had been fitted to No.6000. The last ten of the class were fitted with Timken roller bearing axle boxes. Fourteen of the class were fitted with steam generators for heating passenger trains, though their usage on passenger trains was rarer, and some of the boilers fell out of use, with some removed during service.

*Fig. 274. No.6000 in the service of the N.S. with carriages on the railway yard in Utrecht C.S. City of Utrecht, Creative Commons License.*

There were issues with the production locomotives when running on the Wath to Dunford Bridge section of the line. The trains were normally organised with one locomotive pulling and the other banking the train. This led to a weight transfer issue which damaged the bogie centre pins (including in some extreme examples, complete fracturing of the pins). The trains were originally 850 tons tare; after some time, this was reduced to 750 tons tare to prevent further damage through slippage. Trials on the London Midland Region helped to some extent with understanding the issues further.

The EM1s eventually started their work on the Woodhead route shortly after the new Woodhead Tunnel was opened in June 1954, mainly employed on freight trains. Initial instructions to the drivers were for the use of just one pantograph, but the Woodhead route was subject to many different conditions including soot from steam locomotives, icing of the wires and more, leading to poor pickup on the overhead wires. Both pantographs were eventually raised as standard when running.

The class was reclassified as "Class 76" by British Railways in 1968, with suffixes from 1974 as below:

- 76-aV - EM1 fitted with vacuum brake but no steam heating boiler.

- 76-bX - EM1 fitted with dual brakes.

- 76-cV - EM1 fitted with both vacuum brake and steam heating boiler.

The class was allocated to Reddish depot initially but were redistributed as required to other sheds along the Woodhead route. The EM1s outlived the EM2s (the express passenger equivalent electric locomotive) and from 1968, with the withdrawal of the EM2s, took over their passenger work.

By 1970, however, the passenger services had been withdrawn and the first two EM1s were withdrawn.

By the mid-1970s the Woodhead route was freight only and the EM1s would be pulling the merry-go-round services from the Yorkshire coal fields to the power station at Warrington. Throughout the seventies EM1s would be withdrawn and by 1980 just 38 of the class remained in service. The writing was on the wall for the Woodhead route, however, and when the line closed in July 1981, the rest of the class was immediately withdrawn.

No.26020 was retained for preservation and can be seen currently in the Great Hall at the National Railway Museum. A cab from No.26048 *Hector* can be seen in the Manchester Museum of Science and Industry.

## Wartime Mileages & Availability

Due to the storage of the prototype during the Second World War, no statistics for mileages or availability are available in line with the rest of this publication.

| Class EM1 | | |
|---|---|---|
| Type: | | Bo-Bo |
| Voltage: | | 1500V DC |
| System: | | Overhead |
| Motors: | 4x | M.V. Type 186 |
| Total Power: | 1hr rating: | 1,868 hp |
| | Continuous: | 1,360 hp |
| Tractive Effort: | (starting) | 45,000 lb |
| Wheel diameter: | Bogie: | 4ft 2in |
| Wheelbase: | | 35ft 0in |
| Length over buffers: | | 50ft 4in |
| Weight: | | 87 tons 14cwt |
| Max. Axle Load: | | 22 tons 2cwt |

# New Builds, Rebuilds & Conversions

## Developments from the Grouping of 1923

Fig. 275. An exquisite shot of D16/3 No.62614 at Stratford shed, waiting a turn of duty as a Royal Engine. Photograph by Peter Townend. Colourised by Ian MacCabe, The Gresley Society.

When the LNER was formed at the grouping there were a number of areas where more or better performing locomotives were urgently needed. Where practical Gresley rebuilt existing locomotives or built new locomotives of existing classes that were considered satisfactory. The following is a summary of that area of his work as C.M.E. of the L.N.E.R.

Fig. 276. Many Robinson O4s were re-boilered, creating several sub classes. These were best identified by the round-topped boilers and in some cases replacement smokebox doors. O4/5 No.3816 is shown in this example. The Gresley Society.

## L.N.E.R. Class O4/5 and O4/7 2-8-0 (1923)

The largest fleet of locomotives inherited at the Grouping was from the NER. The largest class, however, was the Robinson designed GCR Class 8K 2-8-0. The GCR had built 126 of these, and no less than 521, with some small differences, notably the fitment of air brakes and lack of water scoops on the tenders, had been built for the Railway Operating Division (R.O.D.) of the Royal Engineers by N.B.L., Nasmyth Wilson and Robert Stephensons. This led to the 8Ks becoming known as "RODs".

By the time of the grouping the G.C.R. had bought more of these locomotives from the R.O.D., whilst the Government had many more on its hands. The L.N.E..R classified both G.C.R. and R.O.D. built locomotives as Class O4 and purchased 125 more from the R.O.D. in December 1923. In February 1925, a further 48 locomotives were purchased, and a final 100 were purchased in February 1927. The rest went to the G.W.R., the L.M.S., Australia and even China. By the end of 1929, the total number of O4s on the L.N.E.R. were 405 locomotives, including some from Class O5 that had been rebuilt as Class O4. These rebuilds were classified as O4/6.

Under Gresley's instruction in 1929, drawings were prepared for the fitting of a round topped O2 type boiler to replace the G.C.R. designed square topped Belpaire version. Two examples were subsequently rebuilt by the end of the year. These were classified as O4/4 and required frame extensions for the new boiler to fit. A shortened O2 boiler that could be fitted without altering the frames was introduced in 1932, and four O4s were converted to this new standard, reclassified as O4/5. The examples of Class O4/4 left were reclassified to O4/5 at the same time.

By 1939, a further revision to the boiler type had been made, and over the next eight years a further 47 of the O4s were converted, this time taking the designation of O4/7.

Fig. 277. Under Gresley's auspices, the L.N.E.R. ordered and built new batches of Robinson's D11 4-4-0s, of which No.6386 Lord Glenallan is a member. The Gresley Society.

## L.N.E.R. Class D11 4-4-0 (1923)

The ex-N.B.R. part of the new L.N.E.R. was in desperate need of some new express passenger locomotives. The G.C.R. "Improved Director" D11 4-4-0s that had been recently brought into service were thought to be a good interim solution by Gresley and so a batch of 24 more D11s were ordered for construction. There were some key differences from the original batch.

The N.B.R. loading gauge was lower than the G.C.R.'s, so a reduction in height was necessary, with lower cabs and boiler mountings provided. The dome was made flatter in profile, and new chimneys to Gresley's specification were fitted. Water pickup gear in the tender wasn't a requirement in Scotland, so this was dispensed with.

Armstrong, Whitworth & Co built 12 examples alongside Kitson & Co who built the other 12, with all 24 locomotives delivered within a five-month period. The L.N.E.R. sub-classified these locomotives as D11/1 and were bestowed with names based on characters in the novels and poems of Sir Walter Scott.

Fig. 278. Raven A2 No.2404 City of York on a passenger train, fitted with the 180lb Gresley A1 boiler and still pulling an N.E.R. six-wheeled tender. The Gresley Society.

## L.N.E.R. Class A2 4-6-2 (1923)

Raven's Pacifics came into being largely as a response to the developments around the G.N.R.'s publicity on the first of its Pacific locomotives. Drawings were prepared swiftly and development of the first two prototype locomotives, anticipating the grouping, was complete by December 1922. Several secondary sources have stated that No.2400 was still in workshop grey at the grouping, and No.2401 was in service from January 1923. The N.E.R. had just missed out on having the first Pacific as a constituent company of the L.N.E.R.

Gresley's involvement in the development of the N.E.R. Pacifics started with the ordering of three more of the class in February 1923. Gresley had these three locomotives modified with a redesign of the rear frames of the Pacifics with a Doncaster style cartazzi fitted, like his A1 design. This was a clear improvement on the Raven design which had experienced issues with overheating due to the closeness of the ashpan to the bearings.

No more modifications were authorised until 1929 when No.2404 was fitted with a slightly modified A1 boiler, requiring the rebuilding of the locomotive by way of a larger cab, wider running plate, and consequently wider footplate in the cab. This boiler was pressed to 180lb and made the locomotive comparable with the original A1 design (the Raven boilers were pressed to 200lb).

Eight-wheel tenders like the non-corridor Gresley tenders replaced the original Raven six-wheel tenders in 1933. In the same year, the Raven Pacifics were getting close to requiring new boilers, and consideration was given to fit new boilers of the A3 type, though this was superseded by a decision to withdraw the locomotives and build more V2s to supplement the existing fleet. No.2400's boiler was used as a stationary boiler for a couple of years at Darlington works before being scrapped around May 1939.

Fig. 279. Raven A2 No.2402, ex-works. Note the inclusion of the Gresley form of the Cartazzi truck underneath the cab. Owing to the size of the firebox and the ashpan, this cartazzi is placed much further forward than on the Gresley Pacifics.

Fig. 279b. Having gained a Gresley tender Raven A2 No.2401 City of Kingston upon Hull stands at New England shed awaiting her next call to arms on 16 June 1935. Strathwood Library Collection

Fig. 280. Raven T1 No.1657 sits on shed. These powerful locomotives were shunters, and the combination of small driving wheels over a long wheelbase gave them better adhesion than other classes. The Gresley Society.

## L.N.E.R. Class T1 4-8-0T (1925)

The N.E.R. had built a series of 4-8-0T locomotives for shunting freight and coal wagons around the docks at Hull, Newport, and Tyne Dock. Originally built in 1909, the T1s shared their boiler design with the A6 4-6-2T. The T1s had some similarities with the contemporary G.C.R. built S1s, with three cylinders of 18 x 26in.

Ten locomotives were built between 1909 and 1910, with a further five examples approved by Gresley for building in 1925. These locomotives worked up until the 1950s, when the reduction of coal exports started to bite and were eventually moved around the ex-N.E.R. area before scrapping. There were two exceptions to this, with two of the original T1s scrapped at Doncaster in 1938.

*Fig. 281. Robinson A5 No.5129 sits waiting its next turn of duty. This is a Robinson built example from the G.C.R. and is distinguishable from the Gresley built variations by the taller boiler fittings including the chimney, dome, and the height of the cab. The Gresley Society.*

## L.N.E.R. Class A5 4-6-2T (1925)

John Robinson's last passenger tank locomotive, which became the L.N.E.R.'s Class A5, was arguably one of his most useful designs. The G.C.R. built the 4-6-2T class in three batches between 1911 and 1917, with all intended for pulling fast suburban trains to and from Marylebone. This was their main work, which they performed for over thirty years.

Robinson become a consultant on the formation of the L.N.E.R. in 1923 and was working in an advisory position alongside Gresley as the new C.M.E. of the company. There was a shortage of suitable passenger tank locomotives in the North East area, and Robinson may have recommended the use of this design to fill that gap.

Gresley ordered a further thirteen locomotives, with some minor alterations to fit the N.E.R. loading gauge, including reduced boiler fittings, cabs, and chimneys. Hawthorn, Leslie & Co were tasked with building the final batch and completed the work between 1925 and 1946, leaving the total built at forty-four.

*Fig. 282 The Hill N7 locomotive was recognized early on by Gresley as a potential standard design for the new L.N.E.R. and he was swift in ordering further batches of the class for use in London and on the ex-G.E.R. lines. No.9711 sits awaiting its next turn of duty. The Gresley Society.*

## L.N.E.R. Class N7 0-6-2T (1925)

Gresley recognised a need for a degree of continuity in locomotive policy in various L.N.E.R. regions. The Hill designed ex-G.E.R. N7 0-6-2Ts were doing excellent work and were one of the first designs to be adopted as a Group Standard. The L.N.E.R. ordered one-hundred-and-twelve more N7s which were built between 1925 and 1928 in five batches, by Doncaster Works, Gorton Works, Robert Stephenson and Company, and W. Beardmore and Company. All these locomotives were built with left hand drive and lowered boiler mountings and cabs for work on the Metropolitan/City Widened Lines. Pony trucks and long travel valve gear was also fitted as something of an upgrade to the last seventy-two examples.

Of these, the last thirty-two N7s built at Doncaster works were built with round topped fireboxes instead of the original Belpaire design, with the Doncaster design becoming the standard for the class, and all but two examples of Class N7 would be rebuilt accordingly.

*Fig. 283. Gresley B12/2 No.8533. These locomotives were based on the S.D. Holden B12 locomotives but were fitted with Lentz valve gear. The Gresley Society.*

## L.N.E.R. Class B12/2 4-6-0 (1928)

By the mid-1920s the ex-G.E.R. region was starting to struggle with increasing train weights. This was particularly felt on the Southend to Tilbury route. Gresley recognised that an interim solution was required and made an order for a batch of ten B12s from Beyer, Peacock & Co. These were different from earlier B12s with the fitting of Lentz gear.

This additional change resulted in a public spat between Gresley and Beyer Peacock where the latter felt the former was asking for something extra in the fitting of Lentz gear. Geoffrey Hughes in his biography of Gresley gives the letter from Sir Sam Fay of Beyer, Peacock & Co, ltd in his appendices. Eventually the disagreement was settled, with the L.N.E.R. paying £1500 to the contractor, half that which had been requested on completion of the contract.

Between 1932 and 1944, all ten of the B12/2 locomotives were rebuilt with larger diameter boilers and long-travel Stephenson piston valves. More information on these rebuilds can be found under the B12/3 section later in this book.

Fig. 284. Holden/Gresley B12/2 No.8520 is turned on the turntable at Gorton in 1931. This is one of the "hikers", fitted with the ACFI feedwater equipment. Strathwood Library Collection.

Fig. 285. Holden/Gresley B12 No.8537 parked up at Stratford in the 1930s. Like No.8520 above, this locomotive has been fitted with the ACFI feedwater equipment. Strathwood Library Collection.

*Fig. 286. Class A8 No.69893 lets off steam as it waits for its next duty, with the driver peering out of the cab. Of note is the British Railways' standard tender to the left and the unmistakable shape of a Gresley A4 Pacific to the right. The Gresley Society.*

## L.N.E.R. Class A8 4-6-2T (1931)

The genesis of the A8s lie in the limitations of the Raven 4-4-4Ts that were working in the North East. Robinson A5s had been ordered to fill a shortage in passenger tank locomotives in 1925. A significant difference in performance and economy was noted between the Class A5 4-6-2Ts and the Raven H1 4-4-4Ts.

Gresley and his team investigated the possibility of rebuilding the H1s with a different wheelbase arrangement, and drawings were in evidence by 1930. In 1931, H1 No.2162 was withdrawn from service and substantially rebuilt with a 4-6-2T arrangement. No.2162 was placed on intensive comparison trials between the remaining H1s and the A5s that were working there, with the outcome being the complete withdrawal of the H1 class to be rebuilt as 4-6-2Ts between 1933 and 1936.

*Fig. 287. Gresley's rebuild of a Raven C7, No.727 as one of the articulated Class C9 locomotives. Note the bogie tender and the booster equipment. Doncaster Works Photograph. The Gresley Society.*

## L.N.E.R. Class C9 4-4-2, Articulated (1931)

Gresley considered that booster technology had potential and installed booster systems on a number of classes, albeit in small numbers. Installations on the C1 and P1 classes had given mixed results, and a particular concern on the C1 Atlantics had been riding problems which were put down to excess weight on the trailing wheels. The Raven C7s were up for rebuilding and became part of this overall development. The redesign gave the C7s a form of articulation between the locomotive and the tender, making the wheel arrangement technically 4-4-4-4, though the Atlantic classification was never dispensed with. No.727 and No.2171 were selected for rebuilding in 1931 after entering Darlington Works for general repairs.

By the end of 1931, the two locomotives had been substantially rebuilt with new round topped Gresley boilers pressed to 200lb (based on the B17 design), the four-axle bogie with booster, and a bogie version of the standard L.N.E.R. six-wheel tender. New smokeboxes and cabs finished the prototypes, looking distinctly like stretched versions of Gresley's Class D49. The rebuilt C7s were classified as C9 when they entered service.

The boosters were used between 1932 and 1936 until they were removed from the two engines. The two engines were withdrawn from service between 1942 and January 1943, No.727 outliving No.2171 by nine months.

*Fig. 288. Robinson S1 No.69905 sits out of use in 1956. Note the word "British" is still extant on the tank side, despite a "Cycling Lion" having been applied to its immediate right. These hump shunters looked like Robinson's Q4 class, sharing many parts, but had three cylinders.*
*The Gresley Society.*

## L.N.E.R. Class S1 0-8-4T (1932)

In the mid-1900s, John Robinson of the G.C.R. designed, and produced a series of 0-8-4T locomotives specifically to shunt the Wath-on-Dearne marshalling yard in South Yorkshire. These locomotives shared some design overlap with Robinson's Q4 0-8-0 tender locomotives but had been fitted with three cylinders and three sets of valve gear instead of two. This allowed for a smoother application of power when shunting uphill. The locomotives were also fitted with a power reversing gear, which was badly needed in a marshalling yard requiring many reversing moves in a working day.

These locomotives were successful at this niche role, but double heading was sometimes required to move heavy trains on wet rails. More S1s were required, and Gresley was already considering a booster fitted bogie for what became the C9 'Atlantics', so a design for the S1s was prepared. This was complicated by the need for the booster to operate in reverse as well as forward. No.6171 was built with the booster in 1930 and became S1/2, with the further two built in 1932 classified S1/3. The engines without the booster were given the classification of S1/1.

In service there were problems with the reverse gear. On No.6171 it was disabled after one month of operation, and it was also removed on the S1/3s. The boosters were removed completely in 1943.

*Fig. 289. Gresley B12/3 No.8510 on a Cambridge express in the 1930s. Note the use of white discs to denote the head code over the L.N.E.R.'s preferred oil lamps, a distinctive feature of ex-G.E.R. workings. The Gresley Society.*

## L.N.E.R. Class B12/3 4-6-0 (1932)

In the early 1930s, Edward Thompson was the mechanical engineer at Stratford. He recognised, together with his assistant, A.E. English, that the B12/2s running on the ex-G.E.R. region could be improved. With Gresley's approval, No.8579 was converted into a prototype of what became classified as B12/3.

This involved the fitting of a round top boiler, Stephenson valve gear with piston valves, larger cabs, and replacement smokeboxes. The resultant locomotive performed exceptionally, with much improved fuel economy. All the B12/1s and B12/2s were to be rebuilt to this standard. There was one exception, No.8534: which was withdrawn from service in 1945 without being rebuilt.

The B12/3s were extensively used during the Second World War on ambulance trains, due to their low axle loading and prodigious performance. Some minor modifications including moving the steps inwards on the running plate allowed them to go across the whole of the country. The first withdrawal came in 1947, with more withdrawn more quickly through the late 1950s, until 1959 when the sole survivor was No.61572. This locomotive hauled a series of rail tours and was fondly known as the "Wandering 1500" (a reference to its original classification). Happily, No.61572 was preserved and at the time of writing is being overhauled to working order at Ian Riley's workshops for the North Norfolk Railway.

*Fig. 290. Gresley D16/3 No.62614 on a stopping passenger train in the 1950s. Note the lack of decorative valances over the driving wheels. The Gresley Society.*

## L.N.E.R. Class D16/3 4-4-0 (1933)

In a similar vein to their work on the B12s, Thompson and English at Stratford Works requested permission from Gresley to investigate the rebuilding of the ex-G.E.R. D15s and D16s (the "Claud Hamiltons") in their area. Gresley threw his full weight behind their approach, with the first D15 to be rebuilt, No.8848, given a similar round topped boiler to the B12/3s.

Over one hundred and four D16/3s were produced until 1949, converted from D15/1s, D15/2s and D16/2s. ten of the D16/3s were given piston valves, but the additional power flexed their frames and caused fractures. Consequently, no more were fitted with piston valves.

One hundred and seventeen of the Clauds were still in service at nationalisation in 1948 (fourteen of which were the last of the unmodified D15s). By 1952, the D15s and D16/2s had all been withdrawn, leaving just the D16/3s remaining. Withdrawals started in 1955 and No.62613 was the last man standing when withdrawn in September 1960.

*Fig. 291. J19 No.64673 is surrounded by Thompson B1s in this shot from the late 1950s. This locomotive has been fitted with the Gresley round topped boiler. The Gresley Society.*

## L.N.E.R. Class J19 0-6-0 (1934)

In 1934 Gresley continued the rebuilding work at Stratford and instructed them to focus on the J19 0-6-0 tender locomotives. These locomotives had been built new from 1912 with more batches built up the grouping. The same large round topped boiler that had been fitted to the D16/3s was used, and a new cab was fitted to suit.

The boilers on the D16/3s were set to 180lb but the J19s were set at 160lb. The J19s that were rebuilt became classified as J19/2. By the end of 1938, all the J19s that had been rebuilt as J19/1s were now part of J19/2.

The classifications were dropped in 1947 when the last J19/1 was rebuilt to J19/2 specification, and all locomotives in the class became simply J19. After twenty years further service, withdrawals started in 1958 and the last two members of the class were withdrawn from traffic on 16 September 1962 as some of the last ex-G.E.R. classes working for British Railways.

*Fig. 292. Gresley ordered the rebuilding of one Raven D20 to this format, modernized with piston valves, high running plate and converted to left hand drive. The prototype, No.2020, was a good locomotive but only three more would be built after Gresley's passing, including this example, No.2360. The Gresley Society*

## L.N.E.R. Class D20/2 4-4-0 (1936)

When Thompson took over at Darlington Works in 1934, the staff there had been investigating the development of the various boilers fitted to this class. Diagram 59 came in two versions: one version fitted to the class in 1928 with a Schmidt superheater, and those to the later diagram 59 fitted from 1932 with a Robinson superheater. This modernisation was happening even though these locomotives had been built around the turn of the century and most were now over thirty years old.

The revised Diagram 59A had a single plate barrel, and from the 113 and 115 tubes of the original boilers, now had 131 tubes, giving more heating surface area. The safety valves were fitted closer together amongst other detail differences.

In 1936, a prototype for a revised version of the D20s was prepared by extensively rebuilding No.2020. This locomotive was one of the oldest, having been built in the first batch of ten locomotives. It was converted to left hand drive, with a new raised running plate (now incorporating separate and smaller splashers over the driving wheels), a larger cab and new bronze axle boxes that were fed by a Fountain type lubricator.

This became Class D20/2, and no more were rebuilt under Gresley, the remaining three D20/2s converted under Thompson as C.M.E. in the 1940s.

*Fig. 293. Raven B16 No.2364 as rebuilt under Gresley's direction to B16/2 specification. Note the use of outside Walschaerts valve gear, in combination with Gresley's conjugated motion.*
*Doncaster Works Photograph.*

## L.N.E.R. Class B16/2 4-6-0 (1937)

Arguably, Sir Vincent Raven's most iconic locomotives were his B16s. These mixed traffic 4-6-0s shared components with the large 0-8-0 mineral locomotives, the Q7s, and used three cylinders in a similar fashion. Three sets of Stephenson valve gear were used, all driving onto the front driving axle. Between 1919 and 1924, Darlington Works built seventy of these useful locomotives.

Gresley decided to investigate updating the B16s in the 1930s. No.2364 was chosen and emerged in 1937 with outside Walschaerts valve gear and conjugated gear for the middle cylinder. This required the front bogie to be moved forward by nine inches and the main frames to be lengthened accordingly. This in turn meant the running plate needed to be raised higher, together with the fitting of a new cab more closely aligned with Gresley's other classes. The rebuild was considered successful, but only six more B16s were converted to this arrangement, becoming classified as B16/2.

*Fig. 294. Three of the Class J45 shunters sit outside in the sun at March shed in early 1948 in between working in Whitemoor yard, notice the slight differences in the battery boxes.*
*Strathwood Library Collection.*

## L.N.E.R. Class J45 0-6-0 (1941)

The L.M.S. were having great success with diesel shunters, and specifically those of English Electric. Gresley and the L.N.E.R. were aware of the trials there and in February 1941 it was proposed at a meeting of the L.N.E.R.'s Wartime Emergency Board that a batch of these shunters should be ordered.

The first batch of four locomotives was built at Doncaster Works, with English Electric advising on the builds and providing the diesel-electric system. Visually, these locomotives were very similar to the L.M.S. locomotives but were a few inches longer. Provision was made for these locomotives to be readily converted to act as mobile generators if required during blackouts or power failures under wartime conditions. The first four locomotives were classified as J45 at first but in 1945 became D.E.S.1 (Diesel Electric Shunter 1).

The four locomotives proved successful, and a further order was made but only more shunter was built as a D.E.S.2 in connection with both Petter and Brush delivering 360 hp numbered as 15004 when delivered in 1949.

*Fig. 295. J45 No15000, now in B.R. dark green. Note the different hatches on the roof, buffer types and hooks on the buffer beam to the Class 08s. R.C.T.S..*

*Fig. 296. One of the remaining J45s parked up at Crewe South in June 1967. Note the differences between this and the cab of the Class 08 behind. Strathwood Library Collection.*

## Overall Production of Locomotives 1923-1939

| Year | No. of Locos Built | No. of Locos Withdrawn | No. of Locos bought | Total Stock | Difference to previous year |
|------|------|------|------|------|------|
| 1923 | 126 | 0 |  | 7399 |  |
| 1924 | 132 | 171 | 125 | 7485 | 86 |
| 1925 | 114 | 178 | 48 | 7469 | -16 |
| 1926 | 104 | 150 |  | 7423 | -46 |
| 1927 | 81 | 166 | 100 | 7438 | 15 |
| 1928 | 116 | 115 |  | 7439 | 1 |
| 1929 | 106 | 152 |  | 7393 | -46 |
| 1930 | 74 | 136 |  | 7331 | -62 |
| 1931 | 69 | 191 |  | 7209 | -122 |
| 1932 | 34 | 136 |  | 7107 | -102 |
| 1933 | 17 | 208 |  | 6916 | -191 |
| 1934 | 60 | 115 |  | 6861 | -55 |
| 1935 | 102 | 161 |  | 6802 | -59 |
| 1936 | 88 | 157 |  | 6733 | -69 |
| 1937 | 69 | 230 |  | 6591 | -142 |
| 1938 | 91 | 149 |  | 6533 | -58 |
| 1939 | 62 | 104 |  | 6491 | -42 |

Fig. 297. Table created from the L.N.E.R.'s annual reports and other associated records at the National Archives. Simon A.C. Martin.

Gresley's reign as C.M.E. saw large numbers of locomotives built in each year, whilst also reducing the overall stock of locomotives the company owned. In 1923, around 7400 locomotives were inherited, and by 1939 the fleet was 1000 locomotives smaller, with many of the oldest pre-grouping locomotives having been withdrawn as new locomotives were introduced. The only notable dip in building came between 1932 and 1934, when locomotive production dropped to incredibly low levels, but there was an acceleration of withdrawals at the same time. Having 1000 less locomotives to maintain represented a saving in overall costs such as fuel, maintenance, and retention of parts.

The overall drop in the locomotive numbers was driven by a significant reduction in the number of 0-6-0 and 4-4-0 tender locomotives. In both cases their overall duties were taken up by mixed traffic classes that did not present a like for like replacement. Greater utilisation of these locomotives by way of improved availability for service likely made the total drop in locomotive numbers achievable.

The majority of Gresley's output for the whole of his career came in the form of mixed traffic locomotives. When looked at in terms of the overall build quantities, year on year, we can see a few trends start to emerge:

# Gresley Locomotive Designs

| | Express Passenger | Secondary passenger | Mixed Traffic | Freight | Shunting | Specalised |
|---|---|---|---|---|---|---|
| 1911 | | | | | | |
| 1912 | | | 11 | | | |
| 1913 | | | 39 | | 10 | |
| 1914 | | | 30 | 5 | 5 | |
| 1915 | | | | | 4 | |
| 1916 | | | 10 | | 5 | |
| 1917 | | | 3 | | 5 | |
| 1918 | | | 22 | 1 | 1 | |
| 1919 | | | 10 | 15 | | |
| 1920 | | 10 | 20 | | | |
| 1921 | | 50 | 25 | 10 | | |
| 1922 | 2 | | 10 | | 5 | |
| 1923 | 10 | | | 10 | 5 | |
| 1924 | 30 | | 25 | 5 | 5 | |
| 1925 | 10 | | 35 | 2 | 5 | 1 |
| 1926 | | | | | 8 | |
| 1927 | | 20 | 44 | 35 | 11 | |
| 1928 | 10 | 6 | | | 13 | |
| 1929 | 11 | 10 | 72 | | 6 | |
| 1930 | 20 | 9 | 36 | | | |
| 1931 | 15 | 19 | 20 | | | |
| 1932 | | 10 | | 8 | | |
| 1933 | 6 | 5 | 25 | | | |
| 1934 | 16 | 16 | 32 | 8 | | |
| 1935 | 18 | 31 | 59 | | | |
| 1936 | 25 | 12 | 9 | | | |
| 1937 | 20 | 15 | 74 | | | |
| 1938 | 1 | 5 | 24 | | | |
| 1939 | | 6 | 77 | | | |
| 1940 | | 5 | 36 | | | |
| 1941 | | | 41 | | | |
| 1942 | | 1 | 25 | 20 | | |
| 1943 | | 2 | 21 | 5 | | |

*Fig. 301. Chart created from the L.N.E.R.'s annual reports and other associated records at the National Archives. Simon A.C. Martin.*

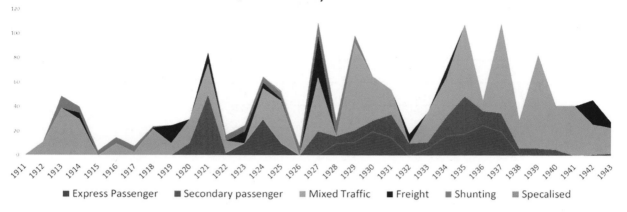

Gresley Locomotive Designs
Build Quantities By Year 1911-1943

■ Express Passenger ■ Secondary passenger ■ Mixed Traffic ■ Freight ■ Shunting ■ Specalised

*Fig. 302. Chart created from the L.N.E.R.'s annual reports and other associated records at the National Archives. Simon A.C. Martin.*

The most obvious trend is that the demand for new mixed traffic locomotives was consistent throughout Gresley's tenure, with larger spikes of building in the late 1920s and the late 1930s In particular, it can be noted that the demand for freight locomotives was far lower, only requiring some small build programmes throughout the 1910s, 1920s and 1930s.

This is likely down to the L.N.E.R.'s purchase of ex-R.O.D. O4 locomotives in the mid-1920s, providing an immediate addition to the available stock of freight locomotives without design, manufacturing, or servicing stages.

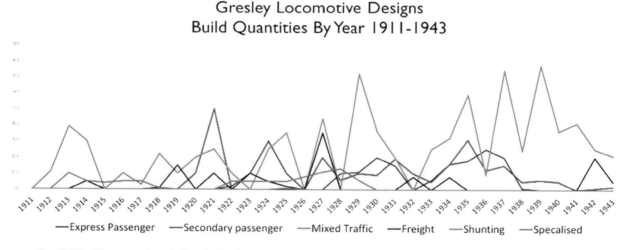

Gresley Locomotive Designs
Build Quantities By Year 1911-1943

—Express Passenger —Secondary passenger —Mixed Traffic —Freight —Shunting —Specalised

*Fig. 303. Chart created from the L.N.E.R.'s annual reports and other associated records at the National Archives. Simon A.C. Martin.*

The statistics show that just over half of Gresley's design output over his career was made up of three-cylinder locomotives, most of these having a form of conjugated motion married to outside Walschaerts valve gear. The exceptions to this rule had Lentz or Reidinger gear. His two-cylinder locomotives in the main used Stephenson's valve gear with piston valves or were rebuilt to this standard.

The three largest locomotives classes produced under Gresley were the Class J39, with 289 examples, the Class K3 with 193 built, and the Class V2 with 184 built. These three classes were considered mixed traffic locomotives by the L.N.E.R. and formed the majority of the new locomotives built for the company. Their combined total was 626 locomotives, with a little over half of these fitted with conjugated valve gear and three-cylinders.

This represents only a slight bias overall in favour of three-cylinder locomotives as a measure of Gresley's total output as C.M.E. of the L.N.E.R. and if anything highlights that he built locomotives that were necessary.

## Steam Locomotive Designs

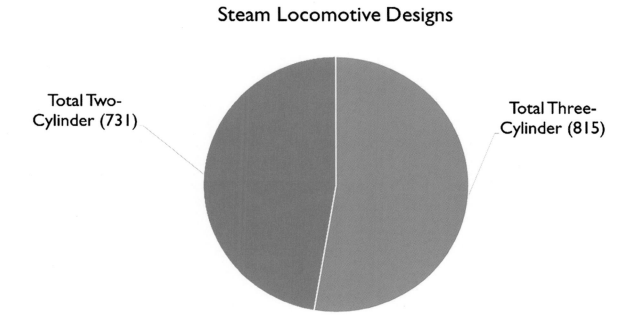

Total Two-Cylinder (731)

Total Three-Cylinder (815)

*Fig. 304. Chart created from the L.N.E.R.'s annual reports and other associated records at the National Archives. Simon A.C. Martin.*

# Chapter 6
# Gresley's Carriage & Wagon Designs

*Fig. 305. Gresley A4 No.4490 Empire of India leads the Coronation train out of Edinburgh Waverley Station in the late 1930s. Willem van de Poll. Creative Commons License.*

## Carriages

This chapter is intended only to provide a summary of the work of Gresley and his design team. Of note is the role of O.V.S. Bulleid and Edward Thompson throughout Gresley's career, both engineers at one time or another, with both providing much technical expertise, advice, and influence towards the improvement of designs. Bulleid in the earlier years of the G.N.R. and then L.N.E.R. provided much of the supervision in the design stages, referring to Gresley on the most important decisions.

Norman Newsome, whose work on development of the *Silver Jubilee* has already been noted, presented a paper to the Gresley Society some years ago in relation to the key philosophies of Gresley's approach to carriage design. In this he noted the following:

- The maximum use of articulation to save overall weight on a given train.

- The maximum use of India-rubber springs to reduce maintenance and replacement of drawgear and buffer components.

- Removing oil gas lighting and reduce overall fire risk as a result.

- Fitting of buckeye couplings between coaches to help prevent telescoping of coaches in accidents.

- Pressure ventilation for improved air flow within the carriages.

- Double glazing for heat insulation.

- Use of an optimised bogie design with good riding qualities.

This led to some early agreed standards for a variety of coach types including the corridor stock. There was one hold out, however: the ex-G.E.R. refused to take on any 60ft coaches for its main line services. This was, it maintained, because its trains out of Liverpool Street served so many different portions to different destinations in Anglia that splitting trains was impossible with this length of coach. Gresley accepted this, and the compromise provided for 51ft corridor coaches that were specific to the needs of the ex-G.E.R. region. There were a few instances when Gresley managed to persuade the region to accept 60ft corridor coaches: in 1925 the new *Hook Continental* train was made up of 60ft coaches, 1929 for the Cromer and again in 1937 when the *East Anglian* and a replacement for the 1925 Hook Continental set was being planned.

The L.N.E.R.'s engineering strategy is recognisable to today's asset engineers and fleet managers in terms of its rolling stock: it would cascade older types to routes as new trains for the premier and most heavily used routes were built or introduced to service. The different areas of authority within the L.N.E.R. were autonomous to the extent that they could submit bids for new construction within the annual programme of activity. It was not until 1942 and with changes undertaken by Thompson that this became centralised.

Gresley produced the first all steel underframes for a carriage vehicle at York in 1934, a significant improvement that eventually led to steel sided coaches and significant improvements in the safety of coaches, arguably carried through by Thompson, and other railways' designers into the amalgamation of best practice that became the B.R. Mk1 series of coaches.

The following table presents the annual new carriage building numbers. Note that the periods 1932-33 and 1933-34 are listed as "building suspended" which is true, strictly speaking, from how the L.N.E.R. recorded the programmes, but there were several new vehicles outshopped including a prototype all steel carriage (No.65000 of 1932), some "Tourist" stock for the replacement of ex-G.N.R. four wheeled passenger stock (1933) and some Gresley designed Buffet cars.

| L.N.E.R. Yearly Carriage Building Programme | | | | | | | | |
|---|---|---|---|---|---|---|---|---|
| Yearly Programme | 1923-24 | 1924-25 | 1925-26 | 1926-27 | 1927-28 | 1928-29 | 1929-30 | 1930-31 | 1931-32 |
| No. of Vehicles | 0 | 100 | 853 | 145 | 313 | 109 | 279 | 280 | 312 |
| Yearly Programme | 1932-33 | 1933-34 | 1934-35 | 1935-36 | 1936-37 | 1937-38 | 1938-39 | 1939-40 | 1940-41 |
| No. of Vehicles | Building Suspended. | Building Suspended. | 270 | 647 | 596 | 711 | 382 | 213 | 155 |

*Fig. 306. Table created from the L.N.E.R.'s annual reports and other associated records at the National Archives. Simon A.C. Martin.*

We are fortunate that we have volunteers in railway preservation that have produced an online catalogue of the surviving rolling stock. Appendix 8 gives a breakdown of the survivors built under Gresley between 1923 and 1941, based on the data collated by the *Railway Heritage Register Online*.

*Fig. 307. Gresley J38 0-6-0 No.65923 heads a train of coal wagons east of Greenhill Junction on the Edinburgh - Glasgow main line. Ben Brooksbank. Creative Commons License.*

## Wagons

The L.N.E.R. at the grouping inherited 284,488 wagons from the following railways:

| Company | No. of Wagons |
|---|---|
| G.C.R. | 35,330 |
| G.E.R. | 27,213 |
| G.N.R. | 38,713 |
| G.N.o.S.R. | 3603 |
| N.E.R. | 123,823 |
| N.B.R. | 55,806 |

*Fig. 308. Table created from the L.N.E.R.'s annual reports and other associated records at the National Archives. Simon A.C. Martin.*

This is best presented in graph form, as below:

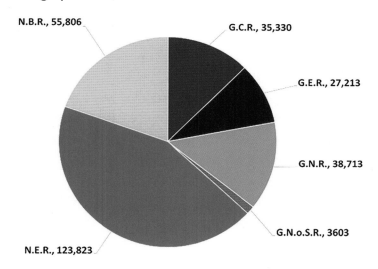

*Fig. 309. Chart created from the L.N.E.R.'s annual reports and other associated records at the National Archives. Simon A.C. Martin.*

The difference in the relative sizes of the constituent railways wagons can be largely explained by the significant difference in the ownership of coal carrying wagons, the N.E.R. owning many of these in house, unlike the other railways where a greater proportion were using private owner wagons together with much smaller quantities of their own.

The N.E.R.'s fleet of coal wagons comprised 64,388 wagons alone, in comparison to the next nearest company, the N.B.R., with 23,439 examples.

The 284,488 wagons inherited in 1923 were made up of the following types:

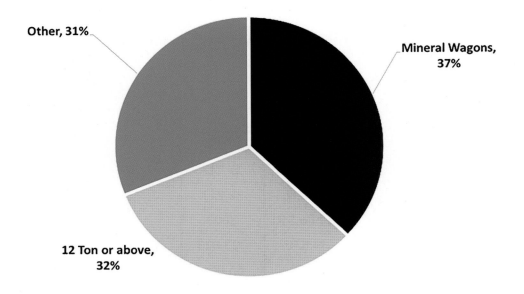

Other, 31%

Mineral Wagons, 37%

12 Ton or above, 32%

*Fig. 310. Chart created from the L.N.E.R.'s annual reports and other associated records at the National Archives. Simon A.C. Martin.*

At the grouping, the L.N.E.R. had several major works that were repairing and building new in almost equal quantities. These works were Shildon (ex-N.E.R.), Faverdale in Darlington (ex-N.E.R. and subsequently became the L.N.E.R.'s main site for new wagon construction), Dukinfield (ex-G.C.R.), some work at York too.

The wagons were generally built to the Railway Clearing House (R.C.H.) standards, including things such as cast-iron split axle boxes, wooden underframes and to specific planking sizes for the wagon bodies. During Gresley's tenure, cast steel open fronted axle boxes were introduced, together with the introduction of all welded steel underframes from 1932. Welding was in its infancy, but Gresley saw the potential of the new technique to reduce weight and increase strength within wagon design, and the first wagon built with welded underframes emerged at Dukinfield in 1930.

In 1936, the Faverdale Wagon Works had been working on some new hopper wagons, the intention being to replace all the timber N.E.R. hoppers with all steel constructed wagons. These wagons were built in large numbers and eventually numbered over 60,000 between those built by the L.N.E.R. and British Railways later. By 1938, the total number of vehicles had reduced substantially to 258,236 items of rolling stock, broken down into the following types:

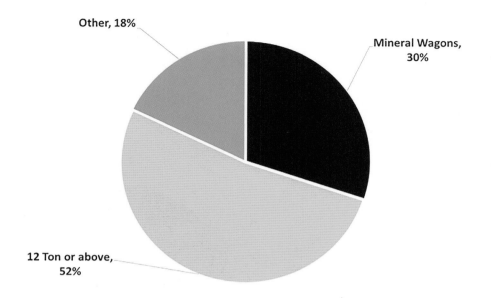

*Fig. 311. Chart created from the L.N.E.R.'s annual reports and other associated records at the National Archives. Simon A.C. Martin.*

This reduction in overall numbers will have been in no small part due to the increasing higher tonnage of railway vehicles together with a reduction in the number of older, smaller wagons being used.

There may also have been some overlap with the reduction in the number of vehicles from private owners across the United Kingdom, with road haulage starting to make inroads to the traffic that was traditionally transported on the railways.

*Fig.311b. The distinctive style of Gresley pattern coaches would be seen albeit in much more limited numbers into the 1970s, here in the carriage sidings at Craigentinny SC16660E was captured on 15 April 1956. Strathwood Library Collection*

# Chapter 7
# The Development of Streamlining

*Fig.312. With a fully streamlined A4 in Garter Blue standing behind P2 No.2001 Cock O' the North at Haymarket we can see a transition towards full streamlining, for the locomotives at least during the latter half of the 1930s. Colourised by Ian MacCabe - The Gresley Society.*

## What is streamlining?

Streamlining in aerodynamics is defined as the contouring of an object (such as an aircraft or locomotive) to reduce its drag or resistance to motion through a stream of air. This leads to two basic principles for streamlining:

* The front of the object should be well rounded.

* The object should gradually curve back from the middle to a tapering rear section.

An efficiently designed object will take on the teardrop shape as an optimum shape. This isn't quite possible for trains, however, which must conform to what is necessary for the purposes of operational requirements. Trains can, however, minimise their drag as much as possible through several methods of drag reduction. These methods are generally accepted as being:

- The streamlining of the front and rear of a train. (In Gresley's work, *The Coronation* was the only train produced where such streamlining was in effect with the observation car attached).

- Making the surface of the train smooth, uniform and free from "protuberances". The latter refers to smaller objects that may protrude out of the bodyshell for functional aspects, such as door handles, pantographs, or the fairings between vehicles.

- Putting a streamlined faring between the bogies of each vehicle to reduce the roughness of air flow and to ensure flow separation around the bogies is reduced as much as possible.

It is generally accepted that the advantages for high-speed trains are obvious with aerodynamic improvements, but modern research into train design suggests that energy savings of as much as 6%-8% are possible with drag reduction of 20%-25% made in the design of suburban commuter trains.

## Optimisation Methods

Trains experience a range of aerodynamic forces and moments whilst in motion, with the total aerodynamic drag of a train the sum of the drag on different parts of the train, including from the front (or "nose"), the rear (or "tail"), the bogies (or driving wheels), gaps between carriages, pantographs, and smoothness of the surface of the train (rougher surfaces increase drag).

To optimise the drag reduction ability of the train, the shape of the train must be optimised. This is noted in the publication *Train Aerodynamics: Fundamentals and Applications* in the modern day as having a very "trial and error" approach throughout railway history, with reliance on the skills of the aerodynamicist (in Gresley's case, Professor Dalby, and Frederick Johansen) to help shape the overall aerodynamic concept.

Where trains are concerned, there are several aerodynamic principles that are also in conflict with one another and changing one aspect of the design may unintentionally add drag to another part. This becomes more complicated when different parts of a train or locomotive may be required to perform different functions aerodynamically.

A good example of this required multi-functionality with some compromises is Gresley's original W1: the front end is aerodynamically designed to scoop in air towards pre-heating for the boiler, together with reducing drag at the front end, and along the boiler sides, and to force smoke and steam up, and away from the boiler casing and the driver's line of sight.

Ultimately it was very successful in two of these variables and in the third there was a compromise which added some drag by way of the locomotive's cab not quite lining up with the tender in terms of its profile, creating additional drag on the entire locomotive as a result.

Gresley identified quite early on compared to other locomotive engineers the requirements for a systematic approach of design, testing through modelling, analysis and then re-design, with comparisons of different aspects of his locomotive, and later full streamlined train designs, requiring appropriate trade-offs to achieve a more streamlined whole.

This is borne out by Frederick Johansen's paper to the iMechE some years later, when describing how the 1/12th scale model of the W1 was compared to a similar model of No.4472 *Flying Scotsman*:

> *The disparity between the resistances of the L.M.S. and L.N.E. tenders is due to the transverse dimensions of the tenders in relation to those of the locomotives. The L.M.S. tender is somewhat narrower and appreciably lower than the engine cab, and consequently is situated in a region of low pressure with the result that, on the whole, it is dragged forward and has a slightly negative air resistance at 0 deg. yaw. An experiment in which small tufts of wool were attached by short silk threads to the L.M.S. tender demonstrated quite clearly the presence of strong air currents over the top of the tender in the direction of the engine cab. The L.N.E. tenders, which are broader and higher than the L.M.S. tender, are much less shielded by the engine cabs in front of them and are, in consequence, subject to positive air resistance. In this connexion it is noteworthy that L.N.E. engine No. 4472, having a greater resistance than No. 10,000 and presumably deflecting the air stream to a greater extent, is associated with a smaller tender resistance, even though the tenders of Nos. 4472 and 10,000 are practically identical. This feature of the shielding influence of a locomotive of bad aerodynamic form (already mentioned on p. 112) leads to the important general conclusion that if only the locomotive of a train is streamlined, the full advantage represented by the reduction of the air resistance of the locomotive will not be attainable since the improved shape of the locomotive will induce the air flow to adhere more closely to the surfaces of the coaches downstream and, if the coaches are of conventional, or bad aerodynamic, form, will cause their air resistance at low angles of yaw to be greater than if they were headed by a locomotive of conventional pattern.*

> *Over the available range of wind tunnel speeds the L.M.S. and L.N.E. one-fortieth scale model trains showed no scale effect on lateral force, nor on longitudinal force at 20 deg. yaw and over. At smaller angles of yaw, however, these trains exhibited some scale effect on longitudinal force, the amount, which was about the same for both types of train and for the standard and modified conditions, being less than that corresponding to the skin friction on a smooth surface. For these trains, therefore, an appropriate proportion of the skin friction correction has been applied as a scale effect correction. In extenuation of this method of estimation, which has been adopted only in default of any established, more certain, procedure, it may be stated that the scale effect so deduced, for 0 deg. yaw, between the model L.M.S. six coach train at 85 ft. per sec. in the wind tunnel and the full-scale train at 100 m.p.h. is less than 6 per cent, while that on the L.M.S. locomotive is only 3 per cent, of the measured coefficient.*

*The one twelfth scale L.N.E. locomotive models showed for the engines slightly diminishing resistance with increased speed, and slightly increasing resistance for the tenders, the resulting scale effect for the complete locomotives being practically zero.*

*The Air Resistance of Passenger Trains, Frederick Johansen, Pages 120 and 121.*

The N.P.L., together with Professor Dalby and Frederick Johansen, worked for nearly a decade on streamlining locomotives and rolling stock, with the first test subject being Gresley's W1, starting from around 1927/1928 with the design finalised by 1929 prior to the locomotive's entry into traffic.

## Gresley's Streamlined Locomotives

Gresley's streamlined locomotives were all, bar one, based on the A4 Pacifics external casing. The one exception to this rule was the W1, whose streamlined casing was the first such streamlined design, and which after much testing in its early years, and with later comparison with the A4 Pacifics, was converted to A4 design philosophy.

The work at the N.P.L. informed the development of the streamlined trains as described in the section on the A4 Pacifics, but perhaps most interesting was the knowledge that came with the testing. Bert Spencer made an interesting presentation to the iMechE in 1947, in which he produced the following figures:

| HORSE POWER SAVED BY STREAMLINING | | | | | | | | | | |
|---|---|---|---|---|---|---|---|---|---|---|
| | Horse-power required to overcome head on air resistance. | | | | | | | | | |
| Speed (mph) | 60 | 70 | 80 | 90 | 100 | 110 | 120 | 130 | 140 | 150 |
| Standard 'Pacific' Type | 97.21 | 154.26 | 230.51 | 328.49 | 450.92 | 599.39 | 778.65 | 988.95 | 1235.87 | 1520.8 |
| Streamlined Type | 56.39 | 89.41 | 133.61 | 190.4 | 261.36 | 347.41 | 451.32 | 573.21 | 716.32 | 881.48 |
| Horsepower saved by Streamlining | 40.82 | 64.85 | 96.9 | 138.09 | 189.56 | 252.98 | 327.33 | 415.74 | 519.55 | 639.32 |

*Fig. 313. Table derived from Bert Spencer's statistics in his 1947 presentation to the iMechE. Simon A.C. Martin.*

What is notable about the figures is how much horsepower is required to overcome air resistance at speeds for which many of the L.N.E.R.'s mixed traffic locomotives, such as the V2s, B17s and similar would be travelling at. The latter class eventually had two members of its class modified to the A4 streamlined form, the V2s were originally designed with it and were then built along more conventional lines.

When presenting the data in graph form, the savings in horse power through applying streamlining are thought provoking:

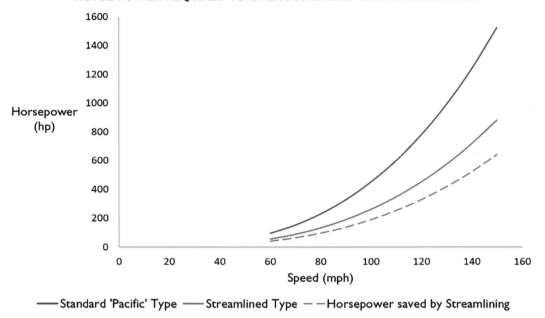

# HORSE POWER SAVED BY STREAMLINING
## HORSE POWER REQUIRED TO OVERCOME HEAD ON AIR RESISTANCE

——Standard 'Pacific' Type ——Streamlined Type − −Horsepower saved by Streamlining

*Fig. 314. Chart derived from Bert Spencer's statistics in his 1947 presentation to the iMechE. Simon A.C. Martin.*

The data that Bert Spencer and the L.N.E.R. collated suggests that streamlining even classes that were unlikely to achieve over 75 mph would have still provided savings in horsepower required when overcoming air resistance. This would lead, all things being equal to fuel economies across the board.

That much was proven by the introduction of the A4 Pacifics, whose water and coal consumptions per mile were shown to be superior to the original Pacifics on test. The streamlining of the A4s was also shown to advantage in later years when several Thompson Pacifics were tested alongside them. The results strongly suggested that if streamlining had been applied to the later Thompson locomotives, better results would have been obtained in fuel economy.

One series of tests undertaken in the late 1940s between A4 Pacific *Sir Ralph Wedgwood* and the Thompson A1 *Great Northern*, emphasize this well in the very close results between the two locomotives, although an additional factor will have been the double Kylchap exhaust of *Great Northern* by comparison with the A4's single chimney. By that time although there may have been encouragement from the C.M.E. to investigate streamlining for locomotive designs, the drawing office was less encouraged and preferred to concentrate on other aspects of design.

*Fig. 315. When the modern day L.N.E.R. started running their Azuma trains, there was a desire to compare the old and the new, and so Gresley A4 No.4468 Mallard was borrowed from the N.R.M. and placed on display. This led to this interesting comparison of front-end shapes. Of note is that Mallard's thin section of streamlining from the bottom of the casing between the buffers, rising up and widening to the top, is similar to the shape of the Azuma. In profile, Gresley's locomotive was remarkably ahead of its time. Considered as an entire train, the high-speed Azuma closely follows the design philosophy of Gresley's high-speed trains, built nearly 100 years earlier. The Gresley Society.*

It remains a shame that the benefits of the A4 Pacific style casing were not more fully realised nor used in any meaningful way towards the production of the British Railways Standard Locomotive classes. It is however interesting to note that in more modern incarnations of the high-speed train, the overall design philosophy of the exterior casing for the entire train follows the very principles that Gresley settled on when developing his streamlined high-speed trains.

# Chapter 8
# Gresley's Legacy

*Gresley's Surviving Locomotive Designs*

The number of locomotives that survive from Gresley's tenure as C.M.E. are but a fraction of the overall output of his life. The locomotives that survive are:

- Class A3 (1) – No. 60103 *Flying Scotsman*, currently operational and owned by the National Railway Museum.

- Class A4 (6) – One operational, appropriately No.60007 *Sir Nigel Gresley*. The other five, *Mallard, Bittern, Dominion of Canada, Union of South Africa*, and *Dwight D. Eisenhower* are all static exhibits currently.

- D49 (1) – No.246 *Morayshire*, currently under overhaul and owned by Scottish Railway Preservation Society (S.R.P.S.)

- K4 (1) – No. 61994 *The Great Marquess*, being prepared to go into her new home, owner John Cameron's museum in Scotland. There she will stand alongside A4 *Union of South Africa*.

- N2 (1) – No.1744, currently under overhaul and owned by The Gresley Society.

- V2 (1) – No.4471 *Green Arrow*, is owned by the National Railway Museum but is interred at the new museum in Doncaster, the Doncaster Museum and Art Gallery (D.A.N.U.M.)

- EM1 (1) – No.26020 is owned by the National Railway Museum and has been on long term display in the Great Hall at York.

Of these, a disproportionate number are from his A4 Pacifics and there are no examples of his 0-6-0, 2-6-0, 2-8-0, 2-6-2T or 4-6-0 designs preserved.

In the modern age, there are several locomotives that are being manufactured new, with the following Gresley era locomotives being recreated:

- B17 (1) – No.61673 Spirit of Sandringham, being built by the B17 Steam Locomotive Trust at C.T.L. Seal Limited in Sheffield. To date the frames have been erected, three tenders procured (one from the defunct other B17 group, who graciously sold their components a few years ago, to the trust) and the driving wheels have been cast.

- P2 (2) – No.2007 *Prince of Wales*, being built by the manufacturers and owners of Peppercorn A1 No.60163 *Tornado*. Their new P2 incorporates many design alterations to enable it to run without issue on the national network, also taking on board lessons learned from the building of *Tornado* and incorporating some standard components such as the boiler and other items. To date it is a rolling chassis, cast cylinders and a tender nearing completion, with a boiler in Meiningen, Germany being manufactured. It will closely resemble No.2001 *Cock O'The North* as built when complete.
The other P2 being built is a replica of No.2001 *Cock O'The North* but in its final streamlined form. Frames have been produced but no further progress has been recorded to date.

- V4 (1) – No.3403 *Highlander*, being built by the manufacturers and owners of Peppercorn A1 No.60163 *Tornado*. This will be the third locomotive out of the new Darlington Works from the same builders. Currently the locomotive is in the design phase whilst the P2 is being completed.

## Gresley's Surviving Carriage & Wagon Designs

The details of the surviving coaching and wagon stock can be found in Appendix 9 at the end of this book, but the L.N.E.R. has, like its locomotive stock, suffered by way of a smaller proportion of its output being preserved in the present day. We are fortunate that several rakes of Gresley teak stock are in use throughout the country, the most notable sets currently on the North Yorkshire Moors and the Severn Valley Railway.

Of note however are the retention and restoration of both of Gresley's beavertail observation coaches from *The Coronation*. No.1719 has been restored in its final form as it was used in Scotland, with the larger rear window and in B.R. maroon livery. It is currently in operation at the Great Central Railway.

No.1729 is currently on display in the Hornby Visitor Centre as part of the Hornby's One:One collection of vehicles on display. It was painstakingly restored over several years to its original shape and format by the Railway Vehicle Preservations group and is owned by the Royal Scot Locomotive & General Trust (R.S.L.G.T.). The work of Andrew Daniels and the rest of the team resulted in the Heritage Railway Association (H.R.A.) awarding them the Chairman's Special Award in 2022.

*Fig. 316. Sir Nigel Gresley on the day of the naming of A4 Pacific No.4498, the hundredth Gresley Pacific, as "Sir Nigel Gresley", surrounded by his colleagues and friends from around the industry and within the L.N.E.R. Left to right: Messer's W. Massey, H. Harper, B. Spencer (Holding Hat), G.A. Musgrave, W.B. Brown (Hand In Pocket), D.R. Edge, A.H. Peppercorn (Rear Row), F. Wintour (Bowler Hat), Sir Nigel Gresley (Holding Model), Messer's R.A. Thom, O.V.S. Bulleid, H. Broughton, F.H. Eggleshaw, Edward Thompson, and T.A. Street. The Gresley Society.*

## The Men behind the Man

Arguably, Gresley's greatest legacy remains in the engineers, draughtsmen, media relations, maintenance, and executive colleagues he left behind, who carried on and worked in a variety of different roles on Britain's railways for many years after.

In the above photograph there are three men who would go on to become C.M.E.s in their own right: Edward Thompson, Arthur Peppercorn and Oliver Bulleid. In the same group there is Bert Spencer, who went on to help develop many of Thompson's and Peppercorn's designs as an advisor and technical assistant. Also in the photograph is Robert Thom who, alongside Spencer, was responsible for helping to develop Gresley's streamlined trains in the form of the carriage designs too.

Some men not in the photograph above but undoubtedly worthy of mention include Frederick Harrison (who, as mentioned earlier in this book, would rise to become the Chief Mechanical & Electrical Engineer of British Railways, responsible for the design of the British Railways Standard 8P, Duke of Gloucester), Alec Emerson (who after being in the L.N.E.R. Electrical Engineers' office went on to take charge of the electrification of the West Coast Main Line some years later), and Norman Newsome, someone Gresley personally hired at Doncaster and then saw out the next fourteen years of his career working on the carriage and wagon designs at the King's Cross office. There are many more that could be mentioned.

Gresley recognised the importance of developing those around him, and though he himself was more in the mind of the practical application of experience, recognised the importance of imparting his knowledge. It is testament to his work that so many of his team went on to have careers that furthered the work he started on the L.N.E.R.

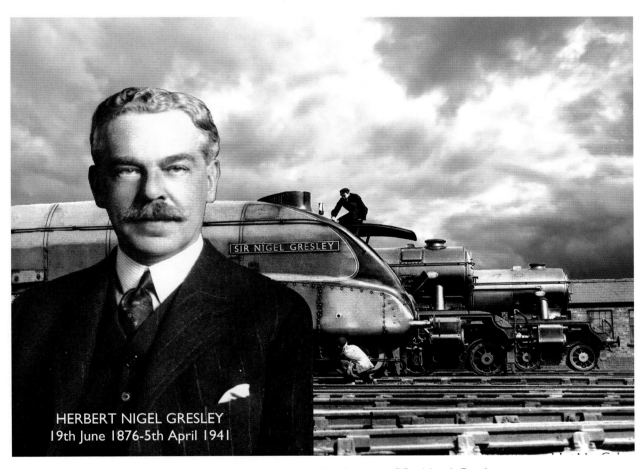

HERBERT NIGEL GRESLEY
19th June 1876-5th April 1941

*Fig.316b. A fine testament to the legacy of Sir Nigel Gresley.*
*Colourised by Ian MacCabe - The Gresley Society.*

Fig. 317. Gresley A3 No.60103 Flying Scotsman about to depart Kings Cross on her final run for British Railways on 14 January 1963. At the front in the duffel coat is a young Ian MacCabe, watching on. The Gresley Society.

## The Gresley Society and its Diamond Jubilee
## (written by Ian MacCabe)

As a founder member of *The Gresley Society* it is difficult to comprehend that we have been in existence for exactly 60 years. The original society was founded in 1963 as *The Gresley A3 Preservation Society*, which was formed to save *Flying Scotsman*, which at the time was an astonishing omission from the list of steam locomotives to be preserved by the British Transport Commission. The sole aim for the society was raising £3000, the scrap asking price from British Railways for the Gresley A3 Pacific.

Of course, Alan Pegler stepped in to save the old girl, much to our relief as we were struggling to raise sufficient funds. The society was relaunched and rebranded in February 1963 with our new purpose established then and remaining our aim today: "to study and celebrate the life and works of Sir Nigel Gresley in particular, and the works and achievements of the London & North Eastern Railway in general."

Although we were not able to save a Gresley Pacific, later in our existence came the opportunity to save one of his earliest designs.

1961
The GA3PS formed to save *Flying Scotsman* from scrap.

1963
January: *Flying Scotsman purchased by Alan Pegler for £3000*
February: The Gresley Society founded; subs set at 3/- per annum (15p).

*Fig. 318. Gresley N2 No.69532 as sold into preservation in 1962. Note the bag tied around the chimney, and the high position of the handrail in relation to the numberplate. The Gresley Society.*

1963
November: N2 No. 69523 purchased by the society for £900.
It was subsequently moved from Doncaster to Harworth Colliery.

1963
November: First Issue of *The Gresley Observer* published.

*Fig. 319. Gresley A3 No.60106 Flying Fox about to depart Kings Cross with the Gresley Society's rail tour "The London and North Eastern Flier". The Gresley Society.*

1964

May: L.N.E.R. Flier special hauled by No. 60106 *Flying Fox* organised by the society.
The locomotive touches 96 mph down Stoke Bank.
November: The N2 steamed for first time.

1965

The N2 moved to the Keighley and Worth Valley Railway (K.W.V.R.).
An L.N.E.R. BSK carriage was purchased for £300.

1966

The Buffet Lounge Carriage was purchased for £450.
The ex-Coronation observation carriage was purchased for £350.
Public service begins at K.W.V.R. using N2 4744.

1969

Our N2 No.4744 featured in the film *The Railway Children*.
Shortly afterwards the N2 suffered a burst boiler tube.
Repairs were beyond the society's income at that time.

1974

Under a new agreement the N2 was moved to the Main Line Steam Trust
(later known as the Great Central Railway, G.C.R.).

The observation carriage was moved to the South Eastern Steam Centre, Ashford.

*Fig. 320. Gresley N2 No.4744 minus its L.N.E.R. branding thunders past the actors of The Railway Children whilst playing the role of the "Scotch Flyer". Simon A.C. Martin.*

## 1978
The N2 was back in service after overhaul,
and the observation coach was moved to the G.C.R.

## 1985
The N2 was withdrawn from service for overhaul.

## 1987
The N2 was back in service back, but now as B.R. No.69523
in the lined out mixed traffic livery.
The BSK was sold to the Railway Vehicle Preservation Society (R.V.P.S.)

## 1990
The N2 began its ten-year overhaul.

*Fig. 321. Chairman Alan Garraway and Tony Roche President IMechE unveil the plaque at the N.R.M. The Gresley Society.*

1992

York plaque unveiled at N.R.M.

1993

100th edition of *The Gresley Observer* published.

1997

English Heritage Blue Plaque unveiled at KX by VP Tim Godfrey

The N2 was sent on tour to a number of heritage railways including the N.N.R. & K.W.V.R.

Fig. 322. Blue plaque, as affixed to the wall at King's Cross station. The Gresley Society.

1998
*Mallard* 126 mph sign unveiled at milepost 90 ¼.

1999
The N2 returns to G.C.R. from K.W.V.R.

2000
*The Gresley Society* signed up as a charity.
The N2 was withdrawn for major overhaul under a new
agreement with the G.C.R.

2001
Edinburgh, Waverley plaque unveiled by Tony Roche (President IMechE).

2002
Buffet Lounge Carriage transferred to Stainmore Railway Co.
on a 25-year lease agreement.

2003
The society exhibited the buffet lounge at *Doncaster 150*.

*Fig. 323. 19 feet high and weighing in at one and a half tons The Gresley Society's memorial sign to Mallard's World Speed Record in place at milepost 90 ¼. The Gresley Society.*

2004
The society attended *Railfest* at the N.R.M.
and gained new members (now 315) and had a successful sales stand.

2005
The decision was taken to replace the N2's firebox with steel.
£2000 was donated from the society towards the restoration of observation coach No.1728.

The N2's overhaul was completed at Loughborough.

2009-2010
N2 on tour: the N.N.R., SVR, NYMR, K.W.V.R., N.R.M. Shildon & Avon Valley Railway were all visited during the course of the year.

1744 stars at *Railfest* at the N.R.M., and the National Exhibition Centre (N.E.C.) as the centrepiece of the Warley Model Railway Exhibition.

The N2 subsequently visits the M.N.R., N.Y.M.R. and the E.L.R.

*Fig. 324. Britannia No. 70013 Oliver Cromwell at Kings Cross now wearing our Gresley Society Golden Jubilee headboard. The society had intended to use an A4 but No.60007 was under repair at the N.Y.M.R. and No.60009 unfortunately failed only days before. The Gresley Society.*

2013
Gresley Society's Golden Jubilee Year.
March: Gresley Lecture at IMechE with presentations by John Cameron & Peter Coster.

June: The N2 visits the Epping Ongar Railway for the
150th Anniversary of London's Underground.
Our first ever photo competition receives over 100 entries and some 300 photos.

October: The N2 returns to Scotland for the first time since being built by NBL Glasgow in
1921. It visits the Bo'ness & Kinneil Railway.

December: Golden Jubilee Special rail tour, King's Cross to Lincoln behind Britannia Standard
Pacific No. 70013
Oliver Cromwell.in lieu of No.60009 Union of South Africa.

*Fig. 325. 2013 December. This was our intended locomotive chosen to haul our Golden Jubilee special. Gresley A4 No.60009 Union of South Africa masquerading as No.60004 William Whitelaw sporting our headboard in the wheel drop shed at Southall the day before the trip.*
*The Gresley Society*

### 2014
The N2 visits the N.N.R., Shildon, E.L.R. and Mid Norfolk Railway (M.N.R.),
And also appears in the BBC's drama *Ripper Street.*

### 2015
The N2 visits the Nene Valley Railway (N.V.R.) and the E.O.R.

### 2016
April: Sir Nigel Gresley Statue unveiled at King's Cross Station
by Sir Peter Hendy of Network Rail.

*Fig. 326. Peter Townend and Dick Hardy stand either side of the bronze statue of Sir Nigel Gresley that was commissioned by the Gresley Society and unveiled at Kings Cross on 5th April 2016. This was the anniversary of Gresley's death in 1941. The Gresley Society.*

*Fig. 327. The plaque commemorating the birth of Sir Nigel Gresley in Edinburgh. The Gresley Society.*

*Fig. 328. Michael Portillo unveils the plaque at Hadley Wood commemorating Gresley and his locomotives. The Gresley Society.*

2016

June: Plaque unveiled at Gresley's birthplace Edinburgh by Bill Reeves.

## 2017
October: Plaque at Hadley Wood unveiled by Michael Portillo.

## 2018
January: A new agreement was signed with the North Norfolk Railway (N.N.R.) to become our N2's new home. The N2 was to be fitted with the equipment necessary to run on Network Rail metals with a view to run Sheringham-Cromer dining trains.

## 2018
November: The N2 was withdrawn from service for its next ten-year overhaul.

## 2023
The N2 overhaul is due to be completed end of this year
and will resume operation at the N.N.R. in the near future.

Ex. LNER officers who became Vice Presidents of the society

T.C.B. Miller

A.H. Emerson

T. Mathewson-Dick O.B.E.

G.F. Fiennes O.B.E.

J.F. Harrison

N. Newsome

E.D. Trask

D.W. Harvey

R.H.N. Hardy

P.N. Townend

## Summary of the Gresley Society

As a charity, we have a remit to educate and this we do through a programme of meetings and talks and by erecting memorials of various kinds at appropriate places. The society publishes *The Gresley Observer*, widely recognized as one of the best society magazines on the market. We own and operate the oldest extant Gresley locomotive in the world, G.N.R. built Gresley N2 No. 1744.

It acts as a flag-bearer for the Society on many heritage railways. No.1744 is now over 100 years old and is about to complete its latest ten-year overhaul. To keep our locomotive in steam costs an enormous sum of money and we need help to keep this priceless engine running and to pay for its next overhaul. So, if you would like to join us, and see us through the next 60 years please contact us through our website:

www. gresley.org

*Fig. 329.The Gresley Society Logo.*

# Chapter 9
# Epilogue

*Fig. 330. Sir Nigel Gresley at Salisbury Hall. This photograph, taken in 1937, shows the great engineer enjoying the company of his wildfowl on his estate. It was apt, then, in 1938 that Mallard would somersault to stardom. The Gresley Society.*

Sir Nigel Gresley remains one of the steam era's most loved and respected cultural icons. Happily, in the modern age, one can take a stroll to King's Cross station and come face to face with Hazel Reeve's beautiful statue of Sir Nigel Gresley, copy of *The Locomotive* in hand, with *Mallard* emblazoned below. Seeing Sir Nigel under the overall roof of the station he will forever be associated with still brings a warm feeling to me, every time I visit.

The purpose of my study has not been to reduce Sir Nigel Gresley's legacy. It was to look at the primary evidence available to us and to see if there was anything further that could be gained in making such a study. In reviewing the files at the N.R.M. and the National Archives, it has been a privilege to review hand written notes, letters, reports, drawings and more that were all from the great man himself. There's also the work of those around him, the interactions that tell as much of his story as that from Gresley himself.

It is perhaps helpful to give a final overview of the different aspects of Gresley's story.

## Was Gresley's conjugated gear his own?

The primary evidence we have suggests strongly that Gresley already had what became the final version of his conjugated valve gear in mind before meeting with Harold Holcroft in 1919 to discuss the development of the valve gear.

Most secondary sources to date on Gresley and Holcroft tie the latter's name to the former's work. In my opinion this is an error that needs to be corrected. Holcroft's and Gresley's conjugated valve gear were different enough for Gresley's patent to be accepted verbatim without challenge or change.

The drawings and descriptions that Gresley gave in that patent relate strongly to the version of the valve gear that was fitted to the production O2 2-8-0s, and in my view that is enough evidence to firmly separate the two men's individual contributions to steam locomotive valve gear design. That the patent showcases the potential for Gresley's later work and predates any meeting between them is something of a smoking gun that Gresley was already on the right lines.

Perhaps more damning is that Gresley went on to build hundreds of locomotives with conjugated valve gear, with each development more refined than the next. Holcroft's contributions to the conjugated valve gear development are far, far more limited: to just a few 2-6-0 tender locomotives produced for the S.E.&C.R. This suggests Holcroft was more theoretical than practical when it came to making the gear workable.

## Was the conjugated valve gear any good?

The conjugated valve gear was very much a success for Gresley and the L.N.E.R. However, its main failures in relation to middle cylinder overrun and middle big end failures only came about because of sustained high-speed running, where the middle valve was allowed to travel further by way of overrun.

This was directly due to the conjugated mechanism by way of slackness in the pins and joints being multiplied by the extra "whip" of the motion levers when at speed. This was managed pre-Second World War by high standards of maintenance and careful observation of the conjugated classes' mechanisms. During the war the number of staff and attention available for these classes fell significantly and therefore their failures were easily highlighted by the operating and design departments.

The data available to us shows conclusively that Gresley's larger classes which operated at lower speeds (namely, his O2 freight and many of his mixed traffic locomotive designs) had better availability during the war than older classes inherited by the L.N.E.R. or in fact newer locomotives turned out to his larger designs of Prairies, Pacifics and Mikados together with better overall mileages.

*Fig. 331. Gresley sits with one of his daughters in a field, a Cocker Spaniel sitting to his left patiently. Dogs featured throughout Gresley's life, the earliest example being a "Blue Roan" Cocker Spaniel named Sam. He was also seen with a black Retriever, Jock, in later years. The Gresley Society.*

This trend is repeated by looking closely at the individual area statistics for certain classes: where speed restrictions were in place on a route, or shorter distances for high speed sustained running were required, Gresley's conjugated valve gear classes had better availability and mileages. In later years, improvements at the major locomotive works using optical equipment to align components (introduced in the main by K.J. Cook), together with improvements to the middle big end and lubrication of the same provided satisfactory results to return the conjugated gear to a level of reliability that was lost during the war years.

## Should Gresley have gone to three cylinders for everything?

The overall argument against Gresley's approach with the use of three cylinders for the majority of his L.N.E.R. locomotive designs is the suggestion that two cylinders were ample for the traffic that most locomotives of the medium sized, or mixed traffic variety encountered. Perhaps overlooked is that Gresley's three-cylinder locomotives with conjugated valve gear in that category were providing a power output for the loading gauge that was normally higher than a similar two-cylinder locomotive. This was certainly true of his O2 2-8-0s, the 2-6-0 K3s and his V1 2-6-2Ts, whose performances in terms of mileages and reliability have been highlighted in this book.

Railway engineering is always a trade-off between different requirements. One thing that my research has made clear to me is that Gresley conjugated valve gear locomotives could work on for longer periods in service than equivalent locomotives, even when run down (the P2s being an obvious exception to this rule), but the wear and tear of the gear required longer periods out of traffic for overhaul. This provides a contrast with the later Thompson and Peppercorn classes, where a more *preventative maintenance* regime was preferred, as opposed to what is notionally *run to failure*.

The argument for having two cylinders and valve gear over three cylinders and conjugated valve gear for small and medium sized locomotives is valid. However, Gresley's contributions to medium sized locomotive design having conjugated valve gear (he made nothing smaller than the Gresley V1/V3 tank engines) seem to be backed by the primary evidence we have available that, where speeds under 60 mph were the norm, conjugated valve gear was as reliable as the two-cylinder setups it worked alongside. This must be considered with the overall benefits of smoother torque, hammer blow and other factors when two and three-cylinder development is analysed. My personal view is that Gresley's solutions to the problems he was presented with were valid approaches that were no less acceptable than that found on other railways.

## What was Gresley's contribution to the future development of the steam locomotive?

There is an argument that British Railways' standard designs ignored Gresley's contributions to steam locomotives when drawing up their standard designs. After all, most of the standard locomotive classes are developments of the London Midland way of thinking. This is not surprising given the background of Robin Riddles and other engineers invested in the programme of new steam locomotives for British Railways.

However, there were some elements of Gresley's thinking that filtered through. The use of 6ft 2in driving wheels for the Britannia Pacifics was an L.N.E.R. standard, coming originally from Gresley's P2s and V2s. The Britannia itself was more closely aligned in layout, rather than detailed design, to the L.N.E.R. Pacifics. However, they did retain some aspects such as the L.N.E.R. styled outside Walschaerts valve gear, initially using an L.N.E.R. design for the return crank whilst maintaining a Southern influence by way of the boiler and trailing truck.

Freddie Harrison maintained that his thinking for the sole 8P British Railways Standard Pacific, *Duke of Gloucester*, had Gresley in mind and the use of Caprotti valve gear married to three cylinders suggests something of Gresley's experimentation with Lentz gear.

Perhaps Gresley's greatest contribution to the future development of the steam locomotive was in his persistence in the support of the building of a national test centre, at which after he had passed, Rugby test centre was opened. The first locomotive on the rollers for testing, observed by many of his friends and former colleagues? No.60007 *Sir Nigel Gresley*.

Fig. 332. It was entirely fitting that No.60007 Sir Nigel Gresley would be the first locomotive on the rollers at the Rugby testing plant. Here the locomotive is being prepared, having been split from its tender and reversed into the building. Colin Underwood/Rail Online.

*Fig. 333. Gresley sits at the window of one of his streamlined trains (likely The Coronation, based on the armchair he is sitting in). The Gresley Society.*

## Was Gresley right to develop streamlined trains?

Gresley was abundantly right to recognise the importance of streamlining in the future of train design, and moreover his recognition of the importance of improving the infrastructure to match the locomotives and trains running is matched by the modern requirements in railway signalling and infrastructure for high-speed trains today. The design of the *Silver Jubilee* in particular, coming in 1935 and with a streamlined front end and full streamlined carriages would not be entirely out of place in terms of the overall shape and design today (accepting that it would be electric and not steam powered, of course).

Gresley's recognition in the 1930s of the benefits of fixed length train units and the use of articulation in improving the capacity for high speed and intensive operation of trains was far ahead of the developments post Second World War. This is perhaps exemplified most in Japan, where the Shinkansen 0 units of the 1960s together with the high-speed rail lines-built echo strongly some of Gresley's presentations, ideas and even train designs to the various engineering societies throughout his life. Indeed, the original Tokaido line was first proposed in the late 1930s just as Gresley's full complement of high-speed trains was running.

Gresley was far ahead of his time, and one can only speculate on what we could have seen on the L.N.E.R., had the war not intervened, and had he been able to do more with the electrification of the railways during his time as C.M.E. of the company.

## Should Gresley have standardised more in locomotive design?

In the development of many of Gresley's locomotive classes he looked at the traffic requirements for the route concerned and developed a specific design to meet the needs of that route. This thinking would be anathema to designers of today, where the broadest possible route availability, interoperability, and standardisation of parts reigns supreme, but in the steam era the locomotive had many forms and ultimately did different work for different routes.

There were internal and external tensions amongst those operating and those designing the locomotives, and in his tenure as C.M.E. Gresley undoubtedly succeeded at tying all the different parts of the new L.N.E.R. together. It is testament to Gresley himself that even as steam died out there were so many engine men, shed staff and engineers so invested in his design ethos, sometimes with great reticence to accept designs or locomotives that followed his.

## Did Gresley help develop those around him?

Sir Nigel Gresley was a man who worked incredibly hard and was supported by a team of fine men, who came from a variety of backgrounds, with differing views on locomotive, rolling stock and infrastructure engineering and yet were trusted enough to get on with the job, and moreover, were allowed to embrace their own passions for railway engineering.

Whether it was Bulleid, being allowed to go to France and help in the development of the large Mikado P2s, or Thompson's pushes for standardising boiler types, piston valves and Walschaerts for rebuilds of older locomotives, Bert Spencer for looking into the issues of the conjugated valve gear and developing the long lap travel valves that unlocked their potential (amongst the huge volume of work he did on his chief's behalf) or Frederick Harrison, whose interest in Gresley's work and his support of the chief's developments led to a locomotive that has been described by some as the natural conclusion of Gresley's Pacifics: No.71000, *Duke of Gloucester*.

Gresley succeeded in producing under his wing some of the steam era's brightest minds and sharpest intellects under one roof: the London & North Eastern Railway. He was passionate about development, and he championed a personal training programme by way of supporting pupillages and premium apprenticeships on the L.N.E.R., together with encouraging apprentices to enrol at the Doncaster Technical College. This was for the purpose of furthering their studies. Gresley was, according to Geoffrey Hughes' biography of him, the president of the Doncaster Pupils and Premium Apprentices Association.

Yet Gresley normally gets little recognition for his support of such educational development, whether through the apprentices or with his technical assistants in their development into designers, heads of engineering departments, and in both Edward Thompson and Arthur Peppercorn's case, developing the next Chief Mechanical Engineers of the L.N.E.R. over a very long period.

In going back to the primary material and seeing how Gresley asked for the views of the individuals that worked for him, and how he moved them around the railway, and around him, developing their skills, knowledge and providing projects that directly benefited the areas of the railway they were responsible for, we find a man who recognised sometime in the mid-1930s that he would be passing the baton on and therefore needed to develop such people who could take on his incredibly demanding role and make a good go of it.

## Did Gresley support electrification, and did he do enough to develop it?

Gresley undoubtedly supported electrification of the railways, and throughout his working life he supported the various engineers of the Electrical Engineering department on the L.N.E.R. in their work. He remained on the government committee for Railway Electrification and towards the end of his career was a proponent of electrification.

Gresley was also a pragmatist and recognised that the more easily available source of fuel, coal, and the capital costs of electrification would render it difficult to achieve wholesale electrification in the United Kingdom.

The success of the 1500 D.C. system that the L.N.E.R. developed together with the EM1 and EM2 locomotives that ran it cannot be ignored. In the modern day, in the United Kingdom we use as a standard for new electrification the 25kV system, but in the 1930s and 40s there were a range of electrical systems on offer, and arguably having overhead electrification that could be converted later to this system was still a positive step forward.

## Overall Conclusions

There is so much focus in secondary sources on just the steam locomotives of Sir Nigel Gresley and a few named express passenger trains that we tend to forget that Gresley wasn't just responsible for steam locomotives. He was also responsible for the developments of new rolling stock, including streamlined carriages and articulated suburban stock, electric multiple units and electric locomotives, wagons, specialised and mass made for domestic markets, the design of new station buildings, in-cab signalling, electrification...

The point being that Sir Nigel Gresley presided over, and had a hand in, so much of the L.N.E.R.'s engineering, public relations, and even financial requirements at times that any suggestion that his legacy was damaged or even destroyed when he passed, and others took over his role is without any basis in fact. It was an impossible task. The L.N.E.R. *was* Gresley. When he died, it had to change and change quickly. The Second World War had changed Gresley, and it changed his railway too going *forward*.

*Fig. 334. Gresley walking with his daughter Violet (right) and his sister Beatrice (far right) shortly after becoming Sir Nigel Gresley at Buckingham Palace. The Gresley Society.*

There were signs of his thinking changing around steam locomotives, when the V4 was designed. A go anywhere, and powerful locomotive that could do everything except, of course, pull the heaviest of the streamlined trains at high speed. It could have been the locomotive that saved the L.N.E.R., in many respects, were it not for a few key decisions on materials choices that pushed up the design's build costs and made it less attractive as a locomotive intended for mass building. It was 1941 and Gresley was near the end of his life, of course, and the war was in its infancy.

That he was able to manage the development of the V4 and the electric EM1 locomotive, prepare arrangements for the succession of the various department heads, design teams, major works facilities and prepare the board for the difficult choices they had ahead of them all whilst suffering from severe, and no doubt debilitating ill health, is testament to how passionate he was about his role, his railway, and his life. The idea that Gresley was not preparing the L.N.E.R. for a life beyond his tenure perhaps overlooks how he singled out Spencer, Thompson, and Peppercorn in different ways for individual development, the latter two supporting Gresley as stand-ins where required at board meetings and similar throughout 1940 and into 1941. Gresley was *always* looking ahead of the curve.

Gresley was broad minded in hearing ideas, and he was supportive in producing the conditions under which the best ideas would be harnessed and used to improve the lot of the railway that he loved. The hands of other Chief Mechanical Engineers were not as tied as Gresley's were to the fortunes of his railway company. Some have argued that financially, Gresley should have made better decisions on his locomotive design and development programmes, and maybe there is some truth in that where the number of classes is concerned.

However, in almost all cases of presenting a locomotive into traffic, Gresley's designs continued to work until the advent of diesel traction, the earliest example of a withdrawal from traffic ahead of this being the two examples of his Class P1. Yet these locomotives are not failures in and of themselves but designed and built for infrastructure improvements and traffic requirements that did not subsequently materialise, something I would argue strongly is not proof of Gresley's folly but of the L.N.E.R. board's lack of foresight in following his vision.

There are some locomotive designs that are attributed to him that shouldn't be: Gresley was not responsible for the design of the Class B17 and so their mixed reputation should ultimately lie, not with him, but with the N.B.L. Co. Ltd. Despite this, the class used Gresley designed components throughout and worked through to the 1960s with minimal modifications.

If anything, Gresley's failure here was to produce a locomotive not unlike that of the Thompson B1 introduced after he had passed. Yet it is difficult to look at the incredibly specific demands of the Great Eastern section and think they were being entirely fair to Gresley or the N.B.L. Co. Ltd. Is that *really* a failure on Gresley's part?

The Class D49, another of Gresley's most questioned designs, did reasonable annual average mileages throughout its life at a cost of overall availability and reliability. Yet they did still do great work and were capable of decent performance too.

His P2 class locomotives could hardly be described as successful designs, but they *were* capable of prodigious performance when in first class condition. Ultimately, they required more design development that was not possible during wartime conditions.

One could argue that Sir Nigel Gresley had only one genuine failure in his design office, that of the water tube boiler fitted W1 locomotive. Yet the W1 managed to achieve its original goals, with superior water and coal efficiency over the original A1 design, albeit with some further development that was made through experimentation on some of his other locomotives.

Without the rapid rise and success of the Class A4, the W1 could have set the tone for future locomotive development on the L.N.E.R. and would not have proved lacking.

*Fig. 335. Sir Nigel Gresley (left) on a group outing. On the far right is his friend and amicable rival, Sir William Stanier of the L.M.S. The Gresley Society.*

Without the W1, it is questionable whether Gresley would have been able to produce the A4 Pacific and the streamlined trains, given its importance in the development of Gresley's thinking and the push for genuine scientific development through things such as wind tunnel testing of models in the design phase.

Much is made of Gresley's largest locomotives and the record holders, but few give credit where it is due for some of his everyday workhorses. Without classes K3, N2, O2 and V1/V3, much of the country would find life that bit harder. These classes proved their worth during the Second World War as some of the best performing steam locomotives on a railway that was truly struggling for availability of working stock.

Of these classes, just a solitary N2 is preserved, the oldest survivor of Gresley's work and arguably just as important (if not more so) than the six preserved A4 Pacifics, including the speed record holder, *Mallard*, representing what life was like for millions of commuters for nearly 50 years in England's capital city and beyond. It is close to steaming again and all enthusiasts of Gresley's work must ensure that this locomotive continues to run and flies the flag for the humblest of Gresley's output now and for the future.

At the other end of the scale, we are so close to a good representation of Gresley's most controversial class, the P2 Mikados. The completion of new build No.2007 *Prince of Wales* will mark the first new Gresley steam locomotive to be built since 1941, an extraordinary achievement. With the experience, knowledge, and track record of some of the big railways' brightest minds and engineers, the new P2 will no doubt prove at last what the Gresley P2 class was capable of, with availability and mileages matching the prodigious hauling capacity of the original locomotives.

Beyond that, we have the new B17 *Spirit of Sandringham*, which is also benefitting from the overall sharing of information and experience that building one Peppercorn A1 and now building a Gresley P2 and V4 in future has accumulated for the A1 Locomotive Trust. Some writers have criticised the number of different designs Gresley provided, 25 in total. However, these designs are spread over a career spanning over 30 years, and his early developments were carefully judged upgrades and improvements of existing designs from his predecessor.

Gresley's longevity and vision were far in advance of many of his contemporaries too, pushing the boundaries in scientific development of locomotive and train design, being the first to utilise wind tunnels in the production of a locomotive and recognising early on the benefits of streamlining. This development ultimately presented the final stage of his high-speed train development, with the fully streamlined *Coronation* train providing the highlight of his career, the world speed record for steam hauled traction behind *Mallard* achieved in July 1938.

Gresley's place in history was assured by the steam speed record exploit of *Mallard*, yet arguably his contribution materially to the locomotive stock of Great Britain is overlooked by some authors in favour of other locomotive engineers with minimal locomotive designs and builds to their name. It is difficult to understand how some railway writers have managed to spectacularly miss the point when reviewing the primary and secondary material on locomotive engineers in this country.

Some writers have missed the obvious: C.M.E.s in their locomotive design role exist to provide railway companies with workable locomotives that provide services on behalf of the railway company. In other words, they are there to *run* a railway company.

The success of a C.M.E. lies not just, or wholly, in the extremes of locomotive performance but in whether their locomotive designs provided their railway with the services that in turn funded their activities further. There is no doubt in my mind that those writers who place Chapelon, Porta, Collett, Stanier and some other railway engineers over Gresley have got it very wrong. Gresley by far exceeded his remit and provided the L.N.E.R. with locomotives that were fully capable of doing the work required, even when run down, with only a few minor exceptions, and pointed directly towards a future of rail transport that is now an everyday sight.

It also does not follow that to praise Gresley for his work before the Second World War automatically means that any later criticism of the conjugated valve gear, for example, was incorrect (as that given during the Second World War by E.S. Cox and Edward Thompson).

Nor does it follow that these criticisms are inaccurate after things improved substantially for the conjugated valve gear classes, with a return to peacetime conditions post 1945 and subsequent improvements in workshop practice and some improved design of certain aspects of the middle big end. The criticisms given were fair and evidenced.

All these things are true and should not be seen as necessarily contradicting each other. The circumstances that *Mallard* encountered in July 1938 were not the same as those found in July 1941 or July 1945 nor were the circumstances ever to be quite the same again by July 1948. It is entirely reasonable to recognise that that the engineering ethos of the time had to ebb and flow with the circumstances that Great Britain found itself under. No more, no less.

Gresley was an engineer with a passion for experimentation, evolution, new kinds of thinking, incremental development by way of experience and was a forward thinker. These aspects of his personality are exemplified by his work with the L.N.E.R. streamlined expresses and their incredibly successful entry into service, one after the other. No train ever had an introduction like the *Silver Jubilee*. No one anywhere else in the world got as close as Gresley did to providing a genuinely high speed, intercity experience. Most modern trains today reflect the early design work in wind tunnels Gresley pushed for and supported throughout his later years.

This required Gresley himself to recognise that a whole system approach must be taken to the railway to improve the services required. He looked at every aspect and improved the L.N.E.R. in many areas, recognising the importance of streamlining, high-speed with ample braking capabilities, signalling equipment improving safety and more. He was more than just a locomotive engineer: today he would be called and recognised as one of the earliest *systems engineers*.

A measure of the love and respect for his life was seen in the choice of No.60007 *Sir Nigel Gresley* being first on the rollers at the new Rugby test plant. Among his friends and former colleagues present were Edward Thompson, Arthur Peppercorn and Sir William Stanier, paying tribute to him by their attendance.

When all is said and done, Sir Nigel Gresley was many things. An intellectual. An innovator. A man of great determination and with courage in his convictions. Always with an eye on the future informing his decisions, ultimately taken with the overall improvement of his railway at the back of his mind.

There are few men who should be accorded the status of hero: Sir Nigel Gresley remains, for me, one of those railway heroes who continues to inspire and will likely do so for all of time.

*Fig.335b. Standing proudly alongside the engine bearing his name. Colourised by Ian MacCabe-The Gresley Society.*

*Fig. 336. Gresley, smoking a pipe, and near the twilight of his railway career. Always impeccably dressed, and in a three-piece suit in virtually all the photographs that exist of him, this was a man of ambition, intellect, and determination. The Gresley Society.*

# Chapter 10
# Strengths and Limitations of the Study

*Formulation of research aims and objectives.*

Following on from the *Edward Thompson: Wartime C.M.E.* project, I was tasked with writing a similar treatment on Sir Nigel Gresley by my publisher. I examined my original bibliography and came up with a series of questions and directions in accordance with the PICO method (Population, Investigation, Comparator and Outcome) in line with the University of York's guidelines in developing protocols for evidence-based research, as part of a systematic review.

Research & Sample Size
The basis of the writing and research for this book is the L.N.E.R.'s *Use of Engine Power* document and the covers the years 1942 to 1946 for the whole of the L.N.E.R.'s locomotive stock. Unless further records are uncovered, we are now unlikely to be able to able to analyse locomotives' availability outside of this data set.

For example: we can create some limited availability data sets for the years before 1942 and after 1946 using the L.N.E.R. Pacifics' Engine Record Cards at York, but we couldn't do the same for other classes where such alternative records do not exist. The amount of data we have however is large and significant (around 60,000 individual entries) with a full comparative study of all the different L.N.E.R. locomotives possible throughout the years given.

There were some known issues with individual data (and where there were issues, they have been highlighted). The number of errors found when collating the spreadsheet originally was minimal: accounting for around 20 individual entries out of the whole of the dataset. For the purposes of this new work, the data was analysed again which allowed for a few further corrections to be made. These corrections however did not affect the statistics for the Gresley, and Thompson designed locomotive classes that have been analysed to date.

This work has the largest dataset collating information not only from statistical analysis from the archives, but also from board minutes, reports, letters, and contemporary documentation such as that found in the railway press. All of which makes this work credible and more reliable.

Since the production of my last book, *Edward Thompson: Wartime C.M.E.*, the original spreadsheet database has been massively upgraded with various additional tools for graphical analysis and comparison and has allowed for a more comprehensive overview of Gresley's locomotives at work during World War Two.

## The Importance of Primary Evidence

In my last book, *Edward Thompson: Wartime C.M.E.*, I devoted some space to explaining the nature of my evidence-based approach to research and writing on the subject. With Thompson's story, there was a significant amount of secondary evidence that has been presented as fact by a multitude of authors over the last sixty years. It was notable that much of it stemmed from a pro-Gresley slant that didn't seem to have a basis in the primary evidence available.

This has remained true with my research into Sir Nigel Gresley, where a number of apocryphal stories and myths have been repeated ad nausea for decades. It is frustrating, given the amount of archive evidence that we have for the L.N.E.R., that we are still today having to unravel the work of myth that has been built up around the three Chief Mechanical Engineers of the railway and their work for the railway.

The importance of the *Use of Engine Power* document cannot be understated, bringing with it a true and accurate picture of the L.N.E.R. fleet in wartime and a real sense of the issues the railway and its staff encountered. As much as it shows us that the performance issues of Edward Thompson's designs were inaccurately reported, it also shows us that most of Gresley's G.N.R. and L.N.E.R. designs were performing magnificently despite the issues of wartime maintenance standards.

The Engine Record cards held at the N.R.M. are incomplete and do not give all the L.N.E.R. classes (only the Pacifics, Mikados and the W1) so to be able to compare so many different classes' day to day performance, even limited as this is to the years 1942 to 1946 in such detail is, frankly, extraordinary.

In this we need to be clear: the current work I have undertaken in transposing the original document into digital form is only available for 1942 to 1946 at present, however future work is likely to include further transposition of original data into digital formats to allow us to analyse more fully the L.N.E.R.'s fleet more closely throughout its working life.

## Previous Studies & Issues

Sir Nigel Gresley and his locomotives have been the subject of hundreds of titles, articles, and opinion pieces, together with documentaries and films recounting his life and work. There is no shortage of previous studies to examine. Those coming from writers such as Peter Townend are significant as they come directly from those who worked on his locomotive designs and include much primary evidence as a basis for their writing. There are also several societies set up dedicated to aspects of the L.N.E.R., one in particular being *The Gresley Society* whose members are amongst the most knowledgeable in this area of study (and without whom, neither this book nor the previous one would have been written to the high standard desired).

One significant pitfall in this area of study, however, can be found in the secondary evidence base for Gresley and the L.N.E.R. in general. Many secondary sources of information (e.g., biographies, books, and magazine articles) lack appropriate primary evidence bases, citations and critical analysis of his work that is rooted in the required disciplines to understand the impact of Gresley as an engineer.

Most of these works have been written in the 1950s, 1960s and 1970s, with updated editions coming later with little regard for any further research or study. These secondary sources have created something of an echo chamber, several of the authors repeating assertions, with greater and greater conviction over several decades despite having little evidence for their writing. This echo chamber is particularly noticeable online now with many unwilling contributors to apocryphal stories and myths pervaded across social media, to the detriment of serious study and debate.

However, it should be noted that in the last ten years there have been some new writers of secondary evidence coming to the fore, applying more academic approaches to writing on Sir Nigel Gresley and the L.N.E.R. and relying more heavily on a primary evidence-based approach. This is an agreeable trend which it is hoped will be helped along further by the support of societies such as The Gresley Society, who in the writing of Edward Thompson: Wartime C.M.E. embraced the research carried out and have done so again in the writing of this book.

## Scope of discussions

There is scope for further research and discussion on the material collated. Debate on the relative importance of the *Use of Engine Power* document and what it tells us about the locomotive classes, their maintainability, and their value to the L.N.E.R., would be welcome.

The study presented here is a first work and will benefit from future discussion and analysis for an updated presentation in years to come.

## Future Work

I am preparing a new book which will comprehensively report on the performances of the entire L.N.E.R. fleet during the Second World War, tentatively titled *The L.N.E.R. Locomotive Fleet in Wartime*. This book will bring together all the statistics and graphical analysis produced for the Gresley and Thompson locomotives and then add in all the remaining locomotive classes working for the L.N.E.R during the war years.

This will include the statistics for various on loan steam locomotive classes (such as the Stanier 8Fs and War Department classes) as well as the more obscure petrol and diesel classes.

I have also begun working on a similar treatment of O.V.S. Bulleid's work for the Southern Railway and am considering a future piece on the locomotives of the G.N.R., together with a study on Robinson or Raven in future.

Fig. 337. Gresley A4 No.4498 Sir Nigel Gresley is posed alongside Stirling Single No.1 at Stevenage Station. Colourised by Ian MacCabe, The Gresley Society.

# SIR NIGEL GRESLEY
## The L.N.E.R.'s First C.M.E.
## SPECIAL THANKS

For all sources, photographs, assistance, discussions, editing and support.

**My sincere thanks and gratitude to the following individuals and groups, without whom this book would not have been written.**

For his wonderful images, support, editing, advice, and help, many thanks to **Ian MacCabe of The Gresley Society,** together with thanks to **Peter Coster** and **Joseph Cliffe** for their review of my material and their recommendations on corrections.

**Ben Godfrey,** for agreeing to write the foreword to this book and for his support and kindness at my lecture given in the spring of 2023 to **The Gresley Society.**

My editor, **Kevin Derrick,** without whom this book, and previous ones, would not have made it to print. Thank you, Kevin, for your kindness and patience.

**Tim Hillier-Graves** for his kind words, support, and information during the latter stages of the book.

**Mark Allatt, Graeme Bunker,** and **Andrew Hardy** for their support and encouragement over the years.

**Peter Townend,** for his writings and first-hand experience of working with the L.N.E.R. Pacifics, as well as some of the photographs included in this book.

With thanks to the late **Richard Hardy,** for his wisdom, writings, and first-hand experiences.

**The Gresley Society, The L.N.E.R.C.A., The A1 and P2 Trusts**

**The R.C.T.S. and David Bird,** for their assistance in locating drawings pertaining to various classes designed under Gresley for the L.N.E.R. as part of the *Locomotives of the L.N.E.R.* series of books.

My **National Preservation Forum** based team of editors and advisors:
**Tom James, Richard Mellish, Jim Champ** for his help in the editing stages of the book.
**Richard Nixon** for his helpful review of the book ahead of publication.

**Colin Mason,** and the **City of Utrecht,** for the source of the EM1 photographs.

**The Mike Morant Photographic Collection, The G.E.R. Society,
The M&GNJR Trust, The G.N.R. Society, The National Preservation Forum**

**The M.N.L.P.S.**

**Chris Ellick, Tom McPherson, James Cummins,** and **Christopher Meredith**
for their encouragement, support and help in the writing of this book, and my lecture series.

**Tim Robbins** for the kind donation of parts of his photographic collection,
for which I give due credit in the captions of this book.

**The National Railway Museum** and their copy services assistants for their help in locating
and examining the dynamometer records for the L.N.E.R.

**The National Archives at Kew**
for their understanding, support, and search of their records.

**George Reeve**, whose patience when helping me edit and proof read is to be commended.

**Lawrence Robbins** for his help both in discussing the many subjects contained within this
book and in editing ahead of printing the book.

**The Martin Family**: **Jill** (my mother), without whom I would have no love of history. **Jerry** (my
father), without whom I would have no love of engineering, DIY, or writing letters into
publications. **Claire** (my sister) who remains an inspirational figure that I love so very much.

My **Uncle Peter** and **Aunty Gillian** for their love, support, and encouragement over many
years.

My father-in-law Anwar and my mother-in-law Nuha for their encouragement and support of
my work towards a PHD. Nezar and Waleed, my brothers-in-law for their humour and help
when working out my ideas.

My late Uncle, **Edwin Holley,** an aeronautical engineer who worked for English Electric, Avro,
Hawker Siddeley, Pratt & Whitney, amongst other well-known engineering firms, together with
helping to restore the Canadian Warplane Heritage Museum's "Bumblebee" in his final years.
Your influence on my love of engineering and engineering restoration has stayed with me
throughout my life. I hope the section devoted to aerodynamics and streamlining would have
met with your approval. (*There always was an Arrow*)

With a million "thank you"(s) to my beloved and incredible wife, **Nada,** who has been my rock
and my muse throughout the writing of this book. She is my best friend and my partner for life.
Without her love and cherished support, I would not have had the strength to continue in my
research and to write every next book. I treasure all our time together and may it always be
thus. I don't know what I would have done without you. Thank you, Nada, I love you.

# SIR NIGEL GRESLEY
# The L.N.E.R.'s First C.M.E.
# BIBLIOGRAPHY

Sources for quotations, images, archive documents and other related information.

## Images

All images have been credited to their copyright owners where applicable.

Some images have been colourised and all are credited to Ian MacCabe & The Gresley Society.

Images from the Tim Robbins Collection are original prints or prints from negatives in the L.N.E.R.'s Photographic Archive, including Works photographs from Doncaster during G.N.R. and L.N.E.R. days.

Line Drawings for the L.N.E.R. Designs have come from the R.C.T.S. archives and have been used under license, courtesy of David Bird.

The Writer and Publisher wish to recognise the City of Utrecht in making available their photographic collection online, which has allowed for the reproduction of several photographs of Gresley's prototype electric locomotive No.6701 at work.

If an error has been made in accreditation, please contact the publisher and future editions of this book will be corrected accordingly, where accreditation can be proven.

## Publications:

'2750, The Legend of a Locomotive', by Harry Webster (1953) Nelson.

'A4 Pacific Locomotives', Peter Tuffrey (2016) Ian Allan Ltd.

'A History of the L.N.E.R.', Volumes 1-3, Michael Bonavia (1983) Allen & Unwin.

'Bill Harvey's 60 Years in Steam', D.W. Harvey (1986) David & Charles Publishing Plc.

'Biographical Dictionary of Railway Engineers', John Marshall, (2nd Edition, 2003) Railway & Canal Historical Society.

'British Locomotives from the footplate', O.S. Nock (1950) Hazell, Watson & Viney Ltd.

'British Pacific Locomotives', Cecil J. Allen (1962) Ian Allan Ltd.

'British Railways Steam Locomotives 1948 – 1968', Hugh Longworth (2007) OPC.

'British Steam Horses', George Dow (1950) Phoenix House.

'Cock O' The North, Gresley's Bold Experiment', Peter Tuffrey (2014) Fonthill Media Limited.

'Dropping the Fire', Philip Atkins (1999) Irwell Press.

'East Coast Pacifics at Work', P.N. Townend (1982) Ian Allan Ltd.

'Edward Thompson of the L.N.E.R.', Peter Grafton (1971 and 2007) Kestrel Books and Oakwood Press.

'Edward Thompson: Wartime C.M.E.', Simon A.C. Martin (2021) Strathwood Publishing

'Enginemen Elite', Norman McKillop 'Torem Beg' (1958) Unwin Brothers Limited.

'Flying Scotsman', Andrew Roden (2007) Aurum Press Ltd.

'FORWARD, The L.N.E.R. Development Programme', L.N.E.R. (1946) Waterlow & Sons Limited.

'From the footplate', O.S. Nock (1984) Book Club Associates and Granada Publishing Limited.

'Genius or Showman? A critical analysis of the work of Sir Nigel Gresley', J.P. Disley (2020) Amazon

Kindle, Kindle Direct Publishing Limited.

'Great Northern', O.S. Nock (1979) Ian Allan Ltd.

'Great Locomotives of the L.N.E.R.', O.S, Nock (1988) Guild Publishing & Patrick Stephens Limited.

'Gresley's Class P2 Locomotives', Andrew Hardy (2016) Ian Allan Publishing Ltd.

'Gresley's Legacy: Locomotives and Rolling Stock', David McIntosh (2015) Ian Allan Publishing Ltd.

'Gresley Locomotives', Brian Haresnape, (1981) Ian Allan Ltd.

'Gresley and his Locomotives', Tim Hillier-Graves (2019) Pen & Sword Books Ltd.

'Gresley's Master Engineer. Bert Spencer, Tim Hillier-Graves (2023) Pen & Sword Books Ltd.

'Gresley's Silver Link', Tim Hillier-Graves and Ronald Hillier (2022) Pen & Sword Books Ltd.

'Hush-Hush: The Story of L.N.E.R. 10000', William Brown (2010) Kestrel Railway Books.

'Top Link Locomotives', Norman McKillop (1957) Nelson.

'Enginemen Elite', Norman McKillop (1958) Ian Allan.

'Nigel Gresley', F.A.S. Brown (1961) Ian Allan.

'L.N.E.R. 4-6-0s at work', Geoffrey Hughes (1988) Ian Allan Ltd.

'L.N.E.R. 4-6-0s at work', Geoffrey Hughes (1988) Ian Allan Ltd.

'L.N.E.R. in Transition', Michael Blakemore (2004) Pendragon Partnership 2004.

'L.N.E.R. Locomotive Development', Jim Armstrong (1974) Peco Publications.

'L.N.E.R. Locomotives', H.C. Casserley (1977) D. Bradford Barton Ltd.

'L.N.E.R. Pacifics Remembered', Peter Townend (2014) Irwell Press Limited.

'L.N.E.R. Passenger Trains and Formations 1923-67', Steve Banks and Clive Carter (2013), Ian Allan Publishing Ltd.

'L.N.E.R. Steam', O.S. Nock (1969) The Chaucer Press Ltd.

'L.N.E.R. Wagons', various editions, Peter Tatlow (1998) Pendragon Partnership.

'L.N.E.R. Workshops, Development, Expansion and Demise', Peter Tuffrey (2018) Crecy Publishing Limited.

'Locomotive Adventure', Harold Holcroft (1962) Ian Allan.

'Locomotive Designers in the Age of Steam', J.N. Westwood (1977) Sidgwick & Jackson.

'Locomotive Engineers of the L.N.E.R.', Ben Webb (1946) Ian Allan Ltd.

'Locomotives of the L.N.E.R.', Volumes 1-11, The Railway Correspondence and Travel Society (R.C.T.S.) (1963-1971).

'Locomotives of the L.N.E.R.', O.S. Nock (1947) London & North Eastern Railway (Publishing).

'Locomotive Panorama, Volumes 1 and 2', E.S. Cox (1965 and 1966) Ian Allan Ltd.

'Mallard and the A4 Class', David McIntosh (2008) Ian Allan Publishing Ltd.

'Mallard: how the blue streak broke the world speed record', Don Hale (2005) Aurem Press.

'Master Builders of Steam', H.A.V. Bulleid (1963) Ian Allan Publishing Ltd.

'Men of Steam', L.A. Summers (2016) Amberley Publishing Ltd.

'Peppercorn: His Life and Locomotives', Tim Hillier-Graves (2021) Pen and Sword Publishing Ltd.

'Nigel Gresley: Locomotive Engineer', F.A.S. Brown (1961) Ian Allan Ltd.

'Non-stop! London to Scotland Steam', A.J Mullay (1989) Alan Sutton Limited.

'Railways in Retrospect', Michael Blakemore (2004) Pendragon Publishing Ltd.

'Sir Nigel Gresley; The Engineer and his family', Geoffrey Hughes (2001) Oakwood Press.

'Sir Vincent Raven and the North Eastern Railway' (2005), Peter Grafton (2005) Oakwood Press.

'Sir Vincent Raven: Visionary Pragmatist, North Eastern Railway Locomotive Engineer' Andrew Everett (2006) Tempus Publishing Limited.

'Sir William Stanier', J.E. Chacksfield, (2001) Oakwood Press.

'Speaking of Steam', E.S. Cox (1971) Ian Allan.

'Steam Days at Haymarket', Harry Knox (2007) Irwell Press Limited.

'Steam in the Blood', Richard Hardy (1971) Ian Allan Ltd.

'Steam was my calling', E.S. Beavor (1974) Ian Allan Ltd.

'Streamlined Steam: Britain's 1930s Luxury Expresses', A.J. Mullay (2002) David & Charles Ltd.

'That was my railway', Frank L. Hick (1991) Silver Link Publishing Ltd.

'The Birth of British Rail', Michael R. Bonavia (1979) George Allen & Unwin Ltd.

'The Book of the A1 and A2 Pacifics', Peter Coster (2013) Irwell Press Limited.

'The Book of the A3 Pacifics', Peter Coster (2008) Irwell Press Limited.

'The Book of the A4 Pacifics', Peter Coster (2013) Irwell Press Limited.

'The Counter Pressure Brake Method of Testing Locomotives'. Journal of the Institution of Locomotive Engineers. T. Robson. (1943).

'The Development of L.N.E.R. Locomotive Design, 1923–1941'. Journal of the Institution of Locomotive Engineers. Bert Spencer (1947).

'The Gresley Influence', Geoffrey Hughes (1983) Ian Allan Ltd.

'The Gresley Pacifics', O.S. Nock (1983), David & Charles Ltd.

'The Locomotive Exchanges', Cecil J. Allen (1949) Ian Allan Ltd.

'The Locomotives of the Great Northern Railways, 1847-1910', G.F. Bird (1910) The Locomotive Pub. Co. Ltd.

'The Locomotive Exchanges', Cecil J. Allen (1949) Ian Allan Ltd.

'The Locomotives of the Great Northern Railways, 1847-1910', G.F. Bird (1910) The

Locomotive Pub. Co.

Ltd.

'The L.M.S. Pacifics', J.W.P. Rowledge (1987) David & Charles Publishers Plc.

'The L.N.E.R. delivers the goods', Peter Tatlow (2022) Lightmoor Press, Black Dwarf Lightmoor

Publications Ltd.

'The L.N.E.R. Remembered', J.S. Whiteley & G.W. Morrison (1979) Morrison and Oxford

Publishing.

'The L.N.E.R. Scene', Maurice Earley (1973) Oxford Publishing Co. Ltd.

'The Power of the A1s', Gavin Morrison (2000) Ian Allan Publishing Ltd.

'The Power of the A2s', Gavin Morrison (2004) Ian Allan Publishing Ltd.

'The Power of the A3s', Gavin Morrison (2002) Ian Allan Publishing Ltd.

'The Power of the A4s', Brian Morrison (Various) Ian Allan Publishing Ltd.

'The Power of the A1s, A2s and A3s', J.S. Whiteley & G.W. Morrison (1982) Ian Allan Publishing

Ltd.

'The Power of the B1s', Peter Swinger (1994) Ian Allan Publishing Ltd.

'The Power of the B17s and B2s', Peter Swinger (1988) Ian Allan Publishing Ltd.

'Trained by Sir Nigel Gresley', Eric Bannister (1984) The Dalesman Publishing Ltd.

'Thompson: His Life and Locomotives', Tim Hillier-Graves (2021) Pen and Sword Publishing Ltd.

'Thompson & Peppercorn: Locomotive Engineers', Colonel H.C.B. Rogers (1979) Ian Allan

Publishing Ltd.

'Trained by Sir Nigel Gresley', Eric Bannister (1984) The Dalesman Publishing Company Ltd.

Yeadon's Register of L.N.E.R. Locomotives: Volumes 1, 2, 3, 4, 5, 6, 7, 8, 9, 10, 11, 14, 15, 16, 17, 18,

22, 23,

24A and 24B, 43A, Willie Yeadon (Various years) Irwell Press Limited & Booklaw

'World Steam in the Twentieth Century', E.S. Cox (1969) Ian Allan.

The Railway Magazine Archives:
The Railway Magazine: Vol.86 January To December 1940

The Railway Magazine: Vol.87 January To December 1941

The Railway Magazine: Vol.88 January To December 1942

The Railway Magazine: Vol.89 January To December 1943

The Railway Magazine: Vol.90 January To December 1944

The Railway Magazine: Vol.91 January To December 1945

The Railway Magazine: Vol.92 January To December 1946

The Railway Magazine: Vol.93 Jan To December 1947

The Railway Magazine: Vol.94 Jan To December 1948

The Railway Magazine: Vol.95 Jan To December 1949

The Railway Magazine: Vol.96 Jan To December 1950

The Railway Magazine: Vol.97 Jan To December 1951

The Railway Magazine: Vol.110 Nov 1963 To December 1964

The Railway Magazine: Vol.114 Jan To December 1968

Engineering Papers & Journals:
'The Development of L.N.E.R. Locomotive Design, 1923-1941', Bert Spencer (1941) in an address to the IMechE.

'The Steam Locomotive: A Machine of Precision', K.J. Cook (1957) Swindon Engineering Society.

'What were the investment dilemmas of the LNER in the inter-war years and did they successfully overcome them?' William Wilson, MA TPM, September 2020.

'The Air Resistance Of Passenger Trains', F. C. Johansen, M.Sc. (Eng.), A.M.I.Mech.E. (1936), iMechE.

Magazines, Bookazines & Other Publications:
'Locomotives Illustrated 38: The A4 Pacifics', (1984) Ian Allan Ltd

'Flying Scotsman – The Locomotive', Geoffrey Hughes, Phillip Benham, and Chris Nettleton (2017) The Amadeus Press Ltd.

'Mallard and the A4 Pacifics', Rob Adamson, and Chris Nettleton (2013) The Amadeus Press Ltd.

National Archive Materials:
*The L.N.E.R. Board, Emergency Board and Locomotive Committee Minutes: File RAIL 390.*

*The L.N.E.R. Assorted Archives (1923-1948): File RAIL 394.*

*Patent no.15,769 of A.D. 1915, "Improvements in Valve Gear for Locomotives and other Steam Engines.*

*The Railway Gazette Archive 1912 through to 1948 inclusive. File RAIL-ZPER 9/15.*

National Railway Museum Materials:
*L.N.E.R. Pacifics Engine Record Cards.*

Brian Reed Interview with Edward Thompson.
The Edward Thompson Archive.

*The W1 File.*

Websites:
University of York Systematic Review Process (PICO)
https://subjectguides.york.ac.uk/systematic-review/expectations

Railway Heritage Register On-Line
https://www.rhrp.org.uk/surveystatus.htm

Heritage Railway Locomotives Database
http://www.heritage-railways.com/locosdb/locos.php

Technical Publications for Railway Engineering:

'Train Aerodynamics', Baker/Johnson/Flynn/Hemida/Johnson/Quinn/Soper/Sterling (2019) Butterworth-Heinemann Publications.

'Fundamentals of Aerodynamics', John D. Anderson Jr. (2019) McGraw Hill.

'Handbook of Railway Vehicle Dynamics, Second Edition', Simon Iwnicki (2019) CRC Press.

# SIR NIGEL GRESLEY
# The L.N.E.R.'s First C.M.E.
# APPENDICES

**Appendix 1: Gresley's Personal Life**

**Appendix 2: Gresley's Railway Career**

**Appendix 3: Gresley's Innovations**

**Appendix 4: Mileages of Locomotives between General Repairs (1937)**

**Appendix 5: Gresley's Patents (Conjugated Valve Gear, 1915, and Articulation Method, United States, 1922)**

**Appendix 6: The E.S. Cox Report (1941)**

**Appendix 7: Abbreviations**

**Appendix 8: Pamphlets for the L.N.E.R. Streamlined Expresses**

**Appendix 9: Surviving L.N.E.R. Rolling Stock 1923-1941**

**Appendix 10: About the Author**

# Appendix I
## Gresley's Personal Life

1876
Born in Edinburgh.

1890
Joined Marlborough College as a pupil (a few years ahead of colleague Edward Thompson).

1899
Meets Ethel Frances Fullagar.

1900
Engaged to Ethel.

1901
Marries Ethel in ceremony at St Anne's Parish

1901
Son, Nigel, born.

1902
Daughter, Violet, born.

1906
Son, Roger, born.

1908
Daughter, Marjorie, born.

1910
Phlebitis due to injury sustained whilst out hunting.

1920
Appointed CBE.

1929
Ethel Frances Gresley passes away.

1936
Appointed "Sir Nigel Gresley".

1941
Gresley passes away in office.

# Appendix 2
## Gresley's Railway Career

### 1893
Joined the L.N.W.R. at Crewe Works as a premium apprentice.

### 1898
Promoted to works fitter at Crewe.

### 1898
Pupillage under John Aspinall, C.M.E. of the L&Y.R.

### 1900
L&Y.R., Assistant Manager of the Carriage & Wagon works (Newton Heath).

### 1902
L&Y.R., Works Manager of the Carriage & Wagon works (Newton Heath).

### 1905
G.N.R., Works Manager of the Carriage & Wagon works (Newton Heath).

### 1911
G.N.R., Locomotive Engineer (Doncaster).
Recruits Oliver Bulleid and Edward Thompson.

### 1922
First Pacific locomotive emerges, No.1470 *Great Northern*.

### 1923
L.N.E.R., hired as the first C.M.E. of the new railway company (Doncaster and King's Cross).

### 1928
First non-stop run between London and Edinburgh in up and down directions, using his patented corridor tender behind No.4472 *Flying Scotsman* and No.2580 *Shotover*.

### 1934
No.4472 *Flying Scotsman* achieves the first authenticated 100mph run.

### 1934
No.2750 *Papyrus* achieves the first authenticated 108mph run.

### 1938
No.4468 *Mallard* achieves the world speed record for steam hauled traction at 126mph.

### 1941
Gresley passes away in office.

# Appendix 3
## Gresley's Innovations

### Locomotive Innovations

- Gresley Conjugated Valve Gear. (1915)

- The largest steam locomotive in the UK, the U1 2-8-0+0-8-2 Garratt. (1925)

- The streamlined locomotive in the U.K. and first in U.K. designed through wind tunnel development, the W1. (1929)

- The first steam locomotive to officially achieve 100mph, the A1 *Flying Scotsman*. *(1934)*

- The largest passenger steam locomotive in the UK, the P2 2-8-2. (1934)

- The fastest authenticated non-streamlined locomotive, at 108mph, the A3 *Papyrus*. *(1935)*

- The fastest steam locomotive in the world, at 126mph, the A4 Mallard. (1938)

- The first use of thermic siphons in a boiler in the U.K. on the V4 locomotives. (1941)

### Rolling Stock Innovations

- The articulated railway carriage, patent included in Appendix 5.

- The corridor tender to allow longer non-stop running. (1928)

- The *Silver Jubilee* and *The Coronation* trains, the first fully streamlined high-speed, long distance and intercity trains (developed through scientific methods).

### Additional Innovations & Influence

- Development of an in-cab signalling apparatus for the A4 Pacifics running on Scottish lines,

- Instigated the L.N.E.R. water softening processes throughout the G.N.R. and L.N.E.R. mainlines; this later became incorporated as a British Standard.

# Appendix 4
## Mileage of Locomotives Between General Repairs (1937)

The *Mileage of Locos Between General Repairs* table below gives figures which have been obtained from an original L.N.E.R. document, which can be found under National Archives File 394 - 228.

<table>
<tr><td colspan="4" align="center">***CIRCULAR No. C.M.E.***<br>***41.***<br><br>*(Revised May, 1937).*<br><br><br>*Chief Mechanical Engineer's Office*<br><br>*King's Cross*</td></tr>
<tr><td colspan="4" align="center"><h2>MILEAGE OF LOCOMOTIVES BETWEEN GENERAL REPAIRS</h2></td></tr>
<tr><td rowspan="2">Type</td><td colspan="3" align="center">MINIMUM MILEAGE</td></tr>
<tr><td>Southern Area</td><td>N.E. Area</td><td>Scottish Area</td></tr>
<tr><td>**A.**</td><td></td><td></td><td></td></tr>
<tr><td>1</td><td>80000</td><td>80000</td><td>75,000</td></tr>
<tr><td>3</td><td>80000</td><td>80000</td><td>75000</td></tr>
<tr><td>4</td><td>80,000</td><td>80000</td><td>75000</td></tr>
<tr><td>5</td><td>75000</td><td>70,000</td><td></td></tr>
<tr><td>6</td><td></td><td>55,000</td><td></td></tr>
<tr><td>7</td><td>50,000</td><td>45,000</td><td></td></tr>
<tr><td>8</td><td></td><td>70,000</td><td></td></tr>
</table>

382

| | | | |
|---|---|---|---|
| **B.** | | | |
| 1, 2, 3, 4 | 70,000 | | |
| 5, 6, 7, 8, 8 | 60,000 | | |
| 12 | 60,000 | | 60,000 |
| 13 | | 75,000 | |
| 15, 16 | | 75,000 | |
| 17 | 75,000 | | |
| **C.** | | | |
| 1 | 70,000 | 70,000 | |
| 4, 5 | 70,000 | | |
| 6 | | 70,000 | |
| 7 | | 80,000 | 75,000 |
| 9 | | 80,000 | |
| 11 | | | 75,000 |
| 12 | 60,000 | 60,000 | |
| 13 | 65,000 | | |
| 14 | 60,000 | | |
| 15, 16 | | 55,000 | 55,000 |
| **D.** | | | |
| 1 | 70,000 | | 65,000 |
| 2, 3 | 70,000 | 70,000 | |
| 6, 7, 9 | 70,000 | | |
| 10 | 65,000 | | |
| 11 | 65,000 | | 65,000 |

383

| | | | |
|---|---|---|---|
| 13, 15, 16 | 65,000 | | |
| 17 | | 75,000 | 75,000 |
| 20, 21 | | 75,000 | |
| 29 | | | 55,000 |
| 30 | | | 65,000 |
| 31, 32 | | 55,000 | 55,000 |
| 33, 34, 36 | | | 55,000 |
| 38 | | | 55,000 |
| 40, 41, 42, 43 | | | 55,000 |
| 49 | | 75,000 | 65,000 |
| **E.** | | | |
| 4 | 55,000 | 55,000 | |
| **F.** | | | |
| 1, 2 | 70,000 | | |
| 3 | 70,000 | | |
| 4 | 55,000 | | 45,000 |
| 5, 6 | 55,000 | | |
| 7 | 70,000 | | 45,000 |
| 8 | | 55,000 | |
| **G.** | | | |
| 4 | 50,000 | | |
| 5 | | 55,000 | |
| 9, 10 | | | 45,000 |
| **J.** | | | |

| | | | |
|---|---|---|---|
| 1, 2 | 60,000 | | |
| 3, 4, 5, 6 | 55,000 | | |
| 10, 11 | 55,000 | | |
| 15, 17, 18 | 55,000 | | |
| 19, 20 | 55,000 | | |
| 21 | 55,000 | 55,000 | 55,000 |
| 23 | | 55,000 | |
| 24 | | 55,000 | 55,000 |
| 25, 26 | | 55,000 | |
| 27 | 55,000 | 55,000 | 55,000 |
| 28 | | 50,000 | |
| 31 | | | 50,000 |
| 33 | | | 50,000 |
| 35 | | 50,000 | 50,000 |
| 36, 37 | | 50,000 | 50,000 |
| 38 | | | 50,000 |
| 39 | 60,000 | 60,000 | 60,000 |
| 50 | 55,000 | | 50,000 |
| 52 | 55,000 | | |
| 60, 62, 63 | 50,000 | | |
| 65, 66, 67, 68 | 60,000 | | |
| 69 | 60,000 | | 55,000 |
| 70 | 25,000 | | |
| 71 | | 60,000 | 55,000 |

| | | | |
|---|---|---|---|
| 72 | 60,000 | 60,000 | 65,000 |
| 73 | | 50,000 | |
| 75 | 55,000 | 55,000 | |
| 77 | 50,000 | 55,000 | |
| 78, 79 | | 30,000 | |
| 83 | | | 55,000 |
| 88 | | | 45,000 |
| **K.** | | | |
| 1 | 60,000 | | |
| 2 | 60,000 | | 50,000 |
| 3 | 65,000 | 70,000 | 55,000 |
| 4 | | | 50,000 |
| **L.** | | | |
| 1 | 55,000 | | |
| **M.** | | | |
| 1 | 50,000 | | |
| **N.** | | | |
| 1 | 60,000 | | |
| 2 | 60,000 | | 50,000 |
| 4, 5, 6 | 50,000 | | |
| 7 | 60,000 | | |
| 8 | | 55,000 | 45,000 |
| 9, 10, 11, 12, 13 | | 55,000 | |
| 14 | | | 45,000 |

| | | | |
|---|---|---|---|
| 15 | | | 50,000 |
| **O.** | | | |
| 1 | 50,000 | | |
| 2 | 50,000 | | |
| 4 | 55,000 | 50,000 | 55,000 |
| 5 | 50,000 | | |
| **P.** | | | |
| 1 | 60,000 | | |
| 2 | | | 70,000 |
| **Q.** | | | |
| 4 | 55,000 | | |
| 5 | | 55,000 | |
| 6 | | 55,000 | 45,000 |
| 7 | | 55,000 | |
| **S.** | | | |
| 1 | 50,000 | | |
| **T.** | | | |
| 1 | 40,000 | 45,000 | |
| 1* | 60,000 | 60,000 | 60,000 |
| **V.** | | | |
| 1 | 60,000 | 60,000 | 60,000 |
| 2 | 75,000 | 75,000 | 75,000 |
| 3 | 75000 | 75000 | 75000 |
| **Y.** | | | |

| | | | |
|---|---|---|---|
| 1 | 40,000 | 40,000 | |
| 3 | 40,000 | 40,000 | 40,000 |
| 4 | 40,000 | 40,000 | 40,000 |
| 6 | 15,000 | 15,000 | 15,000 |
| 7 | | 50,000 | |
| 8 | | 40,000 | |
| 9 | | | 35,000 |
| 10 | 40,000 | | |
| **Z.** | | | |
| 4, 5 | | | |

# Appendix 5
## Gresley's Patents

During my research, I was fortunate in procuring some copies of a few of Gresley's main patents from private collections.

These have not been available to date as full copies, and they are of interest to historians, enthusiasts, and railway modellers for the information they hold within.

I have taken care to try and present the material in as close to its original form as possible, particularly where the images are concerned.

Patent 1: Conjugated Valve Gear, 1915

Pamphlet 2: Articulation Method, United States, 1922

# Patent 1:

# Conjugated Valve Gear Patent

*No. 15,769*                                                                    *A.D. 1915*

*Date of application, 8th Nov., 1915*
*Complete Specification Left, 8th May 1916 – Accepted, 12th Oct., 1916*

*PROVISIONAL SPECIFICATION*
*Improvements in Valve Gear for Locomotives and other Steam Engines*

*I, Herbert Nigel Gresley, of Avenue House, Doncaster, Yorkshire, Locomotive Engineer, do hereby declare the nature of this invention to be as follows:*

*This invention relates to valve gear for locomotive or other reversible steam engines, having three cylinders the piston rods of which are connected with cranks set at suitable angles for instance, is 120°, to each other. The invention consist principally in providing connections between the valves, spindles or rods of two outer cylinders (which might be stipulated outside the engine frame in the case of a locomotive) and the valve spindle or rod of an intermediate or central cylinder whereby the movements given to the valve spindles of the outside cylinders effect the requisite movements of the valve spindle of the intermediate cylinder so that no independent or separate valve care, - such for instance, as that usually employed for each valve of a two cylinder engine, - is required for actuating the distribution valve of the intermediate or central cylinder.*

*Further in one arrangement, according to this invention for the purpose, above-mentioned. I employ two rods or levers of an equal length and arranged transversely of the engine, preferably so as to work in horizontal plains one above the other, these rods or levers being operatively connected one with the other, and with the valve spindles of the three cylinders. Each of these rods is pivotally connected, for instance by pins and links, at or adjacent its outer end to the valve spindle of the adjacent outer cylinder, and the longer rod, or lever pivot, intermediate of its length, on a fixed point at or near the centreline of the engine.*

The shorter rod or lever pivots intermediate its length on or near that of the longer lever opposite to the end connected (as above mentioned) to the valve spindle of one of the outer cylinders, the said short rod or thus being a floating lever. The valve spindle of the intermediate or central cylinder is pivotally connected, for instance, by a link and pins, to the inner end of the aforesaid shorter rod or lever. As an alternative, instead of the above-mentioned, arrangement of rod, or levers, a combination of rocking shafts and levers may be employed.

For instance, in one arrangement adapted for a locomotive with valve chest situated on one side of the central or intermediate cylinder, two rocking shafts of unequal length may be arranged transversely of the engine, in suitable fixed bearings, each of these rocking shafts having fixed on them, at or adjacent the ends, suitable levers or cranks, the levers at the adjacent inner ends of the two rock shafts being pivotally connected to a suitable sway beam or lever one end (which may be the upper end) of which may be connected with the lever or crank on the inner end of the shorter rock shaft, and the lever or crank on the inner end of the longer rock shaft may be pivotally connected to the said sway beam or floating lever at a point intermediate its ends preferably at a point adjacent the end (which may be the lower end) of said sway beam which is pivotally connected, for instance, by a link and pins, to the valve spindle of the intermediate or central cylinder.

There may be two levers or cranks on the outer end of each of the aforesaid rocking shafts, one of which levers may be at the extreme outer end of the shaft, and the other a short distance from said end. This latter lever on one of the rock shafts being pivotally connected with the valve spindle of one of the outside cylinders, the corresponding lever or crank near the outer end of the other rock shaft being similarly connected with the valve spindle of the other outside or outer cylinder.

The levers or cranks on the extreme outer ends of the rock shafts may be pivotally connected with the usual or any suitable valve motion employed for the valves of the outer cylinders.

Dated this eighth day of November 1915.

JOHN P. O'DONNELL
Fel.Chart.Inst.P.A., M.Inst.C.E.,
Agent for the applicant,
Palace Chambers. Westminster, S.W.

COMPLETE SPECIFICATION
Improvements in Valve Gear for Locomotive and Other Steam Engines
I, Herbert Nigel Gresley, of Avenue House, Doncaster, Yorkshire, Locomotive Engineer, do hereby declare the nature of this invention and in what manner the same is to be performed, to be particularly described and ascertained in and by the following statement: -

This invention relates to valve gear for locomotive or other reversible, steam engines. Having three cylinders, the piston rods of which are connected with cranks set suitable angles, for instance, 120°, to each other, the kind, in which the valve of the intermediate cylinder is actuated through lever mechanism by or from the valves of the two outer cylinders without the employment of an independent or separate valve gear for the valve of said intermediate cylinder.

The invention has fought its object to provide a simple and efficient, construction and arrangement of mechanism of the kind above referred to, such as will give to the intermediate *valve, its proper normal travel and correct movements at all times in the running of the engine. The invention consist principally in the combination of a lever having a fixed pivotal point of fulcrum so arranged that such lever has a longer, and a shorter arm, the longer arm being operatively connected to the spindle of the valve of one of the outer cylinders, and a second floating equal armed lever or sway beam having one arm operatively connected to the spindle of the valve of the other outer cylinder and its other arm operatively connected to the spindle of the valve of the intermediate or centre cylinder, this second equal armed lever or sway beam being pivotally connected at its centre to the end of the shorter arm of the first mentioned lever, The position on the engine framework of the fixed pivotal point of the first mentioned lever, and the length of the respective arms of said lever, being such that the movements of the valves of the outer cylinders give, through the said two levers, movement correct as to time and travel to the valve of the intermediate or centre cylinder.*

*The levers may be simple, levers arranged to work in horizontal plains, one above the other, and assuming the length of the travel of the intermediate valve to be the same as that of each of the outer valves, the lever pivoting about a fix point is a "two to one" lever; the said "two to one" lever however, maybe in the form of a rock shaft having half cranks or arms of the required lengths fixed there on at opposite ends, in which case, the connection of the arm of the floating lever to the respective outer valves spindle is also through a rock shaft, having suitably positioned equal length, arms fixed thereon, which letter lever then works in a vertical plane. In the case of the arrangement, according to this invention, in which the levers work in horizontal plains, each of the levers is pivotally, connected, for instance, by pins and links, at or adjacent its outer end to the valve spindle of the adjacent outer cylinder, and one lever pivots, intermediate of its length, on a fixed point at or near the centreline of the engine.*

*The other lever pivots, intermediate its length on, or near that end of the first mentioned lever opposite to the end connected (as above mentioned) to the valve, spindle of one of the outer cylinders, the said other or second mentioned, lever thus being a floating lever. The valve spindle of the intermediate or central cylinder is pivotally connected, for instance by a link and pins, to the inner end of the said second mentioned lever. The above mentioned alternative arrangement, according to this invention, in which a combination of rocking shafts, and levers is employed, is more particularly adapted for a locomotive with the valve chest of the central or intermediate cylinder, situated on one side of such cylinder, and in such arrangement to rocking shots of unequal, length may be arranged transversely of the engine, in suitable fixed bearings, each of these rocking shafts, having fixed on them at or adjacent their ends, suitable levers or cranks, the levers at the adjacent inner ends of the two rock shafts being pivotally connected to a suitable sway beam or lever one end (which may be the upper end) of which is connected with the lever or crank on the inner end of the shorter rock shaft, and the other end of which is pivotally connected, for instance, by a link and pins, to the valve spindle of the intermediate or central cylinder, by the lever or crank on the inner end of the longer rock shaft, being purposely connected to the centre of said, sway beam or floating lever.*

*There may be two levers or cranks on the outer end of each of the aforesaid rocking shafts, one of which levers may be at the extreme outer end of the shaft, and the other a short distance from said end, this latter lever on one of the rock shafts being pivotally connected with the valve, spindle of one of the outside cylinders, the corresponding lever or crank near the outer end of the other rock shaft, being similarly connected with the valve spindle of the other outside, or outer cylinder. The levers or cranks on the extreme outer ends of the rock shafts May be pivotally connected with the usual or any suitable valve gear or valve motion mechanism employed for the valves of the outer cylinders.*

*The lever on the longer rock shaft connected to the outer cylinder is longer than the lever on the inner end of the rock shaft connected to the centre of the sway beam. In order that the invention may be more clearly understood, and readily carried out in practice to embodiments (by way, of example) of the invention will now be described with reference to the accompanying drawings in which, fig.1 is a side elevation, more or less diagrammatic, illustrating, one embodiment of this illustration, as applied to a locomotive engine, fig.2 being a plan view, and fig.3 an end elevation of the embodiment of the invention shown in fig.1. Fig.4 is a similar view to fig.1 but shows an alternative embodiment of the invention. Figs.5 and 6 are respectively, a plan view and an end elevation of the embodiment of the invention shown in fig.4.*

*Like reference numbers indicate corresponding parts in the several figures of the drawings. Referring to figs.1, 2, and 3, 1 indicates the driving wheels of a locomotive engine, to being the crank axle, driving, having the outside cranks three, three, coupled in the usual or any suitable manner with the piston rods of the two outer or outside cylinders 4 and 5 respectively. 6 is the intermediate or central crank on the axle to the piston rod of the intermediate, or inner cylinder, 7 being connected to the crank 6 in the known or any suitable manner. 8 is the valve, of the left hand (outer) cylinder 4 (Fig.2) 9 the valve of right hand (outer) cylinder 5, and 10 the valve of the central or intermediate cylinder 7, these valves, in the example shown, being piston valves.*

*Ordinary D-Slide valves might be employed if desired. The valves 8, 9 and 10 are arranged to work in valve chambers or casings (not shown) of the usual or any suitable kind. The valve motion mechanism or valve mechanism, more or less diagrammatically, is the well-known Walschaerts valve gear, a set of which is as usual provided in connection with each of the valves, 8 and 9. Valve gears of the well-known Joy or Stephenson types are or of other suitable type might however be employed in place of the Walschaerts gears illustrated. In the Walschaerts valve gear illustrated, 11 indicates the eccentric on the main crankshaft two, 12, the eccentric rod connected to the eccentric 11 and to the slot link 13, 14 the radius rod a pin or roller on one end of which works in the slot of the link 13.*

*The other end of the side road being operatively connected with the combination lever 15, which, through the link 16 and arm 17, is operatively connected with the crosshead 18 on the piston rod of the outside cylinder, to which the valve gear applies, for instance, the cylinder 4 (the valve gear of the cylinder 5 being in all respects, identical to that of the cylinder 4), the combination lever 15 being also operatively connected to the spindle of the valve, 8 appertaining to the cylinder, 4. The various parts of the valve gear above described and shown more or less diagrammatically, would be all constructed, combined and adapted to operate in the well-known manner, as in such valve gear is now employed.*

*The apparatus or mechanism according to the embodiment of my invention, illustrated in figs 12 and three of the drawings will now be described, as follows: 19 indicates portions of the underframe of the engine, and 20 a transverse bar or support suitably secured to the portions, 19 of the underframe. 21 and 22 are they here in before mentioned leavers of unequal length, the relatively long lever, 22 being mounted on a pivot, 23, which has its bearing in a hole or suitable, bearing in the crossbar 20, so as to be capable of having a rocking motion, the pivot, 23, forming the centre of fulcrum on which the lever 22 rocks.*

*The outer end of the lever 22 is, as shown, pivotally connected to one end of a link 24, the opposite end of which is pivotally connected to the spindle, 25 of the valve nine, and the inner end of the lever, 22 is pivotally connected, by the pin or pivot 26, to the centre of the relatively* short lever 21: the inner end of the lever 21 is pivotally connected at 27 to one end of the link 28, the other end of which is pivotally connected at 29 to the spindle 30 of the valve, 10, and the outer end of the said lever 21, which is on a floating lever, is pivotally connected, at 31, to one end of the link 32 the other end of which is pivotally connected at 33, to the spindle 34 of the valve 8.

The construction and arrangement of the various parts of the apparatus, according to this invention, as above described with reference to figs 1, 2 and 3 of the drawings, as such that in the working of the engine, the proper movements are given to the valve 10 of the central or intermediate cylinder 7, for admitting steam to and exhausting steam from the said cylinder seven at the proper times by the movements given to the leavers 21 and 22 by the working of the valves 8 and 9 of the outer cylinders, 4 and 5. Further, the usual adjusting movements given to the valves 8 and 9 by the adjustments or notching up of the valve, gears of these valves (by means of the usual reversing lever operable by the engine man), are transmitted, through the levers 21 and 22, to the valve 10 of the central cylinder 7, so that the proper adjustments of the valve 10 are also obtained.

Referring now to the alternative construction and arrangement illustrated in Figs. 4, 5 and 6 of the drawings, in this construction and arrangement 35 and 36 are the hereinbefore mentioned rocking shafts of unequal length the relatively long shaft 36 being supported at or adjacent its opposite ends in suitable fixed bearings (for instance fixed to the under frame of the engine or to a suitable part secured to the under frame) 37, 38, the relatively short rocking shaft 35 being supported in bearings 39, 40.

As clearly shewn in Figs. 5 and 6 the shaft 36 has fixed on it levers or cranks 41, 41$^A$ and 42 the lever 41 being pivotally connected to the sway beam or floating lever 45 at a position, indicated at 45$^A$, between the ends of said lever. The shaft 35 has fixed on its levers or cranks 46, 46$^A$ and 47, the lever 47 being pivotally connected at 48 to the upper end of the sway beam or lever 45 and the lever 46, pivotally connected to links 49, 49$^A$ which are also pivotally connected to a cross head 44$^A$ on the spindle 34 of the valve 8. The lower end of the floating lever or sway beam 45 is pivotally connected to links 50 which are also pivotally connected to the spindle 30 of the valve 10.

The lever or crank 41$^A$ on the shaft 36 is pivotally connected as shewn in Figs. 4 and 6 to the combination lever 15 of the valve motion mechanism or valve gear appertaining to the valve 9 of the right-hand cylinder 5, and the lever or crank 46$^A$ on the shaft 35 is similarly connected to the combination lever 15 of the valve gear appertaining to the valve 8 of cylinder 4. 51, Fig. 6, indicates the valve chambers or casings of the valves 8,9 and 10, and 52, Figs.4 and 5, indicates the ported liners usually fitted in the valve chambers.

The working of the apparatus above described with reference to Figs. 4, 5and 6 of the drawings is the same as described with reference to the apparatus illustrated in Figs. 1, 2 and 3, except that with the apparatus shewn in Figs. 4, 5 and 6 the requisite motions of the valve 10 are transmitted to the said valve, from the valves 8 and 9, through the rocking shafts 35, 36 and floating lever or sway beam 45.

As clearly shewn in Figs 2 and 3 of the drawings the lever 22 is a two-to-one lever the longer arm, to the right of the pivot 23 (Fig. 3), being connected with the spindle of the valve 9 and the shorter arm connected to the floating lever 21 by the pivot 26 at a point equidistant its ends; and the floating lever 21 is an equal lever its arms, to the right and left of the pivot 26, being *connected respectively with the spindles of the valve 8 and 10 as hereinbefore described. Also as clearly shewn in Figs 1, 2, 4 and 5 of the drawings the cranks 3, 3ᴬ and 6 are set relatively to each other on the axle 2 at an angle of 120 degrees.*

*Further, as shewn in Figs. 4 and 6 of the drawings, the lever or crank 41 on shaft 36 is twice the effective length of the lever or crank 42 on the said shaft, thus providing a two-to-one lever, and the crank 42 is pivotally connected to the floating lever 45, at the point 45ᴬ, between the ends of the said floating lever.*

*Variations might be made in the details of construction and arrangement of the parts of the apparatus hereinbefore described and illustrated in the drawings without departing from the main features of the invention. For instance, it is not essential that the hereinbefore mentioned levers 21 and 22 (see Fig. 3) should be of unequal length as shewn. For instance, with the positions of the valves 8, 9 and 10 suitably altered the relative overall lengths of the levers 21, 22 might be suitably altered; or these levers might, if desirable, be equal in length.*

*I may point out that I am aware that it has been heretofore proposed to actuate the valve of the central cylinders of a three cylinder locomotive engine by means of a pivoted "two-to-one" lever and a floating sway beam, the sway beam being arranged transversely of the engine and connected at its ends respectively to the valve spindles of the outer cylinders and being pivoted at its centre to the end of the shorter arm of the "two-to-one" lever which works in a vertical plane and has a fixed pivotal point, the end of the longer arm of said lever being connected to the valve spindle of the central cylinder.*

*Having now particularly described and ascertained the nature of my said invention and in what manner the same is to be performed, I declare that what I claim is: -*

*1. In a steam engine having two outer cylinders and one intermediate or central cylinder, the combination with the distribution valves of the outer cylinders and the valve gear of these valves, of a pivoted lever working about a fixed point on the engine frame and having a longer and shorter arm, the longer arm being operatively connected at or adjacent its end to the valve spindle of one of the outer cylinders, and a floating lever or sway beam connected at or adjacent its ends respectively to the valve spindle of the other outer cylinder and to the valve spindle of the intermediate or central cylinder, said floating lever or sway beam being pivotally connected at its centre to the shorter arm of the other lever at or adjacent the end of said arm, whereby the requisite movements are given to the valve of the intermediate or central cylinder by the movements of the valves and valve gears of the outer cylinders*

*2. In a steam engine having three cylinders the pistons of which are connected to cranks set at 120 degrees to each other on the crank shaft, means operatively connecting the spindle of the distribution valve of the intermediate or central cylinder with the valve spindles, or valve gears, of the distribution valves of the two outer cylinders the said means comprising a two-to-one lever Woking about a fixed point and having its longer arm operatively connected to the valve spindle of one of the said two outer cylinders and its shorter arm operatively connected to the middle point of a floating lever one end of which is operatively connected to the valve spindle of the other of said two outer cylinders and the other end of which is operatively connected with the valve spindle of the intermediate or central cylinder.*

*3. Apparatus of the kind claimed in Claim 1, or in Claim 2, characterised by the fact that the levers are arranged to work in horizontal planes one above the other and are connected to one another and to the respective valve spindles by pins, or pins and inks, substantially as described.*

*4. In a steam engine having three working cylinders each with its own distribution valve, the combination, with the valves and the valve gears of the two outer cylinders of two rocking shafts of unequal length, and each working in fixed bearings, means operatively connecting lever or crank arm at the outer end of the longer rocking shaft with the spindle of the distribution valve of the central cylinder, means operatively connecting the other end of the said floating lever with an arm at the inner end of the shorter rocking shaft, and means operatively connecting a corresponding arm at the other or outer end of the shorter rocking shaft with the spindle of the distribution valve of the other outer cylinder.*

*5. In a steam engine having working three working cylinders each with its own distribution valve and valve motion mechanisms or gears one for each of the two outer cylinders, mechanism, for actuating the distribution valve of the intermediate or central cylinder by the movements of the distribution valves and valve gears of the said outer cylinders, the said mechanism having its parts constructed, combined and adapted to operate substantially as described with reference to and illustrated by Figs. 1, 2 and 3 or by Figs 4, 5 and 6 of the accompanying drawings for the purposes set forth.*

*Dated this 8th Day of May, 1916.*

*John P. O'Donnell*

*Fel.Chart.Inst.P.A., M.Inst.C.E.,*

*Agent for the Applicant*

*Palace Chambers, Westminster, SW.*

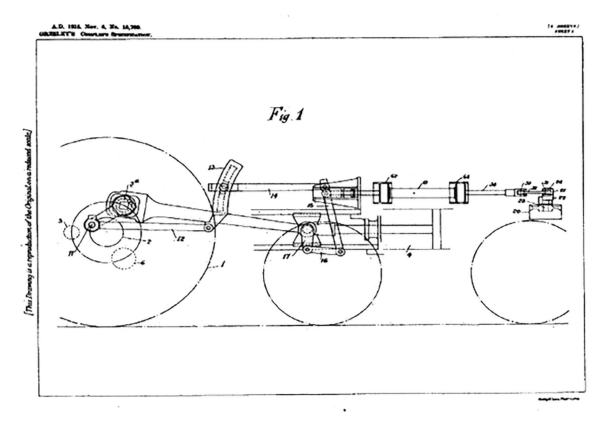

Fig. 338. Images from Gresley's Conjugated Valve Gear Patent. Simon A.C. Martin.

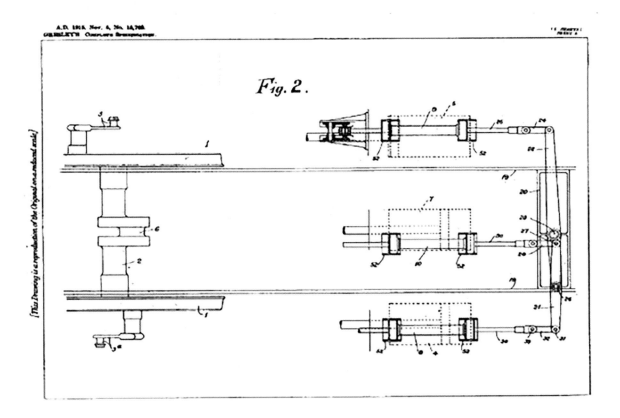

Fig. 339. Images from Gresley's Conjugated Valve Gear Patent. Simon A.C. Martin.

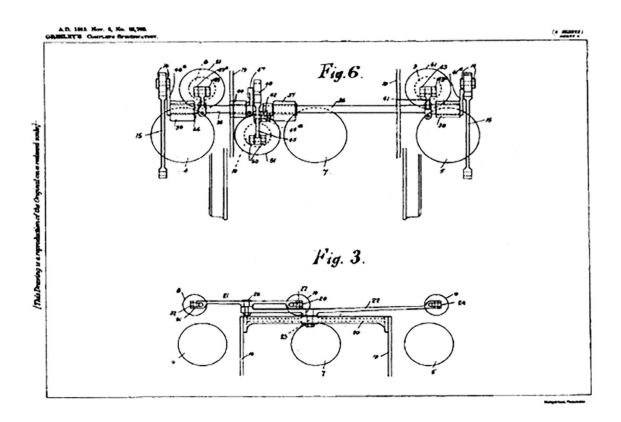

Fig. 340. Images from Gresley's Conjugated Valve Gear Patent. Simon A.C. Martin.

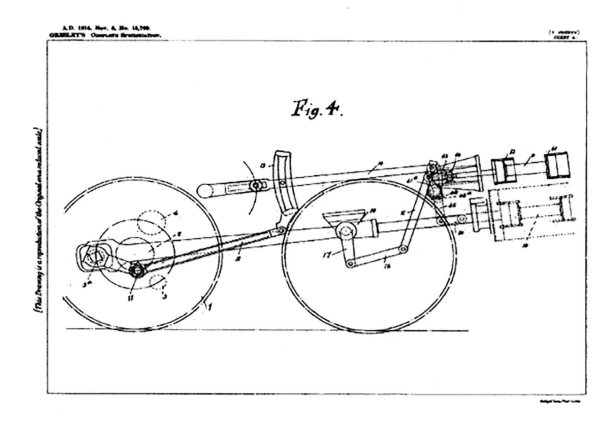

Fig. 341. Images from Gresley's Conjugated Valve Gear Patent. Simon A.C. Martin.

A.D. 1914. Nov. 5. No. 14,765.
GRESLEY'S Conjugated Specification.

(6 SHEETS)
SHEET 5.

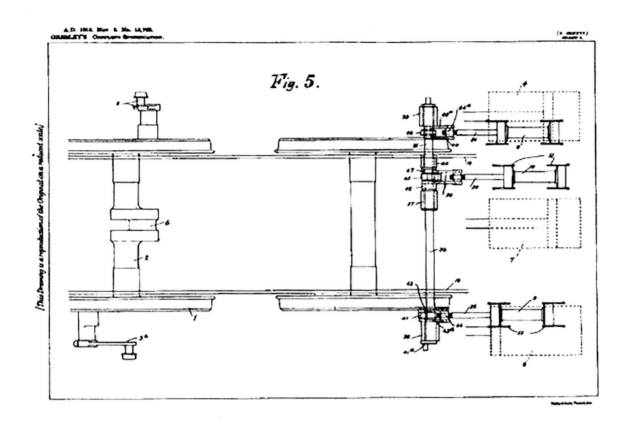

Fig. 342. Images from Gresley's Conjugated Valve Gear Patent. Simon A.C. Martin.

# Patent 2:
## Articulation Method

# UNITED STATES PATENT OFFICE

*HERBERT NIGEL GRESLEY OF DONCASTER, ENGLAND, ASSIGNOR TO THE LEEDS FORGE COMPANY LIMITED OF LEEDS, YORK, ENGLAND, A BRITISH COMPANY*

*RAILWAY AND TRAMWAY VEHICLE*

*1,412,053.*         *Specification of Letters Patent. Patented Apr.11, 1922.*
*Application filed April 26, 1921. Serial 464,620.*

*To all whom it may concern:*

*Be it known that I, Herbert Nigel Gresley, a subject of Great Britain and Ireland, residing at Doncaster, England, have invented certain new and useful improvements in or relating to Railway and Tramway Vehicles: and I do hereby declare the following to be a full, clear and exact description of the invention, such as will enable others skilled in the art to which it appertains to make and use the same.*

*This invention has reference to railway and tramway vehicles of the kind in which the adjacent ends of two vehicles are supported by one common bogie, the other end of either or each of the said vehicles being supported on an independent bogie, or on another bogie which also supports one end of another vehicle.*

*In an arrangement of this kind described in the specification of my prior British Letters Patent No. 4512 of 1907 the two vehicles are supported on and articulated to their common supporting bogie through brackets fixed to the vehicle ends and so formed as to engage one with the other and thereby serve as a coupling or connection between the vehicles.*

*The object of the present invention is to provide an arrangement in which the two vehicles whilst supported on the common bogie by brackets fixed to the respective ends of the two vehicles are connected by draw gear comprising a draw spring or springs so that in a train of vehicles the pull at starting is taken up vehicle by vehicle through the draw springs and gear thereby enabling the load to be advantageously taken up gradually at starting instead of the whole load being taken up at once as is the case where the supporting brackets also constitute the coupling means as described in the said prior specification which do not provide for the movements necessary when draw springs are employed.*

*A further object of the invention is to provide an improved construction and arrangement of supporting brackets embodying lateral co-acting bearing surfaces of considerable area for taking the weight of the vehicles and transmitting the same to the bogie, means being provided for the efficient lubrication of such surfaces.*

*In this way it may be possible to dispense with side brackets fixed to the adjacent ends of the two vehicles, and that either rest on bearing plates fixed to the spring bolster of the supporting* bogie has described in the said prior British Patent specification No.4512 of 1907 or bear one upon the other as described in another specification of British Letters Patent granted to me. For the said purposes, according to the invention, the adjacent ends of the two vehicles connected together by draw gear comprising a draw spring or springs. are supported upon the common bogie by brackets or the like fixed to the respective vehicle ends and mutually engaging one another so as to prevent relative movement in a lateral direction whilst capable not only of relative angular movement to allow E. movement of the two vehicles about the axis of the centre casting or swivel plate of the common bogie but also capable of relative longitudinal movement to allow for movements due to on pression of the draw springs.

One embodiment of such an arrangement comprises a bracket or the like fixed to one vehicle end and adapted to rest on the bogie centre casting or swivel plate and formed with an upwardly extending part cylindrical boss or part annular flange embraced by laterally projecting parts of another racket or the like fixed to the end of the other vehicle and resting upon the first mentioned bracket or the like, the arrangement being such that the two brackets can turn relatively to each other about the axis of the bogie centre casting or swivel plate as well as move longitudinally relatively to each other to provide for compression of the draw springs.

A coupling pin is carried by the bracket or the like fixed to one vehicle engages an eye on the head of a draw bar carried by the other vehicle and associated with a draw spring or springs. The coupling pin may extend centrally through the bogie centre casting or swivel plate and constitute the king bolt or pivot of the bogie. To limit the relative angular movements of the two vehicles about the axis of the bogie centre casting or swivel plate, security chains may connect the adjacent headstocks of the two vehicles near the sides of the vehicles.

If desired side buffers may be fitted so that one or other is compressed when the vehicles are travelling on curved portions of track.

Fig.1 of the accompanying illustrative drawings shows in side elevation the adjacent ends of two railway passenger vehicles supported upon a common bogie, by means embodying the invention. Fig.2 shows in side elevation, to a larger scale, the supporting and coupling arrangement. Fig. 3 is a central vertical longitudinal section on the line A, A of Fig.4 of the supporting and coupling arrangement. Fig. 4 shows the supporting and coupling arrangement in plan, and Fig 5 is a transverse section corresponding to the line B, B of Fig. 4.

1 and 2 indicate the ends of the two vehicles, 3 the bogie, supporting the same through the spring bolster 4, and 5, 6 the brackets fixed by bolts 7 to the headstocks 8 of the vehicle underframes 9. The bracket 5 has a horizontal base 5a which rests directly upon the centre casting or swivel plate 10 of the bolster 4, and which is formed with an annular downwardly extending projection 11 that engages a corresponding annular recess formed in the bolster centre casting or swivel plate 10.

Curved upwardly projecting flanges or webs 12 that connect the vertical wall of the bracket 5 to the base 5a thereof, form a part cylindrical boss the axis of which is in line with the axis of the bogie centre casting or swivel plate 10, and these curved flanges or webs are embraced by corresponding curved flanges or webs 13 connecting the horizontal base portions 6a of the bracket 6 to the vertical wall of such bracket.

The curvature of the flanges or webs 13 does not extend beyond the point of greatest diameter of the curved flanges or webs 12 so that whilst these mutually engaging flanges or webs 12 and 13 prevent any relative side movement of the two brackets and therefore of the two vehicle ends to which the brackets are fixed, they do not prevent relative longitudinal movement of the brackets when the one vehicle is pulled away from the other as in the compression of the draw spring hereinafter referred to, neither do they prevent free relative angular movement of the brackets about the axis of the bogie centre casting or swivel plate. The horizontal base portions 6a of the bracket 6 rest and work on the laterally extended side portions of the base 5a of the bracket 5 and to reduce friction the upper faces of said side portions have formed in them grooves 14 to which lubricant is supplied through grease cups 15 screwed into the horizontal base portions 6a of the brackets 6.

Projecting from the vertical wall of the bracket 5 is a forked boss 16 the horizontally extending jaws of which are formed with holes to receive a coupling pin 17 the axis of which is in line with the axis of the centre casting or swivel plate 10 of the bolster 4. The jaws of the forked boss 16 embrace the head 18 of a draw bar 19 which extends through the bracket 6 and the headstock 8 of the corresponding vehicle 9, a draw spring 20, preferably of the well-known concentric India rubber ring type, being mounted on the draw bar 19 between the back of the headstock 8 and a bearing washer 21 which is backed by a nut 22 on the inner end of the draw rod.

The coupling pin 17 passes through a whole formed therefor in the head 18 of the draw bar 19, and, as will be seen, the forked boss 16, coupling pin 17, and draw bar head 18 are located centrally within the part annular wall formed by the flanges or webs 12.

Normally the draw spring 20, which is considerably stressed by adjustment of the nut 21, pulls the head 18 inwardly so that a flange 18a thereon is pressed against the bracket 6. When, however, the spring 20 is compressed during a drawing operation the bracket 6 is pulled away from the head flange 18a. If desired a rebound spring may be fitted on the drawbar 19 or a cushioning pad of India rubber may be interposed between the head flange 18a and the bracket 6.

In the apparatus illustrated the coupling pin 17 is formed with a downward extension 17a that constitutes the king bolt or pivot of the bogie and engages holes formed therefor in the base 5a of the bracket 5 and in the centre casting or swivel plate of the bogie bolster 4.

It will be seen that the co-acting surfaces of the webs or flanges 12 and 13 of the brackets 5 and 6 prevent relative lateral movement of the adjacent ends of the vehicles whilst allowing free angular movement about the coupling pin and king bolt 17, 17a as also free relative longitudinal movement when the draw spring 20 is compressed. The accurate guides 12 and 13 permit the draw bar 19 to slide longitudinally and compress the spring 20, and the springs 20 in a train of cars relieve the engine of great strain starting, which is found to be very advantageous.

Supporting and coupling means as hereinbefore described may vary considerably in details of construction as will be understood without departure from the invention. What I claim as my invention and desire to secure by Letters Patent is: -

1. The combinations, with the adjacent end portions of two cars, and a supporting carriage arranged under them; of brackets secured to the ends of the cars and provided with arcuate guides which permit one car to move longitudinally and pivotally relative to the other car and which prevent relative lateral movement between the cars, and a spring-controlled draw bar slidable in one of the said brackets and pivoted to the other bracket concentric with the said arcuate guides.

2. The combination, with the adjacent end portions of two cars, and a supporting carriage arranged under them and provided with a bolster; of brackets secured to the ends of the cars and provided with arcuate guides which permit one car to move longitudinally and pivotally relative to the other car and which prevent lateral movement between the cars, means which connect one bracket pivotally with the said bolster, and a spring-controlled draw bar pivoted to the last said bracket concentric with the said arcuate guides, said draw bar being slidable longitudinally in the other bracket.

3. The combination, with the adjacent end portions of two cars, and a supporting carriage arranged under them; of brackets secured to the ends of the cars and provided with arcuate guides the contacting parts of which are portions of vertically arranged cylinders, sail guides operating to prevent one car from moving laterally of the other car and to permit one car to move longitudinally and pivotally relative to the other car, and a spring-controlled draw bar slid able in one of the sail brackets and pivoted to the other bracket concentric with the said arcuate guides.

4. The combination, with the devices as set forth in claim 1, of horizontally arranged base portions on the said brackets, sail base portions being arranged to overlap and bear on each other, and the lower base portion being arranged to bear on the upper part of the supporting carriage.

In testimony whereof I affix my signature, in presence of two witnesses.

**HERBERT NIGEL GRESLEY**

Witnesses:
**BEN DAY,**
**EDWARD FLETCHER**

H. N. GRESLEY.

RAILWAY AND TRAMWAY VEHICLE.

APPLICATION FILED APR. 26, 1921.

1,412,053. Patented Apr. 11, 1922.

2 SHEETS—SHEET 1.

FIG.1.

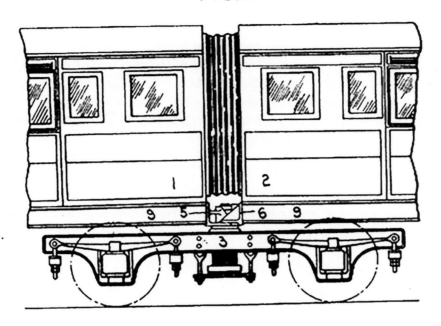

*Fig. 343. Images from Gresley's Articulation Patent. Simon A.C. Martin.*

FIG.2.

Inventor
Herbert N. Gresley
by Herbert W. T. Jenner,
Attorney

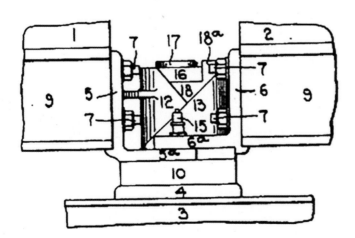

*Fig. 344. Images from Gresley's Articulation Patent. Simon A.C. Martin.*

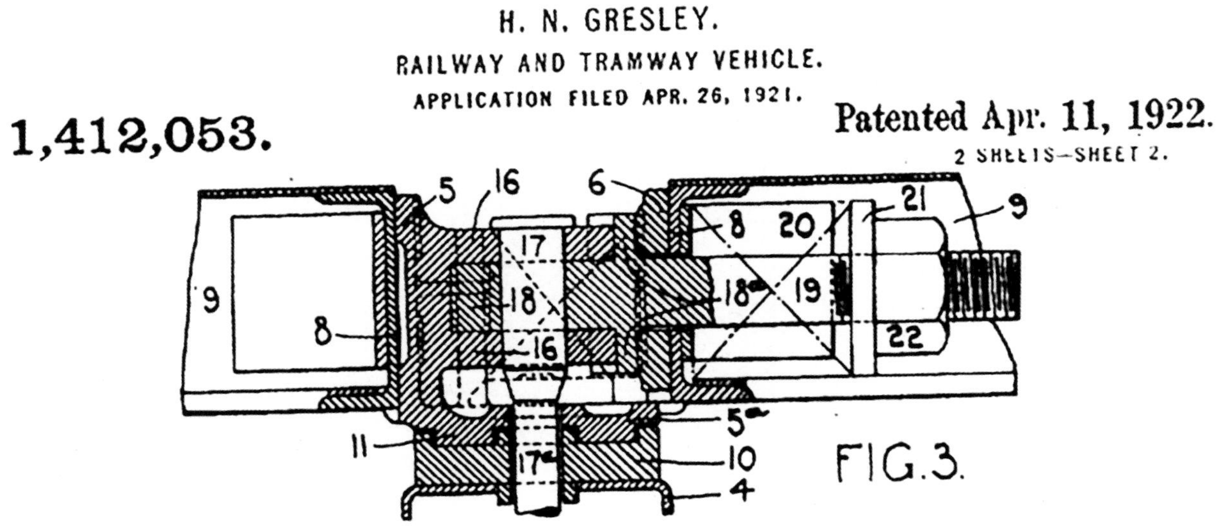

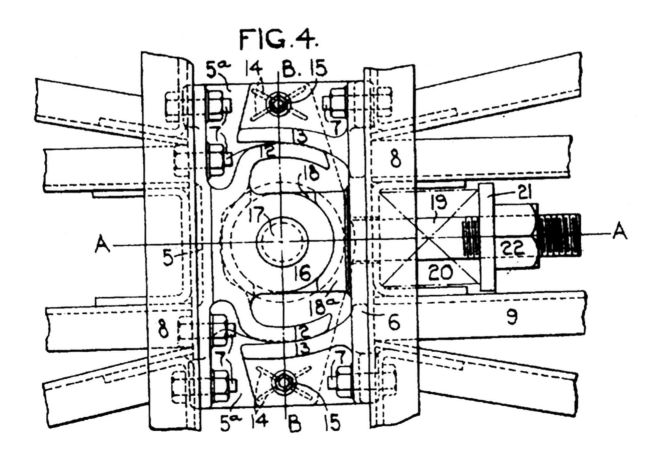

FIG.3.

*Fig. 345. Images from Gresley's Articulation Patent. Simon A.C. Martin.*

FIG.4.

*Fig. 346. Images from Gresley's Articulation Patent. Simon A.C. Martin.*

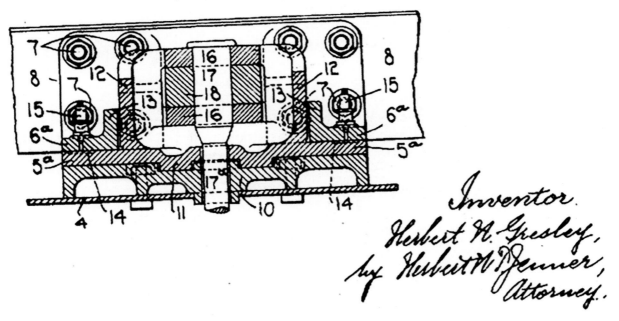

Fig. 347. Images from Gresley's Articulation Patent. Simon A.C. Martin.

# Appendix 6
## The E.S. Cox
## Report (1942)

In June 1942 the L.N.E.R.'s Emergency Board was presented with a "not to be published" internal report that had been ordered by Sir Charles Newton and Edward Thompson towards the development of a future strategy in locomotive design, building and maintenance.

Thompson approached Sir William Stanier for a report into the railway's conjugated valve gear fleet. Stanier accepted, and deputised E.S. Cox for writing the report. The two men were shown around the main locomotive works of the L.N.E.R., with various parts of conjugated valve gear covering the largest classes laid out for them to inspect. Cox ultimately wrote the report, and Stanier signed off on it.

The original report was dated 8th June 1942 and titled *"Report on the "2 to 1" Gresley valve gear on L.N.E.R. 3-cylinder locomotives".*

The report was presented to the L.N.E.R. Emergency Board and the L.N.E.R.'s Locomotive Committee at its July 1942 meetings. After careful consideration of its points, the L.N.E.R. Emergency Board gave Edward Thompson permission to proceed with the recommendations that had been made.

*REMIT: There are 652 3-cylinder locomotives on the L.N.E.R. on which the inside valve is driven by an arrangement of rocking levers known as the 'Gresley' valve gear. Mechanical trouble has been experienced with these engines, and I have been asked to give a considered opinion on the merits or demerits of this gear and its influence on the mechanical trouble in question.*

*THE VALVE GEAR:*

*I have carefully examined the design of the gear from information placed at my disposal by the L.N.E.R. and have supplemented this by an independent investigation into the valve events under various conditions. I find there is an inherent defect which will prevent any such a gear from giving correct steam distribution in the inside cylinder under any circumstances, and that this is supplemented by two defects in application which further aggravate the defective distribution.*

*In theory the movement of the outside valves, as directly driven by normal walschaert gear, is reproduced exactly on the inside valve, suitably phased to allow for the 120 spacing of the cranks, and the correctness of this movement can be proved mathematically.*

*In practice, on the other hand, the various leverages are such that any play existing at the various pin joints, adds, and in some cases multiples in its effect on the middle valve, the final result being that unit play at each of the eight pin joints in the gear is multiplied by eleven by the time it reaches the middle valve. Diagrams prepared by the L.N.E.R. to illustrate this fact have been carefully checked and are correct.*

*When an engine is new out of the shops, with no more than the normal manufacturing clearances allowed by the L.N.E.R. in pins and links, namely, 0.004in. at each joint, the lost motion at the middle valve amounts to 0.044in. With the clearances due to wear which are common experience on engines as returned to the shops for repairs, this lost motion can amount to more than 3/8in.*

*The effect of this varies with the cut-off, speed, and friction of the valve in its liner. The nominal cut-off is exceeded in full gear (65%) by only 3%, but in the case of a nominal 20% the usual cut-off for high-speed working, the actual inside cylinder cut-off may be increased to 28%.*

*The steam port opening associated with this longer cut-off varies under different circumstances. At low speeds or if friction between valve and liner is high, the inside valve only moves a portion of its normal travel, and then pauses while the remaining movement of the outside gear is absorbed by the lost motion.*

*In full gear or late cut-offs this effect is not serious, but in the case of an engine working at early cut-off, where due to the accumulation of carbon or other reasons, the valve is stiff in its liner, the port opening at 20% nominal may be only 1/10in. instead of the designed 1/4in. so that the steam entering the cylinder is severely throttled and the power developed may be up to 30% below that of the outside cylinders.*

*On the other hand, at high speeds, the valve, by reason of its inertia, overshoots expected normal travel by the amount of lost motion, so that the port opening is that corresponding to the increased cut off of 28%, namely, about 7/16in. instead of the designed 1/4in. and the power developed may now be theoretically up to 30% above that of the outside cylinders.*

*Between these two extremes, according to various conditions, the power output of the inside cylinder can vary widely from time to time on a given engine. Indicator cards taken by the L.N.E.R. Confirm that at late cut offs the variation in power development in the inside cylinder is not serious, but at the highest speeds and early cut offs the power output is sometimes as much as 50% above that of the outside cylinders, showing that in addition to the over-travel of the valve due to lost motion, there is probably still further over-travel due to the whip in the long arms of the rocking lever. There is thus a kind of 'supercharge' effect in the centre cylinder, which may have some bearing on the good haulage performance of these engines in fast running.*

*Mechanically, the design is unsound because the inherent multiplication of the play in the pins promotes the development of still further play by wear, and the gear can be expected to, and in does in fact, become 'run down' at much lower mileage than in the case of the normal walschaert gear originating the motion in which the leverages are such that the play at various pins is actually reduced several times by the time it reaches the valve.*

*Added to the inherent defect described above are the results of two defects in application. First to the various pins and the roller bearings where employed are not adequate in size to offer the greatest resistance to wear resulting from the special circumstances of high leverage and small angle of movement. The following comparison is given with practice on L.M.S. 4-cylinder engines where, of course, the length of the rocking arms is much less than in the '2 to 1' valve gear:*

| L.N.E.R. | L.M.S. |
|---|---|
| Main Rocking Lever Pivot Pin Diameter | |
| 1 ½ in. | 2 1/8 in. |
| Inside diameter of ball race | |
| 1 ¾ in. | 2 7/8 in. |
| Other pin joints | |
| 1 ½ in. plain bearing | 1 ¾ in. plain bearing, 1 9/16 in. needle bearing |

*Secondly, on most of the engines concerned, the drive to the inside valve is taken from the outside valve spindles after they have passed through the steam chests subject to steam temperature. It is possible to compensate for this to some extent in the setting of the valves, but however set, the variation in steam temperature, which may amount to some 260 degrees Fahrenheit or more in a single run, is sufficient in conjunction with the multiplication afforded by the '2 to 1' valve gear, to effect the moment of the inside valve by a further 1/16 in. The result at early cut-offs is to shorten the effective cut-off at the forward stroke of the piston and to increase it at the backward stroke.*

*In simple terms, therefore, with this particular valve gear the steam distribution to the inside cylinder will inevitably be irregular and wear of its parts will be rapid. Practical support for this contention is found in the fact that although it was at first applied widely to 3-cylinder engines throughout the world, including large numbers in America and Germany, it has been successively abandoned wherever it was applied, and the provision of three separate gears is now standard practice in every important application except on the L.N.E.R.*

*HOT BIG ENDS*

*Statistics furnished by the L.N.E.R. Show that last year, on the 652 engines concerned, ten times as many hot bearings occurred on the inside as on the outside big ends. The number of the former appears to be about 6 times as many as were experienced by the L.M.S., in the same year with 591 3-cylinder locomotives. The high-speed engines of the 4-6-2 class of the L.N.E. suffered the highest proportion of failures, the 2-6-2 and 2-8-2 types also being high.*

*I have carried out a very careful investigation into the probable loading of the inside big end on a typical L.N.E.R. 3-cylinder locomotive, allowing for the inertia forces and the increased steam loading arising from the over-travel of the inside valve which is permitted by a badly worn '2 to 1' valve gear, and I have worked out corresponding figures for the inside big end on the L.M.S. 'Royal Scot' which is an engine comparable in nominal piston loading to the L.N.E.R. 'V2' 2-6-2 and which has been very free from hot inside big ends over the 15 years the class has been in service.*

*I find that the maximum bearing pressure in the two cases at high speed, and allowing for the effects of severe wear in the valve gear of the L.N.E.R engine, is if anything, slightly higher in the case of the 'Royal Scot' engine which has actually a narrower bearing than the former engine, and from a scrutiny of the character of the load diagrams throughout a whole revolution, I cannot say that the poor distribution in the L.N.E inside cylinder is likely to contribute other than in a minor way to the overheating which has been experienced.*

*Examination of the design of the inside connecting rod big end, which is common to the whole of the engines in question, does, however, show certain defects. The most serious are lack of stiffness in the big end strap, and the possibility of the marine type bolts stretching in service, both of which features can cause play between the split brass and its housing, which experience shows can distort the two halves of the brass so that they tend to nip the bearing and cause heating. The L.N.E.R have realised this, and I was shown alternative designs of inside connecting rod which should obviate this trouble in future. Even in the new designs there remain, however, certain features, common also to the original design, which experience on the L.M.S has shown to be conducive to hot big ends.*

*These are:-*

*1.a brass strip, 1 ½ in. wide, is allowed to bear on the crank pin on the horizontal centre line instead of continuing the white metal all round each half of the bearing. L.M.S experience has shown this to be undesirable since if the adjacent white metal is heated sufficiently it can flow over the brass strip, reduce the clearance, and eventually cause a hot big end.*

*2.The white metal used contains 5% lead. Investigation by the L.M.S. Research department has shown that the matrix of such a metal will contain a constituent which becomes completely molten at around 185 degrees Celsius.*

*If the working temperature of the big end reaches 100C, as is possible when the loading bears* heavily on the brass strip, this fusible constituent which honeycombs the alloy will begin to flow and smear. The L.M.S. uses a white metal in which the lead is limited to 0.2% maximum. In this metal the easily fusible constituent is not formed, and no melting occurs until a temperature of 239C has been reached.

Mechanical tests show that this alloy has great rigidity and resistance to creep at working temperature than the somewhat similar alloy containing 5% lead. Some years ago the L.M.S had several big end bearing failures where exfoliation of the white metal occurred at which the alloy in use was similar to the L.N.E metal.

3.The felt pads which come between the oil tube outlet and the journal, continue right across to the outside of the bearing, presumably to give some side lubrication. If badly fitted or worn, much of the oil may escape sideways without getting onto the journal. L.M.S practice is to enclose the felt pads entirely within the brass.

It is appreciated, of course, that the above three features are also present on the L.N.E outside big ends which do not experience so much trouble, but under the more unfavourable circumstances of the split inside brasses, and based on a good deal of L.M.S experience it is felt they may at least be one contributory feature.

CONCLUSIONS and RECOMMENDATIONS

1.      The '2 to 1' valve gear although theoretically correct is, in practice, incapable of being made into a sound mechanical job, and rapid wear of the pins, and incorrect steam distribution, are the inevitable results of its use. In view of the inherent defects and the discontinuance of its use throughout the world, a case can be made for not perpetuating it in any future design.

2.      It is certain that with this arrangement of valve gear it will be necessary to give the engines a frequent overhaul in the shops and even then, it is not possible to eliminate the effect of lost motion due to running clearance required in the pin joints and the effect of expansion on the outside valve spindles on the inside valve. It is a matter of consideration, therefore, as to whether certain of the classes should not be fitted with an independent inside valve gear.

3.      The excessive big end trouble experienced is in my opinion due mainly to the design of the big end. The alternative designs already developed by the L.N.E.R should bring about considerable improvement. The use of higher-grade white metal and the elimination of the brass strip across the bearing are also, in my view, worthy of consideration in view of an extensive experience with 3-cylinder engines on the L.M.S.

(sgd) W.A. Stanier

# Appendix 7
## Abbreviations

A.B. –Acceptance Body

A.C.F.I.–Auxiliaires des Chemins de Fer(feedwater heater)

C.E.E. –Chief Electrical Engineer

C.M.E. –Chief Mechanical Engineer

E.C.J.S.R. –East Coast Joint Stock

E.C.M.L–East Coast Main Line

G.C.R. –Great Central Railway

G.E.R. –Great Eastern Railway

G.N.O.S.R.–Great North of Scotland Railway

G.N.R. –Great Northern Railway

G.W.R. –Great Western Railway

HS2 –High Speed 2

K.W.V.R–Keighley and Worth Valley Railway

L.M.S. –London, Midland, and Scottish Railway

L.N.E.R. –London and North Eastern Railway

L.N.W.R. –London and North Western Railway

L & Y.R. –Lancashire and Yorkshire Railway

M.E. –Mechanical Engineer

M.R. –Midland Railway

N.B.L. –North British Locomotive Co. Ltd

MPH –Miles Per Hour

N.B.R. –North British Railway

N.E.R. –North Eastern Railway

N.N.R. –North Norfolk Railway

N.P.L. –National Physics Laboratory

N.R.M. –National Railway Museum

R.C.T.S. –Railway Correspondence and Travel Society

R.O.D. –Railway Operating Division

S.E.C.R. –South East & Chatham Railway

U.S.A. –United States of America

# Appendix 8
## Pamphlets for the L.N.E.R. Streamlined Expresses

During my research, I was fortunate in procuring copies of the L.N.E.R.'s publicity pamphlets for their streamlined trains. These have not been available to date as full copies, and they are of interest to historians, enthusiasts, and railway modellers for the information they hold within. The scans do not of course convey the exceptional shine that the gold and silver effects of the pamphlets, which are of excellent quality despite their years. The pages make interesting reading to see that tickets for the services were also being sold via several outside concerns including Thomas Cook and Pickfords. Likewise, the duties of train attendants (all male back then) included sending telegrams and posting letters and supplying bespoke stationary for the train on behalf of the L.N.E.R. as well. Should any of the souvenirs offered from the time have survived we would be suprised.

Some blank pages have been omitted from the scans, and therefore some page numbers are missing. The numbers are Figs. 348-92 inclusive.

Pamphlet 1: The Silver Jubilee

Pamphlet 2: The Coronation

Pamphlet 3: The West Riding

# "THE SILVER JUBILEE"

## BRITAIN'S FIRST STREAMLINE TRAIN

## NEWCASTLE
## DARLINGTON
## KING'S CROSS

WEEKDAYS (Saturdays excepted)
FROM MONDAY,
30TH SEPTEMBER, 1935

LONDON & NORTH EASTERN RAILWAY

Printed in Great Britain at The Baynard Press, London, S.W.9

# "THE SILVER JUBILEE"

has been designed to run at exceptionally high speeds, and at the same time to give the travelling public a special degree of comfort. It is the first train running on a British railway to be "streamlined" throughout. Travelling for long distances at an average speed of over seventy miles an hour, "The Silver Jubilee" will occupy an exceptional share of the running lines and must be well loaded, if it is to pay its way. The retention of the train as a permanent feature of the timetable will depend upon its popularity.

"The Silver Jubilee" is intended for the use of passengers to and from London only. To avoid possible disappointment, a special seat allocation system has been inaugurated and, to ensure the comfort of passengers, seat reservations are limited to 158 (62 First Class, 96 Third Class). Intending passengers are invited to make reservations in advance as early

3

as possible at the undermentioned offices :—

NEWCASTLE            Telephone
Inquiry Office, Central Station      23567

DARLINGTON
Station Booking Office          2594

LONDON
Inquiry Office, King's Cross Station    Terminus 4200
59, Piccadilly, W.1            Regent 3437
71, Regent Street, W.1         Regent 6423

Thos. Cook & Son, Ltd.,     } Grosvenor 4000
Berkeley Street, W.1, & Branches

Dean & Dawson Ltd.,      } Mansion House
163, Fenchurch Street, E.C.3      4432/3
& Branches

If intending passengers do not find it convenient to obtain their reservation tickets at the above-mentioned offices, seats may be reserved through any of the Company's Passenger Agencies or stations, provided that sufficient notice is given before the date of the journey.

A small supplementary charge per seat (5s. First Class, 3s. Third Class) will be made in view of the exceptionally fast service afforded : this payment includes the fee for seat reservation, and may be made at the time of booking or to the train attendant.

4

# DESCRIPTION OF ENGINE AND TRAIN

The outward appearance of the engine and train vehicles is entirely new. The engine, of the Pacific type, is streamlined and painted grey in several tones : it is named " Silver Link." The tender is built up to the loading gauge and has a corridor through it. The leading dimensions are as follows :—

> Length over buffers, 70' 6⅛".
> Weight, working order, 165 tons.
> Boiler pressure, 250 lbs./sq. in.
> Diameter of driving wheels, 6' 8".
> Cylinder diameter, 18½".
> Stroke, 26".
> Tractive effort, 35,500 lbs.

The train is composed of seven articulated vehicles consisting of a Twin Brake First, Triplet Restaurant Car Set and Twin Brake Third. The sides are covered in Silver Rexine outside, whilst the exterior mouldings, window frames and lettering are in stainless steel. The spaces between the articulated carriages are covered with special Indiarubber

5

sheeting to reduce the wind resistance ; wherever possible outside projections have been suppressed.

\* \* \*

A system of pressure ventilation is employed by means of which filtered air, heated in winter to a comfortable temperature, is supplied to the Restaurant Cars and compartments. The windows consist of double glass with an intervening air space, which reduces noise to a minimum.

\* \* \*

A novel arrangement of lighting using tubular lights has been installed and the decoration of the interior of the train strikes a new note in railway carriage decoration by the employment of flat surfaces and the suppression of all mouldings. The First Class Restaurant is veneered in quartered Australian Maple and the Third Class in Burmah Teak. The ceilings are finished to harmonise with the colour scheme used. Separate arm chairs are provided in the First Class Restaurant Car. The compartments are tastefully decorated in Rexine to match the upholstery

6

materials. An electric speedometer for the convenience of passengers interested in the speed of the train has been fitted in the First Class Restaurant Car.

❅ ❅ ❅

The Kitchen Car is provided with improved electric cooking and refrigerating apparatus in accordance with the most recent practice. No attempt has been made to produce a lightweight train at the expense of the passengers' comfort : the weight, excluding the engine, is 220 tons, and the length 392' 0". Seats are provided for 78 First and 120 Third Class passengers.

❅ ❅ ❅

The weight of the complete train, including the engine, is 385 tons, and the overall length over buffers is 462' 2$\frac{3}{8}$".

7

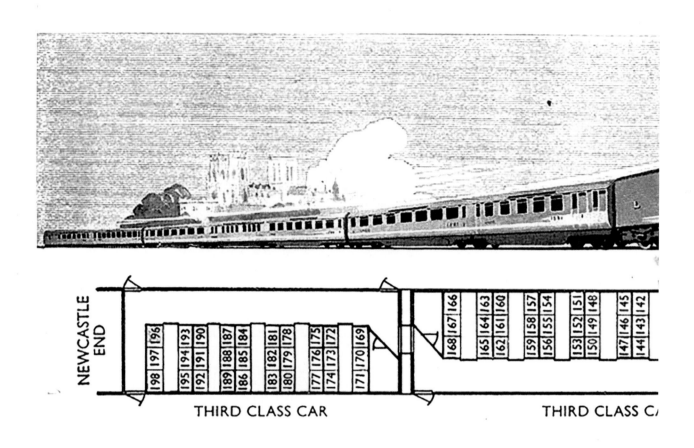

NEWCASTLE END

THIRD CLASS CAR

THIRD CLASS CA...

| 198 | 197 | 196 |
| 195 | 194 | 193 |
| 192 | 191 | 190 |
| 189 | 188 | 187 |
| 186 | 185 | 184 |
| 183 | 182 | 181 |
| 180 | 179 | 178 |
| 177 | 176 | 175 |
| 174 | 173 | 172 |
| 171 | 170 | 169 |

| 168 | 167 | 166 |
| 165 | 164 | 163 |
| 162 | 161 | 160 |
| 159 | 158 | 157 |
| 156 | 155 | 154 |
| 153 | 152 | 151 |
| 150 | 149 | 148 |
| 147 | 146 | 145 |
| 144 | 143 | 142 |

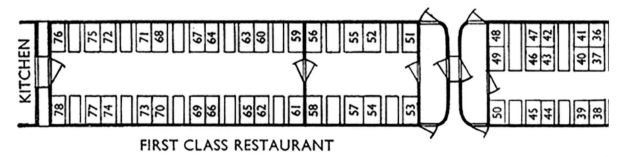

KITCHEN

FIRST CLASS RESTAURANT

| 76 | 75 72 | 71 68 | 67 64 | 63 60 | 59 | 56 | 55 52 | 51 | 49 48 | 47 | 46 43 | 42 | 40 41 | 37 36 |
| 78 | 77 74 | 73 70 | 69 66 | 65 62 | 61 | 58 | 57 54 | 53 | 50 | 45 44 | 39 | 38 | | |

SEAT PLAN OF "T...

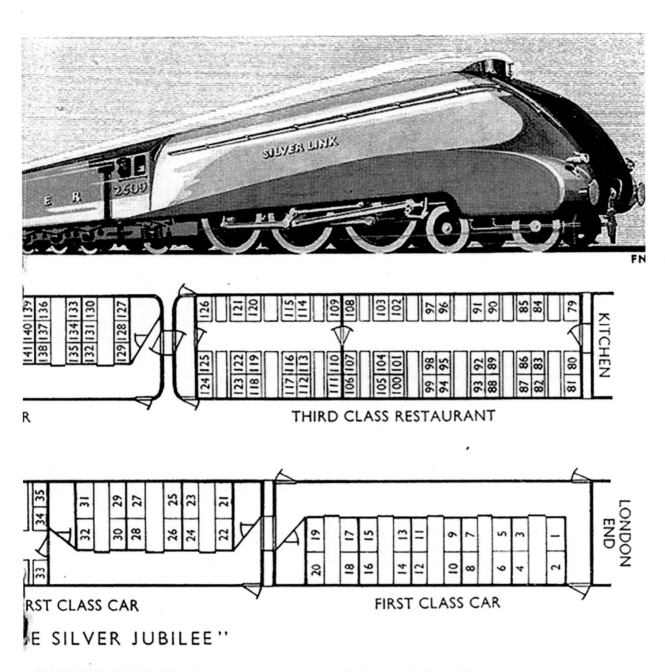

SILVER LINK

E R 2509

FN

KITCHEN

141 140 139
138 137 136
135 134 133
132 131 130
129 128 127

126
124 125
123 122
118 119
117 116
112 113
111 110
106 107
105 104
100 101
99 98
94 95
93 92
88 89
87 86
82 83
81 80
121 120
115 114
109 108
103 102
97 96
91 90
85 84
79

R

THIRD CLASS RESTAURANT

LONDON END

34 35
33
31
32
29
30
27
28
25
26
23
24
21
22

19
20
17
18
15
16
13
14
11
12
9
10
7
8
5
6
3
4
1
2

RST CLASS CAR

FIRST CLASS CAR

E SILVER JUBILEE"

LNER

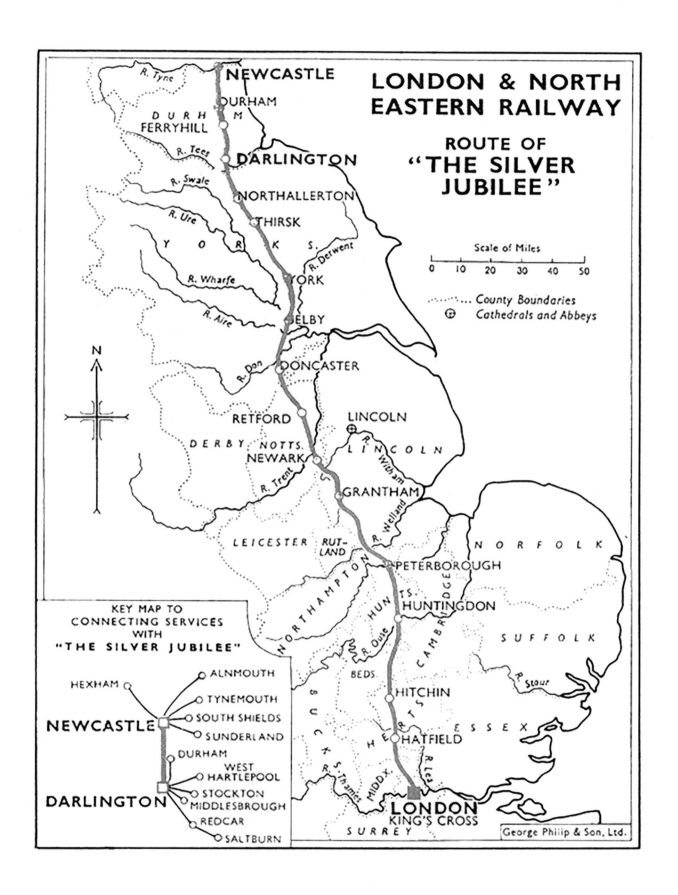

LONDON & NORTH EASTERN RAILWAY

ROUTE OF "THE SILVER JUBILEE"

Scale of Miles
0    10    20    30    40    50

..... County Boundaries
⊕ Cathedrals and Abbeys

KEY MAP TO
CONNECTING SERVICES
WITH
"THE SILVER JUBILEE"

George Philip & Son, Ltd.

419

## "THE SILVER JUBILEE"

POINT TO POINT MILEAGES
RUNNING TIMES
AND SPEEDS

### NEWCASTLE, DARLINGTON, KING'S CROSS

| Distance from Newcastle Mls. Chns. | Station | | Point to Point | | |
|---|---|---|---|---|---|
| | | | Time Mins. | Distance Mls. Chns. | Speed Miles per hour |
| | | a.m. | | | |
| | Newcastle (Central) | dep. 10. 0 | | | |
| 5  39 | Birtley | pass 10. 8 | 8 | 5  39 | 41·2 |
| 14   3 | Durham | pass 10.18 | 10 | 8  44 | 51·3 |
| 23  18 | Ferryhill | pass 10.28 | 10 | 9  15 | 55·1 |
| 36   6 | Darlington | arr. 10.40 | 12 | 12  68 | 64·2 |
| | ,, | dep. 10.42 | | | |
| 50  20 | Northallerton | pass 10.55 | 13 | 14  14 | 65·4 |
| 58   – | Thirsk | pass 11. 1 | 6 | 7  60 | 77·5 |
| 69   2 | Alne | pass 11. 9 | 8 | 11   2 | 82·7 |
| 80  16 | York | pass 11.19 | 10 | 11  14 | 67·1 |
| 94   2 | Selby | pass 11.33 | 14 | 13  66 | 59·3 |
| 112  30 | Doncaster (Central) | pass 11.49 | 16 | 18  28 | 68·8 |
| | | p.m. | | | |
| 129  57¾ | Retford | pass 12. 3 | 14 | 17  27¾ | 74·3 |
| 148  18¾ | Newark | pass 12.19 | 16 | 18  41 | 69·4 |
| 162  70½ | Grantham | pass 12.32 | 13 | 14  51¾ | 67·6 |
| 191  78 | Peterborough (North) | pass 12.56 | 24 | 29   7½ | 72·7 |
| 209  37¼ | Huntingdon (North) | pass  1.12 | 16 | 17  39¼ | 65·6 |
| 236  33¼ | Hitchin | pass  1.33 | 21 | 26  76 | 77·0 |
| 250  52½ | Hatfield | pass  1.44 | 11 | 14  19¼ | 77·7 |
| 268  27 | King's Cross | arr.  2. 0 | 16 | 17  54½ | 66·3 |

Over-all speed 67·08 miles per hour

11

# "THE SILVER JUBILEE"

## POINT TO POINT MILEAGES
## RUNNING TIMES
## AND SPEEDS

## KING'S CROSS, DARLINGTON, NEWCASTLE

| Distance from King's Cross Mls. Chns. | | Station | | Point to Point | | |
|---|---|---|---|---|---|---|
| | | | | Time Mins. | Distance Mls.Chns. | Speed Miles per hour |
| | | | p.m. | | | |
| | | King's Cross | dep. 5.30 | | | |
| 17 | 54½ | Hatfield | pass 5.48 | 18 | 17 54½ | 58·9 |
| 31 | 73¾ | Hitchin | pass 5.59 | 11 | 14 19¼ | 77·7 |
| 58 | 69¾ | Huntingdon (North) | pass 6.19 | 20 | 26 76 | 80·8 |
| 76 | 29 | Peterborough (North) | pass 6.35 | 16 | 17 39¼ | 65·6 |
| 105 | 36½ | Grantham | pass 6.59½ | 24½ | 29 7½ | 71·3 |
| 120 | 8¼ | Newark | pass 7.11½ | 12 | 14 51¾ | 73·2 |
| 138 | 49¼ | Retford | pass 7.27 | 15½ | 18 41 | 71·7 |
| 155 | 77 | Doncaster (Central) | pass 7.41 | 14 | 17 27¾ | 74·3 |
| 174 | 25 | Selby | pass 7.56½ | 15½ | 18 28 | 71·0 |
| 188 | 11 | York | pass 8. 9 | 12½ | 13 66 | 66·4 |
| 199 | 25 | Alne | pass 8.20 | 11 | 11 14 | 60·9 |
| 210 | 27 | Thirsk | pass 8.29 | 9 | 11 2 | 73·5 |
| 218 | 7 | Northallerton | pass 8.35 | 6 | 7 60 | 77·5 |
| 232 | 21 | Darlington | arr. 8.48 | 13 | 14 14 | 65·4 |
| | | " | dep. 8.50 | | | |
| 245 | 9 | Ferryhill | pass 9. 3 | 13 | 12 68 | 59·3 |
| 254 | 24 | Durham | pass 9.15 | 12 | 9 15 | 45·9 |
| 262 | 68 | Birtley | pass 9.23 | 8 | 8 44 | 64·1 |
| 268 | 27 | Newcastle (Central) | arr. 9.30 | 7 | 5 39 | 47·0 |

### Over-all speed 67·08 miles per hour

12

## "THE SILVER JUBILEE"

CONNECTING
SERVICES

WILL BE GIVEN IN EACH DIRECTION WITH THE
FOLLOWING TOWNS BY THE TRAINS INDICATED

*TO LONDON*

|  |  | a.m. |  |
|---|---|---|---|
| Alnmouth | dep. | 8.44 | |
| Hexham | ,, | 9.16 | |
| Tynemouth | ,, | 9.30 | VIA NEWCASTLE |
| South Shields | ,, | 9.10 | |
| Sunderland | ,, | 9.30 | |
| | | | |
| Durham | ,, | 9.54 | |
| West Hartlepool | ,, | 9.35 | |
| Stockton | ,, | 10. 0 | VIA DARLINGTON |
| Saltburn | ,, | 9.12 | |
| Redcar | ,, | 9.25 | |
| Middlesbrough | ,, | 10. 0 | |

*FROM LONDON*

|  |  | p.m. |  |
|---|---|---|---|
| Middlesbrough | arr. | 9.27 | |
| Redcar | ,, | 9.51 | |
| Saltburn | ,, | 10. 5 | VIA DARLINGTON |
| Stockton | ,, | 9.32 | |
| West Hartlepool | ,, | 9.55 | |
| Durham | ,, | 9.48 | |
| | | | |
| Sunderland | ,, | 10.18 | |
| South Shields | ,, | 10.13 | |
| Tynemouth | ,, | 10.18 | VIA NEWCASTLE |
| Hexham | ,, | 10.40 | |
| Alnmouth | ,, | 11.55 | |

13

## SEAT RESERVATIONS

Every seat in the train is numbered, and reservations can be made at the offices mentioned on page 4. The supplementary charges per seat are 5s. First Class and 3s. Third Class.

## BANK HOLIDAYS, ETC.

"The Silver Jubilee" train will run each weekday, Monday to Friday inclusive, except on the following dates :—

December 20th to 27th inclusive, 1935
April 9th to 13th inclusive, 1936

## A TRAIN ATTENDANT

travels with the train and will be happy to render to the passengers any service which will be helpful in ensuring the fullest possible comfort on the journey. He will undertake the posting of letters or dispatch of telegrams.

## NOTEPAPER AND ENVELOPES

are provided for the use of passengers and can be obtained free of charge from the Train Attendant.

## MEALS AND REFRESHMENTS

will be served in the Restaurant Cars or, if desired, at the tables in the ordinary carriages.

14

# RESTAURANT TARIFF

## LUNCHEON

| | |
|---|---|
| Table d'Hôte 1st Class . . . | 3/6 |
| Table d'Hôte 3rd Class . . . | 3/6 |
| Two Course Meal . . . . | 2/6 |

## DINNER

| | |
|---|---|
| Table d'Hôte 1st Class . . | 5/– |
| Table d'Hôte 3rd Class . . | 4/6 |
| Three Course Meal . . . | 3/6 |

## AFTERNOON TEA

| | |
|---|---|
| Tea or Coffee, Toast or Tea Cake, Bread and Butter, Cake or Pastry . | 1/– |
| Tea or Coffee, Bread and Butter, or Cake or Toast . . . . | 9d. |
| Pot of Tea . . . . . | 6d. |

*For children travelling with half-fare tickets, half-price only is charged for luncheon or dinner, with a minimum charge of 1/9.*

"THE SILVER JUBILEE"

15

SOUVENIRS OF
# "THE SILVER JUBILEE"

A Silver-plated Paperweight
Model of "SILVER LINK"
Locomotive No. 2509

With a base measurement of 5½ inches by 1½ inches

**2/6**

A real photograph Postcard
of the Locomotive

**2d.**

A real photograph Postcard
of the Train

**2d.**

A Jig-saw Puzzle of the Train

Size 12½ inches by 10 inches

(150 pieces)

**2/6**

Obtainable at L·N·E·R Offices

16

True love's the gift which God has given
To man alone beneath the heaven.

\* \* \* \* \* \* \*

It is the secret sympathy,
The silver link, the silken tie,
Which heart to heart, and mind to mind
In body and in soul can bind

*Lay of the Last Minstrel*
*Canto V, Stanza 13*

# LONDON & NORTH
# EASTERN RAILWAY

# "THE CORONATION"

## THE FIRST STREAMLINE TRAIN

## KING'S CROSS

### FOR

## SCOTLAND

### WEEKDAYS

(except on Saturdays and 30th July and 2nd August, 1937)

## FROM MONDAY, 5th JULY, 1937

LONDON & NORTH EASTERN RAILWAY

1

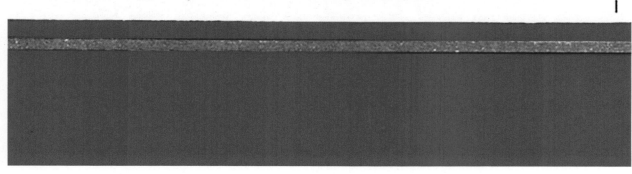

The travelling public are themselves the soundest judges of new facilities. Their patronage of Britain's first streamline train—" The Silver Jubilee "—has proved that high speed, when it goes with punctuality and comfort, makes a strong appeal. The popularity of " The Silver Jubilee " has encouraged the London & North Eastern Railway Company to plan a high-speed service between London and Edinburgh. The new trains are styled " The Coronation " and cover the 392 miles between the capitals in six hours. One stop only is made—at York on the down journey and at Newcastle on the southbound trip. The average throughout speed is $65\frac{1}{2}$ miles an hour and over some sections of the route the trains travel at eighty miles an hour.

The times of arrival and departure are :—

| | | |
|---|---|---|
| King's Cross | dep. | 4. 0 p.m. |
| York | dep. | 6.40 p.m. |
| Edinburgh (Waverley) | arr. | 10. 0 p.m. |
| | | |
| Edinburgh (Waverley) | dep. | 4.30 p.m. |
| Newcastle | dep. | 6.33 p.m. |
| King's Cross | arr. | 10.30 p.m. |

The accommodation on the trains is limited to 216 passengers (48 First Class, 168 Third Class). In view of the exceptionally fast service provided, a small supplementary charge per seat is made. Charges, varying

"THE CORONATION"

3

# EASTERN RAILWAY

**"THE CORONATION"**

according to the journey made, are as follow for each single journey :

|  | First Class | Third Class |
|---|---|---|
| London and Edinburgh | 6/- | 4/- |
| London to York | 4/- | 2/6 |
| Edinburgh to Newcastle | 3/- | 2/- |
| Newcastle to London | 5/- | 3/- |
| York to Edinburgh | 4/- | 2/6 |

The supplementary charge, payable at the time of booking, includes a fee for seat reservation.

Those intending to travel by " The Coronation " are urged to make reservations in advance as early as possible at the undermentioned offices :

| | Telephone |
|---|---|
| **LONDON** | |
| King's Cross (Enquiry Office) | Terminus 4200 |
| 59 Piccadilly, W.I. | Regent 3437 |
| 71 Regent Street, W.1 | Regent 6423 |
| Messrs. Thos. Cook & Son, Ltd., | |
| Berkeley Street & Branches | Grosvenor 4000 |
| Messrs. Dean & Dawson, Ltd. | |
| 163 Fenchurch Street, E.C.3 | Monument 4432/3 |
| Messrs. Pickfords, Ltd. | |
| 205/206 High Holborn & Branches | Holborn 7091 |

and at any L.N.E.R. London Office or Agency and stations in the London Suburban Area.

| | |
|---|---|
| **YORK** | |
| Station Enquiry Office | 2001 |
| Messrs. Thos. Cook & Son, Ltd. | |
| 38 Coney Street | 2486 |
| **NEWCASTLE** | |
| Central Station Enquiry Office | 23567 |
| Messrs. Thos. Cook & Son, Ltd. | |
| 2 Northumberland Street | 22464/5 |

4

LONDON & NORTH

**EDINBURGH**

| | |
|---|---|
| Waverley (Seat Reservation Office) | 23081 Ex.32 |
| Messrs. Thos. Cook & Son, Ltd. <br> 54 Princes Street | 25152/3 |
| Messrs. Mackay Bros. & Co. <br> 29/31 Hanover Street | 20151 |
| Messrs. Pickfords, Ltd. <br> 18 So. St. Andrew Street | 20108 |

**DUNDEE**

| | |
|---|---|
| Station Master's Office, <br> Tay Bridge Station | 4892 |
| L.N.E.R. Town Office, <br> 18 South Union Street | 5855 |
| Messrs. Mackay Bros. & Co. <br> 9 Whitehall Crescent | 5490 |

**ABERDEEN**

| | |
|---|---|
| Town Booking Office <br> 9 Bridge Street | 3214 |
| Station Master's Office | 1904 |
| Messrs. Mackay Bros. & Co. <br> 35a Union Street | 825 |

If it is not convenient for intending passengers to reserve at the above offices, they may do so at any L.N.E.R. Passenger Agency or station if reasonable notice is given.

An outstanding feature of each train is the rear observation car from which can be had an uninterrupted view of the receding scenery as the train progresses. The car is available for the use of all passengers. Although seats in the observation car cannot be reserved throughout the whole journey, the use of a chair for a session of one hour is ensured by payment of a charge of 1s. to the observation car attendant on the train.

## "THE CORONATION"

5

# EASTERN RAILWAY

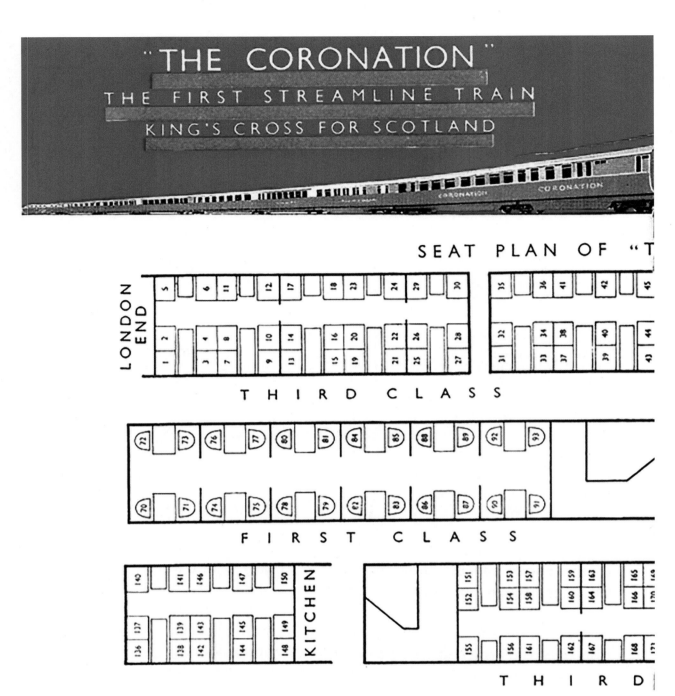

**"THE CORONATION"**

THE FIRST STREAMLINE TRAIN

KING'S CROSS FOR SCOTLAND

SEAT PLAN OF "T

LONDON END

THIRD CLASS

FIRST CLASS

KITCHEN

THIRD

IN ADDITION THERE IS AN OBS

6

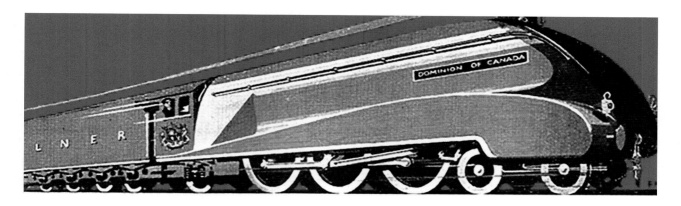

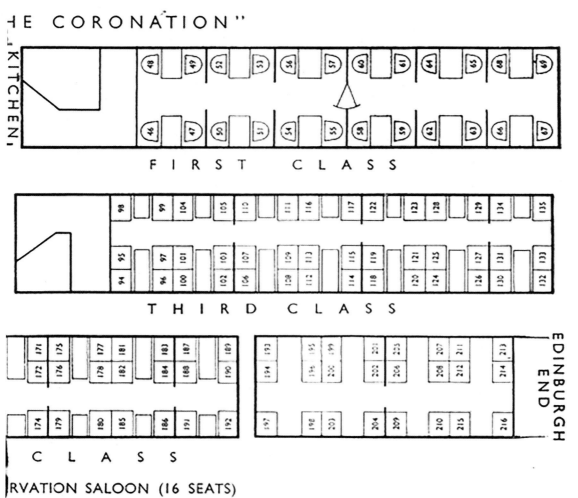

HE CORONATION"

KITCHEN

FIRST CLASS

THIRD CLASS

EDINBURGH END

CLASS

RVATION SALOON (16 SEATS)

7

LONDON & NORTH
EASTERN RAILWAY

**"THE CORONATION"**

" The Coronation " trains each consist of nine carriages, the last being a fully-streamlined observation saloon fitted with large windows and comfortable armchairs.

The exteriors are distinctive. Painted in Marlborough blue above the waist and Garter blue below, they have mouldings and fittings of stainless steel. Great care has been taken to reduce the wind resistance as much as possible by making the sides of the carriages perfectly smooth and by streamlining the rear end of the tail car. The spaces between the carriages are covered by indiarubber sheeting of the same colours as the body sides.

\*     \*     \*

Something quite new in railway coach design is the division of the interior of each train into sections. Each passenger has the privacy usually associated with a compartment while enjoying the advantages and spaciousness of a saloon.

In the first-class carriages the sections each accommodate four passengers, two at each table arranged on either side of a central gangway. Ornamental screen wings projecting from the partitions give the effect of alcoves for two people. Two swivelling chairs are placed at specially shaped tables, and are so arranged that passengers when dining are facing diagonally towards the windows.

In the third-class part of the train each section seats twelve passengers.

In both the first- and third-class coaches it is unnecessary for the passengers to leave their seats for the purpose of taking meals. (For tariff see page 12.)

\*     \*     \*

The interior of the train has been laid out and decorated on original lines. Three different colour schemes are employed incorporating decorative Rexine with aluminium ornaments finished by the Alumilite process.

A system of ventilation provides filtered air at a comfortable temperature. The controlled air, entering each vehicle at floor level, is extracted through roof grilles, and is completely changed every three minutes.

The spaces between the sides, roof and floor have been filled with sound-insulating material, and double windows with a small air space between have been provided, thereby reducing noise to a minimum.

8

# LONDON & NORTH

All meals are prepared in two up-to-date all-electric kitchens. The electricity used for cooking, lighting, ventilating and refrigerating is supplied by axle-driven generators, the total power generated being 32 kilowatts.

\* \* \*

To haul " The Coronation " trains, five streamlined locomotives, named after countries of the British Empire, have been built. Their names are :

|                          | No.  |
|--------------------------|------|
| Dominion of Canada       | 4489 |
| Commonwealth of Australia| 4491 |
| Dominion of New Zealand  | 4492 |
| Union of South Africa    | 4488 |
| Empire of India          | 4490 |

The engines have been finished in Garter blue with stainless steel lettering and mouldings, the wheels being coloured a dark red.

By permission of the respective Governments, the armorial bearings of each country are displayed on the cab of the engine concerned.

*Empire of India* bears an emblem comprising a plain shield with the Star of India surmounted by the Imperial Crown. The engines are further distinguished by the fact that the whistle of *Dominion of Canada* has been specially sent from Canada by the Canadian Pacific Railway Company and has the distinctive note of the whistles heard in that country. *Union of South Africa* is fitted with a whistle as used on the South African Railways.

The leading dimensions are :—

| | |
|---|---|
| Length over Buffers | 71' 0⅜" |
| Weight in working order | 167 tons |
| Boiler Pressure | 250 lbs. per sq. in. |
| Diameter of Driving Wheels | 6' 8" |
| Cylinder Diameter | 18½" |
| Stroke | 26" |
| Tractive Effort | 35,500 lbs. |

The corridor tender follows the general scheme of streamlining. It carries 8 tons of coal and 5,000 gallons of water.

\* \* \*

The weight of a train alone is 312 tons, and its length over buffers 513' 2½". The weight with an engine attached is 479 tons, and the overall length 584' 1¾".

"THE CORONATION"

9

EASTERN RAILWAY

“THE CORONATION”

# POINT TO POINT MILEAGES RUNNING TIMES AND SPEEDS

## LONDON (KING'S CROSS) YORK AND EDINBURGH

| Distance from King's Cross Mls. | Chns. | Station | | Point to Point Times Mins. | Distance Mls. | Chns. | Speed Miles per hr. |
|---|---|---|---|---|---|---|---|
| | | KING'S CROSS | p.m. dep. 4. 0 | | | | |
| 17 | 54½ | Hatfield | pass 4.18½ | 18½ | 17 | 54½ | 57.3 |
| 31 | 73¾ | Hitchin | pass 4.29½ | 11 | 14 | 19¼ | 77.7 |
| 58 | 69¾ | Huntingdon (North) | pass 4.48½ | 19 | 26 | 76 | 85.1 |
| 76 | 29 | Peterborough (North) | pass 5. 3½ | 15 | 17 | 39¼ | 70.0 |
| 105 | 36½ | Grantham | pass 5.27½ | 24 | 29 | 7½ | 72.7 |
| 120 | 8¼ | Newark | pass 5.39½ | 12 | 14 | 51¾ | 73.2 |
| 138 | 49¼ | Retford | pass 5.54½ | 15 | 18 | 41 | 74.0 |
| 155 | 77 | Doncaster (Central) | pass 6. 8½ | 14 | 17 | 27¾ | 74.3 |
| 174 | 25 | Selby | pass 6.24 | 15½ | 18 | 28 | 71.0 |
| 188 | 11 | YORK | arr. 6.37<br>dep. 6.40 | 13 | 13 | 66 | 63.9 |
| 210 | 27 | Thirsk | pass 7. 1½ | 21½ | 22 | 16 | 61.9 |
| 218 | 7 | Northallerton | pass 7. 8½ | 7 | 7 | 60 | 66.4 |
| 232 | 21 | Darlington | pass 7.21 | 12½ | 14 | 14 | 68.1 |
| 245 | 9 | Ferryhill | pass 7.33 | 12 | 12 | 68 | 64.2 |
| 254 | 24 | Durham | pass 7.45 | 12 | 9 | 15 | 46.0 |
| 268 | 27 | Newcastle (Central) | pass 8. 0 | 15 | 14 | 3 | 56.1 |
| 284 | 77 | Morpeth | pass 8.21 | 21 | 16 | 50 | 47.5 |
| 303 | 16 | Alnmouth | pass 8.37 | 16 | 18 | 19 | 68.4 |
| 319 | 79 | Belford | pass 8.51½ | 14½ | 16 | 63 | 69.5 |
| 335 | 27 | Berwick | pass 9. 5 | 13½ | 15 | 28 | 68.1 |
| 346 | 49 | Reston Junction | pass 9.17 | 12 | 11 | 22 | 56.4 |
| 351 | 49 | Grantshouse | pass 9.22 | 5 | 5 | 0 | 60.0 |
| 363 | 49 | Dunbar | pass 9.32 | 10 | 12 | 0 | 72.0 |
| 375 | 9 | Drem Junction | pass 9.41½ | 9½ | 11 | 40 | 72.6 |
| 379 | 49 | Longniddry Junction | pass 9.45½ | 4 | 4 | 40 | 67.5 |
| 386 | 57 | Monktonhall Junction | pass 9.51½ | 6 | 7 | 8 | 71.0 |
| 389 | 69 | Portobello | pass 9.55 | 3½ | 3 | 12 | 54.0 |
| 392 | 69 | EDINBURGH (Waverley) | arr. 10. 0 | 5 | 3 | 0 | 36.0 |

Average speed between London and York 71.9 miles per hour.
Overall speed 65.5 miles per hour.

# KING'S CROSS FOR SCOTLAND

## POINT TO POINT MILEAGES RUNNING TIMES AND SPEEDS

### EDINBURGH (WAVERLEY), NEWCASTLE AND LONDON (KING'S CROSS)

| Distance from Edinburgh Mls. | Chns. | Station | | p.m. | Point to Point Times Mins. | Distance Mls. | Chns. | Speed Miles per hr. |
|---|---|---|---|---|---|---|---|---|
| | | EDINBURGH (Waverley) | dep. | 4.30 | | | | |
| 3 | 0 | Portobello | pass | 4.34½ | 4½ | 3 | 0 | 40.0 |
| 6 | 12 | Monktonhall Junction | pass | 4.38 | 3½ | 3 | 12 | 54.0 |
| 13 | 20 | Longniddry Junction | pass | 4.44 | 6 | 7 | 8 | 71.0 |
| 17 | 60 | Drem Junction | pass | 4.48 | 4 | 4 | 40 | 67.5 |
| 29 | 20 | Dunbar | pass | 4.57½ | 9½ | 11 | 40 | 72.6 |
| 41 | 20 | Grantshouse | pass | 5.10½ | 13 | 12 | 0 | 55.4 |
| 46 | 20 | Reston Junction | pass | 5.15 | 4½ | 5 | 0 | 66.7 |
| 57 | 42 | Berwick | pass | 5.25 | 10 | 11 | 22 | 67.7 |
| 72 | 70 | Belford | pass | 5.38½ | 13½ | 15 | 28 | 68.1 |
| 89 | 53 | Alnmouth | pass | 5.53 | 14½ | 16 | 63 | 69.5 |
| 107 | 72 | Morpeth | pass | 6. 9 | 16 | 18 | 19 | 68.4 |
| 124 | 42 | NEWCASTLE (Central) | arr. / dep. | 6.30 / 6.33 | 21 | 16 | 50 | 47.5 |
| 138 | 45 | Durham | pass | 6.51½ | 18½ | 14 | 3 | 45.6 |
| 147 | 60 | Ferryhill | pass | 7. 1½ | 10 | 9 | 15 | 55.1 |
| 160 | 48 | Darlington | pass | 7.13 | 11½ | 12 | 68 | 67.0 |
| 174 | 62 | Northallerton | pass | 7.26 | 13 | 14 | 14 | 65.4 |
| 182 | 42 | Thirsk | pass | 7.33 | 7 | 7 | 60 | 66.4 |
| 204 | 58 | York | pass | 7.53 | 20 | 22 | 16 | 66.6 |
| 218 | 44 | Selby | pass | 8. 7 | 14 | 13 | 66 | 59.3 |
| 236 | 72 | Doncaster (Central) | pass | 8.22½ | 15½ | 18 | 28 | 71.0 |
| 254 | 19¾ | Retford | pass | 8.36½ | 14 | 17 | 27¾ | 74.3 |
| 272 | 60¾ | Newark | pass | 8.51½ | 15 | 18 | 41 | 74.0 |
| 287 | 32½ | Grantham | pass | 9. 3½ | 12 | 14 | 51¾ | 73.2 |
| 316 | 40 | Peterborough (North) | pass | 9.27 | 23½ | 29 | 7½ | 74.3 |
| 333 | 79¼ | Huntingdon (North) | pass | 9.42 | 15 | 17 | 39¼ | 70.0 |
| 360 | 75¼ | Hitchin | pass | 10. 3 | 21 | 26 | 76 | 77.0 |
| 375 | 14½ | Hatfield | pass | 10.14 | 11 | 14 | 19¼ | 77.7 |
| 392 | 69 | KING'S CROSS | arr. | 10.30 | 16 | 17 | 54½ | 66.3 |

Average speed between Newcastle and King's Cross 68.0 miles per hour.
Overall speed 65.5 miles per hour.

"THE CORONATION"



EASTERN RAILWAY

# RESTAURANT TARIFF

## AFTERNOON TEA

Tea or Coffee, Toast or Tea Cake, Bread
    and Butter, Cake or Pastry   .     .     1/-

Tea or Coffee, Bread and Butter, or Cake
    or Toast   .    .    .    .    .    9d

Pot of Tea   .    .    .    .    .    6d

## DINNER

Table d'Hote First Class   .    .    .    5/-

Table d'Hote Third Class   .    .    .    4/6

## A LA CARTE MEALS ALSO AVAILABLE

*For children travelling with half-fare tickets, half-price only is charged for dinner or a la carte meals, with a minimum charge of 1/9.*

## TRAIN ATTENDANTS

travel with the train and will be happy to render to the passengers any service which will be helpful in ensuring the fullest possible comfort on the journey. They will undertake the posting of letters or dispatch of telegrams.

12

*The Baynard Press*

LONDON & NORTH EASTERN RAILWAY

"WEST RIDING LIMITED"

THE FIRST STREAMLINE TRAIN

BRADFORD LEEDS LONDON
KING'S CROSS

LONDON & NORTH EASTERN RAILWAY

# "WEST RIDING LIMITED"

## THE FIRST STREAMLINE TRAIN

### BRADFORD—LEEDS

AND

### LONDON (KING'S CROSS)

## WEEKDAYS
(except on Saturdays and 23rd to 27th December, 1937, inclusive,
and 14th to 18th April, 1938, inclusive)

## FROM MONDAY, 27th SEPTEMBER, 1937

LONDON & NORTH EASTERN RAILWAY

# "WEST RIDING LIMITED"

Since their inception the L.N.E.R. streamline train services between London and Newcastle ("The Silver Jubilee") and London and Edinburgh ("The Coronation") have won their place in the list of the world's most famous trains. With every confidence in the public patronage of further services of this character, combining high speed with high standard of comfort and punctuality, the London & North Eastern Railway Company introduce this autumn the "West Riding Limited" between London, Leeds and Bradford.

The times of departure and arrival are :—

| | | |
|---|---|---|
| Bradford (Exchange) | dep. | 11.10 a.m. |
| Leeds (Central) | dep. | 11.31 a.m. |
| London (King's Cross) | arr. | 2.15 p.m. |
| | | |
| London (King's Cross) | dep. | 7.10 p.m. |
| Leeds (Central) | arr. | 9.53 p.m. |
| Bradford (Exchange) | arr. | 10.15 p.m. |

*(See pages 10 and 11 for Mileage Tables.)*

3

## THE FIRST STREAMLINE TRAIN
### BRADFORD LEEDS AND LONDON (KING'S CROSS)

The " West Riding Limited " is intended for the use of passengers to and from London only.

The accommodation on the trains is limited to 216 passengers (48 First Class, 168 Third Class). In view of the exceptionally fast service provided, a small supplementary charge per seat is made. Charges are as follow for each single journey.

|  | First Class | Third Class |
| --- | --- | --- |
| Bradford and London | 4/- | 2/6 |
| Leeds and London | 4/- | 2/6 |

The supplementary charge, payable at the time of booking, includes a fee for seat reservation.

Those intending to travel by the " West Riding Limited " are urged to make reservations in advance as early as possible at the following offices :

4

**LONDON** — Telephone

King's Cross (Enquiry Office) — Terminus 4200   Ex. 3610
59 Piccadilly, W.1 — Regent 3437
71 Regent Street, W.1 — Regent 6423
Thos. Cook & Son, Ltd.,
Berkeley Street & Branches } — Grosvenor 4000
Dean & Dawson, Ltd.,
7 Blandford Square, N.W.1, and Branches } — Paddington 8051
Pickfords, Ltd.,
205/206 High Holborn & Branches } — Holborn 7091
and at any L.N.E.R. London Office or Agency
and stations in the London Suburban Area.

**LEEDS** — Telephone

Central Station (Booking Office) — 30091
Thos. Cook & Son, Ltd.,
55 Boar Lane } — 29071
Dean & Dawson, Ltd.,
137 Briggate } — 30321/2

**BRADFORD** — Telephone

Exchange Station (Booking Office) — 9446 or 1369
Thos. Cook & Son, Ltd.,
19 Market Street } — 8144
Dean & Dawson, Ltd.,
24 Market Street } — 1114/5

**HALIFAX** — Telephone

Old Station (Booking Office) — 4207

If it is not convenient for intending passengers to reserve at the above offices, they may do so at any L.N.E.R. Passenger Agency or station if reasonable notice is given.

"WEST RIDING LIMITED"

5

# "WEST RIDING LIMITED"

SEAT PLAN OF "WES[T]

LONDON END

THIRD CLASS

FIRST CLASS

KITCHEN

THIRD

BETWEEN BRADFORD AND LE[EDS]

FIRST CLASS

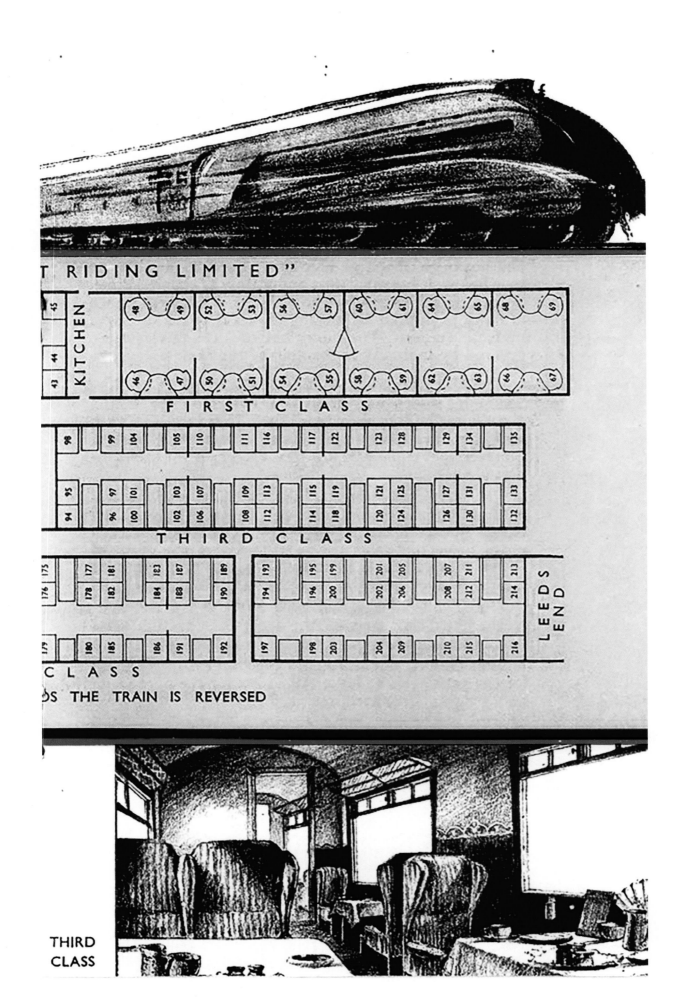

T RIDING LIMITED"

KITCHEN

FIRST CLASS

THIRD CLASS

LEEDS END

CLASS

DS THE TRAIN IS REVERSED

THIRD
CLASS

The train consists of eight carriages. The exterior is distinctive.

Finished in Marlborough blue above the waist and Garter blue below, it has mouldings and fittings of stainless steel. Great care has been taken to reduce the wind resistance as much as possible by making the sides of the carriages perfectly smooth. The spaces between the carriages are covered by indiarubber sheeting of the same colours as the body sides.

\* \* \*

Something quite new in railway coach design is the division of the interior of each train into sections. Each passenger has the privacy usually associated with a compartment while enjoying the advantages and spaciousness of a saloon.

In the first-class carriages the sections each accommodate four passengers, two at each table arranged on either side of a central gangway. Ornamental screen wings projecting from the partitions give the effect of alcoves for two people. Two swivelling chairs are placed at specially shaped tables, and are so arranged that passengers when dining are facing diagonally towards the windows.

In the third-class part of the train each section seats twelve passengers.

In both the first and third-class coaches it is unnecessary for the passengers to leave their seats for the purpose of taking meals. (For tariff see page 12.)

\* \* \*

The interior of the train has been laid out and decorated on original lines. Three different colour schemes are employed incorporating decorative Rexine with aluminium ornaments finished by the Alumilite process.

8

## BRADFORD LEEDS

A system of ventilation provides filtered air at a comfortable temperature. The controlled air, entering each vehicle at floor level, is extracted through roof grilles, and is completely changed every three minutes.

The spaces between the sides, roof and floor have been filled with sound-insulating material, and double windows with a small air space between have been provided, thereby reducing noise to a minimum.

All meals are prepared in two up-to-date all-electric kitchens. The electricity used for cooking, lighting, ventilating and refrigerating is supplied by axle-driven generators, the total power generated being 72 kilowatts.

\*   \*   \*

Two new streamlined "Pacific" locomotives of the latest design have been constructed to haul, each in its turn, the "West Riding Limited."

The engines have been finished in Garter blue with stainless steel lettering and mouldings, the wheels being coloured a dark red.

The leading dimensions are :—

| | |
|---|---|
| Length over Buffers | 71' 0⅜" |
| Weight in working order | 167 tons |
| Boiler Pressure | 250 lb. per sq. in. |
| Diameter of Driving Wheels | 6' 8" |
| Cylinder Diameter | 18½" |
| Stroke | 26" |
| Tractive Effort | 35,500 lb. |

The corridor tender follows the general scheme of streamlining. It carries 8 tons of coal and 5,000 gallons of water.

\*   \*   \*

The weight of a train alone is 278 tons, and its length over buffers 459' 7½". The weight with an engine attached is 445 tons, and the overall length 530' 6¾".

9

# "WEST RIDING LIMITED" THE

"WEST RIDING LIMITED"

## POINT TO POINT MILEAGES RUNNING TIMES AND SPEEDS
### BRADFORD (EXCHANGE) LEEDS (CENTRAL) AND LONDON (KING'S CROSS)

| Distance from Bradford Mls. Chns. | Station | | Point to Point Times Mins. | Point to Point Distance Mls. Chns. | Point to Point Speed Miles per hr. |
|---|---|---|---|---|---|
| | BRADFORD (Exchange)* | dep. a.m. 11.10 | | | |
| 9 34¾ | LEEDS (Central) | arr. 11.27<br>dep. 11.31 | 17 | 9 34¾ | 33.3 |
| 19 26¾ | Wakefield (Westgate) | pass 11.47 | 16 | 9 72 | 37.1 |
| 39 14½ | Doncaster (Central) | pass p.m. 12.6 | 19 | 19 67¾ | 62.7 |
| 56 42¼ | Retford | pass 12.21 | 15 | 17 27¾ | 69.4 |
| 75 3¼ | Newark | pass 12.36 | 15 | 18 41 | 74.0 |
| 89 55 | Grantham | pass 12.48 | 12 | 14 51¾ | 73.2 |
| 118 62½ | Peterborough (North) | pass 1.11½ | 23½ | 29 7½ | 74.3 |
| 136 21¾ | Huntingdon (North) | pass 1.26½ | 15 | 17 39¼ | 70.0 |
| 163 17¾ | Hitchin | pass 1.47½ | 21 | 26 76 | 77.0 |
| 177 37 | Hatfield | pass 1.58½ | 11 | 14 19¼ | 77.7 |
| 195 11½ | KING'S CROSS | arr. 2.15 | 16½ | 17 54½ | 64.3 |

Average speed between Leeds and London 67.9 miles per hour.
Overall speed 63.3 miles per hour.

* Connecting train leaves Halifax (Old) 10.40 a.m., arrives Bradford 11.2 a.m.



# BRADFORD LEEDS

# FIRST STREAMLINE TRAIN BETWEEN

## POINT TO POINT MILEAGES RUNNING TIMES AND SPEEDS LONDON (KING'S CROSS) LEEDS (CENTRAL) AND BRADFORD (EXCHANGE)

| Distance from King's Cross Mls. Chns. | Station | | | Point to Point Times Mins. | Point to Point Distance Mls. Chns. | Speed Miles per hr. |
|---|---|---|---|---|---|---|
| | KING'S CROSS | dep. | p.m. 7.10 | | | |
| 17 54½ | Hatfield | pass | 7.28½ | 18½ | 17 54½ | 57.3 |
| 31 73¾ | Hitchin | pass | 7.39½ | 11 | 14 19¼ | 77.7 |
| 58 69¾ | Huntingdon (North) | pass | 7.58½ | 19 | 26 76 | 85.1 |
| 76 29 | Peterborough (North) | pass | 8.13½ | 15 | 17 39¼ | 70.0 |
| 105 36½ | Grantham | pass | 8.37½ | 24 | 29 7½ | 72.7 |
| 120 8¼ | Newark | pass | 8.49½ | 12 | 14 51¾ | 73.2 |
| 138 49¼ | Retford | pass | 9.4½ | 15 | 18 41 | 74.0 |
| 155 77 | Doncaster (Central) | pass | 9.19 | 14½ | 17 27¾ | 71.8 |
| 175 64¾ | Wakefield (Westgate) | pass | 9.38 | 19 | 19 67¾ | 62.7 |
| 185 56¾ | LEEDS (Central)* | arr.<br>dep. | 9.53<br>9.57 | 15 | 9 72 | 39.6 |
| 195 11½ | BRADFORD (Exchange) | arr. | 10.15 | 18 | 9 34¾ | 31.4 |

Average speed between London and Leeds 68.4 miles per hour.
Overall speed 63.3 miles per hour.

* Connecting train leaves Leeds (Central) 10.14 p.m., arrives Halifax (Old) 10.51 p.m.

"WEST RIDING LIMITED"

11

# AND LONDON

## "WEST RIDING LIMITED"

## RESTAURANT TARIFF

### LUNCHEON

| | | |
|---|---|---|
| Table d'Hôte First Class . . . | 3/6 |
| Table d'Hôte Third Class . . | 3/6 |

### DINNER

| | | |
|---|---|---|
| Table d'Hôte First Class . . . | 5/- |
| Table d'Hôte Third Class . . | 4/6 |

### À LA CARTE MEALS ALSO AVAILABLE

*For children travelling with half-fare tickets, half-price only is charged for dinner or à la carte meals, with a minimum charge of 1/9.*

### TRAIN ATTENDANTS

travel with the train and will be happy to render to the passengers any service which will be helpful in ensuring the fullest possible comfort on the journey. They will undertake the posting of letters or dispatch of telegrams.

## THE FIRST STREAMLINE TRAIN
### BRADFORD LEEDS AND LONDON (KING'S CROSS)

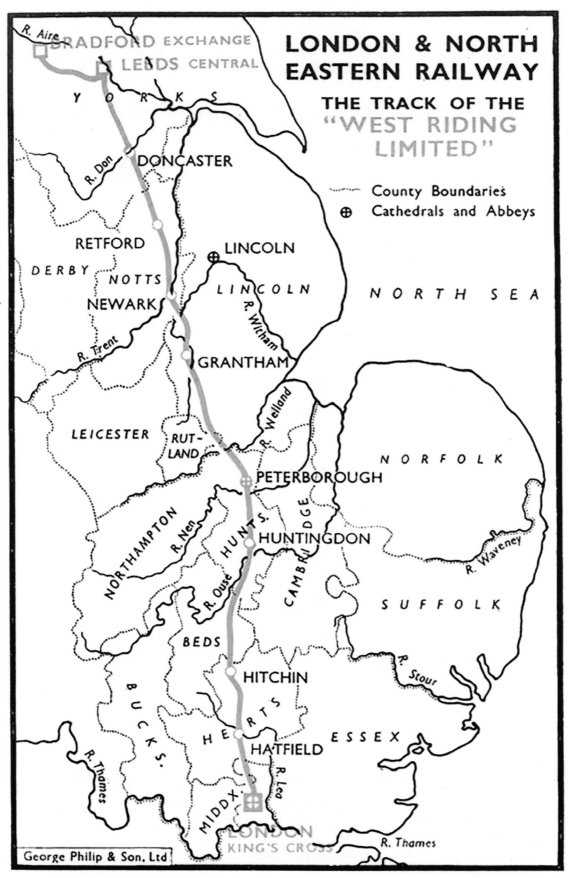

## LONDON & NORTH EASTERN RAILWAY

### THE TRACK OF THE "WEST RIDING LIMITED"

········· County Boundaries
⊕ Cathedrals and Abbeys

*BRADFORD* EXCHANGE
*LEEDS* CENTRAL
R. Aire
Y O R K S
R. Don
DONCASTER
RETFORD
DERBY
NOTTS
NEWARK
LINCOLN
L I N C O L N
R. Witham
R. Trent
GRANTHAM
LEICESTER
RUT-LAND
R. Welland
NORTH SEA
R. Nen
NORTHAMPTON
H U N T S.
PETERBOROUGH
HUNTINGDON
C A M B R I D G E
NORFOLK
R. Waveney
S U F F O L K
R. Ouse
BEDS
R. Stour
BUCKS.
HITCHIN
H E R T S
ESSEX
R. Lea
HATFIELD
R. Thames
MIDDX.
LONDON
KING'S CROSS
R. Thames

George Philip & Son, Ltd

*The Baynard Press*

452

# Appendix 9
## Surviving L.N.E.R. Rolling Stock
## 1923-1941

The following is a list of surviving L.N.E.R. rolling stock, ordered by way of date of manufacture. This list excludes items of rolling stock where either the body or underframe only survives.

### *Carriages*

L.N.E.R. 10155 Corridor Composite, built 1924.
L.N.E.R. 62515 Brake Corridor Third, built 1924.
L.N.E.R. 10178 Gresley Brake Corridor Composite, built 1924.
L.N.E.R. 10021 Third Corridor, built 1924.
L.N.E.R. 22219 Suburban Third, built 1925.
L.N.E.R. 61634 Corridor Third, built 1926.
L.N.E.R. 3641 Brake Third, built 1926.
L.N.E.R. 6259 Four-wheel PMVY, converted to Crane Runner, built 1926.
L.N.E.R. 3107 Brake Third, built 1926.
L.N.E.R. 22313 Brake Third, now Crane Runner, built 1927.
L.N.E.R. 61684 Third, built 1927.
L.N.E.R. 6282 Four-wheel PMVY, converted to Crane Runner, built 1927.
L.N.E.R. 62565 Gresley Brake Corridor Third, built 1927.
L.N.E.R. 4163 Corridor Brake First, built 1928.
L.N.E.R. 42972 Pantry Third, built 1929.
L.N.E.R. 42969 Gresley Restaurant First, built 1929.
L.N.E.R. 6843 Four-wheel Passenger Brake (Pigeon Van), built 1929.
L.N.E.R. 1222 Gresley Restaurant First, built 1929.
L.N.E.R. 3291 Gresley Corridor Third, built 1930.
L.N.E.R. 3669 Gresley Brake Third Corridor, built 1930.
L.N.E.R. 6854 BYP, then 'Sunshine Coach', built 1930.
L.N.E.R. 32480 Non-Gang Lavatory Composite (now Prototype CCTY), built 1930.
L.N.E.R. 1299 Gresley Third Convertible Sleeper, built 1930.
L.N.E.R. 3132 Gresley Corridor Third, built 1931.
L.N.E.R. 6777 Gresley Gangway fitted Passenger Brake (later POT), built 1931.
L.N.E.R. 3395 Gresley Corridor Third, later Exhibition Coach, built 1931.
L.N.E.R. 43600 Gresley Open Third, built 1934.
L.N.E.R. 3188 Gresley Corridor Third, built 1934.
L.N.E.R. 1459 Gresley Corridor Third, built 1934.
L.N.E.R. 43612 Gresley Open Third, built 1934.
L.N.E.R. 43654 Gresley Open Third converted to Restaurant Car, built 1935.
L.N.E.R. 52255 Gresley Open Third, built 1935.
L.N.E.R. 43632 Gresley Open Third, later Control Train Vehicle, built 1935.
L.N.E.R. 43571 Gresley Brake Third Open, built 1935.
L.N.E.R. 43567 Gresley Brake Third Open, built 1935. 460
L.N.E.R. 23896 Gresley Corridor Third, later Control Train Vehicle, built 1935.
L.N.E.R. 23890 Gresley Corridor Third, built 1935.
L.N.E.R. 1211 Gresley bogie First Sleeper, built 1935.
L.N.E.R. 52256 Gresley TO (ex-Control Train), built 1935.
L.N.E.R. 1591 First Sleeper, built 1936.
L.N.E.R. 7960 Kitchen Composite, built 1936.
L.N.E.R. 900580 Engineer's Saloon, later West Highland Observation car, built 1936.
L.N.E.R. 24109 Gresley Open Third, built 1936.
L.N.E.R. 3857 Gresley Corridor Third, built 1936.
L.N.E.R. 4149 Gresley Gangway fitted Passenger Brake (Pigeon Van), built 1936.
L.N.E.R. 1592 First Sleeper, built 1936.
L.N.E.R. 24105 Gresley Open Third, built 1936.
L.N.E.R. 24082 Gresley Buffet Car, built 1936.
L.N.E.R. 24079 Gresley Buffet Car, built 1936
L.N.E.R. 60505 'Short' Tourist Third Open, built 1936.
L.N.E.R. 23956 Gresley Open Third, later Control Train Vehicle, built 1936.
L.N.E.R. 23953 Gresley Tourist Third Open, built 1936.
L.N.E.R. 24080 Gresley Buffet Car, built 1936.
L.N.E.R. 23981 Gresley Open Third, built 1936.
L.N.E.R. 1729 Coronation 'Beavertail' Observation Car, built 1937.
L.N.E.R. 24278 Gresley Buffet Car, built 1937.
L.N.E.R. 24279 Gresley Buffet Car, built 1937.
L.N.E.R. 24068 Brake Composite Corridor, built 1937.

L.N.E.R. 24280 Gresley Buffet Car, built 1937.
L.N.E.R. 1719 Coronation 'Beavertail' Observation Car, built 1937.
L.N.E.R. 641 Gresley Buffet Car, built 1937.
L.N.E.R. 643 Gresley Buffet Car, built 1937.
L.N.E.R. 644 Gresley Buffet Car, built 1937.
L.N.E.R. 650 Gresley Buffet Car, built 1937.
L.N.E.R. 51769 Gresley Buffet Car, built 1937.
L.N.E.R. 2441 Post Office Sorting Van, built 1937.
L.N.E.R. 649 Gresley Buffet Car, built 1937.
L.N.E.R. 4247 Gresley Gangway fitted Passenger Brake (Pigeon Van), built 1938.
L.N.E.R. 56856 Gresley Open Third, built 1938.
L.N.E.R. 41384 5-compartment Brake Third Corridor, built 1938.
L.N.E.R. 43556 Gresley BTO, built 1938.
L.N.E.R. 1852 RB ('Flying Scotsman' set), built 1938.
L.N.E.R. 24287 Gresley Buffet Car, built 1939.
L.N.E.R. 1298 Four-wheel CCT (Covered Carriage Truck), built 1939.
L.N.E.R. 57451 Gresley Brake Third Corridor, built 1939.
L.N.E.R. 4274 Gresley Gangway fitted Passenger Brake (Pigeon Van), built 1940.
L.N.E.R. 4271 Gresley Gangway fitted Passenger Brake (Pigeon Van), built 1940.
L.N.E.R. 4050 Gresley Gangway fitted Passenger Brake (Pigeon Van), built 1941.

## Wagons

L.N.E.R. FB 228 Flat.
L.N.E.R. EWA 564 Mineral Wagon.
L.N.E.R. ARMY 47700 Goods Van. 461.
L.N.E.R. E 1xxxxx Double Bolster.
L.N.E.R. ARMY 47109 Goods Van.
L.N.E.R. AD 47749 Goods Van.
L.N.E.R. ARMY 47893 Goods Van.
L.N.E.R. KDE 202183 Plate Wagon.
L.N.E.R. ARMY 47729 Goods Van.
L.N.E.R. AD 47726 Goods Van.
L.N.E.R. 3285 Flat Wagon.
L.N.E.R. FM 637E Frozen Meat Container.
L.N.E.R. NCB 71846 Mineral Wagon.
L.N.E.R. ARMY 47107 Goods Van.
L.N.E.R. 13 Ballast Hopper.
L.N.E.R. ADE 941766 Crane Jib Runner.
L.N.E.R. 9300/4032 Coal Hopper.
L.N.E.R. E 141183 Goods Van, built 1925.
L.N.E.R. EWA 58 Mineral Wagon, built 1925.
L.N.E.R. ADRR 95224 Breakdown Crane, built 1926.
L.N.E.R. 320952 Four-wheel PMVY, converted to Crane Runner, built 1926.
L.N.E.R. DE 633433 Rail/Sleeper Carrier, built 1927.
L.N.E.R. 95091 Mineral Wagon, built 1927.
L.N.E.R. DE321051 Four-wheel PMVY, converted to Crane Runner, built 1927.
L.N.E.R. 157214 Goods Van, built 1928.
L.N.E.R. ADE 941751 Crane Runner, built 1928.
L.N.E.R. E 164690 Goods Van, built 1928.
L.N.E.R. 6843 Four-wheel Passenger Brake (Pigeon Van), built 1929.
L.N.E.R. 157787 Goods Brake Van, built 1929.
L.N.E.R. 164745 Goods Van, built 1930.
L.N.E.R. E 16xxxx (chassis only) Plate Wagon, built 1930.
L.N.E.R. E 160658 Goods Van, built 1930.
L.N.E.R. 161278 Goods Van, built 1930.
L.N.E.R. E 159918 Fish Van, built 1930.
L.N.E.R. NCB 471 Mineral Wagon, built 1930.
L.N.E.R. E70268E Gresley Gangway fitted Passenger Brake, built 1931.
L.N.E.R. E 166497 Goods Van, built 1931.
L.N.E.R. DE 960602 Rail/Sleeper Carrier, built 1931.
L.N.E.R. DE 900332 Personnel Carrier, built 1932.
L.N.E.R. E 167459 Goods Van, built 1932.
L.N.E.R. E 168064 Brake Van, built 1932.
L.N.E.R. 960209 Personnel Carrier, built 1933.
L.N.E.R. E 170890 Plate Wagon, built 1934.
L.N.E.R. E 171213 Plate Wagon, built 1934.
L.N.E.R. E 193254 Coal Hopper, built 1935.
L.N.E.R. E 181358 Tube Wagon, built 1935.
L.N.E.R. E 181524 Goods Van, built 1935.
L.N.E.R. E 178xx6 Crane Runner, built 1935.

L.N.E.R. E 1xxxxx Goods Van, built 1935.
L.N.E.R. E 187851 Pipe Wagon, built 1936.
L.N.E.R. ADRC 95223 Breakdown Crane, built 1936.
L.N.E.R. LDE 187774 Brake Van, built 1936.
L.N.E.R. 2704 Gresley Gangway fitted Passenger Brake (Pigeon Van), built 1936. 462 remove
L.N.E.R. 187994 Grain Hopper Van, built 1937.
L.N.E.R. E70294E Post Office Sorting Van, built 1937.
L.N.E.R. E 205005 Single Bolster, built 1937.
L.N.E.R. E 212315 Plate Wagon, built 1937.
L.N.E.R. E 193xxx Coal Hopper, built 1937.
L.N.E.R. E 184957 Loco Coal Wagon, built 1937.
L.N.E.R. E 210890 Goods Van, built 1937.
L.N.E.R. B 222814 Fruit Van, built 1938.
L.N.E.R. BK 1xxx Furniture Container, built 1938.
L.N.E.R. E 222418 Fruit Van, built 1938.
L.N.E.R. E 21xxxx Goods Van, built 1938.
L.N.E.R. 203834 Grain Hopper Van, built 1938.
L.N.E.R. E 225641 Mineral Wagon, built 1938.
L.N.E.R. DRG 80111 Heavy Duty Crane, built 1938.
L.N.E.R. E 21xxxx Goods Van, built 1938.
L.N.E.R. E 216013 Goods Van, built 1938.
L.N.E.R. E70470E Gresley Gangway fitted Passenger Brake (Pigeon Van), built 1938.
L.N.E.R. 203814 Grain Hopper Van, built 1938.
L.N.E.R. 1298 Four-wheel CCT (Covered Carriage Truck), built 1939.
L.N.E.R. DR 80000 Light Duty Crane, built 1939.
L.N.E.R. DRG 80117 Heavy Duty Crane, built 1939.
L.N.E.R. E 230965 Machinery Flat, built 1939.
L.N.E.R. ADRC 96719 Heavy Duty Crane, built 1939.
L.N.E.R. 217315 Machinery Flat, built 1939.
L.N.E.R. DE 230908 Well Trolley, built 1939.
L.N.E.R. TS200 Machinery Flat, built 1939.
L.N.E.R. E 230943 Machinery Flat, built 1939.
L.N.E.R. ADE 230966 Machinery Flat, built 1939.
L.N.E.R. BD 1459E Furniture Container, built 1939.
L.N.E.R. DE 230964 Machinery Flat, built 1939.
L.N.E.R. ADE 230935 Machinery Flat, built 1939.
L.N.E.R. ADE 230931 Machinery Flat, built 1939.
L.N.E.R. E 230927 Machinery Flat, built 1939.
L.N.E.R. Gresley Gangway fitted Passenger Brake (Pigeon Van), built 1940.
L.N.E.R. DE 549931 Ballast Hopper, built 1940.
L.N.E.R. 860E Ballast/Plough Brake Van, built 1940.
L.N.E.R. FM 216E Frozen Meat Container, built 1940.
L.N.E.R. Gresley Gangway fitted Passenger Brake (Pigeon Van), built 1940.
L.N.E.R. E 20xxxx Coal Hopper, built 1940.
L.N.E.R. E 239666 Plate Wagon, built 1940.
L.N.E.R. 4050 Gresley Gangway fitted Passenger Brake (Pigeon Van), built 1941.
L.N.E.R. E 243462 Goods Van, built 1941.
L.N.E.R. E 246710 Brake Van, built 1941.
L.N.E.R. DE 246837 Rail/Sleeper Carrier, built 1941.

# Appendix 10
# About the Author

*Fig. 393. The author and his wife enjoying a rare day out in London alongside A3 No. 60103 Flying Scotsman, doing the same! This locomotive and its fame continue to endure.*
*Simon A.C. Martin*

Simon A.C. Martin is an Asset Engineer (Renewals and Enhancements) working for Network Rail, Anglia Route, specialising in signalling asset management and major project development. In his spare time, he is the treasurer of the Merchant Navy Locomotive Preservation Society (M.N.L.P.S.) which runs the steam locomotive no.35028 *Clan Line,* a rebuilt member of Bulleid's Merchant Navy Class.

After ten years in financial services, a change of scene was needed. Simon was inspired to follow his passion in railways after appearing on Channel 4's *The Biggest Little Railway In The World.* This was followed a couple of years later by appearing in Channel 5's *Great Model Railway Challenge*. He has also authored a series of children's books, *The British Railway Stories*, which were originally presented as short films on YouTube and to date have amassed millions of views worldwide.

Simon's extensive research work on Edward Thompson and Sir Nigel Gresley has been presented as a series of lectures to a variety of railway societies including *The Gresley Society, The Model Railway Club* and the R.C.T.S. over the years.

Simon lives in West London with his wife Nada, an NHS Doctor, who has been a constant source of support and reason throughout the latter stages of the book's development.